s	Where	Finish	(Crowd Count)	$	Stars	
ANCE T. STORM	PONOKA, ALB	1.5 min Time Limit	130	30	☆☆½	
Steve Gillespi + Ed Langley	STRATHMORE, ALB	PINNED LANGLEY	250	50	☆	TVIP
Steve BRETT Como	AGASSIZ, BC	LOST BY PINFALL (PULLED TIGHTS)	60	25	☆☆☆½	
Steve Gillespie vs Boys In BLACK	PONOKA, ALB	LOST BY PINFALL (WITH ÆTHER)	140	30	☆☆	TVI
Texas Terminators	STRATHMORE, ALB	WON BY DQ	70	20	☆☆☆½	
Brett Como	CALGARY, ALB	10 min Time Lim	350	50	☆☆	S
Brett Como + Don Bozo McCullough	CALGARY, ALB	PINNED BOZO (ROCKET LAUNCHER)	200	50	☆☆½	S
Brad Young	CALGARY, ALB	DRAW (DCW Finish)	300	50	☆☆	
Heroes, Jimmy Jordan	CALGARY, ALB	WON By Sunset	275	50	☆☆½	C
BOYS IN BLACK	OLDS, ALB	2 of 3 Lost 3 with poster	55	50	☆☆☆	
Jim RUDD JIM JORDAN	CALGARY, ALB	PINNED JORDAN (ROCKET LAUNCHER)	225	50	☆☆☆	
SHANE CROFT	CALGARY, ALB	WON BY SUNSET FROM TOP	150	50	☆☆½	
BOYS IN BLACK	DEVMILLE, ALB	2 of 3 Lost with poster	50	50	☆☆☆	C
Jim RUDD + SHANE CROFT	CALGARY, ALB	Pinned Croft (small package)	200	50	☆☆☆½	
Jimmy JORDAN + BRETT COMO	CALGARY, ALB	PINNED COMO (Fair Jordan)	205	50	☆☆☆½	
Bozo McCullough	CALGARY, ALB	LOST BY F⊙	200	50	☆ ½	TVID
Jimmy JORDAN	CALGARY, ALB	Time Limit	200	50	☆☆	TVID
Jimmy Jordan + BRETT Como	CALGARY, ALB	WON by Reverse Pin (Storm/Como)	200	5CO	☆☆☆	TVIO
BY Brad Young vs Brett Como + Lenny St. CLAIR	CAL, ALB	YOUNG PINNED	220	50	☆☆	
Bulldog Bob Brown + Chi Chi Cruz	CAL, ALB	STORM PINNED DI (FO)	200	50	☆☆	
Lenny ST. CLAIRE	CAL, ALB	Won By School boy	200	50	☆☆½	TVIF
Bulldog Bob Brown + Brett Como	CAL, ALB	STORM PINNED COMO	150	50	☆ ½	TVI
w/ Mike Lozanski vs Bob Brown, Kerry Brown, Chi Chi Cruz CAL, ALB		Lost by CO	150	50		
Johnny Smith + GREAT GAMA CAL, ALB		Lost By Pinfall (Clothesline from behind)	250	50	☆☆☆☆	
w/ Mike Lozanski vs Brett Como + Kris Jerkey Pomona, Cal		LOZANSKI Pinned Key	850	100	☆☆☆	TVID
CAPTAIN JONES	Wpg, Man	Won with Vault over top	250	50	☆☆½	TV
STAN SAXON	Wpg, Man	Won with elbow From top	250	50	☆☆☆	TV
Kerry Brown	Wpg, Man	Won By DQ	250	50	☆☆	TV
STAN SAXON	Winkler, Man	Won with Dropkick from top	285	50	☆☆	
w/ Mike Lozanski vs Bob Brown + Kerry Brown Wpg, Man		Draw (Countout)	110	50	☆☆☆	
w/ Mike Lozanski vs Bob Brown + Kerry Brown Deer Creek, Man		Draw (Double DQ)	130	50	☆☆☆	

THIS BOOK IS DEDICATED TO PAT PATTERSON.

Without your guidance and influence, this book would not have been written. What I learned from you about the psychology of how to put together a wrestling match enabled me to be involved in some of the greatest matches in history. What I gained from knowing you as a person was a better sense of humor, a better direction on how to navigate my way through the choppy waters of wrestling politics, and a better understanding of how to work the room at a karaoke bar. Thanks Patrick. "Je t'aime!"

THIS BOOK IS ALSO DEDICATED TO BRODIE LEE.

Whether you were called Brodie, Luke Harper, or Jon Huber — a nicer man and a better worker I haven't encountered in this job. I'm so happy I was able (in a small way) to help you realize your destiny of becoming a legit main event headliner and I appreciate you for helping me become a better father and for showing me the way to Mecca. Thanks Big Rig. I love you.

THE COMPLETE
LIST OF
JERICHO

30 YEARS
OF SMASHES,
MATCHES
& HITS

CHRIS JERICHO
WITH PETE FORNATALE
& ALEX MARVEZ

LIONCREST
PUBLISHING

AUSTIN, TX

ISBN: 978-1-5445-2003-2

COVER DESIGN BY ABDULMALIK ALI
(@97Abdulmalik on Twitter/Instagram)
BOOK DESIGN BY SAM POTTS

SPECIAL THANKS TO BARRY BLOOM

FOREWORD

Alex Marvez

The first time Chris Jericho wrestled in Corpus Christi, Texas, he worked with the late Eddy Guerrero in February 1998. At the time, there was no way Chris could know that almost 22 years later, the "Sparkling City by the Sea" would serve as the backdrop for the start of this project.

After writing announcer notes for our All Elite Wrestling *Dynamite* show on December 18, 2019, I ran into Chris backstage at the American Bank Center. After doing internet research, I told Chris that on the day his opponent "Jungle Boy" Jack Perry was born in 1997, he was wrestling in his 387th career match against one of his all-time favorite opponents, Ultimo Dragon. That's when "Le Champion" told me such information might not be accurate and the reason he knew that. Chris had been keeping a handwritten journal documenting every match he had worked on his way to becoming one of pro wrestling's biggest stars.

One thing led to another, and I began inputting all of Chris' 2,722 matches into a database in anticipation of his 30-year anniversary inside the ring. This included several undocumented bouts that weren't listed on websites that I was cross-checking. Chris also displayed incredible recall of details about when and where he wrestled, as well as the quality of his matches (i.e., personal star ratings where Chris is his own worst critic).

I would never have had the chance to help write this book without AEW president and longtime friend Tony Khan hiring me for his company after I had spent the previous 30 years as a journalist covering the industry. I want to thank my wife, Sherry Bartz-Marvez, for helping assemble the final list as well as the various Jericho factoids sprinkled throughout the book. She did an incredible job, and

I wouldn't have been able to finish this project without her. Our kids, Nicholas and Natalya, provided inspiration as well. AEW digital director Jeff Jones helped arrange for the acquisition of pictures, and we thank him and those who shot the photos. *The Complete List of Jericho* editor Pete Fornatale did yeoman's work in helping put everything together.

And despite his comments about my "fat head" during our AEW interviews, I want to thank Chris for trusting me to chronicle what is a Hall of Fame career by any measure and one that shows no signs of slowing down as he enters his fourth decade inside the squared circle. If there are any mistakes on the list, such as a match result or date/city discrepancy, I take ownership of them.

Alex Marvez
All Elite Wrestling announce team

FOREWORD

Tony Khan

There is nobody else who could have released a book like *The Complete List of Jericho*. Nobody else has had a career spanning 30 years wrestling at a top level for virtually every major wrestling promotion worldwide, and nobody else has kept such a complete record of their matches and the details.

What Chris Jericho has assembled in this book is miraculous, and the contents have touched people around the world as countless fans have attended at least one of these thousands of matches live, and millions have seen many of them on television or, more recently, streaming, as Chris has built an indelible legacy of excellence throughout the planet and documented it for posterity.

For a fan who is newer to Jericho, this is a complete history of his bouts, and it will serve as a reference point and educational material for so many young fans learning about Chris' unprecedented career. For those of us who have followed Chris for a long time, decades for some of us, this is a record of our memories, countless matches we watched on television and pay-per-view, but also the great live wrestling experiences we've had.

I attended my first and second Chris Jericho matches at ECW with my father when I was 13 years old, and for Chris, those were matches #584 (Sabu) and #585 (2 Cold Scorpio).

I later attended two WWF championship matches — #1378 (The Rock for the WCW world title) and #1420 (Triple H for the undisputed WWF title at Wrestle-Mania 18) — and was at matches #2057 (Shawn Michaels), #2498 (the late Luke Harper, who became Brodie Lee in All Elite Wrestling), and #2550 (Jericho, A.J. Styles, and Mark Henry vs. New Day) with Chris in the renamed WWE.

Chris signs his AEW contract on the day of his surprise appearance at the kickoff press conference in Jacksonville, Florida on January 8, 2019.

Jericho is now a top star in All Elite Wrestling. I've not only attended, but I've booked and overseen all of his AEW matches, numbers #2691 to #2722, minus two matches he did for New Japan Pro-Wrestling during that span (#2692 and #2702).

I consider myself fortunate to have worked with Chris in AEW every day for the past two years, and, outside of work, we've built a lasting friendship that I treasure. I'm grateful he asked me to write the foreword, and I hope that you find this book as informative and enjoyable to read as I have.

Congratulations to Chris Jericho on 30 amazing years in the wrestling business, and here's to 30 more!

Tony Khan
All Elite Wrestling president

INTRODUCTION

Chris Jericho

In July of 1990, when I first reported for duty at the Hart Brothers Pro Wrestling Camp in Calgary, Alberta (Lance Storm™), I found myself freaking out. There I was, standing in the middle of a REAL wrestling ring talking to a REAL Stampede Wrestling superstar in Keith Hart, the older brother of Bret and Owen and a seasoned vet of the grappling game! After a brief synopsis of what we could expect from the camp over the next few months, he asked if the motley crew of miscreants and wannabes assembled before him had any questions. When it was my turn, I nervously asked him what I considered to be a legitimate question. "How many matches have you had?" Keith stared at me like I had Ed Whalen growing out of the side of my head and said in an ornery tone, "I have no idea. Nobody keeps track of those types of things." He seemed honestly annoyed at my innocent question ... and a few seconds later, I realized he really was. "What a gearbox," Hart muttered to himself (what kind of an insult is that?) and proceeded to throw me off the ropes for a backdrop. Keep in mind, it was the first day of wrestling school, and we hadn't learned how to hit the ropes OR to take a backdrop, so things didn't end well for me. When he pushed me into the air, I over-rotated and landed on my feet. I thought for sure I had impressed Keith with my agility and had instantly become his favorite student. Keith didn't agree and instead decided to stretch me for what he took as my show of disrespect.

After Keith finished tying me up and trying to literally use my upper teeth to break my lower teeth (don't ask), I scurried back in terror to the safety of the ring apron and pondered his blow-off answer to my serious query. I thought his reply was a strange one because if I wanted to know how many hockey games

Wayne Gretzky played in, I could go into a library (remember those, kids?) and find the exact number in a matter of minutes in a record book. The fact there was no documentation of Keith's (or any other wrestler's) total career bouts seemed ludicrous to me. So right then, I made a pact with myself that I would keep a log of every match I ever had for the duration of my career. And I did. What you hold in your sweaty little hands right now is the culmination of 30 years of my taking out a white binder from my gear bag after each wrestling show, grabbing a blue pen (yes, every entry in that binder is written in the same color ink) and entering the details of that evening's bout onto the page, underneath the details of the previous one. I still remember going into the upstairs room I was living in at Bev and Jerry Palko's house in Okotoks, Alberta, long after midnight on October 3, 1990, and taking a sheet of typewriter paper (now known as computer paper) to begin writing out the day's events with the following details:

Oct 2, 90 1. Lance T Storm Ponoka, AB 15 Min Time Limit 130 30 2.5

I'm literally looking at that 30-year-old piece of paper right now as I write this and after perusing through the rest of this book, the exact "date, match number, opponent, city, finish, crowd number, payoff and star rating" order of info has remained the same over the past three decades. And if you're so inclined, you can now read those stats from all of the 2,722 matches I've had from October 2, 1990, to October 7, 2020, all of which are included in this tome. I'm very proud of this journal because, quite simply, there is nothing else like it in the entire history of the pro wrestling business. It's rare for a performer to last 30 years in this job — but there are a handful of us who have lasted three decades and are still at the top of our game. However, I can honestly say that NOBODY with the longevity I have has kept a record like this of EVERY match they have ever had.

From Canadian indies to Japan, to Mexico, to Germany, to Smoky Mountain Wrestling, to ECW, to WCW, to WWE, to New Japan, to AEW, you will find every single one of the bouts I had in all those companies and countries documented here. You'll notice at certain stages that details I once documented (like crowd size and payoffs) disappear, as I stopped recording that info along the way and my goal was to replicate the journal exactly how I originally wrote it. Also included are over 100 extremely rare photos (many of which have never been seen before) from my personal collection, a gaggle (fun word) of exclusive Top 10 lists from my career, infographics, and assorted other worthy MacGuffins for you to sink your teeth into.

But this book is so much more than just a list of my matches. It's a history lesson. It's a journal (obviously more sacred than the Dead Sea Scrolls) of a 30-year career in a business that, when I first entered it, still enforced kayfabe, had secret handshakes, barred going over highspots, and thought being seen in public with your opponent was a cardinal sin. Now, 30 years later, it's more about wrestling websites and newsletters revealing every bit of minutiae about the behind-the-scenes workings of the business, podcasts explaining and describing every detail about big matches; a time when heels and babyfaces are almost rolled into one. There are certainly pros and cons from both of those eras and ALL the others I've experienced in between, but the one thing that's the same about the pro wrestling business is that it's still the pro wrestling business!

It's still the perfect amalgamation of story and fantasy, athleticism and Shakespeare, comedy and tragedy, acting and realism, and it's nothing like any other form of sport or entertainment out there. And I love it all! Wrestling is what I've mostly done for a living since I was 19 years old, and it's still mostly what I do for a living as I near my 50th birthday. Obviously, I won't be in the ring forever, but I think I'll always be involved with this business in some way or another until the day I shuffle off this mortal coil. And if there's wrestling in heaven, then I'm challenging Owen Hart and Randy Savage right here and now!

Wrestling has allowed me to live out all my dreams and provided an amazing life for my amazing family, and I can't thank it enough. But here's the best part.

Wrestling has allowed me to meet all of you.

Now, we might never have met face to face, but you feel you know me regardless. And whether you've watched one of my matches or one thousand, whether you bought a Jericho T-shirt or a Jericho action figure (or bowling ball), whether you've cheered me on or booed the shit out of me, I want to say it's been a fuckin' honor to be a part of your life. Thanks to every one of you who bought this book and every one of you who has been a part of this amazing 30-year journey. And just know it's not over yet, as there's plenty more Jericho to come. So thank you for being a part of these 30 years of Smashes, Matches, and Hits! (I hope Gene Simmons and Paul Stanley don't sue me for that, but I couldn't resist!)

So, as a tribute to all of you, allow me to pop open a Little Bit of the Bubbly and propose a toast to YOU: the true Friends of Jericho!

More cheers, more beers, guys!

P.S. — Let the record show that my top ten lists are in no particular order. Every person, place, and thing I discuss in the book is of equal importance and relevance to me.

CJ
October 4, 2020

MY TOP 10 FAVORITE MATCHES

(IN NO PARTICULAR ORDER)

#2702, HIROSHI TANAHASHI
JAN. 5, 2020, TOKYO DOME, TOKYO

Most people talk about the Omega match as THE Jericho NJPW classic, but this one is just as near and dear to me. It was the perfect example of a true "dream match." Two longtime main-event, fan favorite "legendary" performers who had NEVER spent one second in the ring prior, locking horns in the biggest show of the year. And what a match it was — dynamic, psychologically perfect, safe, and exciting. Tana was the perfect opponent for me and, in my opinion, it led to a flawless night for both of us. If that's my last ever New Japan match, I can't think of a better way to say goodbye to my second wrestling home.

#2710, STADIUM STAMPEDE
MAY 23, 2020, TIAA BANK FIELD, JACKSONVILLE, FL

Quite simply one of my favorite matches ever. This had everything: creativity, danger, comedy, chemistry, flow, story, wackiness, and genius. It was 10 guys with months of brilliant story lines behind us, creating a masterpiece on the blank canvas of a match that had never existed prior. We filmed this over the course of eight wild hours overnight and finished at 5:15 a.m., only mere minutes before the sun came up. A classic in every sense of the word and a match I will remember and cherish forever.

#2705, JON MOXLEY, AEW WORLD TITLE MATCH
FEB. 29, 2020, WINTRUST ARENA, CHICAGO

Taking place only a few weeks before the world locked down, this was a great finish to the 13-week-long story Mox and I told revolving around his injured eye. After wearing a patch for six weeks (including four days straight on the second Jericho Cruise), Mox outsmarted me by feigning blindness and using it against me to get the pin and become the second-ever AEW champion. This night also featured my all-time favorite ring entrance: I found a gospel choir online, and they did an incredible a cappella version of "Judas."

#2685, KENNY OMEGA
JAN. 4, 2018, TOKYO DOME, TOKYO
I'm the oldest North American performer to ever have a five-star match in the Wrestling Observer Newsletter, and this bout was the reason why. The chance to headline the Tokyo Dome with Kenny, another dude from Winnipeg who had made a gigantic impact in wrestling outside of the WWE system, was something I couldn't pass up. Coupled with the fact that my old WAR tag partner Gedo was the booker of New Japan, it made this a "meant to be" match. Alpha vs. Omega was a huge box office success both in ticket sales and streaming subscriptions and, more importantly, it solidified the fact that at 47 years old, I was better than ever, both in and out of the ring. This was also the match that opened the door for the inception of AEW. (Thanks to Don Callis for helping get the match in the ring.)

#2003, SHAWN MICHAELS, LADDER MATCH FOR WWE TITLE
OCT. 5, 2008, ROSE GARDEN, PORTLAND, OR
This was the culmination of one of the best angles of my career, an angle that was only supposed to last for one week, that ended up going for seven months. It's also been called "the best wrestling match ever" by *Bleacher Report,* and is my go-to whenever somebody asks me what my all-time favorite is. Shawn is possibly the best I've ever been in the ring with, and the story we told and our passion behind the scenes for this angle only cements this match's place on this list. Plus, Metallica's "All Nightmare Long" was the theme song for the show.

#1291, STEVE AUSTIN
JUNE 3, 2001, WINNIPEG ARENA, WINNIPEG, MANITOBA
Returning home to challenge for the WWF title in the arena I grew up watching wrestling in made this one of the biggest nights of my career. Combine that with the fact that Steve and I drew the largest house in Winnipeg wrestling history AND had a great match to boot, and you can see what made this night one of my all-time favorites.

#2045, JOHN CENA, CAGE MATCH
DEC. 28, 2008, MADISON SQUARE GARDEN, NEW YORK CITY
Howard Finkel told me this was the best cage match he had ever seen, and it drew the highest gate in MSG history up to that point. We also got yelled at after the show for going too long, which caused WWE to get fined by the MSG union. The next day Vince told me the fines were

irrelevant as the most important thing was having a classic match that would be talked about for many years. "That … is what we do."

#1284, TAG MATCH WITH CHRIS BENOIT VS. TRIPLE H AND STEVE AUSTIN
MAY 21, 2001, COMPAQ CENTER, SAN JOSE, CA

This was voted the best match in *Raw* history and has become even more legendary due to the fact that Triple H tore his quad toward the end. Not only one of the greatest tag team matches I've ever been involved with, it was also the beginning — and the end — of my big babyface push in that era.

#1415, THE ROCK
MARCH 1, 2002, YOKOHAMA ARENA, YOKOHAMA, JAPAN

This was my big return to Japan (as the WWF champion, no less), against another of my all-time favorite opponents. It was a classic house show match with a 20-minute bit of improv banter afterward between Rocky and me. So much fun and the epitome of what pro wrestling is all about.

#1152, TRIPLE H, LAST MAN STANDING
JULY 23, 2000, REUNION ARENA, DALLAS

My first PPV "main event" match and still one of the greatest of its kind. It was one of many great matches I had with Hunter … even though I totally should've gone over.

#468, ULTIMO DRAGON
JULY 7, 1995, RYŌGOKU SUMO HALL, TOKYO

This was the match that got me booked in both ECW and WCW. Mick Foley and Jimmy Hart are among the many who still talk about this bout today. Dragon still remains one of my all-time favorite dance partners.

#	Date	Opponent	Location	Result	Pay	Rating
995	Sept 12, 99	KEN SHAMROCK	SAN DIEGO, CA	LOST BY ANKLE LOCK	10,000	★★ 1/4
996	Sept 20, 99	MR. ASS	HOUSTON, TX	WON BY DQ J	10,000	★★★
997	Sept 21, 99	KEN SHAMROCK FIRST BLOOD MATCH	DALLAS, TX	WON BY SPLASH	12,000	★★★
998	Sept 25, 99	X PAC	CHARLOTTE, NC	LOST BY DQ	8,000	★★ 1/4
999	Sept 26, 99	ROCK	AUGUSTA, GA	LOST BY ELBOW	4,000	★★ 3/4
1000	Sept 27, 99	BIG SHOW	GREENSBORO, NC	LOST BY DQ	8,000	★★
1001	Sept 28, 99	ROAD DOGG	RICHMOND, VA	LOST BY DQ	8,000	★★ 1/4
1002	Oct 2, 99	ROAD DOGG	BIRMINGHAM, UK	WON WITH BALL SHOT	10,000	★★★ 1/2
1003	Oct 4, 99	ROCK	NEWARK, NJ	LOST BY ELBOW	9,000	★★ 1/2
1004	Oct 5, 99	w/ Hughes vs Dudleys	UNIONDALE, NY	HUGHES PIN	9,000	★★
1005	Oct 10, 99	ROAD DOGG	MIAMI, FLA	LOST BY PIN	10,000	★★ 1/2
1006	Oct 11, 99	w/ Hughes vs Headbangers	ATLANTA, GA	HUGHES PIN	35,000	★★ 1/2
1007	Oct 12, 99	Hughes	BIRMINGHAM, AB	WON WITH PIN	8,000	★★
1008	Oct 16, 99	ROAD DOGG	DAYTON, OH	LOST BY PUMP HANDLE	4,000	★★
1009	Oct 19, 99	D'LO BROWN	LOUISVILLE, KY	LOST BY TOP ROPE BOMB	8,000	★★
1010	Oct 23, 99	MANKIND	CHICAGO, IL	WON WITH PIN	12,000	★★ 1/2
1011	Oct 24, 99	MANKIND	ST. LOUIS, MS	WON WITH PIN	8,000	★★ 1/4
1012	Oct 25, 99	w/ STEVIE RICHARDS vs CHYNA D'LO BROWN	PROVIDENCE, RI	STEVIE PIN	8,000	★★ 1/2
1013	Oct 26, 99	STEVIE RICHARDS	SPRINGFIELD, MA	LOST BY PIN	5,000	★★
1014	Oct 30, 99	ROCK	MSG, NYC	LOST BY ELBOW	20,000	★★★
1015	Oct 31, 99	CHYNA	NEW HAVEN, CT	LOST BY ROLLUP	7,000	★★★
1016	Nov 2, 99	GODFATHER	PHILADELPHIA, PA	LOST BY HO TRAIN	15,000	★★ 1/2
1017	Nov 14, 99	CHYNA	DETROIT, MI	LOST BY TOP ROPE PEDIGREE	17,000	★★★ 1/2
1018	Nov 15, 99	GANGREL	PITTSBURGH, PA	LOST BY NORTHERN LIGHTS	10,000	★★★
1019	Nov 16, 99	MARK HENRY	CINCINATTI, OH	WON BY LAWSTULT	10,000	★★ 1/2

SECTION ONE
EARLY YEARS

OCT. 02, 1990 - MAR. 02, 1994
MATCHES 1 - 285

1	Oct. 02	Ponoka, Alberta		★★1/2	
	Lance T. Storm				
DR	15 minutes		CROWD: 130		PAYOFF: $30

2	Oct. 02	Ponoka, Alberta		★★	
	"The Royal Rumble" battle royal				
L	Lance Storm won		CROWD: 130		PAYOFF: $0

3	Oct. 16	Strathmore, Alberta		★	
	Tag with Lance Storm vs. Steve Gillespie & Ed Langley				
W	pinned Langley		CROWD: 250		PAYOFF: $50

4	Oct. 24	Agassiz, British Columbia		★★★1/2	
	Brett Como				
L	trunks pulled		CROWD: 60		PAYOFF: $25

5	Oct. 27	Ponoka, Alberta		★★	
	Tag with Steve Gillespie vs. Boys in Black (Skull Mason & Randy Rudd)				
L	ether		CROWD: 140		PAYOFF: $30

My first promo shot (Stryper tights and mullet included) taken in an Okotoks hotel room in the fall of 1990 by Ed Langley. Note the blue blanket that we taped to the wall for a background.

Getting suplexed by Lance in the summer of 1990 in the Silver Dollar Action Center, where the Hart Brothers Pro Wrestling Camp was based.

NOVEMBER 1990

6	Nov. 10	Strathmore, Alberta	★★★1/2

Tag with Lance Storm vs. Texas Terminators

W by DQ — CROWD: 70 — PAYOFF: $20

DECEMBER 1990

7	Dec. 21	Calgary, Alberta	★★

Brett Como

DR 10-minute — CROWD: 350 — PAYOFF: $50

JANUARY 1991

8	Jan. 11	Calgary, Alberta	★★1/2

Tag with Lance Storm vs. Brett Como & Don "Bozo" McCullough

W pinned Bozo/rocket launcher — CROWD: 200 — PAYOFF: $50

9	Jan. 25	Calgary, Alberta	★★

Brad Young

DR — CROWD: 300 — PAYOFF: $50

FEBRUARY 1991

10	Feb. 01	Calgary, Alberta	★★1/2

"Gentleman" Jimmy Jordan

W — CROWD: 275 — PAYOFF: $50

11	Feb. 07	Olds, Alberta	★★★

Tag with Lance Storm vs. Boys in Black (Skull Mason & Randy Rudd)

L 2-of-3 falls/pinned 3rd fall/powder — CROWD: 55 — PAYOFF: $50

12	Feb. 08	Calgary, Alberta	★★★

Tag with Lance Storm vs. Randy Rudd & Jimmy Jordan

W pinned Jordan/rocket launcher — CROWD: 225 — PAYOFF: $50

13	Feb. 15	Calgary, Alberta	★★

Shane Croft

W top-rope sunset flip — CROWD: 150 — PAYOFF: $50

14	Feb. 16	Drumheller, Alberta	★1/2

Tag with Lance Storm vs. Boys in Black

L 2-of-3 falls/pinned 3rd fall/powder used — CROWD: 50 — PAYOFF: $50

15	Feb. 23	Calgary, Alberta	★★★

Tag with Lance Storm vs. Randy Rudd & Shane Croft

W pinned Croft/small package — CROWD: 200 — PAYOFF: $50

MARCH 1991

16	Mar. 01	Calgary, Alberta	★★★1/2

Tag with Lance Storm vs. Jimmy Jordan & Brett Como

W pinned Como/powerslam — CROWD: 205 — PAYOFF: $50

17	Mar. 08	Calgary, Alberta	★1/2

Bozo McCullough

L foreign object — CROWD: 200 — PAYOFF: $50

18	Mar. 15	Calgary, Alberta	★★

Jimmy Jordan

DR CROWD: 200 — PAYOFF: $50

19	Mar. 22	Calgary, Alberta	★★★

Tag with Lance Storm vs. Jimmy Jordan & Brett Como

W Storm pinned Como — CROWD: 200 — PAYOFF: $50

20	Mar. 29	Calgary, Alberta	★★

Tag with Brad Young vs. Brett Como & Lenny St. Clair

L Young pinned — CROWD: 220 — PAYOFF: $50

APRIL 1991

21	Apr. 05	Calgary, Alberta	★★

Tag with Lance Storm vs. Bulldog Bob Brown & Chi Chi Cruz

L Storm pinned/foreign object — CROWD: 200 — PAYOFF: $50

22	Apr. 12	Calgary, Alberta	★★1/2

Lenny St. Clair

W schoolboy   **CROWD:** 200   **PAYOFF:** $50

23	Apr. 20	Calgary, Alberta	★★1/2

Tag with Lance Storm vs. Bulldog Bob Brown & Brett Como

W Storm pinned Como   **CROWD:** 150   **PAYOFF:** $50

24	Apr. 26	Calgary, Alberta	★1/2

6-man with Lance Storm & Mike Lozanski vs. Bulldog Bob Brown, Kerry Brown & Chi Chi Cruz

L countout   **CROWD:** 150   **PAYOFF:** $50

MAY 1991

25	May 03	Calgary, Alberta	★★★★

Tag with Lance Storm vs. Johnny Smith & Great Gama

L Jericho pinned/clothesline from behind   **CROWD:** 250   **PAYOFF:** $50

26	May 05	Pomona, CA	★★★

Tag with Mike Lozanski vs. Brett Como & Krusher Key

W Lozanski pinned Key   **CROWD:** 850   **PAYOFF:** $150

What a motley-looking crew this is! Local Calgary guys assembled for an FMW tryout in front of Japanese talent scout and magazine writer Kiaki Sakai. Besides Lance and I, check out Dr. Luther with the fancy jams.

Los Gatos Salvaje (The Wildcats) with the late Mike Lozanski in 1992. Mike was one of my first mentors and took me under his wing many times during my first three years in the business. He also made me drive all night and insisted on playing Firehouse's "Don't Treat Me Bad" over and over again ad nauseam.

27	May 27	Winnipeg, Manitoba		★★1/2
	Captain Jones			
W	vault over top		CROWD: 250	PAYOFF: $50
28	May 27	Winnipeg, Manitoba		★★★
	Stan Saxon			
W	top-rope elbow		CROWD: 250	PAYOFF: $50
29	May 27	Winnipeg, Manitoba		★★★
	Kerry Brown			
W	by DQ		CROWD: 250	PAYOFF: $50
30	May 28	Winkler, Manitoba		★★
	Stan Saxon			
W	top-rope dropkick		CROWD: 285	PAYOFF: $50

Lance and I with Ed Langley, in the summer of 1991 when we essentially were the trainers for the Hart Brothers camp that year ... after only one year in the business!

JUNE 1991

31	June 05	Winnipeg, Manitoba		★★★
	Tag with Mike Lozanski vs. Bulldog Bob Brown & Kerry Brown			
DC	DOUBLE COUNTOUT		CROWD: 110	PAYOFF: $50

32	June 08	Winnipeg, Manitoba		★★★
	Tag with Mike Lozanski vs. Bulldog Bob Brown & Kerry Brown			
DQ	DOUBLE DQ		CROWD: 130	PAYOFF: $50

33	June 11	Winnipeg, Manitoba		★★★
	The Natural (aka Don Callis)			
W	reverse decision		CROWD: 40	PAYOFF: $50

34	June 12	Winnipeg, Manitoba		★★
	Tag with Mike Lozanski vs. Bulldog Bob Brown & Kerry Brown			
L	foreign object		CROWD: 200	PAYOFF: $50

AUGUST 1991

35	Aug. 10	Sundre, Alberta		★★★
	Tag with Lance Storm vs. Brett Como & Lenny St. Clair			
W	2-of-3 falls/3rd fall complex schoolboy		CROWD: 250	PAYOFF: $60

36	Aug. 18	Selma, CA	★★1/2

Tag with Lance Storm vs. Brett Como & Lenny St. Clair (payoff included hotel & transportation)

L

CROWD: 15   PAYOFF: $40

MATCH NOTES #36

The four of us drove the 35 odd hours to Selma (just outside of Fresno) in my beat-up 1976 Volare. When I took the car in for an inspection before the trip, the mechanic wrote, "Get a new …" and then crossed it out. The match was in a barn in front of about 10 people, but we had a blast and then decided to take a drive down to Los Angeles before heading home. Admiring the beauty of Venice Beach, I vowed I was never going back to Canada and threw my car keys in the ocean. After Como said, "So how do you plan to get around L.A. with no car?" I freaked out, found my car keys, and drove the entire 38 hours back to Calgary in my salty swim trunks.

SEPTEMBER 1991

37	Sept. 27	Grand Marias, Manitoba	★★★

Tag with Lance Storm vs. The Natural & Bulldog Bob Brown

L Storm pinned/DDT

CROWD: 220   PAYOFF: $50

38	Sept. 28	Eriksdale, Manitoba	★1/2

Bob Brown

L COUNTOUT

CROWD: 200   PAYOFF: $30

39	Sept. 29	Brandon, Manitoba	★1/2

Stan Saxon

L submission

CROWD: 125   PAYOFF: $40

40	Sept. 30	Peguis, Manitoba	★★1/2

Tag with Lance Storm vs. The Natural & Brian Jewel

L Jericho pinned/DDT

CROWD: 100   PAYOFF: $40

OCTOBER 1991

41	Oct. 10	Kanagawa, Japan	★★★1/2

6-man with Lance Storm & Mark Starr vs. Atsushi Onita, Katsuji Ueda & Sambo Asako

L Starr pinned/powerbomb

CROWD: 2,200   PAYOFF: $160

42	Oct. 11	Aichi, Japan	★★★

Tag with Lance Storm vs. Eiji Ezaki & The Shooter

W Storm pin/complex schoolboy

CROWD: 2,600   PAYOFF: $160

43	Oct. 12	Nara, Japan	★★★

Tag with Lance Storm vs. Tarzan Goto & Ricky Fuji

L pinned/facebuster

CROWD: 1,800   PAYOFF: $160

Drunk and half naked on the bus during my first tour of Japan in 1991. It pretty much became a habit after that. The FMW referee, Ito, ended up getting his pants ... and then his underwear ... stripped off shortly afterward.

Singing karaoke at a bar in Tokyo in 1991. What's more impressive in this picture above: a) Ricky Fuji's majestic mullet, b) My tie-dyed jeans, or c) Lance Storm on the dance floor?

On the back of the FMW bus eating apples and drinking Tequila (as you do) with Lance Storm, the late Mike Awesome, and the late Mark Starr in 1991.

On the streets of Tokyo with Lance, Ricky Fuji, Damian 666, and a young Hayabusa.

Backstage somewhere in Japan in 1991 with the FMW crew, including Mark Starr, Horace Boulder, Damian 666, and Pandita ... a guy who wrestled in a fuckin Panda costume.

The illustrious Hart Brothers Pro Wrestling Camp – Class of 1990! (from top to bottom) Edwin Barrel, Big Dave, Paul, Vic DeWilde, Jericho, Wilf Wolfman, Lance T Storm, Deb, Big Bossman Eric, Mike

44	Oct. 14	Fukuoka, Japan		★★★
	6-man with Lance Storm & Ultraman vs. Ricky Fuji, Masashi Honda &			
	The Shooter			
W	pinned Honda/complex schoolboy		CROWD: 3,500	PAYOFF: $160

45	Oct. 16	Nagasaki, Japan		★★★
	6-man with Lance Storm & Mark Starr vs. Sambo Asako, Tarzan Goto			
	& Masashi Honda			
L	pinned/facebuster		CROWD: 350	PAYOFF: $160

46	Oct. 17	Nagasaki, Japan		★★1/2
	Tag with Lance Storm vs. Tarzan Goto & Eiji Ezaki			
W	pinned Ezaki/complex schoolboy		CROWD: 2,300	PAYOFF: $160

47	Oct. 20	Aichi, Japan		★★1/2
	Tag with Lance Storm vs. Tarzan Goto & The Shooter			
L	pinned/clothesline		CROWD: 2,100	PAYOFF: $160

48	Oct. 22	Nagano, Japan	★★★	
L	**Tag with Lance Storm vs. Tarzan Goto & Masashi Honda**			
	facebuster		CROWD: 3,000	PAYOFF: $160

49	Oct. 23	Ibaraki, Japan	★★★	
	6-man with Lance Storm & Mark Starr vs. Tarzan Goto, The Shooter & Ricky Fuji			
L	Storm pinned/facebuster		CROWD: 700	PAYOFF: $160

50	Oct. 24	Saitama, Japan	★★★★	
	Tag with Lance Storm vs. Horace Boulder & The Gladiator			
W	pinned Gladiator/backslide		CROWD: 2,200	PAYOFF: $160

JANUARY 1992

51	Jan. 10	Calgary, Alberta	★★1/2	
	Mixed tag with Desiree Peterson vs. Great Gama & Rhonda Sing			
L	Peterson/splash		CROWD: 250	PAYOFF: $50

FEBRUARY 1992

52	Feb. 21	North Battleford, Saskatchewan	★★★	
	Tag with Lance Storm vs. Lenny St. Clair & Gerry Morrow			
L	2-of-3 falls/Storm pinned/powder		CROWD: 200	PAYOFF: $150

53	Feb. 25	Winnipeg, Manitoba	★★1/2	
	Tag with Lance Storm vs. Lenny St. Clair & Jimmy Jordan			
W	pinned Jordan/complex schoolboy		CROWD: 275	PAYOFF: $100

54	Feb. 25	Winnipeg, Manitoba	★★1/2	
	Tag with Lance Storm vs. Red Bastien Jr. & Pampero El Felipo			
W	Storm pinned Felipo/double dropkick		CROWD: 275	PAYOFF: $100

55	Feb. 25	Winnipeg, Manitoba	★★★	
	6-man with Lance Storm & Gene Kiniski vs. Bob Brown, The Natural & Gerry Morrow			
DR			CROWD: 275	PAYOFF: $100

MATCH NOTES #55: GENE KINISKI'S FINAL MATCH BEFORE RETIREMENT

Gene was a classic old-school brother, who was sitting in the dressing room buck naked and smoking a cigarette (or drinking a beer or eating a sandwich ... I know for sure he had something in his hand) without a care in the world, until I told him, "Excuse me, sir, that's our ring music; we have to go out now!" He said, "Wow, I have ring music?" finished his smoke/beer/sandwich, pulled up his tights, and muttered, "Well, we better get out there." And with that, the illustrious career of NWA champion Gene Kiniski was a wrap.

56	Feb. 25	Winnipeg, Manitoba	★★

Tag with Lance Storm vs. Lenny St. Clair & Randy Rudd

W Storm pinned St. Clair/small package CROWD: 275 PAYOFF: $100

57	Feb. 28	Cloverdale, British Columbia	★★★

Lenny St. Clair

W front dive CROWD: 150 PAYOFF: $75

MARCH 1992

58	Mar. 21	Vulcan, Alberta	★★

Colin Hawes

W top-rope splash CROWD: 120 PAYOFF: $30

APRIL 1992

59	Apr. 15	Long Plain First Nation, Manitoba	★★★

Tag with Lance Storm vs. Stan Saxon & The Natural

W double pin CROWD: 60 PAYOFF: $67

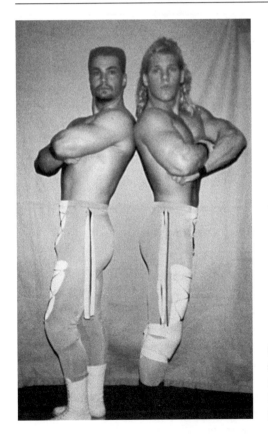

Our second photo shoot, which was held in same hotel room in Okotoks with the same blue blanket taped on the wall. Gotta dig Lance's goatee, the only time in my life I saw him with facial hair.

60	Apr. 16	Morden, Manitoba		★★
W	**Tag with Lance Storm vs. Stan Saxon & The Natural**			
	double pin		CROWD: 70	PAYOFF: $67

61	Apr. 18	Dauphin, Manitoba		★★★
DR	**The Natural**			
	15 minutes		CROWD: 225	PAYOFF: $67

62	Apr. 18	Dauphin, Manitoba		★★1/2
W	**Tag with Lance Storm vs. Stan Saxon & The Natural**			
	double pin		CROWD: 225	PAYOFF: $67

63	Apr. 20	Killarney, Manitoba		★★
W	**Tag with Lance Storm vs. Gerry Morrow & The Natural**			
	Storm pinned Morrow		CROWD: 120	PAYOFF: $67

64	Apr. 21	Melita, Manitoba		★★★
W	**Tag with Lance Storm vs. Gerry Morrow & The Natural**			
	Storm pinned Morrow		CROWD: 250	PAYOFF: $67

65	Apr. 22	Beausejour, Manitoba		★★1/2
W	**Tag with Lance Storm vs. Gerry Morrow & The Natural**			
	Storm pinned Morrow		CROWD: 150	PAYOFF: $67

66	Apr. 23	Steinbach, Manitoba		★★★
W	**Tag with Lance Storm vs. Gerry Morrow & The Natural**			
	Storm pinned Morrow		CROWD: 60	PAYOFF: $67

67	Apr. 24	Winnipeg, Manitoba		★★★
W	**Tag with Lance Storm vs. Gerry Morrow & The Natural**			
	Storm pinned Morrow		CROWD: 175	PAYOFF: $87

MY TOP 10 CANADIAN INDIE OPPONENTS

• LANCE T. STORM

The "T" stands for THUNDER! If it hadn't been for Lance, I'm not sure my career would've followed the path it has. He always pushed me to be better during my early years, but it was hard to keep up with him because he was naturally so damn good.

• LENNY ST. CLAIRE

Lenny went on to become Dr. Luther in Japan and AEW, but when I first started, Lenny was a whiny heel, and a match between him and Brett Como against Lance and Jericho was a hot ticket on the Alberta indies in the early '90s.

• BRETT COMO

I wrestled many of my first matches against "Da Comoooo." He was a high-flying pioneer who reached his biggest fame as Black Dragon in WAR and The Canadian Butcher in Monterrey, Mexico. More importantly, when I didn't want to be "Cowboy Chris Jericho" for my first match, he gave me the sage advice of "Well, just don't do it." So I didn't.

• "THE NATURAL" DON CALLIS

A close friend to this day, he totally jobbed me out when I first met him in the locker room of a Gold's Gym in Winnipeg in 1989 — a year before I got into the business.

• JOHNNY SMITH

The first "big-time" Stampede Wrestling star I ever worked with. I was so nervous and I kept apologizing during the match for stiffing him.

• BIFF WELLINGTON

Biff was a regular tag partner of Chris Benoit in Stampede and coincidentally passed away the same weekend Benoit did. He was a really good worker for his time and bumped and moved a lot like Benoit.

• GERRY MORROW

Very underrated, should have been a bigger star. He taught me a lot about ring psychology and babyface comebacks, and he took the best back drop I've ever seen to this day.

• STAN SAXON

Solid meat-and-potatoes performer out of Winnipeg who was a good base for my high-flying moves at the time.

• ERIC FREEZE

Eric replaced Lance for Sudden Impact's second and last appearance in FMW, a match at Yokohama Stadium in 1992. He obviously wasn't as good as Lance, but had a great look and worked really hard to prepare for our big Japanese bout.

• "BULLDOG" BOB BROWN

I never had a good match with him, but he taught me a lot about what to do (always put over your opponent in a promo) and what NOT to do (pretty much everything else, including abuse of power) to survive in the business. He was also the booker of most of the companies I worked for at the time, and he had a penchant for paying the boys while he was completely naked.

68	Apr. 25	Melfort, Saskatchewan		★★★1/2
	Steve Gillespie			
W	front dive		CROWD: 300	PAYOFF: $75

MAY 1992

69	May 31	Winnipeg, Manitoba		★★1/2
	Wild Thing			
W	front dive		CROWD: 300	PAYOFF: $51

70	May 31	Winnipeg, Manitoba		★★
	Big Mike Manson			
W	front dive		CROWD: 300	PAYOFF: $51

71	May 31	Winnipeg, Manitoba		★1/2
	Pampero El Felipo			
W	front dive		CROWD: 300	PAYOFF: $51

JUNE 1992

72	June 01	Brandon, Manitoba		★★
	The Natural			
DR	15 minutes		CROWD: 125	PAYOFF: $51

73	June 03	The Pas, Manitoba		★★★
	The Natural			
DR	15 minutes		CROWD: 225	PAYOFF: $51

74	June 04	Flin Flon, Manitoba		★★★
	The Natural			
DR	15 minutes		CROWD: 170	PAYOFF: $51

75	June 05	Thompson, Manitoba		★★
	The Natural			
DR	25 minutes		CROWD: 140	PAYOFF: $51

76	June 06	Cross Lake, Manitoba		★★
	The Natural			
DR	20 minutes		CROWD: 120	PAYOFF: $51

77	June 07	Winnipeg, Manitoba		★★1/2
	The Natural			
W	flying fist		CROWD: 200	PAYOFF: $51

78	June 07	La Broquerie, Manitoba		★★★
	Chicago Bull			
W	top-rope elbow		CROWD: 140	PAYOFF: $51

79	June 08	Beausejour, Manitoba		★★
W	**Chicago Bull**			
	flying fist		CROWD: 75	PAYOFF: $51

80	July 19	Winnipeg, Manitoba		★★1/2
DR	**Lenny St. Clair**			
	10 minutes		CROWD: 500	PAYOFF: $125

81	July 19	Winnipeg, Manitoba		★★
DC	**Tag with Chi Chi Cruz vs. Lenny St. Clair & Bryan Jewel**			
	DOUBLE COUNTOUT		CROWD: 500	PAYOFF: $125

82	July 19	Winnipeg, Manitoba		★★★
L	**Lenny St. Clair**			
	cross-body reverse		CROWD: 500	PAYOFF: $125

83	July 19	Winnipeg, Manitoba		★★★1/2
W	**6-man with Bobby Jay & Gene Swan vs. Lenny St. Clair, Big Mike & Pampero El Felipo**			
	pinned St. Clair/front dive		CROWD: 500	PAYOFF: $125

84	Aug. 07	Newark, CA		★★★
W	**Shane Kody**			
	DQ/hit by cowbell		CROWD: 100	PAYOFF: $0

85	Aug. 21	Newark, CA		★★1/2
W	**Handsome Al**			
	flying fist		CROWD: 100	PAYOFF: $0

86	Aug. 21	Newark, CA		★★
L	**Spanish Hitman**			
	side slam/Mae Young held foot		CROWD: 100	PAYOFF: $0

87	Aug. 29	Sundre, Alberta		★★
W	**Tag with Ken Johnson vs. Boys in Black**			
	crossbody on Mason		CROWD: 200	PAYOFF: $0

88	Sept. 19	Kanagawa, Japan		★★★
W	**Tag with Eric Freeze vs. Eiji Ezaki and Koji Nakagawa**			
	pinned Ezaki/top-rope double dropkick		CROWD: 35,000	PAYOFF: $800

89	Oct. 16	Calgary, Alberta		★★★
Bill Jodoin				
W	moonsault		CROWD: 105	PAYOFF: $30

90	Oct. 23	Calgary, Alberta		★★1/2
Biff Wellington				
DQ	DOUBLE DQ		CROWD: 110	PAYOFF: $50

91	Oct. 30	Calgary, Alberta		★★★
Gerry Morrow				
W	DQ		CROWD: 100	PAYOFF: $50

92	Nov. 06	Calgary, Alberta		★★1/2
P.J. Walker				
W	moonsault		CROWD: 150	PAYOFF: $50

93	Nov. 13	Calgary, Alberta		★★★★
Lance Storm (Storm wins vacant CRMW junior heavyweight title)				
L	top-rope power bomb		CROWD: 200	PAYOFF: $50

94	Nov. 21	San Felipe, Mexico		★★
6-man with Canadian Tiger & Latin Lover vs.				
Sanguinario, Blue Fish & Ranger				
W	pinned Ranger/moonsault		CROWD: 800	PAYOFF: $250

95	Nov. 22	Monterrey, Mexico		★★
6-man with Canadian Tiger & Mil Mascaras vs. Sanguinario, Ranger & Castro				
W	pinned Ranger/moonsault		CROWD: 6,000	PAYOFF: $357

96	Nov. 29	Reynosa, Mexico		★1/2
6-man with Canadian Tiger & Latin Lover vs.				
Fabuloso Blondy, Nacha & Falcon de Oro				
W	DQ/Lover fouled		CROWD: 150	PAYOFF: $150

97	Nov. 29	Monterrey, Mexico		★★1/2
6-man with Canadian Tiger & Latin Lover vs.				
Fabuloso Blondy, Sanguinario & Viking				
W	Lover pinned Blondy		CROWD: 3,000	PAYOFF: $580

98	Dec. 06	Monterrey, Mexico		★★★★
Black Magic				
L	cross-body reverse		CROWD: 9,000	PAYOFF: $1,000

99	Dec. 13	Monterrey, Mexico		★★1/2
W	**Tag with Canadian Tiger vs. Los Misioneros de la Muerte**			
	moonsault		CROWD: 11,000	PAYOFF: $333

100	Dec. 13	Monterrey, Mexico		★★
W	**Tag with Vampiro vs. Fabuloso Blondy & Rick Patterson**			
	pinned Patterson/small package		CROWD: 800	PAYOFF: $200

101	Dec. 18	Monterrey, Mexico		★★
W	**Tag with Canadian Tiger vs. Sanguinario & Blue Fish**			
	pinned Blue Fish/powerslam		CROWD: 10,000	PAYOFF: $200

102	Dec. 19	Monterrey, Mexico		★★1/2
L	**6-man with Canadian Tiger & Rick Patterson vs.**			
	Fabuloso Blondy, Sangre Chicana & Valente			
	Vampiro pinned		CROWD: 6,000	PAYOFF: $400

All bloody after the first-ever barbed wire match in Canadian history, with Biff Wellington in Calgary in 1993. My nails are painted black, but I was the newly crowned Rocky Mountain Wrestling Champion and it was my God-given right to do so dammit!

103	Dec. 20	Monterrey, Mexico		★★1/2
	6-man with Canadian Tiger & Tigra Universitario vs.			
	Ranger, Sanguinario & Karonte			
W	pinned Sanguinario/moonsault		CROWD: 15,000	PAYOFF: $333

104	Dec. 20	Monterrey, Mexico		★★1/2
	Tag with Canadian Tiger vs. Los Misioneros de la Muerte			
W	moonsault		CROWD: 10,000	PAYOFF: $400

JANUARY 1993

105	Jan. 15	Calgary, Alberta		★★★
	Biff Wellington			
W	DQ		CROWD: 150	PAYOFF: $50

106	Jan. 29	Calgary, Alberta		★★★★
	Biff Wellington (Won CRMW heavyweight title/barbed wire match)			
W	clothesline		CROWD: 275	PAYOFF: $135

107	Jan. 30	Stand Off, Alberta		★
	Biff Wellington (cage match)			
W			CROWD: 150	PAYOFF: $50

FEBRUARY 1993

108	Feb. 05	Calgary, Alberta		★★1/2
	Bill Jodoin			
W	moonsault		CROWD: 200	PAYOFF: $40

109	Feb. 12	Calgary, Alberta		★★★
	Jason the Terrible (lost CRMW heavyweight title)			
L	powerbomb		CROWD: 175	PAYOFF: $50

MY TOP 11 IN-RING INFLUENCES

• JIMMY HART

Jimmy taught me to be colorful in the ring with my costumes and the value of reading the crowd's signs. "You can't force people to make signs, darlin'. They do them on their own, for who they wanna see."

• HULK HOGAN

After being a huge Hulkamaniac in 1987, it was a thrill to be one of his trusted opponents 15 years later. So much so that Hulk let me put together all the matches we had together, including taking a lionsault, a Walls Of Jericho off his leg drop attempt, and even giving me a superplex (albeit from the second rope).

• RICKY "THE DRAGON" STEAMBOAT
His move set and selling are still some of the best and most exciting ever. Working with him at WrestleMania 25 (#2084) and beyond was a career highlight for me.

• RANDY "MACHO MAN" SAVAGE
The epitome of committing to your character, Randy is still one of the best to ever do it. Great psychology and ring costumes too! I never worked with him, but I saw him a few months after I left WCW and he said, "I would've liked to have had a match with you, kid." Doh!

• OWEN HART
I never got to work with Owen, but he was the single biggest inspiration for me to get into the business. I first saw him in a highlight package on *Stampede Wrestling* in 1987 to the tune of "Hearts on Fire" by Bryan Adams, and his pioneering high-flying moves left me breathless. My dream was to be tag team champions with him someday.

• SHAWN MICHAELS
From his early Rockers days to his breaking out as a singles star in 1992, Shawn had the look, style, and promo skills that I wanted to emulate. I even wanted to call myself "Shawn Skywalker" at some point, before I came to my senses and decided on "Jack Action." Thankfully Lance Storm put a stop to that one!

• VINCE MCMAHON
Vince always insisted he didn't want to just teach me "wrestling lessons," he wanted to teach me "life lessons" as well. That he did, and I never learned as much about the business and about myself as I did from Vince. I miss working with him, but even though those days are in the past, I have nothing but love and respect for him.

• "ROWDY" RODDY PIPER
Still one of the best promos and heat-getting heels in history. The last great Piper promo, in my opinion, was with me in Spokane on a *Raw* in 2009 that left people crying. I still kicked him in the shins afterward, though.

• BRIAN PILLMAN
The one interaction I had with Brian was in ECW in 1995, and he gave me some serious advice. "If you wanna make it in wrestling, you have to do something different." I've been following and living by those words ever since.

• PAT PATTERSON

I learned 90 percent of what I know about ring psychology from Pat. A literal pro-wrestling Jedi, Pat has influenced and helped more main-event stars than you can count. He was a master karaoke singer as well.

• THE BRITISH BULLDOGS

I was obsessed with Davey and Dynamite as a teenager and used to wait outside the Winnipeg Arena with a tight shirt on, hoping they would see me and make me the third member of the team. Thankfully they didn't!

---

110 Feb. 21 Monterrey, Mexico ★★
6-man with Canadian Tiger & Juarez vs. Karloff Lagarde Jr., Sanguinario & René Guajardo Jr.
W DQ CROWD: 4,000 PAYOFF: $600

---

111 Feb. 26 Apodaca, Mexico ★★1/2
6-man with Canadian Tiger & Juarez vs. Butcher, Corona & Sanguinario
W pinned Butcher/moonsault CROWD: 500 PAYOFF: $200

---

112 Feb. 27 Guadalupe, Mexico ★★
6-man with Canadian Tiger & Juarez vs. Butcher, Karonte & Blue Fish
W pinned Butcher/powerbomb CROWD: 500 PAYOFF: $200

---

113 Feb. 28 Monterrey, Mexico ★★★
6-man with Canadian Tiger & Pierroth Jr. vs. Butcher, Jaque Mate & Masakre
W DQ CROWD: 5,000 PAYOFF: $500

MARCH 1993

114 Mar. 05 Apodaca, Mexico ★★
6-man with Canadian Tiger & Bronco vs. Sanguinario, Butcher & Corona
W CROWD: 550 PAYOFF: $234

---

115 Mar. 06 San Felipe, Mexico ★★★1/2
Tag with Canadian Tiger vs. Butcher & Astro Negro
W pinned Astro/powerbomb CROWD: 1,000 PAYOFF: $200

---

116 Mar. 07 Guadalupe, Mexico ★★★
6-man with Canadian Tiger & Vampiro vs. Butcher, Blue Fish & Valente
W pinned Valente/moonsault CROWD: 2,000 PAYOFF: $317

---

117 Mar. 07 Monterrey, Mexico ★★★1/2
6-man with Canadian Tiger & Bronco vs. Sanguinario, Butcher & Valente
L DQ CROWD: 10,000 PAYOFF: $500

118	Mar. 09	Matamoros, Mexico	★1/2
W	**Tag with Canadian Tiger vs. Butcher & Blue Fish**		
	pinned Butcher/backslide	CROWD: 1,000	PAYOFF: $200

119	Mar. 19	Monterrey, Mexico	★★★
W	**6-man with Canadian Tiger & Ninja vs. Blue Fish, Stuka & Johnny Fiero**		
		CROWD: 6,000	PAYOFF: $500

120	Mar. 20	Guadalupe, Mexico	★★1/2
W	**6-man with Canadian Tiger & Latin Lover vs. Blue Fish, Butcher & Sanguinario**		
	pinned Butcher/flipsault	CROWD: 300	PAYOFF: $200

121	Mar. 21	Monterrey, Mexico	★★★
L	**6-man with Bronco & Valente vs. Butcher, Blue Fish & René Guajardo Jr.**		
	pinned by Butcher/top-rope leg drop	CROWD: 5,000	PAYOFF: $500

122	Mar. 26	Calgary, Alberta	★★1/2
W	**Jason Helton**		
	moonsault	CROWD: 100	PAYOFF: $50

The Atomic Punk (Dr. Luther) and I show off our matching GOLD backstage in Standoff, Alberta. I'm sure the 150 people in attendance that night lost their SHIT when we walked through the curtain, daddy!

123	Apr. 02	Calgary, Alberta	★★★1/2

W Atomic Punk (Lenny St. Clair)
DQ/cricket bat   CROWD: 200   PAYOFF: $70

124	Apr. 09	Calgary, Alberta	★★★1/2

L Atomic Punk
cross-body reverse   CROWD: 100   PAYOFF: $0

125	Apr. 23	Mexico City	★★★1/2

W 6-man with Lazertron & Ciclón Ramirez vs. Javier Cruz, Titan & Felino
pinned Cruz/moonsault   CROWD: 2,200   PAYOFF: $290

126	Apr. 24	Mexico City	★★

L 6-man with Lazertron & El Dandy vs. Pirata Morgan, MS-1 & Javier Cruz
El Dandy fouled   CROWD: 500   PAYOFF: $290

127	Apr. 28	Mexico City	★★

W 6-man with Ultimo Dragon & Atlantis vs. Negro Casas, Fabuloso Blondy & Black Magic
DQ   CROWD: 500   PAYOFF: $290

128	Apr. 30	Mexico City	★★★

W 6-man with Oro & Ciclón Ramirez vs. Negro Casas, Javier Cruz & Felino
pinned Cruz/plancha   CROWD: 4,000   PAYOFF: $223

129	May 01	Mexico City	★★★

W Tag with El Dandy vs. Javier Cruz & Bestia Salvaje
pinned Salvaje/plancha   CROWD: 700   PAYOFF: $223

130	May 02	Mexico City	★★★

W 6-man with Ultimo Dragon & Lazertron vs.
Negro Casas, Masakre & Sangre Chicana
DQ/Casas foul   CROWD: 3,000   PAYOFF: $223

131	May 03	Mexico City	★★1/2

L 6-man with Dos Caras & Super Astro vs. Villano IV, Villano V & Inferno
CROWD: 500   PAYOFF: $220

132	May 04	Mexico City	★★1/2

W 6-man with Ultimo Dragon & Oro vs. Sangre Chicana, Bestia Salvaje &
Emilio Charles Jr.
DQ/fouled by Salvaje   CROWD: 6,000   PAYOFF: $235

133	May 05	Mexico City	★★1/2
L	6-man with Negro Casas & The King vs. Villano IV, Villano V & Inferno		
	DQ	**CROWD:** 400	**PAYOFF:** $266

134	May 06	Mexico City	★★
L	6-man with Dos Caras & Enrique Vera vs. Villano IV, Villano V & Inferno		
	Caras pinned	**CROWD:** 500	**PAYOFF:** $235

135	May 08	Mexico City	★★★
W	6-man with Lazertron & Atlantis vs. Negro Casas, Mano Negro & Fabuloso Blondy		
	DQ	**CROWD:** 1,000	**PAYOFF:** $235

136	May 09	Mexico City	★★★
L	6-man with Lazertron & Mascara Magica vs. Negro Casas, Masakre & Black Magic		
	DQ/Casas fake foul	**CROWD:** 5,000	**PAYOFF:** $235

137	May 09	Aragon, Mexico	★1/2
W	Tag with Cuchillo vs. Los Cavernicolas		
	moonsault cross-body	**CROWD:** 300	**PAYOFF:** $333

MATCH NOTES #137

Arena Aragon is probably the darkest, dumpiest, and scariest arena I ever wrestled at in Mexico City, so much so that I always dreaded seeing my name attached to it on the booking sheet. Funny thing is, 27 years later, I found out that Aragon was the venue where the teenage Pentagón and Fénix used to watch matches and decided to become wrestlers.

138	May 10	Leon, Mexico	★1/2
W	6-man with Oro & Pierroth Jr. vs. Negro Casas, Mano Negro & Black Magic		
	pinned Casas/sunset flip	**CROWD:** 1,000	**PAYOFF:** $244

139	May 11	Mexico City	★
L	6-man with Pierroth Jr. & El Dandy vs. Sangre Chicana, Bestia Salvaje & Emilio Charles Jr.		
	DQ/El Dandy fouled Salvaje	**CROWD:** 4,000	**PAYOFF:** $244

140	May 12	Acapulco, Mexico	★★1/2
W	6-man with Pierroth Jr. & Atlantis vs. Fabuloso Blondy, Titan & Mano Negra		
	pinned Blondy/moonsault	**CROWD:** 2,000	**PAYOFF:** $244

141	May 16	Mexico City	★★★
W	6-man with Plata & Bronce vs. Las Cavernicolas		
	DQ/fouled by Cavernicola III	**CROWD:** 4,500	**PAYOFF:** $244

142	May 18	Pachuca, Mexico	★★
W	6-man with Plata & Bronce vs. Bestia Salvaje, Felino & Ulysses		
	pinned Salvaje/moonsault	**CROWD:** 5,000	**PAYOFF:** $252

Press conference in Mexico City, 1993. The gentleman on the mic is Señor Bonales, who was the liaison for the "gringos" in CMLL.

143	May 19	Acapulco, Mexico		★★1/2
L	**Tag with Pierroth Jr. vs. Mano Negra & Jaque Mate**			
	pinned by Negra/foreign object		CROWD: 1,200	PAYOFF: $200

144	May 20	Cuernavaca, Mexico		★★1/2
W	**6-man with El Dandy & Oro vs. Sangre Chicana, Bestia Salvaje & Emilio Charles Jr.**			
	DQ		CROWD: 500	PAYOFF: $200

145	May 21	Mexico City		★
W	**6-man with Pierroth Jr. & Atlantis vs. Black Magic, Negro Casas & El Satanico**			
	pinned Casas/moonsault		CROWD: 5,000	PAYOFF: $200

146	May 22	Mexico City		★★1/2
L	**6-man with El Dandy & Oro vs. Sangre Chicana, Bestia Salvaje & Emilio Charles Jr.**			
	El Dandy pinned		CROWD: 600	PAYOFF: $199

147	May 23	Mexico City		★★1/2
L	**6-man with Triton & Mascara Magica vs. Los Cavernicolas**			
	camel clutch		CROWD: 1,000	PAYOFF: $198

148	May 26	Acapulco, Mexico		★★★
L	**6-man with Haku & Ultimo Dragon vs. Negro Casas, Fiera & Mano Negra**			
	Dragon pinned		CROWD: 1,000	PAYOFF: $297

149	May 28	Mexico City		★★1/2
L	**6-man with El Dandy & El Texano vs. MS-1, Sangre Chicana & Bestia Salvaje**			
	pinned MS-1/powerslam		CROWD: 5,000	PAYOFF: $297

150	May 29	Mexico City		★★★
W	**Cavernicola III**			
	small package		CROWD: 6,000	PAYOFF: $298

ALFREDO ESPARZA'S TOP 10 CORAZÓN DE LEÓN LUCHA MATCHES

Alfredo Esparza is the head writer for Luchaworld.com

10. #152, 6-MAN TAG MATCH WITH VAMPIRO & ULTIMO DRAGON VS. MS-1, JAVIER CRUZ & PIRATA MORGAN, JUNE 11, 1993, ARENA MÉXICO, MEXICO CITY

This was a wild brawl from start to finish, with everyone going in and out of the ring and into the crowd. Even after the match ended, Chris and MS-1 fought.

9. #145, 6-MAN TAG MATCH WITH PIERROTH JR. & ATLANTIS VS. BLACK MAGIC (NORMAN SMILEY), NEGRO CASAS, & EL SATANICO, MAY 21, 1993, ARENA MÉXICO, MEXICO CITY

Just a few weeks into his first run in CMLL, Chris got a pin on Negro Casas in the third fall with one of Casas' own finishers, "La Casita." This showed how highly CMLL's programming department at the time thought of Chris, and we'd see that continue.

8. #486, 6-MAN WITH ULTIMO DRAGON & EL HIJO DEL SANTO VS. NEGRO CASAS, EMILIO CHARLES JR., & EL SATANICO, SEPT. 15, 1995, ARENA MÉXICO, MEXICO CITY

The rematch between these two trios: This time around the *tecnico* trio got some revenge on their rivals. Casas was left bloody.

7. #418, ULTIMO DRAGON, NWA WORLD MIDDLEWEIGHT TITLE MATCH, MAR. 17, 1995, ARENA COLISEO, MEXICO CITY

Chris dominated most of this match, winning the first fall but then late in the second fall, momentum started to swing in the other direction with Ultimo Dragon evening it all up and taking fall two. The third fall had a lot of near finishes, including Chris kicking out of La Casita, which surprised the fans. Ultimo Dragon would end up winning what was a very good third fall to retain the title.

6. #482, 6-MAN WITH ULTIMO DRAGON & EL HIJO DEL SANTO VS. NEGRO CASAS, EMILIO CHARLES JR., & EL SATANICO, SEPT. 8, 1995, ARENA MÉXICO, MEXICO CITY

Chris was part of a match where El Hijo del Santo made his way back to CMLL after a long stint with rival promotion AAA, and upon his return, Negro Casas decided to turn *rudo* to face his longtime rival. The match was about 15 minutes long, but the crowd heat and everyone in the match going after each other was quite the scene.

5. #385, 6-MAN TAG MATCH WITH DOS CARAS AND NEGRO CASAS VS. ATLANTIS, SILVER KING, & EL TEXANO, DEC. 2, 1994, ARENA MÉXICO, MEXICO CITY

This was an all-*tecnico* (babyface) trio match, and it was fantastic. This match had a cool blending of styles with Chris bringing in a faster, high-flying style that combined a little of everything he was doing at this time in Japan, Mexico, and the U.S. Along with Silver King, El Texano, and Negro Casas brought the fast-paced style of lucha, and Dos Caras and Atlantis had more of a traditional technical style. There was a lot of variety in this match, and the fans appreciated it.

4. #178, TAG WITH ULTIMO DRAGON VS. NEGRO CASAS & EL DANDY, JULY 16, 1993, ARENA COLISEO, MEXICO CITY

This match featured three *tecnicos* (babyfaces) and Negro Casas as the lone *rudo* (heel). They wrestled the match clean, with Casas teasing that he was going to resort to his evil ways to win the match and also try to get El Dandy to go along with him. But they stuck to the rules and had a great technical match, which the fans appreciated. They threw money into the ring at the conclusion. A few days later, Chris teamed with El Dandy to win the WWA World Tag Team titles from Los Cowboys (Silver King and El Texano) and were considered one of the best tag teams in Mexico that year.

3. #128, 6-MAN WITH ORO & CICLÓN RAMIREZ VS. NEGRO CASAS, JAVIER CRUZ, & FELINO, APR. 30, 1993, ARENA COLISEO, MEXICO CITY

One week after his CMLL debut, Chris teamed with two of the best high-flyers of that era in the late Oro (who would pass away later in the year) and Ciclón Ramirez, against a pretty awesome *rudo* trio. This was an absolutely fast-paced match, with Chris getting put in against the legend Negro Casas as his rival.

2. #409, 6-MAN WITH ULTIMO DRAGON & FELINO VS. NEGRO CASAS, EL DANDY, AND BESTIA SALVAJE, MAR. 3, 1995, ARENA MÉXICO, MEXICO CITY

Chris ended up winning the Copa Campeón de Campeones (Champion of Champions Cup). This was an elimination rules match with Ultimo Dragon and El Dandy picking their teams. It came down to Chris having to beat El Dandy, followed by Negro Casas, to win the trophy. The post-match celebration included the five other participants tossing Chris up in the air, which was a pretty great visual as the show was coming to an end.

1. #489, APOLO DANTÉS, CMLL WORLD HEAVYWEIGHT TITLE, SEPT. 19, 1995, ARENA COLISEO, MEXICO CITY

Chris moved up in weight class, having spent most of his time in Mexico as a middle-weight, to challenge for the CMLL World Heavyweight title held by Dantés. This was a great match, including a strong third fall with a crazy spot where Chris tried to suplex Apolo back into the ring, but Apolo was able to gain the upper hand and send Chris out of the ring all the way to the floor. That looked very painful! Chris got some near falls, but Dantés surprised him with a pin to retain the title.

JUNE 1993

151	June 04	Calgary, Alberta		★★
W	**Tag with Jason Anderson vs. Shane Croft & Randy Rudd**			
	pinned Rudd/moonsault cross-body	CROWD: 200	PAYOFF: $0	

152	June 11	Mexico City		★★1/2
W	**6-man with Vampiro & Ultimo Dragon vs. MS-1, Javier Cruz & Pirata Morgan**			
	pinned MS-1/small package	CROWD: 9,000	PAYOFF: $333	

153	June 12	Puebla, Mexico		★★
W	**6-man with Brazo de Plata & El Dandy vs. Black Magic, Mano Negra & Emilio Charles Jr.**			
	pinned Magic/moonsault cross-body	CROWD: 900	PAYOFF: $332	

154	June 13	Merida, Mexico		★★
W	**6-man with Vampiro & Atlantis vs. Black Magic, Negro Casas & Pirata Morgan**			
	pinned Magic/small package	CROWD: 8,000	PAYOFF: $332	

155	June 13	Mexico City		★★1/2
W	**6-man with Super Astro & Oro vs. Titan, Pirata Morgan & Mano Negra**			
	DQ/fouled by Morgan	CROWD: 1,200	PAYOFF: $332	

156	June 15	Mexico City		★★★
W	**6-man with El Dandy & Atlantis vs. Negro Casas, Black Magic & Gran Markus Jr.**			
	pinned Gran Markus Jr./moonsault & Negro faceplant	CROWD: 6,000	PAYOFF: $181	

157	June 17	Cuernavaca, Mexico		★★★
L	**6-man with El Dandy & Brazo de Oro vs. Negro Casas, MS-1 & Emilio Charles Jr.**			
	pinned Casas	CROWD: 600	PAYOFF: $181	

158	June 18	Mexico City		★1/2
L	**6-man with Vampiro & Pierroth Jr. vs. Fiera, Dr. Wagner Jr. & Sangre Chicana**			
	DQ	CROWD: 8,000	PAYOFF: $181	

159	June 19	Tlaxcala, Mexico		★★
W	**6-man with Atlantis & Rayo de Jalisco Jr. vs. MS-1, Masakre & Emilio Charles Jr.**			
	pinned Masakre/moonsault	CROWD: 1,500	PAYOFF: $181	

160	June 20	Guadalajara, Mexico		★★1/2
W	**6-man with Ciclon Ramirez & Oro vs. Bestia Salvaje, Gran Markus Jr. & Javier Cruz**			
	DQ/foul by Salvaje	CROWD: 4,000	PAYOFF: $486	

161	June 22	Mexico City	★★★

6-man Ringo Mendoza vs. Bestia Salvaje, Gran Markus Jr. & Mano Negra

W DQ/Mendoza fouled · CROWD: 6,500 · PAYOFF: $130

162	June 23	San Luis, Mexico	★★

Tag with Americo Rocca vs. Gran Markus Jr. & Kahoz

W pinned Markus/moonsault · CROWD: 300 · PAYOFF: $459

163	June 24	Mexico City	★★★

6-man with Ciclon Ramirez & Oro vs. Felino, Javier Cruz & Jaque Mate

W pinned Cruz/moonsault · CROWD: 12,000 · PAYOFF: $130

164	June 24	Cuernavaca, Mexico	★★★

Tag with Ultimo Dragon vs. Negro Casas & Javier Cruz

W pinned Cruz/moonsault · CROWD: 500 · PAYOFF: $130

165	June 27	Guadalajara, Mexico	★★1/2

Tag with Atlantis vs. Bestia Salvaje & Mano Negra

W DQ/foul by Salvaje · CROWD: 4,000 · PAYOFF: $335

166	June 30	Acapulco, Mexico	★★

6-man with Brazo de Plata & Atlantis vs. Negro Casas, Felino & Javier Cruz

W DQ/Brazo de Plata fake foul · CROWD: 500 · PAYOFF: $229

JULY 1993

167	July 01	Mexico City	★★★1/2

6-man with Atlantis & Ultimo Dragon vs. Silver King, El Texano & Dos Caras

L Atlantis pinned · CROWD: 600 · PAYOFF: $236

168	July 02	Mexico City	★★★

6-man with Oro & El Brazo vs. Mogur, Tornado Negro & Mano Negra

W · CROWD: 7,000 · PAYOFF: $228

169	July 03	Mexico City	★★★

6-man with Pierroth Jr. & Americo Rocca vs. Bestia Salvaje, Emilio Charles Jr. & Sangre Chicana

L Pierroth Jr. fouled · CROWD: 800 · PAYOFF: $228

170	July 04	Guadalajara, Mexico	★★★★

Bestia Salvaje

W belly-to-back suplex from top-rope reversal · CROWD: 4,500 · PAYOFF: $351

171	July 05	Leon, Mexico	★★1/2

Tag with Vampiro vs. Gran Markus Jr. & Masakre

W DQ/Vampiro fouled · CROWD: 2,000 · PAYOFF: $239

172	July 07	Ciudad Lopez Mateos, Mexico	★★1/2

Tag with Pierroth Jr. vs. Negro Casas & Sangre Chicana

W pinned Casas/moonsault — CROWD: 300 — PAYOFF: $239

173	July 09	Mexico City	★★★

6-man with El Dandy & Atlantis vs. Mano Negra, Black Magic & Javier Cruz

W pinned Magic/tope — CROWD: 12,000 — PAYOFF: $239

174	July 10	Mexico City	★★

6-man with Vampiro & Pierroth Jr. vs. Sangre Chicana, Bestia Salvaje & Emilio Charles Jr.

W DQ — CROWD: 1,000 — PAYOFF: $239

175	July 11	Mexico City	★★1/2

6-man with Americo Rocca & Ciclon Ramirez vs. Felino, Cavernicola & Gladiador

L DQ — CROWD: 1,200 — PAYOFF: $239

176	July 13	Toluca, Mexico	★★

6-man with Ultimo Dragon & Atlantis vs. Dos Caras, Super Astro & Transformer

DR — CROWD: 300 — PAYOFF: $214

177	July 15	Cuernavaca, Mexico	★★

6-man with Atlantis & Fiera vs. Sangre Chicana, Bestia Salvaje & Emilio Charles Jr.

L DQ — CROWD: 1,200 — PAYOFF: $265

178	July 16	Mexico City	★★★★

Tag with Ultimo Dragon vs. Negro Casas & El Dandy

L pinned by El Dandy — CROWD: 2,000 — PAYOFF: $294

179	July 17	Puebla, Mexico	★★1/2

Tag with Ultimo Dragon vs. Gran Markus Jr. & Jaque Mate

W pinned Mate/killsault — CROWD: 800 — PAYOFF: $265

180	July 18	Mexico City	★★

Tag with Dos Caras vs. Canek & Yamato

L pinned by Yamato/Samoan drop — CROWD: 1,000 — PAYOFF: $494

181	July 19	Puebla, Mexico	★★1/2

6-man with Ultimo Dragon & Pierroth Jr. vs. Canek, Villano IV & Villano V

L DQ — CROWD: 3,000 — PAYOFF: $220

182	July 21	Ciudad Lopez Mateos, Mexico	★★★

Tag with El Dandy vs. El Texano & Silver King (won WWA world tag team titles)

W pinned El Texano/powerslam — CROWD: 450 — PAYOFF: $282

183	July 22	Cuernavaca, Mexico	★★★

6-man with El Dandy & Oro vs. Jaque Mate, Kahoz & Javier Cruz

W pinned Cruz/moonsault — CROWD: 1,000 — PAYOFF: $305

184	July 23	Mexico City	★★★

6-man with El Dandy & Fiera vs. Negro Casas, Felino & Dr. Wagner Jr.

L

CROWD: 3,000   PAYOFF: $305

185	July 24	Puebla, Mexico	★★

6-man with El Dandy & Americo Rocca vs. Emilio Charles Jr., Mano Negra & Cachorro Mendoza

L   DQ

CROWD: 800   PAYOFF: $304

186	July 25	Mexico City	★★★

6-man with Oro & Transformer vs. Villano IV, Villano V & Masakre

L   pinned by Villano IV after switch with Villano V/legdrop   CROWD: 2,000   PAYOFF: $491

187	July 26	Puebla, Mexico	★★

6-man with Dos Caras & Enrique Vera vs. Yamato, Canek & Killer

W

CROWD: 3,100   PAYOFF: $257

188	July 28	Acapulco, Mexico	★★★

6-man with El Dandy, Pierroth Jr. & Brazo de Oro vs. Negro Casas, Dr. Wagner Jr. & Emilio Charles Jr.

W   DQ/came late, worked with Casas, huge pop   CROWD: 1,500   PAYOFF: $221

189	July 29	Ecatepec, Mexico	★★

6-man with El Dandy & Atlantis vs. Javier Cruz, Jaque Mate & Mano Negra

W   El Dandy pinned Cruz   CROWD: 500   PAYOFF: $221

190	July 30	Mexico City	★★★1/2

6-man with Atlantis & Ultimo Dragon vs. Silver King, El Texano & El Dandy

W   Atlantis pinned El Dandy   CROWD: 6,000   PAYOFF: $222

191	July 31	Mexico City	★★★

6-man with Gran Hamada & Blue Demon Jr. vs. Gladiador, Tornado Negro & Kahoz

W   pinned Gladiador/top-rope elbow   CROWD: 1,400   PAYOFF: $222

AUGUST 1993

192	Aug. 01	Mexico City	★★★

6-man with Oro & Atlantis vs. Villano IV, Villano V & El Signo

W

CROWD: 10,000   PAYOFF: $491

193	Aug. 20	Mexico City	★★★

6-man with Ciclón Ramirez & Fiera vs. Gladiador, Sangre Chicana & Gran Markus Jr.

W   pinned Markus/moonsault   CROWD: 5,000   PAYOFF: $279

194	Aug. 21	Mexico City	★★★

6-man with Atlantis & Vampiro vs. Negro Casas, Cachorro Mendoza & Mano Negra

W   pinned Casas/moonsault   CROWD: 1,700   PAYOFF: $278

195	Aug. 22	Mexico City	★★

6-man with Haku & Fiera vs. Gladiador, Gran Markus Jr. & Dr. Wagner Jr.

L Haku pinned — CROWD: 4,000 — PAYOFF: $278

196	Aug. 23	Puebla, Mexico	★★1/2

6-man with Dos Caras & Gran Hamada vs. Negro Casas, Miguel Perez & Yamato

W pinned Perez/moonsault — CROWD: 2,000 — PAYOFF: $232

197	Aug. 24	Mexico City	★★★

6-man with El Dandy & Ultimo Dragon vs. Dr. Wagner Jr., Gladiador & Gran Markus Jr.

L — CROWD: 5,500 — PAYOFF: $336

198	Aug. 25	Naucalpan, Mexico	★★1/2

6-man with Ciclon Ramirez & Pantera vs. Villano IV, Villano V & Kraneo

L — CROWD: 800 — PAYOFF: $380

MATCH NOTES #198

This arena was another rough one, and on this night the Villanos literally left the ring mid-match to fight with drunken fans in the crowd. They even climbed up to the second deck to catch them, even though it had literal spikes on the balcony to keep such incidents from happening. The Villanos, Tommy and Raymond, didn't give a shit, however, and hauled themselves over the spikes and kicked the shit out of the drunken loudmouths to the point that they suddenly couldn't speak anymore.

199	Aug. 27	Mexico City	★★1/2

6-man with Atlantis & American Rocca vs. Felino, Bestia Salvaje & Mano Negra

W pinned Felino/reverse tope — CROWD: 4,000 — PAYOFF: $337

200	Aug. 28	Mexico City	★★★

6-man with Vampiro & Pierroth Jr. vs. Gladiador, Dr. Wagner Jr. & Gran Markus Jr.

L — CROWD: 2,200 — PAYOFF: $337

201	Aug. 29	Mexico City	★1/2

6-man with Blue Demon & Ciclon Ramirez vs. Emilio Charles Jr., Felino & Mano Negra

W by DQ/Ciclon fouled — CROWD: 400 — PAYOFF: $220

202	Aug. 29	Guadalajara, Mexico	★★

6-man with Blue Demon & Cesar Dantes vs. Mano Negra, Emilio Charles Jr. & Cachorro Mendoza

W El Dandy pinned Negra — CROWD: 5,000 — PAYOFF: $394

203	Aug. 30	Tampico, Mexico	★1/2

6-man with Vampiro & Pierroth Jr. vs. Black Magic, Dr. Wagner Jr. & Canek

W DQ/Pierroth Jr. fouled — CROWD: 4,000 — PAYOFF: $318

TOP 10 CITIES
TO WRESTLE IN

- Sydney
- London
- Tokyo
- New York
- Philadelphia
- Mexico City
- Chicago
- Toronto
- Osaka, Japan
- Winnipeg, Manitoba

204	Aug. 31	Mexico City	★★
6-man with Silver King & El Texano vs. Black Magic, Bestia Salvaje & Emilio Charles Jr.			
W DQ/El Texano fouled		CROWD: 3,000	PAYOFF: $329

SEPTEMBER 1993

205	Sept. 01	Mexico City	★★★
Tag with El Dandy vs. Silver King & El Texano (lost WWA world tag team titles)			
L figure four		CROWD: 400	PAYOFF: $226

206	Sept. 02	Cuernavaca, Mexico	★★1/2
6-man with Atlantis & Pierroth Jr. vs. Kahos, Jaque Mate & Masakre			
L abdominal stretch		CROWD: 400	PAYOFF: $227

207	Sept. 03	Mexico City	★★1/2
6-man with El Dandy & Pierroth Jr. vs. Dr. Wagner Jr., Gran Markus Jr. & Gladiador			
L arm stretch		CROWD: 3,000	PAYOFF: $227

208	Sept. 07	Hamburg, Germany	★★★
Brick Crawford			
W moonsault		CROWD: 200	PAYOFF: $140

209	Sept. 08	Hamburg, Germany	★★
Indio Guajardo			
DR 20 minutes		CROWD: 60	PAYOFF: $140

210	Sept. 09	Hamburg, Germany	★★1/2
Mad Mac			
DR 20 minutes		CROWD: 100	PAYOFF: $140

211	Sept. 10	Hamburg, Germany		★★1/2
	Johnny South			
DR	20 minutes		CROWD: 300	PAYOFF: $140

212	Sept. 11	Hamburg, Germany		★★1/2
	Tag with Robbie Brookside vs. Indio Guajardo & Brick Crawford			
DR	30 minutes		CROWD: 400	PAYOFF: $149

213	Sept. 12	Hamburg, Germany		★★
	Moondog Rex			
W	DQ		CROWD: 100	PAYOFF: $140

214	Sept. 14	Hamburg, Germany		★★1/2
	Johnny South			
W	moonsault		CROWD: 200	PAYOFF: $140

215	Sept. 15	Hamburg, Germany		★★
	Rip Morgan			
DR	20 minutes		CROWD: 175	PAYOFF: $140

216	Sept. 16	Hamburg, Germany		★★★
	Tag with Boston Blackie vs. Johnny South & Mad Mac			
W	pinned South/top-rope elbow		CROWD: 400	PAYOFF: $146

217	Sept. 17	Hamburg, Germany		★★
	Tag with Boston Blackie vs. Rene Lasartesse & Moondog Rex			
W	DQ		CROWD: 400	PAYOFF: $140

218	Sept. 18	Hamburg, Germany		★★★1/2
	Rip Morgan			
W	DQ/neck in ropes		CROWD: 600	PAYOFF: $140

219	Sept. 19	Hamburg, Germany		★★★
	Brick Crawford			
DR	20 minutes		CROWD: 150	PAYOFF: $140

220	Sept. 21	Hamburg, Germany		★★
	Moondog Rex			
W	DQ		CROWD: 125	PAYOFF: $140

221	Sept. 22	Hamburg, Germany		★★1/2
	"Royal Rumble"			
L	backdropped out by Doc Dean		CROWD: 670	PAYOFF: $140

222	Sept. 23	Hamburg, Germany		★★1/2
	Rip Morgan			
DR	20 minutes		CROWD: 600	PAYOFF: $190

223	Sept. 24	Hamburg, Germany	★★1/2
DR	**Moondog Rex** 20 minutes	**CROWD:** 250	**PAYOFF:** $190

224	Sept. 25	Hamburg, Germany	★★★
W	**Brick Crawford** moonsault	**CROWD:** 500	**PAYOFF:** $190

225	Sept. 26	Hamburg, Germany	★★
W	**Johnny South** DQ	**CROWD:** 150	**PAYOFF:** $278

226	Sept. 28	Hamburg, Germany	★★1/2
W	**Indio Guajardo** top-rope elbow	**CROWD:** 200	**PAYOFF:** $166

227	Sept. 30	Hamburg, Germany	★★★
W	**Moondog Rex** DQ	**CROWD:** 200	**PAYOFF:** $140

OCTOBER 1993

228	Oct. 01	Hamburg, Germany	★★
L	**Rip Morgan** DQ	**CROWD:** 300	**PAYOFF:** $140

229	Oct. 02	Hamburg, Germany	★★
L	**"Royal Rumble"** Moondog elimination	**CROWD:** 275	**PAYOFF:** $140

230	Oct. 03	Hamburg, Germany	★★★★
DR	**Mad Mac** 25 minutes	**CROWD:** 300	**PAYOFF:** $140

231	Oct. 04	Hamburg, Germany	★★1/2
W	**Tag with Boston Blackie vs. Rene Lasartesse & Moondog Rex** COUNTOUT	**CROWD:** 100	**PAYOFF:** $146

232	Oct. 06	Hamburg, Germany	★★1/2
L	**Rip Morgan** face-buster suplex	**CROWD:** 575	**PAYOFF:** $140

233	Oct. 07	Hamburg, Germany	★★★1/2
W	**Moondog Rex** sunset flip	**CROWD:** 500	**PAYOFF:** $160

234	Oct. 08	Hamburg, Germany	★★★
W	**Mad Mac**		
	reverse victory roll from top rope	CROWD: 300	PAYOFF: $140

235	Oct. 09	Hamburg, Germany	★★1/2
L	**Tag with Boston Blackie vs. Rene Lasartesse & Moondog Rex (lumberjack match)**		
	DQ/injured/couldn't continue	CROWD: 300	PAYOFF: $140

236	Oct. 10	Hamburg, Germany	★★★
W	**Mad Mac**		
	DQ/referee bump	CROWD: 250	PAYOFF: $164

237	Oct. 12	Hamburg, Germany	★
W	**Tag with Boston Blackie vs. Rene Lasartesse & Moondog Rex**		
	Blackie pinned Rene/reverse pin	CROWD: 200	PAYOFF: $140

238	Oct. 13	Hamburg, Germany	★★★
L	**Moondog Rex**		
	hit by bone	CROWD: 500	PAYOFF: $140

239	Oct. 14	Hamburg, Germany	★★★
L	**Mad Mac**		
	cross-body roll-up	CROWD: 400	PAYOFF: $140

240	Oct. 15	Hamburg, Germany	★★★1/2
L	**Rip Morgan**		
	clothesline	CROWD: 400	PAYOFF: $140

241	Oct. 16	Hamburg, Germany	★★★
L	**Mad Mac**		
	missed moonsault	CROWD: 750	PAYOFF: $176

242	Oct. 29	Calgary, Alberta	★★
W	**Tag with Atomic Punk vs. Jason Helton & Dylan Powers**		
	DQ	CROWD: 200	PAYOFF: $25

MATCH NOTES #242

During the week, Lenny (aka Punk) received a cryptic message that because he had heat with Calgary booker Karl Moffat, Moffat's stooge Shane Croft was gonna attack him and shoot on Len after the match. Their stupid plan leaked, and part of it was that as part of the match, I would fight both Powers and Helton out of the arena, leaving Len alone for Croft to attack from behind. Lenny and I made a deal that if he needed help, he would give me a sign, and I'd come in for the save. Croft was a big, burly farm boy who topped the scales at about 350, so as soon as he hit the ring, he got the upper hand on Len pretty fast. I did the run-in and started flailing fists down upon the big man. I was pulling his hair as hard as I could but he wasn't reacting, until I realized it was actually Len's weeds that I was tugging. I quickly let go and then grabbed Croft by the nuts and squeezed as hard as I could. Even though this was actually Croft's crotch, once again, he still wasn't selling it in the least, and he actually looked at me and laughed. He smacked my face and I rolled to floor, grabbed a chair, came back in, and walloped him in the head as hard as I could. Finally, he backed down and retreated. But the fun was just beginning for Lenny and me as we proceeded to destroy Croft's merch table and called his wife the most awful of names before heading downstairs to threaten Moffat with a hockey stick with nails driven through it (a creation I conceived and constructed earlier that week). Eventually, we kicked him out of his own office.

NOVEMBER 1993

243	Nov. 05	Mexico City	★★1/2
W	**6-man with Atlantis & Ultimo Dragon vs. Mocho Cota, Black Magic & Emilio Charles Jr.**		
	pinned Magic/cross-body to the floor	CROWD: 4,000	PAYOFF: $268

244	Nov. 06	Ecatepec, Mexico	★★1/2
L	**6-man with Justiciero & Football Man vs. Black Magic, Tiger de Oro & Skinhead**		
	submitted by Magic	CROWD: 600	PAYOFF: $254

245	Nov. 06	Mexico City	★★★
W	**6-man with Sombra & La Fiera vs. Negro Casas, Cachorro Mendoza & Dr. Wagner Jr.**		
	pinned Wagner/cross-body to the floor	CROWD: 800	PAYOFF: $268

246	Nov. 07	Mexico City	★★1/2
L	**6-man with Sombra & Atlantis vs. Black Magic, Felino & Supremo**		
	Sombra pinned	CROWD: 4,000	PAYOFF: $269

247	Nov. 10	Acapulco, Mexico	★★★
W	**6-man with El Dandy & Atlantis vs. Black Magic, Negro Casas & Mano Negra**		
	pinned Magic/finesse press	CROWD: 600	PAYOFF: $245

248	Nov. 12	Mexico City	★★1/2
L	**6-man with El Dandy & Rayo de Jalisco Jr. vs. Black Magic, Negro Casas & Mano Negra**		
	El Dandy pinned	CROWD: 5,000	PAYOFF: $429

249	Nov. 13	Puebla, Mexico	★★1/2
L	**6-man with El Dandy & Blue Demon vs. Gran Markus Jr., Dr. Wagner Jr. & Gladiador**		
	back suplex	CROWD: 1,000	PAYOFF: $245

250	Nov. 14	Guadalajara, Mexico	★★★
W	**6-man Ringo Mendoza & Atlantis vs. Negro Casas, Bestia Salvaje & Mano Negra**		
	DQ/Mendoza fouled	CROWD: 7,000	PAYOFF: $246

I love this picture! I hadn't seen it in about 25 years but I totally remember this night. A star-studded lineup at Allegro discotheque in Mexico City in 1993 featuring Negro Casas, Norman Smiley, Haku, Jado, Gedo, Jaque Mate, Masakre, and the best of all ... the American kid in the black shirt at the front who just happened to be there and got super fucked up. We never saw him again.

251	Nov. 17	Cancun, Mexico	★★★1/2
W	**6-man with Rayo de Jalisco Jr. & Atlantis vs. Mano Negra, Mocho Cota & Pierroth Jr.**		
	pinned Cota/moonsault	CROWD: 3,000	PAYOFF: $246

252	Nov. 19	Mexico City	★1/2
W	**6-man Ringo Mendoza vs. Emilio Charles Jr., Felino & Sangre Chicana**		
	DQ	CROWD: 3,500	PAYOFF: $355

253	Nov. 20	Mexico City	★1/2
W	**6-man with Vampiro & El Dandy vs. Dr. Wagner Jr., Gladiador & Emilio Charles Jr.**		
	pinned Charles/sunset flip	CROWD: 200	PAYOFF: $254

254	Nov. 20	Mexico City	★★
W	**Tag with Ringo Mendoza vs. Red Man & Spike**		
	top-rope elbow	CROWD: 300	PAYOFF: $254

255	Nov. 20	Mexico City	★★1/2

6-man Ringo Mendoza vs. Gladiador, Dr. Wagner Jr. & Gran Markus Jr.

W pinned Markus/reverse tope · CROWD: 450 · PAYOFF: $247

256	Nov. 21	Mexico City	★★★

Tag with Ciclon Ramirez vs. Negro Casas & Black Magic

L CROWD: 4,000 · PAYOFF: $247

257	Nov. 23	Mexico City	★★

6-man Ringo Mendoza & Fiera vs. Black Magic, Dr. Wagner Jr. & Emilio Charles Jr.

W Mendoza pinned Wagner · CROWD: 3,000 · PAYOFF: $216

258	Nov. 24	Acapulco, Mexico	★★1/2

6-man with El Dandy & Ultimo Dragon vs. Negro Casas, Mocho Cota & Emilio Charles Jr.

W DQ/Dragon fouled · CROWD: 300 · PAYOFF: $216

259	Nov. 25	Toluca, Mexico	★★1/2

Tag with El Dandy vs. Yamato & Engendro

W DQ/fouled by Yamato · CROWD: 200 · PAYOFF: $223

260	Nov. 26	Mexico City	★★1/2

6-man with Silver King & Brazo de Plata vs. Yamato, El Texano & Killer

W Silver King fouled · CROWD: 600 · PAYOFF: $483

261	Nov. 27	Mexico City	★★

6-man with Fiera & Rayo de Jalisco Jr. vs. Mano Negra, Sangre Chicana & Mocho Cota

W DQ · CROWD: 350 · PAYOFF: $216

262	Nov. 28	Mexico City	★★1/2

6-man with Rayo de Jalisco Jr. & Pantera vs. Black Magic, Mocho Cota & Tornado Negro

W CROWD: 3,500 · PAYOFF: $217

DECEMBER 1993

263	Dec. 01	Acapulco, Mexico	★★★

6-man with Atlantis & El Dandy vs. Emilio Charles Jr., Sangre Chicana & Mocho Cota

W DQ/fouled by Charles · CROWD: 600 · PAYOFF: $255

264	Dec. 03	Mexico City	★★★

6-man with King Haku & Rayo de Jalisco Jr. vs. Earthquake, Dr. Wagner Jr. & Pierroth Jr.

L pinned by Wagner/splash · CROWD: 6,000 · PAYOFF: $255

265	Dec. 04	Mexico City	★★1/2

Mano Negra (won NWA world middleweight title)

W TKO · CROWD: 600 · PAYOFF: $255

266	Dec. 05	Merida, Mexico		★★1/2

6-man with King Haku & Vampiro vs. Dr. Wagner Jr., Pierroth Jr. & Emilio Charles Jr.

W pinned Wagner/crucifix sunset flip   CROWD: 2,000   PAYOFF: $254

267	Dec. 07	Mexico City		★★★

6-man Ringo Mendoza & America Rocca vs. Mogur, Gladiador & Emilio Charles Jr.

W pinned Charles/reverse tope   CROWD: 3,800   PAYOFF: $231

268	Dec. 08	Acapulco, Mexico		★★1/2

6-man with King Haku & Atlantis vs. Emilio Charles Jr., Black Magic & Pierroth Jr.

L pinned by Magic/reverse top-rope cross-body block   CROWD: 450   PAYOFF: $231

269	Dec. 11	Mexico City		★★★

6-man with Atlantis & Kato Kung Lee vs. Mano Negra, Mocho Cota & Sangre Chicana

W DQ/fouled by Negra   CROWD: 450   PAYOFF: $232

270	Dec. 12	Guadalajara, Mexico		★★1/2

6-man with Ciclon Ramirez & Rayo de Jalisco Jr. vs. Felino, Cachorro Mendoza & Jaque Mate

L Felino pinned Ramirez   CROWD: 4,000   PAYOFF: $327

271	Dec. 14	Mexico City		★★

6-man with El Brazo & Brazo de Plata vs. Kahoz, Jaque Mate & Bestia Salvaje

DC DOUBLE COUNT   CROWD: 3,000   PAYOFF: $239

272	Dec. 15	Acapulco, Mexico		★★★

Black Magic

W reversed top-rope belly-to-belly suplex   CROWD: 400   PAYOFF: $239

273	Dec. 16	Cancun, Mexico		★★

Tag with Fiera vs. Kato Kung Lee & El Hijo del Solitario

W DQ/Fiera fouled   CROWD: 400   PAYOFF: $239

274	Dec. 18	Ecatepec, Mexico		★★

6-man with Justiciero & Grizzly vs. Jaque Mate, Tigre de Oro & King Xanadu

W DQ/Justiciero fouled by Mate   CROWD: 175   PAYOFF: $256

275	Dec. 18	Mexico City		★★★

6-man with Ciclon Ramirez & Ultimo Dragon vs. Negro Casas, Bestia Salvaje & Cadaver

L pinned by Bestia/messed up Lionsault   CROWD: 300   PAYOFF: $239

MATCH NOTES #275

The finish was supposed to be Negro missing a headbutt off the top rope and me rolling him up as a result. Instead, when he came off the top, I forgot to move, and he flew down expecting me to move. He landed about two feet to the left of me, making us both look *muy stupido*. I forced the great Negro Casas to look like an idiot, and then even worse, I forgot I was supposed to roll him up, which he tried to tell me three times before finally basically pinning himself. It was the stinker of all stinker finishes for a match that had gone quite well up to the end. Afterwards I was despondent, until Negro said, "Don't worry. I told the announcers to say I was dizzy from the match and lost my balance." When that still didn't help me cheer up, he said, "It's a good lesson. Take what you can learn from tonight and use it to make sure this never happens again. And tomorrow is a new match and your chance to make this one go away." He was right, and that's been my mindset ever since when I have a match I don't care for.

276	Dec. 19	Mexico City	★★★

6-man with Ultimo Dragon & Blue Demon vs. Negro Casas, Dr. Wagner Jr. & Gran Markus Jr.

W	DQ/fouled by Wagner after backflip	**CROWD:** 3,800	**PAYOFF:** $240

JANUARY 1994

277	Jan. 07	Calgary, Alberta	★★★1/2

Steve Rivers (won CRMW mid-heavyweight title)

W	spinning DDT	**CROWD:** 200	**PAYOFF:** $45

278	Jan. 14	Calgary, Alberta	★★1/2

Lance Storm

W	DQ/fake foul on Storm	**CROWD:** 150	**PAYOFF:** $50

279	Jan. 21	Calgary, Alberta	★★1/2

Lance Storm

DQ	DOUBLE DQ	**CROWD:** 150	**PAYOFF:** $50

280	Jan. 28	Calgary, Alberta	★★★1/2

Lance Storm

L	4-3 in seven-fall iron man match	**CROWD:** 150	**PAYOFF:** $50

FEBRUARY 1994

281	Feb. 04	Calgary, Alberta	★★★★

Lance Storm (lost CRMW mid-heavyweight title/ladder match)

L		**CROWD:** 150	**PAYOFF:** $50

282	Feb. 24	Tokyo	★★1/2

Rio, Lord of the Jungle

W	lionsault	**CROWD:** 1,600	**PAYOFF:** $400

283	Feb. 25	Toyota, Japan	★★★

Masao Orihara

W	lionsault	**CROWD:** 2,200	**PAYOFF:** $400

Doing the Fabulous Fargo strut
with my old friend Masa Horie
somewhere in Japan circa 1996.
Note "Blue Meanie Hart" written
at the top, as I was imitating
Da Blue Guy who was using the
strut in ECW at the time.

284	Feb. 26	Ito City, Japan		★★
L	**Kim Duk**			
	submission		CROWD: 3,200	PAYOFF: $400

MARCH 1994

285	Mar. 02	Tokyo		★★1/2
L	**Super Strong Machine**			
	flying headbutt		CROWD: 12,000	PAYOFF: $400

SECTION TWO
MEXICO-JAPAN

MAR. 07, 1994 - AUG. 03, 1996

MATCHES 286 - 585

286	Mar. 07	Dungannon, VA	★★1/2
Tag with Lance Storm vs. The Infernos			
W	Storm pin/top-rope double dropkick	CROWD: 300	PAYOFF: $40

287	Mar. 07	Dungannon, VA	★★1/2
Tag with Lance Storm vs. Mike Sampson & Larry Santo			
W	powersault	CROWD: 300	PAYOFF: $41

288	Mar. 07	Dungannon, VA	★★
Tag with Lance Storm vs. Mike Sampson & Hornet			
W	Storm pin/electric chair cross-body	CROWD: 300	PAYOFF: $40

289	Mar. 11	Paintsville, KY	★★
Tag with Lance Storm vs. Infernos			
W	Storm pin/electric chair cross-body	CROWD: 350	PAYOFF: $140

290	Mar. 12	Johnson City, TN	★★
Tag with Lance Storm vs. Infernos			
W	Storm pin/splash	CROWD: 800	PAYOFF: $200

291	Mar. 13	Knoxville, TN	★★1/2
Tag with Lance Storm vs. Infernos			
W	powersault	CROWD: 1,000	PAYOFF: $143

292	Mar. 15	Albany, KY	★★1/2
Tag with Lance Storm vs. Infernos			
W	powersault	CROWD: 500	PAYOFF: $120

293	Mar. 17	Hayden, KY	★★1/2
Tag with Lance Storm vs. Well Dunn			
W	pinned Well/sunset flip	CROWD: 250	PAYOFF: $107

294	Mar. 18	Barbourville, KY	★★★
Tag with Lance Storm vs. Well Dunn			
W	pinned Well/sunset flip	CROWD: 650	PAYOFF: $140

295	Mar. 19	Harlan, KY	★★★
Tag with Lance Storm vs. Well Dunn			
W	pinned Well/sunset flip	CROWD: 300	PAYOFF: $140

296	Mar. 26	Kumamoto, Japan	★1/2
Tag with Yamato vs. Hiromichi Fuyuki & Ultimo Dragon			
L	pinned by Asai/spinning roll-up	CROWD: 1,500	PAYOFF: $300

297	Mar. 27	Nobeoka, Japan		★★1/2
L	**The Great Kabuki**			
	clothesline		CROWD: 1,700	PAYOFF: $300

298	Mar. 28	Miyakonojo, Japan		★★1/2
W	**Norman Smiley**			
	lionsault		CROWD: 2,700	PAYOFF: $300

299	Mar. 29	Hakata, Japan		★1/2
L	**Norman Smiley**			
	missed moonsault		CROWD: 2,500	PAYOFF: $300

300	Mar. 30	Ohita, Japan		★★★
W	**Nobukazu Hirai**			
	lionsault		CROWD: 1,700	PAYOFF: $300

APRIL 1994

301	Apr. 01	Tokyo		★★★★
L	**Jado**			
	top-rope Frankensteiner		CROWD: 2,100	PAYOFF: $300

302	Apr. 04	Clinton, TN		★★★
W	**Tag with Lance Storm vs. Well Dunn**			
	small package		CROWD: 500	PAYOFF: $35

303	Apr. 04	Clinton, TN		★★
W	**Tag with Lance Storm vs. Chris Hamrick & Hornet**			
	pinned Hamrick/face-first superplex		CROWD: 500	PAYOFF: $35

304	Apr. 04	Clinton, TN		★★1/2
W	**Tag with Lance Storm vs. Inferno & Killer Kyle**			
	pinned Inferno/top-rope spin kick		CROWD: 500	PAYOFF: $35

TAZ'S TOP 5 JERICHO MOVES

5. TRIANGLE DROPKICK
One of Chris' signature offensive maneuvers for decades, this springboard twisting dropkick from the second rope showcases his speed, balance, footwork, and accuracy on impact.

4. GERMAN SUPLEX
It's not part of Jericho's normal offense, but he possesses a very potent German suplex with impactful hip surge on the throw and a strong back bridge.

Backstage with Ultimo Dragon in Japan, one of my greatest rivals and opponents ever.

3. LIONSAULT
Chris has always been known for excellent athleticism. He utilizes it with this springboard moonsault from the middle rope. He can basically hit this no matter where his opponent is. It's impressive and deadly!

2. WALLS OF JERICHO
There have been hundreds of wrestlers over the years that have done impressive Boston crabs. I have been in many myself, but there are none like this version. It produces an insane amount of pain — I'm speaking from experience!

1. JUDAS EFFECT
One underrated thing about Chris is his very quick feet. That's the key with this awesomely impressive spinning back elbow strike.

305	Apr. 06	Acapulco, Mexico	★★★1/2
W	**Tag with El Dandy & Emilio Charles Jr. vs. El Texano**		
		CROWD: 600	PAYOFF: $443

In the cage with Fuyuki and Gedo with WAR in 1994. It was my first night with the team after replacing an injured Jado, which is why I didn't have a fancy matching jacket.

306	Apr. 08	Mexico City	★★1/2
	6-man with Negro Casas & Fiera vs. Bestia Salvaje, Mocho Cota & Emilio Charles Jr.		
W	DQ/fake foul on Storm	CROWD: 8,000	PAYOFF: $444
307	Apr. 09	Mexico City	★★★1/2
	6-man with Haku & Vampiro vs. Dr. Wagner Jr., Black Magic & Miguel Perez		
DR	double pin	CROWD: 1,000	PAYOFF: $437
308	Apr. 10	Mexico City	★★
	6-man with Ultimo Dragon & Vampiro vs. Miguel Perez, Mano Negra & Pierroth Jr.		
L	pinned by Pierroth Jr./clothesline	CROWD: 3,500	PAYOFF: $464
309	Apr. 15	Mexico City	★★1/2
	Atlantis		
L	powerbomb	CROWD: 8,000	PAYOFF: $589

310	Apr. 16	Huamantla, Mexico	★★★

6-man with Atlantis & Rayo de Jalisco Jr. vs. Pierroth Jr., Killer & Enrique Vera

W pinned Killer/top-rope elbow   **CROWD:** 2,500   **PAYOFF:** $589

311	Apr. 17	Mexico City	★★★

6-man with Haku & El Texano vs. Dr. Wagner Jr., Yamato & Miguel Perez

W Haku pinned Yamato   **CROWD:** 3,000   **PAYOFF:** $595

312	Apr. 21	Gifu, Japan	★★

Tag with Ultimo Dragon vs. Mil Mascaras & Dos Caras

L pinned by Mascaras/top-rope cross body   **CROWD:** 3,000   **PAYOFF:** $366

313	Apr. 23	Kanazawa, Japan	★★1/2

6-man with Gado & King Haku vs. Ultimo Dragon, Mil Mascaras & Dos Caras

L pinned by Mascaras/top-rope cross body   **CROWD:** 500   **PAYOFF:** $366

314	Apr. 24	Fukui, Japan	★★★★

Ultimo Dragon

L German suplex   **CROWD:** 2,500   **PAYOFF:** $367

315	Apr. 25	Niigata, Japan	★★1/2

Tag with Gedo vs. Mil Mascaras & Dos Caras

L Mascaras pinned Gedo   **CROWD:** 2,800   **PAYOFF:** $367

316	Apr. 26	Iwate, Japan	★★★★

King Haku

L powerbomb   **CROWD:** 3,400   **PAYOFF:** $367

317	Apr. 27	Tokyo	★★

Tag with Koji Ishinriki vs. Mil Mascaras & Dos Caras

L pinned by Mascaras/top-rope cross body   **CROWD:** 2,000   **PAYOFF:** $367

MAY 1994

318	May 19	Morganton, NC	★★

Tag with Lance Storm vs. Well Dunn

W pinned Dunn/top-rope sunset flip   **CROWD:** 100   **PAYOFF:** $100

319	May 20	Knoxville, TN	★★★

Tag with Lance Storm vs. Well Dunn

W Storm pinned Dunn   **CROWD:** 2,000   **PAYOFF:** $100

320	May 21	Morristown, TN	★★1/2

Tag with Lance Storm vs. Well Dunn

W pinned Dunn/flying forearm   **CROWD:** 650   **PAYOFF:** $100

321	May 22	Marietta, GA	★★

Tag with Lance Storm vs. Well Dunn

W pinned Dunn/flying elbow   CROWD: 400   PAYOFF: $100

322	May 27	Duff, TN	★★1/2

Tag with Tracy Smothers vs. Chris Candido & Brian Lee

W DQ/fake foul on Storm   CROWD: 200   PAYOFF: $50

323	May 27	Duff, TN	★1/2

Battle Royal

W   CROWD: 200   PAYOFF: $50

324	May 28	Virgie, KY	★1/2

Steve Dunn

W   CROWD: 200   PAYOFF: $50

325	May 28	Virgie, KY	★★

Battle Royal

W   CROWD: 200   PAYOFF: $50

JUNE 1994

326	June 02	Hyden, KY	★★

Tag with Lance Storm vs. Well Dunn

W   CROWD: 100   PAYOFF: $125

327	June 02	Hyden, KY	★★

Battle Royal

W   CROWD: 100   PAYOFF: $125

328	June 04	Barbourville, KY	★★★

Tag with Lance Storm vs. Well Dunn

W   CROWD: 450   PAYOFF: $250

329	June 06	Dalton, KY	★★

Tag with Lance Storm vs. Well Dunn

W   CROWD: 60   PAYOFF: $250

330	June 07	Loudon, TN	★★1/2

Tag with Lance Storm vs. Larry Santo & Chris Hamrick

W suplex/cross-body   CROWD: 325   PAYOFF: $250

331	June 07	Loudon, TN	★★

Tag with Lance Storm vs. Larry Santo & James Adkins

W   CROWD: 325   PAYOFF: $250

332	June 10	Paintsville, KY	★★1/2

Tag with Lance Storm vs. Chris Candido & Steve Dunn

W pinned Dunn/sunset flip   CROWD: 325   PAYOFF: $250

333	June 11	Morristown, TN	★★★

Tag with Lance Storm vs. Brian Logan & Steve Dunn

W pinned Logan/cross-body electric chair   CROWD: 300   PAYOFF: $250

334	June 12	Beckley, WV	★★1/2

Tag with Lance Storm vs. Brian Logan & Steve Dunn

W pinned Logan/cross-body electric chair   CROWD: 200   PAYOFF: $250

335	June 13	Albany, KY	★★1/2

Tag with Lance Storm vs. Chris Candido & Steve Dunn

W pinned Dunn/top-rope sunset flip   CROWD: 200   PAYOFF: $250

336	June 16	Lenoir, NC	★★1/2

Tag with Lance Storm vs. Chris Candido & Steve Dunn

W pinned Dunn/top-rope sunset flip   CROWD: 250   PAYOFF: $250

337	June 17	Knoxville, TN	★★1/2

Tag with Lance Storm vs. Steve Dunn & Killer Kyle

W pinned Dunn/drop splash   CROWD: 700   PAYOFF: $250

338	June 18	Johnson City, TN	★★★

Tag with Lance Storm vs. Steve Dunn & Killer Kyle

W pinned Dunn/drop splash   CROWD: 600   PAYOFF: $250

339	June 24	Fallsburg, KY	★★1/2

Tag with Lance Storm vs. Steve Dunn & Killer Kyle

W pinned Dunn/drop splash   CROWD: 100   PAYOFF: $250

340	June 25	Hickory, NC	★1/2

Tag with Lance Storm vs. Jeff Victory & Chris Candido

W pinned Victory/cross-body electric chair   CROWD: 200   PAYOFF: $250

341	June 30	Sendai, Japan	★★

6-man with Dos Caras & Brett Como vs. Super Strong Machine, Ashura Hara & Arashi

W decision   CROWD: 5,500   PAYOFF: $433

342	June 30	Sendai, Japan	★★★1/2

6-man with Dos Caras & Brett Como vs. Gedo, Jado & Hiromichi Fuyuki

W Como pinned Gedo   CROWD: 5,500   PAYOFF: $433

343	June 30	Sendai, Japan	★★

6-man with Dos Caras & Brett Como vs. Great Sasuke, Masao Orihara & Shiryu

W Como pinned Sasuke   CROWD: 5,500   PAYOFF: $433

DAVE LAGRECA'S TOP 10 FAVORITE JERICHO MATCHES

Dave LaGreca is the host of Busted Open Radio *on SiriusXM Fight Nation*

10. #1285, 4-WAY TLC WITH CHRIS BENOIT VS. THE DUDLEY BOYZ VS. THE HARDY BOYZ VS. EDGE AND CHRISTIAN, SMACKDOWN 2001, MAY 22, 2001, ANAHEIM, CA
Remember when the tag team division actually meant something in the WWE? This underrated match closed the book not only on true tag team wrestling in the company but was also the final exclamation point of the Attitude Era. I love this match because it is truly a document of a bygone era.

9. #2687, TETSUYA NAITO, DOMINION, JUNE 9, 2018, OSAKA
This was the first time Chris Jericho ever won the IWGP Intercontinental Championship — even more impressive, he became the first wrestler to ever hold the Intercontinental title in both New Japan and the WWE.

8. #2698, CODY, AEW FULL GEAR, NOV. 9, 2019, BALTIMORE
To me, this match contributed to the foundation of AEW. This set the tone of a company that was going to be a combination of old-school storytelling with new-school athleticism, and this match defined it. The match kept the world championship on the mainstream star, Chris Jericho, while setting up a story with the heart and soul of AEW, Cody, going against the newest and biggest heel in pro wrestling, MJF.

7. #2690, TETSUYA NAITO, WRESTLE KINGDOM 13, JAN. 4, 2019, TOKYO
Always changing his character and appearance, Chris Jericho had an all-new persona with his Alice Cooper/Malcolm McDowell look for Wrestle Kingdom 13 in the Tokyo Dome. A rematch of their classic at Dominion, where Jericho made Naito a star to an American audience that may have been seeing him for the first time.

6. #2130, REY MYSTERIO JR., THE BASH 2009, JUNE 28, 2009, SACRAMENTO, CA
To me, this was one of the greatest intercontinental championship matches of all time. It's almost impossible to have a bad match with these two legends, but the fast pace of this effort kept you on the edge of your seat from start to finish.

5. #2352, CM PUNK, WRESTLEMANIA 28, APR. 1, 2012, MIAMI GARDENS, FL

To me, this was the best match at WrestleMania 28 by a mile. The story going in was a straight-edge CM Punk being harassed by Chris Jericho about his father's alcoholism. It was real, it was dark, and — oh, by the way, it was for the WWE Championship.

4. #1227, CHRIS BENOIT, ROYAL RUMBLE, JAN. 21, 2001, NEW ORLEANS

When you look back to the greatest ladder matches in history, this bout has to be listed near the top. Chris may be one of the best ever in ladder matches, and this one was special even by his own high standards.

3. #1582, SHAWN MICHAELS, WRESTLEMANIA 19, MAR. 30, 2003, SEATTLE

My personal favorite match from one of the best WrestleManias ever. Old-school psychology meets pure adrenaline. A classic match that, instead of ending with an embrace, ended with a literal kick to the groin.

2. #2685, KENNY OMEGA, WRESTLE KINGDOM 12, JAN. 4, 2018, TOKYO

As a fan, THANK GOD Chris left the WWE. Arguably this is the greatest match in his career. If you look at his run in New Japan, not only did it show a dimension, but it may have also been his best run period. This match is as close to perfection as you could possibly get.

1. #2003, SHAWN MICHAELS, NO MERCY, OCT. 5, 2008, PORTLAND, OR

Two of the top 10 greatest of all time in the ring with a ladder for the World Heavyweight Championship. Enough said.

JULY 1994			
344	July 01	Knoxville, TN	★★1/2
W	**Tag with Lance Storm vs. Well Dunn (penalty box match)** Storm pinned Well	**CROWD:** 1,000	**PAYOFF:** $225
345	July 02	Barbourville, KY	★1/2
W	**Tag with Lance Storm vs. Well Dunn (penalty box match)** Storm pinned Well	**CROWD:** 850	**PAYOFF:** $225
346	July 03	Marietta, GA	★★1/2
W	**Tag with Lance Storm vs. Well Dunn (penalty box match)** pinned Dunn/sunset flip	**CROWD:** 400	**PAYOFF:** $225

347	July 04	Paintsville, KY	★★

Tag with Lance Storm vs. Well Dunn (penalty box match)

W pinned Dunn/sunset flip   CROWD: 400   PAYOFF: $225

348	July 05	Warrensville, NC	★★1/2

Tag with Lance Storm vs. Hornet & Steve Skyfire

W turbo Thesz press   CROWD: 400   PAYOFF: $225

349	July 05	Warrensville, NC	★

Tag with Lance Storm vs. Anthony Michaels & Chris Hamrick

W   CROWD: 400   PAYOFF: $225

350	July 07	Harlan, KY	★★★

Tag with Lance Storm vs. Well Dunn (penalty box match)

W   CROWD: 200   PAYOFF: $225

351	July 08	Beckley, WV	★★

Tag with Lance Storm vs. Well Dunn (penalty box match)

W   CROWD: 200   PAYOFF: $225

352	July 09	Johnson City, TN	★★1/2

Tag with Lance Storm vs. Well Dunn (penalty box match)

W   CROWD: 500   PAYOFF: $225

353	July 15	Koriyama, Japan	★★1/2

Ultimo Dragon

L moonsault   CROWD: 1,000   PAYOFF: $1,150

354	July 17	Tokyo	★★★1/2

6-man with Warlord & Vampiro vs. Genichiro Tenryu, Atsushi Onita & Bam Bam Bigelow

L pinned by Onita/powerbomb   CROWD: 12,000   PAYOFF: $1,150

355	July 22	Fairlea, WV	★1/2

Tag with Lance Storm vs. The Batten Twins

W   CROWD: 100   PAYOFF: $225

356	July 23	Chilhowie, VA	★★

Tag with Lance Storm vs. The Batten Twins

W   CROWD: 300   PAYOFF: $225

357	July 24	Inez, KY	★★

Tag with Lance Storm vs. The Batten Twins

W   CROWD: 200   PAYOFF: $225

358	July 29	Albany, KY		★1/2
W	**Tag with Lance Storm vs. Inferno & Killer Kyle**		**CROWD:** 300	**PAYOFF:** $225

AUGUST 1994

359	Aug. 01	Lebanon, KY		★★
W	**Tag with Lance Storm vs. The Gangstas**			
	DQ		**CROWD:** 150	**PAYOFF:** $500

360	Aug. 02	Jamestown, KY		★★
W	**Tag with Lance Storm vs. The Gangstas**			
	DQ		**CROWD:** 350	**PAYOFF:** $500

361	Aug. 04	Harlan, KY		★★1/2
W	**Tag with Lance Storm vs. The Gangstas**			
	DQ		**CROWD:** 250	**PAYOFF:** $500

362	Aug. 05	Knoxville, TN		★★★★
W	**Tag with Lance Storm vs. The Heavenly Bodies (street fight)**			
	pinned Jimmy Del Rey/roll-up		**CROWD:** 4,500	**PAYOFF:** $500

MATCH NOTES #362, HELPED SMOKY MOUNTAIN WRESTLING SELL OUT "NIGHT OF THE LEGENDS"

During the summer of 1994, I convinced myself that if I couldn't do a shooting star press, I would never make it in pro wrestling. After the encouragement of Ultimo Dragon, who told me I could do it no problem, I spent the summer trying the move off diving boards and build up the courage to give it a try. After a few rough attempts where I narrowly avoided disaster in house show rings, I decided I was going to debut it in this huge match on this huge show. I got to the arena early and gave it a try ... with no crash pad and no spotter. I landed wrong on my side and instantly knew I was hurt. I went to the hospital to find out I had indeed fractured my right forearm. I was scheduled for surgery immediately, but I was able to postpone it to the next morning by telling the doctor I had to make an appearance at the wrestling show that evening to "sign autographs." Instead I left the hospital, went straight to the dressing room to put on my gear and wouldn't take no for an answer from anybody who suggested I not do the match (promoter Jim Cornette wasn't one of them.). The contest that followed was a clinic on how to lead an injured idiot through a good match. Jimmy Del Ray and Dr. Tom Pritchard literally made a one-armed man look like Superman. I'm still amazed, and I was in the damn thing! It was my last ever SMW match, but what a way to go out!

Hakata Star Lanes with WAR in Fukuoka, 1994. The funny thing is, I trained in Canada in a bowling alley, only to travel across the world to wrestle in Japan ... in a bowling alley.

SEPTEMBER 1994

363	Sept. 29	Tokyo		★★1/2
L	**Vampiro**			
	powerbomb		CROWD: 1200	PAYOFF: $600

364	Sept. 30	Fukuoka, Japan		★★
L	**Dos Caras**			
	top-rope cross-body		CROWD: 2,300	PAYOFF: $600

365	Oct. 01	Oita, Japan		★★★
L	**Ultimo Dragon**			
	twisting moonsault		CROWD: 3,000	PAYOFF: $600

366	Oct. 05	Kumamoto, Japan		★★
W	**Masanobu Kurisu**			
	flying fist		CROWD: 1,500	PAYOFF: $600

367	Nov. 02	Yonezawa, Japan	★★
W	**Hiroshi Itakura** timber headbutt	CROWD: 1,500	PAYOFF: $333

368	Nov. 03	Kuroishi, Japan	★★
L	**Tag with Yuji Yasuraoka vs. Rock 'N Roll Express** Yasuraoka pinned	CROWD: 2,000	PAYOFF: $333

369	Nov. 04	Aomori, Japan	★★★
W	**Tag with Ultimo Dragon vs. Rock 'N Roll Express**	CROWD: 3,000	PAYOFF: $333

370	Nov. 05	Sakata, Japan	★★★1/2
L	**6-man with Rock 'N Roll Express vs. Jado, Gedo & Hiromichi Fuyuki**	CROWD: 1,600	PAYOFF: $333

371	Nov. 06	Chiba, Japan	★★★1/2
W	**Ultimo Dragon** lionsault	CROWD: 2,300	PAYOFF: $334

372	Nov. 08	Tokyo	★★★★★
L	**Ultimo Dragon (lost NWA world middleweight title)** Cancun tornado	CROWD: 2,000	PAYOFF: $334

373	Nov. 11	Mexico City	★★
W	**Tag with Atlanis vs. Rayo de Jalisco Jr. & El Hijo del Solitario** pinned Atlantis	CROWD: 5,000	PAYOFF: $461

374	Nov. 12	Puebla, Mexico	★★
W	**Tag with El Dandy vs. Dr. Wagner Jr. & El Satanico** DQ	CROWD: 500	PAYOFF: $461

375	Nov. 13	Mexico City	★★★
W	**6-man with Ultimo Dragon & El Dandy vs. Black Magic, Pierroth Jr. & Emilio Charles Jr.** pinned Magic/top-rope elbow	CROWD: 1,200	PAYOFF: $460

376	Nov. 16	Acapulco, Mexico	★★
W	**Tag with Atlantis vs. Emilio Charles Jr. & Dr. Wagner Jr.** pinned Wagner/lionsault	CROWD: 850	PAYOFF: $332

377	Nov. 18	Mexico City	★★1/2
W	**Tag with Atlantis vs. Fiera & Shocker** pinned Shocker/Canadian supercrusher	CROWD: 4,000	PAYOFF: $332

378	Nov. 19	Puebla, Mexico	★★1/2

Tag with Silver King vs. Dr. Wagner Jr. & Emilio Charles Jr.

L Wagner **CROWD:** 450 **PAYOFF:** $333

379	Nov. 20	Guadalajara, Mexico	★★

6-man with Apolo Dantes & Rayo de Jalisco Jr. vs. Emilio Charles Jr., Gran Markus Jr. & El Satanico

L **CROWD:** 400 **PAYOFF:** $333

380	Nov. 25	Mexico City	★

Tag with Atlantis vs. Emilio Charles Jr. & El Satanico

L pinned/missed tope **CROWD:** 2,000 **PAYOFF:** $354

381	Nov. 26	Mexico City	★1/2

6-man with Negro Casas & El Dandy vs. Bestia Salvaje, Javier Cruz & Mano Negra

W DQ/Negra **CROWD:** 300 **PAYOFF:** $354

382	Nov. 27	Mexico City	★★★

6-man with Negro Casas & El Texano vs. Black Magic, Emilio Charles Jr. & Gran Markus Jr.

W pinned El Texano **CROWD:** 2,500 **PAYOFF:** $354

383	Nov. 27	Mexico City	★★1/2

Tag with El Texano vs. Black Magic & Emilio Charles Jr.

W DQ/Charles **CROWD:** 400 **PAYOFF:** $354

384	Nov. 30	Acapulco, Mexico	★★★★

Tag with Silver King vs. Negro Casas & El Dandy

L Casas pin **CROWD:** 1,200 **PAYOFF:** $332

DECEMBER 1994

385	Dec. 02	Mexico City	★★★

6-man with Negro Casas & Dos Caras vs. Silver King, El Texano & Atlantis

L pinned Silver King/moonsault body-block **CROWD:** 3,000 **PAYOFF:** $332

386	Dec. 03	Mexico City	★★1/2

6-man with El Dandy & Negro Casas vs. Black Magic, Emilio Charles Jr. & Pierroth Jr.

L pinned Magic/cross-body rollover **CROWD:** 350 **PAYOFF:** $333

387	Dec. 04	Mexico City	★★★

6-man with El Texano & Kato Kung Lee vs. Gran Markus Jr., Dr. Wagner Jr. & El Brazo

L pinned El Texano **CROWD:** 2,000 **PAYOFF:** $333

388	Dec. 09	Mexico City	★★1/2

6-man with Atlantis & Dos Caras vs. Dr. Wagner Jr., Emilio Charles Jr. & El Satanico

L pinned Wagner **CROWD:** 2,500 **PAYOFF:** $443

For some reason, this is my twin daughters' favorite picture of me and they break out in giggle fits whenever they see it. Big Titan, Lance, and me in Japan in 1995.

389	Dec. 10	San Pedro, Mexico	★★1/2
	Tag with Solar vs. Pierroth Jr. & Mocha Coto		
W	DQ	CROWD: 300	PAYOFF: $116

390	Dec. 10	Mexico City	★★1/2
	6-man with El Dandy & Ringo Mendoza vs. Pierroth Jr., El Satanico & Dr. Wagner Jr.		
W		CROWD: 350	PAYOFF: $443

391	Dec. 11	Mexico City	★★1/2
	6-man with Vampiro & Brazo de Plata vs. Black Magic, Emilio Charles Jr. & Pierroth Jr.		
W	beat Pierroth Jr./Inoki stretch	CROWD: 1,500	PAYOFF: $443

392	Dec. 13	Mexico City	★★
	6-man with Apolo Dantes & Brazo de Plata vs. Sangre Chicano, El Brazo & Mogur		
L	Dantes	CROWD: 1,000	PAYOFF: $470

393	Dec. 14	Acapulco, Mexico	★1/2
	6-man with Silver King & El Texano vs. Dr. Wagner Jr., Black Magic & Sangre Chicana		
W	DQ	CROWD: 1,500	PAYOFF: $471

394	Dec. 16	Mexico City	★★
	6-man with Vampiro & Mil Mascaras vs. Dr. Wagner Jr., Pierroth Jr. & Gran Markus Jr.		
W	beat Wagner/Inoki stretch	CROWD: 6,000	PAYOFF: $470

395	Dec. 17	Mexico City	★★★
	6-man with Ringo Mendoza & Fiera vs. Black Magic, El Satanico & Dr. Wagner Jr.		
W	beat Fiera	CROWD: 300	PAYOFF: $471

396	Dec. 18	Mexico City	★★★1/2

6-man with Vampiro & Ringo Mendoza vs. Bestia Salvaje, Black Magic & Gran Markus Jr.

W	beat Salvaje/Inoki stretch	**CROWD:** 4,000	**PAYOFF:** $470

JANUARY 1995

397	Jan. 06	Shizuoka, Japan	★★★

Ultimo Dragon

L		**CROWD:** 2,500	**PAYOFF:** $383

398	Jan. 07	Kanagawa, Japan	★★1/2

Ciclon Ramirez

W	lionsault	**CROWD:** 2,000	**PAYOFF:** $383

399	Jan. 08	Tokyo	★★★1/2

Masao Orihara

DR	30 minutes	**CROWD:** 2,200	**PAYOFF:** $383

400	Jan. 10	Saitama, Japan	★★1/2

Ciclon Ramirez

W	lionsault	**CROWD:** 700	**PAYOFF:** $383

401	Jan. 10	Saitama, Japan	★★

Felino

W	Canadian super-crusher	**CROWD:** 700	**PAYOFF:** $383

402	Jan. 11	Ibaraki, Japan	★★1/2

Felino

W	lionsault	**CROWD:** 500	**PAYOFF:** $383

403	Jan. 27	Chilliwack, British Columbia	★★★

Firefighter Adrian

DR	25 minutes	**CROWD:** 250	**PAYOFF:** $75

FEBRUARY 1995

404	Feb. 06	Tokyo	★★★1/2

Tag with Nobukazu Hirai vs. Eliminators

L	Hirai pinned	**CROWD:** 2,200	**PAYOFF:** $420

405	Feb. 08	Osaka, Japan	★★1/2

Tag with Kim Duk vs. Eliminators

L	Duk pinned	**CROWD:** 1,000	**PAYOFF:** $420

406	Feb. 10	Shingu, Japan	★★1/2

Tag with Hiroshi Itakura vs. Eliminators

L	Itakura pinned	**CROWD:** 2,000	**PAYOFF:** $420

FUMI SAITO'S TOP 10
JERICHO MOMENTS IN JAPAN

(IN CHRONOLOGICAL ORDER)

Fumi Saito is a legendary Japanese pro wrestling journalist.

10. #41, 6-MAN WITH LANCE STORM & MARK STARR VS. ATSUSHI ONITA, KATSUJI UEDA, & SAMBO ASAKO, OCT. 10, 1991, KANAGAWA

At the age of 21, Jericho made his first trip to Japan, touring with Atsushi Onita's FMW (Frontier Martial Arts Wrestling) with Lance Storm (his Sudden Impact tag team partner), "The Gladiator" Mike Awesome, Horace Boulder, Mark Starr, Amigo Ultra, and Pandita. His very first match was a non-televised small spot show in Ebina, Kanagawa.

9. #88, TAG MATCH WITH ERIC FREEZE VS. EIJI EZAKI & KOJI NAKAGAWA, SEPT. 19, 1992, KANAGAWA

A year later, he came back to work for FMW's Supershow at Yokohama Stadium. His match was the opening match of the evening, a tag team match against Eiji Ezaki and Koji Nakagawa. Ezaki, of course, would become the legendary Hayabusa later on in his career. Useless trivia: this was the only time any wrestling company held a big show at Yokohama Stadium, the home of the Yokohama BayStars of NPB (Nippon Professional Baseball, Japan's major league baseball).

8. #282, RIO, LORD OF THE JUNGLE, FEB. 24, 1994, TOKYO

At the age of 23, Jericho returned to Japan as Lion Heart, this time for Genichiro Tenryu's WAR (Wrestle and Romance, later Wrestle Association R). Between 1994 and 1996, he made a total of 25 tours with Aikido and Karatedo. He had participated in the famous Super J-Cup Tournament, along with junior heavyweight superstars including Jushin "Thunder" Liger, Wild Pegasus, Ultimo Dragon, Dos Caras, El Samurai, Shinjiro Otani, and Funaki. It was during this WAR run that Jericho became a part of heel faction Fuyuki-Gun with Kodo Fuyuki, Jado, and Gedo and changed his ring name to Lion Do. "Do" in Japanese means "the way of" as in Judo, Kendo, Aikido, Karatedo. Also, he held the NWA World Middleweight, WAR International Junior Heavyweight, and WAR International Junior Heavyweight tag team titles (with partner Gedo) during this run.

7. #647, KOJI KANEMOTO, JAN. 4, 1997, TOKYO

Jericho made his New Japan Pro-Wrestling debut as the masked Super Liger at the

Wrestling World 1997 show. He beat Koji Kanemoto. This new character, Super Liger, was short-lived. Between 1997 and September of 1998, he returned to NJPW as Chris Jericho without the mask and made a total of five tours with the company.

6. #1415, THE ROCK, MAR. 1, 2002, YOKOHAMA

Jericho returned to Japan as a part of a big WWE SmackDown Live tour at Yokohama Arena. This time, he was the Undisputed WWE and WCW World Heavyweight Champion, with two titles on his shoulder. He defended his double championships against The Rock. It was a big moment for Japanese fans, who have known Jericho from the beginning. Also, it was the first WWE tour in Japan since the infamous "WWF Mania" tour in 1994, which was far from a success. From that point on, Jericho would come back to Japan every summer as a part of a "WWE Raw Live" and/or "WWE SmackDown Live" tour group even while he was not on regular domestic U.S. tours.

5. SPECIAL VIDEO APPEARANCE, NOV. 5, 2017, OSAKA

At NJPW's big show Power Struggle at Osaka Castle Hall, Jericho made a surprise appearance on the video screen, challenging Kenny Omega for an "Alpha vs. Omega" singles match. Jericho signing a match contract with NJPW was huge news and shook the entire wrestling world.

4. #2685, KENNY OMEGA, JAN. 4, 2018, TOKYO

At Wrestle Kingdom 12 at the Tokyo Dome, the Jericho vs. Omega dream match took place. This fateful encounter ultimately contributed to the formation of AEW.

3. #2687, TETSUYA NAITO, JUNE 9, 2018, OSAKA

At NJPW's annual Dominion supershow at Osaka Castle Hall, Jericho beat Tetsuya Naito to win the IWGP Intercontinental championship. Shortly after this title match, Jericho had a closed-door meeting with Vince McMahon and pitched the idea of promoting an IWGP IC Champion against WWE IC Champion double title match at that year's SummerSlam. The plan never materialized.

2. #2692, KAZUCHIKA OKADA, JUNE 9, 2019, OSAKA

At NJPW's annual Dominion supershow at Osaka Castle Hall, Jericho challenged Kazuchika Okada for the IWGP World Heavyweight championship. Simply put, a historic match.

1. #2702, HIROSHI TANAHASHI, JAN. 5, 2020, TOKYO

At Wrestle Kingdom 14 at the Tokyo Dome, another dream match took place. This time Jericho had a one-time-only singles match against Japan's biggest superstar of this era, Hiroshi Tanahashi. He beat Tanahashi with his signature Walls of Jericho. Another one for the history books.

407	Feb. 11	Yui, Japan	★★

Tag with Osamu Tachihikari vs. Eliminators

L Tachihikari pinned   CROWD: 2,200   PAYOFF: $420

408	Feb. 12	Hiroshima, Japan	★★1/2

Tag with Warlord vs. Eliminators

L Warlord pinned   CROWD: 3,000   PAYOFF: $420

MARCH 1995

409	Mar. 03	Mexico City	★★★★

6-man with Ultimo Dragon & Felino vs. Negro Casas, El Dandy & Bestia Salvaje (Copa Campeon de Campeones torneo cibernetico elimination match)

Elimination order: 1 Salvaje, 2 Felino, 3 Dragon, 4 Dandy (victory roll), 5 Casas/Canadian super-crusher

W   CROWD: 8,000   PAYOFF: $193

410	Mar. 04	Puebla, Mexico	★★★

Tag with Mil Mascaras vs. Dr. Wagner Jr. & Gran Markus Jr.

W Mascaras fouled   CROWD: 700   PAYOFF: $193

411	Mar. 05	Mexico City	★★★

6-man with Ultimo Dragon & Fiera vs. Jason the Terrible, Sangre Chicana & Mano Negra

L Fiera pinned   CROWD: 3,500   PAYOFF: $193

412	Mar. 05	Mexico City	★★★

Tag with Sombra vs. Pirata Morgan & Espectro

W Sombra fouled   CROWD: 450   PAYOFF: $193

413	Mar. 09	Cuernavaca, Mexico	★★1/2

6-man with Hector Garza & Atlantis vs. Emilio Charles Jr., El Brazo & Kahoz

W   CROWD: 400   PAYOFF: $193

414	Mar. 10	Mexico City	★★1/2

6-man with Vampiro & Fiera vs. Sangre Chicana, Emilio Charles Jr. & Bestia Salvaje

L Fiera pinned   CROWD: 4,000   PAYOFF: $193

415	Mar. 11	Mexico City	★★★

6-man with Rayo de Jalisco Jr. & El Dandy vs. Bestia Salvaje, Emilio Charles Jr. & Gran Markus Jr.

W   CROWD: 500   PAYOFF: $193

416	Mar. 12	Mexico City	★★★

6-man with Rayo de Jalisco Jr. & Silver King vs. Dr. Wagner Jr., El Satanico & Mano Negra

W   CROWD: 2,000   PAYOFF: $193

417	Mar. 13	Acapulco, Mexico	★★1/2
Tag with Ultimo Dragon vs. Emilio Charles Jr. & El Satanico			
W	DQ/fouled by Charles	CROWD: 1,500	PAYOFF: $193

418	Mar. 17	Mexico City	★★★★★
Ultimo Dragon			
L	top-rope sunset powerbomb	CROWD: 8,500	PAYOFF: $193

419	Mar. 18	Mexico City	★★
6-man with Dos Caras & Rayo de Jalisco Jr. vs. Gran Markus Jr., Jaque Mate & Jason the Terrible			
W	Rayo pinned Jason	CROWD: 400	PAYOFF: $193

420	Mar. 19	Mexico City	★★★
6-man with Mil Mascaras & Rayo de Jalisco Jr. vs. Dr. Wagner Jr., El Satanico & Pierroth Jr.			
W	pinned Wagner/crucifix	CROWD: 3,000	PAYOFF: $193

421	Mar. 21	Mexico City	★★★
3-way vs. Ultimo Dragon vs. Vampiro			
L		CROWD: 2,000	PAYOFF: $193

422	Mar. 26	Tokyo	★★1/2
Masao Orihara			
W	lionsault	CROWD: 7,500	PAYOFF: $358

423	Mar. 26	Tokyo	★★★
Ultimo Dragon			
W	roll-up	CROWD: 7,500	PAYOFF: $358

424	Mar. 26	Tokyo	★★★★★
Gedo			
L	top-rope Frankensteiner	CROWD: 7,500	PAYOFF: $358

425	Mar. 27	Okayama, Japan	★★1/2
Tag with Yuji Yasuraoka vs. Ultimate Dragon & Masao Orihara			
L	Orihara pinned Yasuraoka	CROWD: 2,500	PAYOFF: $358

426	Mar. 30	Nagoya, Japan	★★
Tag with Yuji Yasuraoka vs. Ultimate Dragon & Masao Orihara			
W	pinned Dragon/lionsault	CROWD: 3,000	PAYOFF: $358

427	Mar. 31	Nagahama, Japan	★★
Tag with Ultimo Dragon vs. Ultimate Dragon & Masao Orihara			
W	pinned Dragon/Saddledome suplex	CROWD: 1,500	PAYOFF: $358

428	Apr. 01	Gifu, Japan	★★★

6-man with Gedo & Hiromichi Fuyuki vs. Genichiro Tenryu, Ryuma Go & Nobukazu Hirai

W Fuyuki pinned Hirai CROWD: 4,000 PAYOFF: $358

429	Apr. 02	Tokyo	★★★★1/2

Tag with Gedo vs. Nobukazu Hirai & Koji Kanemoto

L pinned by Hirai/tiger suplex CROWD: 2,200 PAYOFF: $358

430	Apr. 04	Mexico City	★★

6-man with Rayo de Jalisco Jr. & Brazo de Oro vs. El Brazo, Sangre Chicana & Mano Negra

L Brazo CROWD: 1,500 PAYOFF: $193

431	Apr. 05	Acapulco, Mexico	★★★

Tag with Hector Garza vs. El Dandy & Apolo Dantes

W pinned El Dandy/small package CROWD: 500 PAYOFF: $193

432	Apr. 07	Actopan, Mexico	★

Tag with Brazo de Plata vs. Gran Markus Jr. & Jaque Mate

W CROWD: 200 PAYOFF: $193

433	Apr. 09	Mexico City	★★

6-man with El Dandy & Hector Garza vs. Sangre Chicana, Bestia Salvaje & El Brazo

W pinned Brazo/lionsault CROWD: 300 PAYOFF: $193

434	Apr. 09	Aragon, Mexico	★

Tag with Tiger Lee vs. Gladiador & Super Brazo

W pinned Super Brazo/splash CROWD: 30 PAYOFF: $193

435	Apr. 12	Acapulco, Mexico	★★★★

El Dandy

L magistral cradle CROWD: 2,200 PAYOFF: $193

436	Apr. 14	Mexico City	★★1/2

6-man with Shocker & Silver King vs. Astro Jr., Dr. Wagner Jr. & Emilio Charles Jr.

L Silver King pinned CROWD: 1,500 PAYOFF: $193

437	Apr. 15	Mexico City	★★1/2

6-man with Vampiro & El Dandy vs. Gladiador, Gran Markus Jr. & Mono Negra

W pinned Negra/lionsault CROWD: 300 PAYOFF: $193

438	Apr. 18	Shizuoka, Japan	★★

6-man with Hiromichi Fuyuki & Gedo vs. Genichro Tenryu, Koki Kitahara & Nobukazu Hirai

L Kitahara pinned Gedo CROWD: 2,000 PAYOFF: $528

MY TOP 10 OPPONENTS IN JAPAN

• ULTIMO DRAGON

Dragon recruited me to tour Japan with the strangely named Wrestle and Romance promotion after working with me in Mexico in 1994. It was a great move for both of us as we had excellent chemistry and a similar viewpoint about the business. We became close rivals and friends as a result.

• EIJI EZAKI

Ezaki gained huge fame when he became Hayabusa later in his career, but when I first worked with him in 1991, we were both rookies with less than a year in the business. I feel he would've been a much bigger star had he worked with a bigger company, but he was loyal to FMW, the company that broke him in.

• GEDO

Gedo was both a good opponent and tag partner. My favorite match with him (#455) was in Korakuen Hall in 1995, a WAR IJ title bout that went 19:59. Even though it was a great match that got amazing reviews, I was despondent afterward because our boss, Tenryu, asked us to go 20 minutes and I felt I had let him down by going one second short.

• GENICHIRO TENRYU

One of top three legends in 1980s Japanese wrestling, Tenryu wasn't only an awesome boss (always pushed me and gave me bonuses), but he was also a great adversary. He did everything he could to make me look good whenever we worked, including catching me on my wacky dives and actually selling for me, which a star of his caliber didn't have to do. He also left bootlace imprints on my forehead from kicking me so hard from time to time.

• HIROSHI TANAHASHI

A true gentleman and ring technician. One of the best of all time, Tana is a master of getting the most out of the least, and after our Tokyo Dome encounter (#2702) I'd gladly wrestle him a dozen times more.

• TETSUYA NAITO

During my two-year run as a New Japan headliner in 2018 to 2019, I spent the most time with Naito, who definitely has the most American-style character and personality of the modern NJPW headliners. We beat the shit out of each other in a pair of excellent matches, one of which (#2690) co-headlined the Tokyo Dome in 2019.

• MASAAKI MOCHIZUKI

Mochizuki was a student and understudy of Koji Kitao, a giant former yokozuna sumo champion and as stiff a pro wrestler you'll find. Whenever I had to wrestle Kitao, which was often, I was always relieved when Mochi was his partner as he was a good performer who understood how to portray a karate expert without actually kicking like one.

• JADO

Jado was a solid worker in the ring, but with his intelligence and inquisitive nature he was perfectly cut out to be a behind-the-scenes executive — which he is to this day in NJPW. He also serves as my personal manager when I'm in Japan.

• EL SAMURAI

Samurai wouldn't say shit if he had a mouthful, and he always smelled like smoke. But I never saw him have a bad match, and our contest in the 1997 Best of the Super Junior tournament (#711) was my favorite of the tour.

• YUJI YASURAOKA

Yuji was a naturally shy young rookie who was just coming into his own in 1995. But I worked with him a lot, and when I finally put him over in Korakuen Hall, he was the first in a long list of names who became a bigger star after working with (and beating) me.

439	Apr. 20	Sapporo, Japan	★★1/2
W	**Tag with with Hiromichi Fuyuki vs. Koji Kitao & Masaaki Mochizuki**		
	Fuyuki pinned Mochizuki	CROWD: 3,500	PAYOFF: $528

440	Apr. 22	Hakodate, Japan	★★★
L	**6-man with Hiromichi Fuyuki & Gedo vs. Shiro Koshinaka, Tatsutoshi Goto & Akitoshi Saito**		
	pinned by Koshinaka/powerbomb	CROWD: 2,700	PAYOFF: $528

441	Apr. 24	Aomori, Japan	★★★
W	**6-man with Hiromichi Fuyuki & Gedo vs. Eliminators & Warlord**		
	Fuyuki beat Saturn	CROWD: 2,000	PAYOFF: $528

442	Apr. 25	Akita, Japan	★★1/2
W	**6-man with Hiromchi Fuyuki & Gedo vs. Eliminators & Warlord (cage match)**		
	Fuyuki beat Saturn	CROWD: 1,600	PAYOFF: $528

443	Apr. 26	Ryotsu, Japan	★★1/2
W	**6-man with Hiromichi Fuyuki & Gedo vs. Shiro Koshinaka, Tatsutoshi Goto & Michiyoshi Ohara**		
	Fuyuki pinned Ohara	CROWD: 1,000	PAYOFF: $528

Bringing down the hardware at the Victoria Community Center in Calgary, in early 1995. This was the sequel to the first ladder match Lance and I had in 1994 ... two months before Shawn and Razor had their classic at WrestleMania 10.

444	Apr. 27	Murakami, Japan	★★★

6-man with Hiromichi Fuyuki & Gedo vs. Shiro Koshinaka, Tatsutoshi Goto & Michiyoshi Ohara

L Koshinaka beat Gedo **CROWD:** 800 **PAYOFF:** $528

445	Apr. 28	Sendai, Japan	★★★

6-man with Hiromchi Fuyuki & Gedo vs. Eliminators & Warlord (cage match)

W Fuyuki beat Saturn **CROWD:** 1,000 **PAYOFF:** $528

446	Apr. 30	Tokyo	★★★

Tag with with Hiromichi Fuyuki vs. Koji Kitao & Masaaki Mochizukiki

L pinned by Kitao/stuff piledriver **CROWD:** 2,200 **PAYOFF:** $528

MAY 1995

447	May 11	Strathmore, Alberta	★★★

Eric Freeze

W roll-up **CROWD:** 20 **PAYOFF:** $100

448	May 12	Calgary, Alberta	★★★
W	**Lance Storm (won vacant CRMW mid-heavyweight title/2nd time)**		
	tiger suplex/3rd fall	CROWD: 60	PAYOFF: $100

449	May 19	Calgary, Alberta	★★★
DC	**Lance Storm**		
	DOUBLE COUNTOUT	CROWD: 60	PAYOFF: $100

450	May 26	Calgary, Alberta	★★★★
L	**Lance Storm (lost CRMW mid-heavyweight title/ladder match)**		
		CROWD: 150	PAYOFF: $100

451	May 29	Kawasaki, Japan	★★1/2
W	**Nobukazu Hirai**		
	lionsault	CROWD: 400	PAYOFF: $511

JUNE 1995

452	June 01	Kasama, Japan	★★1/2
L	**6-man with Hiromichi Fuyuki & Nobutaka Araya vs. Shiro Koshinaka, Tatsutoshi Goto & Michiyoshi Ohara**		
	pinned by Koshinaka/powerbomb	CROWD: 1,000	PAYOFF: $511

453	June 02	Shibukawa, Japan	★★
W	**Hiroshi Itakura**		
	lionsault	CROWD: 1,000	PAYOFF: $510

454	June 03	Ito, Japan	★★★★
L	**8-man with Hiromichi Fuyuki, Gedo & Nobutaka Araya vs. Shiro Koshinaka, Tatsutoshi Goto, Akitoshi Saito & Michiyoshi Ohara**		
	Araya pinned	CROWD: 2,500	PAYOFF: $510

455	June 04	Tokyo	★★★
W	**Gedo (won WAR international junior-heavyweight title)**		
	dragon suplex	CROWD: 2,200	PAYOFF: $511

456	June 08	Winkler, Manitoba	★★★
W	**Eric Freeze**		
	German suplex	CROWD: 500	PAYOFF: $100

457	June 09	Portage la Prairie, Manitoba	★★
W	**Steve Gillespie**		
	lionsault	CROWD: 500	PAYOFF: $50

458	June 09	Portage la Prairie, Manitoba	★★★
W	**Tag with Lance Storm vs. Gerry Morrow & Great Gama**		
	pinned Morrow/sunset flip	CROWD: 400	PAYOFF: $50

459	June 24	Fukuoka, Japan	★★★

Tag with Hiromichi Fuyuki vs. Koji Kitao & Masaaki Mochizukiki

L	pinned by Kitao/Samoan drop		**CROWD:** 2,500	**PAYOFF:** $440

460	June 26	Oita, Japan	★★★

Tag with Nobutaka Araya vs. Eliminators

L	pinned Saturn/electric chair		**CROWD:** 1,000	**PAYOFF:** $440

461	June 27	Kitakyushu, Japan	★★1/2

8-man with Hiromichi Fuyuki, Gedo & Nobutaka Araya vs. Shiro Koshinaka, Tatsutoshi Goto, Akitoshi Saito & Michiyoshi Ohara

L	Araya pinned		**CROWD:** 1,000	**PAYOFF:** $440

462	June 28	Nagasaki, Japan	★★★

Ultimo Dragon

L	top-rope sunset flip		**CROWD:** 1,000	**PAYOFF:** $440

463	June 29	Shimane, Japan	★★★★

Ultimo Dragon

L	roll-up		**CROWD:** 1,500	**PAYOFF:** $440

464	June 30	Hiroshima, Japan	★★★

Hector Garza

W	lionsault		**CROWD:** 1,400	**PAYOFF:** $440

JULY 1995

465	July 02	Daigo, Japan	★★1/2

Hector Garza

W	lionsault		**CROWD:** 2,800	**PAYOFF:** $440

466	July 04	Yokkaichi, Japan	★★★1/2

Arashi

L	powerbomb		**CROWD:** 1,000	**PAYOFF:** $440

467	July 05	Toyohashi, Japan	★★

Nobukazu Hirai

W	lionsault		**CROWD:** 600	**PAYOFF:** $440

468	July 07	Tokyo	★★★★★

Ultimo Dragon

W	super chicken g-plex		**CROWD:** 9,500	**PAYOFF:** $440

469	July 28	Tokyo	★★★★★

Ultimo Dragon (lost WAR international junior-heavyweight title)

L	rockarana		**CROWD:** 2,100	**PAYOFF:** $405

470	July 31	Osaka, Japan	★★★
L	**Ultimo Dragon**		
	magistral cradle	CROWD: 1,100	PAYOFF: $405

471	Aug. 01	Onomichi, Japan	★★1/2
L	**6-man with Hiromichi Fuyuki & Jado vs. Koji Kitao, Masaaki Mochizuki & Koki Kitahara**		
	pinned by Kitao/piledriver	CROWD: 800	PAYOFF: $406

472	Aug. 02	Nagato, Japan	★★
W	**Tamura (young boy)**		
	lionsault	CROWD: 400	PAYOFF: $406

473	Aug. 04	Hyuga, Japan	★★1/2
L	**Arashi**		
	powerbomb	CROWD: 1,800	PAYOFF: $406

474	Aug. 05	Kagoshima, Japan	★★★★
W	**Ultimo Dragon**		
	tiger suplex	CROWD: 2,400	PAYOFF: $406

475	Aug. 11	Calgary, Alberta	★★1/2
L	**Lance Storm**		
	Northern Lights suplex	CROWD: 120	PAYOFF: $100

476	Aug. 27	Tokyo	★★★
W	**Hiroshi Itakura**		
	super double arm-plex	CROWD: 2,400	PAYOFF: $807

477	Aug. 29	Shizuoka, Japan	★★
W	**Tag with Jado vs. Nobutaka Araya & Yuji Yasuraoka**		
	Jado pinned Araya	CROWD: 2,700	PAYOFF: $807

478	Aug. 31	Nagoya, Japan	★★★
L	**8-man with Hiromichi Fuyuki, Gedo & Jado vs. Genichiro Tenryu, Nobutaka Araya, Koki Kitahara & Ultimo Dragon (elimination match)**		
	pinned by Dragon/magistral cradle	CROWD: 2,500	PAYOFF: $808

479	Sept. 01	Mexico City	★★1/2
L	**6-man with Atlantis & Vampiro vs. Ricky Santana, Miguel Perez & El Boricua**		
	pinned Vampiro	CROWD: 8,000	PAYOFF: $259

MY TOP 10 OPPONENTS
IN MEXICO

• "BLACK MAGIC" NORMAN SMILEY

He's not Mexican by birth, but was one of my best rivals in CMLL. We never had a bad match or a cross word, and it was my match with him in Monterrey in 1992 (#98), that put me on the map and got me hired by CMLL. I later repaid him by recommending him for a trainer's job in WWE — a job that he still has to this day.

• NEGRO CASAS

Negro is the Ric Flair of Mexico and an early mentor of mine. I can't put into words how much I learned from him and how patient he was with me. After I screwed up a finish terribly one night, he said, "The only thing you can do is learn from this and have a better match tomorrow." I still give that advice to this day.

• EL DANDY

We were frequent partners and won the WWA World tag team championships (#182) together. Roberto Gutiérrez Frías (I didn't have to Google that, by the way) loved Bryan Adams and was always available to give me a ride to the next town if I needed it.

• EMILIO CHARLES JR.

Emilio kind of looked like a crazy version of Carvelli from *Welcome Back, Kotter* (Google it), but he was a great worker and super-hilarious in the ring.

• BESTIA SALVAJE

He used to beat the shit out of me when I first arrived in CMLL in 1993. But once I earned his respect, he led me through some killer matches. He also had the biggest, ugliest nose I've ever seen.

• DR. WAGNER JR.

One of the best workers I faced in Mexico, Wagner and his brother, Silver King, came from a great family and were taught to be good wrestlers and people. I once woke up in the middle of the night to hear Manny screaming like a madman as he trashed his room (which was next to mine) during a tour of Japan. In the morning when I saw him at check-out, he calmly apologized for waking me up as he paid the hotel manager 10,000 yen for the damage he caused.

• SILVER KING

I always loved working with Silver and his partner El Texano (Los Cowboys), but you always knew afterward that you had been in the ring with them. They weren't careless, just very solid with their work, and so fast in the ring with incredible double-team moves. I feel they could've made it in the States for sure, especially in 2020, with size not being an issue.

• EL TEXANO

Juan, or Johnny, was the comedian of Los Cowboys and a blast to be around. He once asked me if I needed a pill for a sore knee after a match. I said, "What do you have?" He replied, "Well, I have green ones, blue ones, red ones ... I'm not sure which is which, but I'm sure one of them will work." Needless to say, my knee was fine that night.

• HÉCTOR GARZA

I met Héctor and the entire Garza family in Monterrey in 1992 and followed Héctor's career from that moment on. He was a tremendous high-flyer right out of the gate and became a big star in Mexico before passing away way far too young in 2013. However, his legacy lives on through his nephews, WWE stars Humberto Carrillo and Angel Garza.

• MANO NEGRA

I beat Black Hand (he wore a single leather glove in the ring) for the NWA world middleweight championship (#265) in December 1993 — a title that was originally held by Eddy's father, Gory Guerrero.

480	Sept. 03	Mexico City	★★★
W	**6-man with Vampiro & Rayo de Jalisco Jr. vs. Ricky Santana, Miguel Perez & El Boricua**		
	Vampiro fouled	CROWD: 2,000	PAYOFF: $259

481	Sept. 04	Laredo, Mexico	★★1/2
W	**6-man with Bestia Salvaje & Sangre Chicana vs. Ultimo Dragon, Humberto Garza & Atlantis**		
	pinned Drago/spinning victory roll	CROWD: 300	PAYOFF: $259

482	Sept. 08	Mexico City	★★★
W	**6-man with Ultimo Dragon & El Hijo del Santo vs. Negro Casas, Emilio Charles Jr. & El Satanico**		
	DQ	CROWD: 8,000	PAYOFF: $259

483	Sept. 10	Mexico City	★★
W	**6-man with Atlantis & Silver King vs. Miguel Perez, El Boricua & Dr. Wagner Jr.**		
	DQ	CROWD: 350	PAYOFF: $259

484	Sept. 12	Mexico City	★★1/2
W	**6-man with Vampiro & Fiera vs. Gran Markus Jr., Mano Negra & Apolo Dantes**		
	pinned Dantes/small package	CROWD: 1,000	PAYOFF: $259

485	Sept. 13	Acapulco, Mexico	★★1/2
W	**6-man with El Santo & El Dandy vs. Negro Casas, Scorpio Jr. & Emilio Charles Jr.**		
		CROWD: 3,000	PAYOFF: $259

486	Sept. 15	Mexico City	★★
W	**6-man with Ultimo Dragon & El Hijo del Santo vs. Negro Casas, Emilio Charles Jr. & El Satanico**		
	pinned Charles/lionsault	CROWD: 3,000	PAYOFF: $259

487	Sept. 16	Tizayuka, Mexico	★★
W	**6-man with Vampiro & Brazo de Oro vs. Negro Casas, Bestia Salvaje & Apolo Dantes**		
	pinned Bestia/backslide	CROWD: 2,000	PAYOFF: $259

488	Sept. 17	Guadalajara, Mexico	★★
W	**6-man with Hector Garza & Shocker vs. Emilio Charles Jr., Dr. Wagner Jr. & Foreign Exchange (Jose Estrada)**		
	pinned Exchange/plancha	CROWD: 2,000	PAYOFF: $259

489	Sept. 19	Mexico City	★★★★
L	**Apolo Dantes**		
	pinned Northern Lights suplex	CROWD: 1,800	PAYOFF: $259

490	Sept. 29	Chiba, Japan	★★
L	**Tag with Jado vs. Akio Sato (Great Shinja) & Typhoon**		
	pinned by Sato/Northern Lights suplex	CROWD: 3,000	PAYOFF: $500

OCTOBER 1995

491	Oct. 01	Saku, Japan	★★1/2
L	**Ultimo Dragon**		
	top-rope victory roll	CROWD: 3,300	PAYOFF: $500

492	Oct. 03	Tokyo	★★1/2
L	**Tag with Jado vs. Koji Kitao & Masaaki Mochizuki**		
	submission/Kitao	CROWD: 300	PAYOFF: $500

493	Oct. 04	Hamamatsu, Japan	★★1/2
W	**Masayoshi Motegi**		
	tiger suplex	CROWD: 2,000	PAYOFF: $500

494	Oct. 05	Omiya, Japan	★★
W	**Tag with Jado vs. Masaaki Mochizuki & Shigeo Okumura**		
	Jado pinned Okumura	CROWD: 600	PAYOFF: $500

495	Oct. 21	Hirosaki, Japan	★★1/2

6-man with Jado & Hiromichi Fuyuki vs. Arashi, Koti Kitihara & Nobutaka Araya

L Kitihara pinned Jado — CROWD: 2,000 — PAYOFF: $357

496	Oct. 23	Koriyama, Japan	★★

Tag with Dr. Wagner Jr. vs. Ultimo Dragon & Hiroshi Itakura

L Dragon pinned Wagner — CROWD: 400 — PAYOFF: $357

497	Oct. 24	Akita, Japan	★★★

Hiroshi Itakura

W lionsault — CROWD: 400 — PAYOFF: $357

498	Oct. 25	Aomori, Japan	★★1/2

6-man with Jado & Hiromichi Fuyuki vs. Arashi, Koti Kitihara & Nobutaka Araya

L Kitahara powerbomb — CROWD: 2,000 — PAYOFF: $357

499	Oct. 26	Shizukuishi, Japan	★★1/2

Tag with Dr. Wagner Jr. vs. Ultimo Dragon & Negro Casas

L Dragon pinned Wagner — CROWD: 800 — PAYOFF: $357

500	Oct. 27	Murakami, Japan	★★★

Negro Casas

W reverse roll-up bridge — CROWD: 400 — PAYOFF: $357

501	Oct. 29	Tokyo	★★

6-man with Jado & Dr. Wagner Jr. vs. Ultimo Dragon, Yuji Yasuraoka & Hiroshi Itakura

L Dragon pinned Wagner — CROWD: 2,100 — PAYOFF: $357

NOVEMBER 1995

502	Nov. 14	Winnipeg, Manitoba	★★1/2

Ultimo Dragon

L Frankensteiner — CROWD: 300 — PAYOFF: $100

503	Nov. 15	Gimli, Manitoba	★★★

Ultimo Dragon

L magistral cradle — CROWD: 400 — PAYOFF: $100

504	Nov. 16	Morris, Manitoba	★★★

Ultimo Dragon

L magistral cradle — CROWD: 400 — PAYOFF: $100

505	Nov. 21	Tokyo	★★★

Tag with Gedo vs. Ultimo Dragon & Yuji Yasuraoka

W Gedo pinned Yasuraoka — CROWD: 1,800 — PAYOFF: $630

Celebrating after the finish of the super successful Super J-Cup Second Stage in Tokyo. I was wasted out of my gourd from the scoop of GHB Benoit gave me 60 minutes prior. Note Dos Caras' amazingly swank brown dress pants.

506	Nov. 26	Tsu, Japan		★★1/2
	Tag with Gedo vs. Great Shinja & Typhoon			
L	pinned by Shinja/press splash		**CROWD:** 1,800	**PAYOFF:** $630

507	Nov. 27	Gifu, Japan		★★1/2
	Yuji Yasuraoka			
W	reverse roll-up bridge		**CROWD:** 2,000	**PAYOFF:** $630

508	Nov. 28	Niigata, Japan		★★1/2
	Takashi Okamura			
W	sleeper		**CROWD:** 1,800	**PAYOFF:** $630

509	Nov. 30	Kochi, Japan		★★★
	Tag with Hiromichi Fuyuki vs. Genichiro Tenryu & Ultimo Dragon			
W	Fuyuki pinned Dragon		**CROWD:** 1,500	**PAYOFF:** $630

From the classic first-time meeting of Jericho & Benoit from the Super J-Cup Second Stage at the Tokyo Sumo Hall in December 1995.

DECEMBER 1995			
510	Dec. 01	Saijo, Japan	★★
W	**Takashi Okamura**		
	clothesline	**CROWD:** 1,000	**PAYOFF:** $630
511	Dec. 04	Hakata, Japan	★★★1/2
W	**Tag with Gedo vs. Ultimo Dragon & Lance Storm**		
	pinned Storm/reverse roll-up bridge	**CROWD:** 2,200	**PAYOFF:** $631

512	Dec. 05	Kumamoto, Japan		★★1/2
L	**Nobukazu Hirai**			
	second-rope elbow		CROWD: 1,000	PAYOFF: $631

513	Dec. 06	Mihara, Japan		★★
W	**Nobukazu Hirai**			
	lionsault		CROWD: 500	PAYOFF: $631

514	Dec. 06	Mihara, Japan		★★★
	8-man with Hiromichi Fuyuki, Jado & Gedo vs. Genichiro Tenryu, Arashi, Osamu Tachihikari & Koki Kitahara			
W	Fuyuki pinned Tachihikari		CROWD: 500	PAYOFF: $631

515	Dec. 08	Tokyo		★★★★
L	**Lance Storm**			
	victory roll-up		CROWD: 4,000	PAYOFF: $631

516	Dec. 13	Tokyo		★★1/2
W	**Hanzo Nakajima (WAR 1995 Super J-Cup)**			
	lionsault		CROWD: 11,500	PAYOFF: $631

517	Dec. 13	Tokyo		★★★★
L	**Wild Pegasus (Chris Benoit – WAR 1995 Super J-Cup)**			
	top-rope tombstone		CROWD: 11,500	PAYOFF: $631

JANUARY 1996

518	Jan. 23	Tokyo		★★★
W	**Lance Storm**			
	tiger suplex		CROWD: 2,000	PAYOFF: $625

519	Jan. 24	Nagano, Japan		★★★
L	**Osamu Tachihikari**			
	chokeslam		CROWD: 1,000	PAYOFF: $625

520	Jan. 25	Joetsu, Japan		★★★
	Tag with Lance Storm vs. Ultimo Dragon & Yuji Yasuraoka			
L	Storm pinned by Dragon		CROWD: 1,000	PAYOFF: $625

521	Jan. 27	Ito, Japan		★★★1/2
W	**Masaaki Mochizuki**			
	lionsault		CROWD: 2,500	PAYOFF: $625

522	Feb. 02	Reading, PA	★★1/2

L **Tag with Rob Van Dam vs. Perry Saturn & John Kronus**

pinned by Kronus/total elimination   CROWD: 350   PAYOFF: $175

MATCH NOTES #522, ECW DEBUT

I had been trying to get into ECW for a whole year, so when I finally got booked, I was nervous and excited. The good news was that for my first match in the company, I was in the ring with one of the best tag teams of the mid '90s in the Eliminators, with whom I'd also worked with a ton in WAR. I remember the crowd was into it and knew most of my stuff. Even though RVD had only started a week or two before as well, we were the hot young upstarts in the company, and we lived up to the hype. I used to do a standing suplex and then remove one arm to encourage the fans to cheer with my newly freed hand. After the match, Tommy Dreamer approached and said in his dry, sardonic voice, "Don't beg for cheers ever again. Our fans hate that."

523	Feb. 03	New York City	★★★

W **Rob Van Dam**

lionsault   CROWD: 1,100   PAYOFF: $175

524	Feb. 12	Chiba, Japan	★★1/2

L **Tag with Gedo vs. Lance Storm & Yuji Yasuraoka**

pinned by Yasuraoka/German suplex   CROWD: 400   PAYOFF: $450

525	Feb. 13	Kisarazu, Japan	★

W **Kamikaze**

lionsault   CROWD: 200   PAYOFF: $450

526	Feb. 14	Fukuya, Japan	★★★

6-man with Gedo & Masaaki Mochizuki vs. Negro Casas, Ultimo Dragon & Gran Naniwa

DR 30 minutes   CROWD: 350   PAYOFF: $450

527	Feb. 16	Atami, Japan	★★★

W **Tag with Gedo vs. Masaaki Mochizuki & Gran Naniwa**

Gedo pinned Mochizuki   CROWD: 250   PAYOFF: $450

528	Feb. 17	Chiba, Japan	★★

W **Tag with Gedo vs. Takashi Okamura & Battle Ranger**

Gedo pinned Ranger   CROWD: 500   PAYOFF: $450

529	Feb. 20	Fukushima, Japan		★★
W	**Kamikaze**			
	lionsault		CROWD: 500	PAYOFF: $450

530	Feb. 21	Shiokawa, Japan		★★★
L	**Tag with Gran Naniwa vs. Ultimo Dragon & Negro Casas**			
	pinned by Dragon/magistral cradle		CROWD: 300	PAYOFF: $450

531	Feb. 23	Sendai, Japan		★★★1/2
W	**Tag with Gedo vs. Ultimo Dragon & Negro Casas**			
	Gedo pinned Casas		CROWD: 1,000	PAYOFF: $450

532	Feb. 23	Sendai, Japan		★★★
W	**Tag with Gedo vs. Lance Storm & Yuji Yasuraoka**			
	(won WAR international junior heavyweight tag team title tournament)			
	Gedo pinned Storm		CROWD: 1,000	PAYOFF: $450

533	Feb. 24	Iwanuma, Japan		★★★
W	**Takashi Okamura**			
	sleeper		CROWD: 500	PAYOFF: $450

534	Feb. 25	Matsushima, Japan		★★★
W	**Battle Ranger**			
	lionsault		CROWD: 600	PAYOFF: $450

Sapporo in the winter is beautiful. Standing in front of a life-sized ice sculpture, February of 1996.

MY TOP 10 ENTRANCE THEMES

- **"OVERNIGHT SENSATION," FIREHOUSE** (FMW)

I got in big trouble when I held up the bus to the airport on my first tour of Japan because I couldn't find my Firehouse cassette. "Fuck, I'll buy you a new one," a furious Mark Starr yelled at me.

- **"ELECTRIC HEAD PT. 2," WHITE ZOMBIE** (ECW)

The opening line, "I just said, 'Up yours, baby!'" always put me in the perfect, arrogant mood while heading to the ring.

- **"UNSKINNY BOP," POISON** (CANADIAN INDIES)

I liked the cool opening drum/bass groove for my walk to the ring. I stopped using it when the music guy somehow played it backward before my second match.

- **"SILENT JEALOUSY," X JAPAN** (FMW)

I thought I would get a huge pop for my return to FMW in 1992 (#88) when I used this song by Japan's all-time biggest metal band for the Yokohama Stadium match. Instead, crickets chirped and nobody cared.

- **"BREAK THE WALLS DOWN," JIM JOHNSTON** (WWE)

The classic WWE Jericho song was written and composed by Jim Johnston, the best wrestling ring-song writer ever. This tune completely captured the Jericho vibe.

- **"BREAK THE WALLS DOWN," ZAKK WYLDE** (WWE)

I wanted a change when I returned in 2007, but Vince HATED Zakk's interpretation. I thought it was cool — and I need to find this so you guys can hear it!

- **"ENTER SANDMAN," METALLICA** (CMLL)

I didn't choose this tune. It was given to me because I was a "rockero," and it was the biggest rock song in the world at the time. It worked for my vibe and character, so I went with it.

- **"TEASE ME, PLEASE ME," SCORPIONS** (CANADIAN INDIES)

I remember stage managers literally trying to push me through the curtain in the bowling alley we used as the CNWA venue because I kept waiting for the extended intro to kick in. "Not yet! Just a few seconds longer ..."

- **"JUDAS," INNER CIRCLE CHOIR, FEAT. MEREDITH BELL, AEW REVOLUTION 2020 (#2705)**

My favorite and most powerful ring entrance of all time, put together by a 10-piece choir from Philly that I discovered on Instagram. Absolutely magical.

- **"JUDAS," FOZZY**

I first used this at the Tokyo Dome for the Omega match in 2018 (#2685), and it gave me goosebumps. Once again, the music perfectly fit with my character's vibe. A few years later, having 2,500 people singing MY song at the top of their lungs as I walked to the ring of MY wrestling company in the middle of MY cruise (#2703) was one of the greatest moments of my life!

535	Feb. 26	Tokyo		★★★★★
W	**Tag with Gedo vs. Jushin "Thunder" Liger & Tatsuhito Takaiwa**			
	Gedo pinned Takaiwa		CROWD: 2,200	PAYOFF: $450

MARCH 1996

536	Mar. 01	Compton, CA		★★
L	**6-man with Crazy Boy & Falcon de Oro vs. Bestia Salvaje, Principe Joel & Poison**			
	DQ		CROWD: 200	PAYOFF: $200
537	Mar. 03	Los Angeles		★★1/2
L	**6-man with Pilota Suicida & Mecurio vs. Crazy Boy, Super Boy & Capitan**			
	pinned by Crazy Boy/German suplex		CROWD: 300	PAYOFF: $200
538	Mar. 08	New York City		★★★★
W	**Cactus Jack (Big Ass Extreme Bash)**			
	German suplex		CROWD: 1,100	PAYOFF: $225
539	Mar. 09	Philadelphia		★★★★1/2
W	**Taz (Big Ass Extreme Bash)**			
	DQ		CROWD: 1,100	PAYOFF: $225
540	Mar. 15	Jim Thorpe, PA		★★1/2
W	**Stevie Richards**			
	lionsault		CROWD: 600	PAYOFF: $187
541	Mar. 16	Glenolden, PA		★★★
W	**Stevie Richards**			
	lionsault		CROWD: 350	PAYOFF: $188

542	Mar. 19	Toyohashi, Japan		★★
L	**Tag with Gedo vs. Yuji Yasuraoka & Ultimo Dragon**			
	Yasuraoka pinned Gedo/German suplex		CROWD: 200	PAYOFF: $455

543	Mar. 20	Shingu, Japan		★★1/2
W	**Tag with Gedo vs. Yuji Yasuraoka & Lance Storm**			
	Gedo pinned Storm		CROWD: 1,200	PAYOFF: $455

544	Mar. 21	Owase, Japan		★★★1/2
W	**Yuji Yasuraoka**			
	lionsault		CROWD: 700	PAYOFF: $455

545	Mar. 22	Hamamatsu, Japan		★★1/2
L	**Yuji Yasuraoka**			
	German suplex		CROWD: 500	PAYOFF: $455

546	Mar. 24	Sabae, Japan		★★1/2
W	**Masayoshi Motegi**			
	lionsault		CROWD: 1,000	PAYOFF: $455

547	Mar. 26	Takaoka, Japan		★★★1/2
W	**Lance Storm**			
	lionsault		CROWD: 1,000	PAYOFF: $454

548	Mar. 27	Nagoya, Japan		★★★1/2
L	**Tag with Gedo vs. Yuji Yasuraoka & Lance Storm (lost WAR international junior heavyweight tag team titles)**			
	Gedo pinned by Yasuraoka		CROWD: 1,000	PAYOFF: $455

549	Mar. 28	Yokkaichi, Japan		★★★
W	**Tag with Gedo vs. Ultimo Dragon & Masaaki Mochizuki**			
	Gedo pinned Mochizuki		CROWD: 300	PAYOFF: $454

550	Mar. 29	Omihachiman, Japan		★★1/2
L	**Lance Storm**			
	power bomb		CROWD: 800	PAYOFF: $454

551	Mar. 30	Gifu, Japan		★★
L	**Tag with Masayoshi Motegi vs. Yuji Yasuraoka & Lance Storm**			
	Motegi pinned		CROWD: 2,500	PAYOFF: $454

552	Mar. 31	Tokyo		★★★★
L	**Tag with Dr. Luther vs. Arashi & Osamu Tachihikari**			
	Tachihikari pinned Luther		CROWD: 2,000	PAYOFF: $454

553   Apr. 12   Glenolden, PA   ★★★

Damian

W   tiger suplex   **CROWD:** 350   **PAYOFF:** $200

---

554   Apr. 13   New York City   ★★★

Taz (Massacre on Queens Blvd./shoot fight rules)

L   Tazmission   **CROWD:** 800   **PAYOFF:** $200

---

555   Apr. 19   Sapporo, Japan   ★★★

Tag with Damian vs. Yuji Yasuraoka & Ultimo Dragon

L   Damian pinned   **CROWD:** 4,000   **PAYOFF:** $433

---

556   Apr. 20   Hakodate, Japan   ★★

Battle Ranger

W   lionsault   **CROWD:** 2,000   **PAYOFF:** $433

---

557   Apr. 21   Toyoura, Japan   ★★

Masaaki Mochizuki

W   lionsault   **CROWD:** 400   **PAYOFF:** $433

---

558   Apr. 23   Iwate, Japan   ★★★

Tag with Psicosis vs. Ultimo Dragon & Rey Mysterio Jr.

L   pinned by Dragon/magistral cradle   **CROWD:** 300   **PAYOFF:** $433

---

559   Apr. 24   Aomori, Japan   ★★1/2

Masayoshi Motegi

W   tiger driver   **CROWD:** 250   **PAYOFF:** $434

---

560   Apr. 26   Tokyo   ★★★★

Masaaki Mochizuki

L   top-rope karate kick   **CROWD:** 1,800   **PAYOFF:** $434

---

561   Apr. 28   Los Angeles   ★★1/2

6-man with Mercurio & Piloto Suicida vs. Super Boy, Capitan Oro & Acero Dorado

W   **CROWD:** 300   **PAYOFF:** $200

MAY 1996

562   May 10   Reading, PA   ★★1/2

Mikey Whipwreck

W   tiger suplex   **CROWD:** 350   **PAYOFF:** $225

---

563   May 11   Philadelphia   ★★★1/2

Mikey Whipwreck (A Matter of Respect)

W   super double-arm suplex   **CROWD:** 1,200   **PAYOFF:** $225

564	May 17	Glenolden, PA	★★1/2
L	**Too Cold Scorpio**		
	moonsault legdrop	CROWD: 300	PAYOFF: $212

565	May 18	Allentown, PA	★★★
L	**Raven**		
	DDT on chair	CROWD: 2,000	PAYOFF: $213

JUNE 1996

566	June 01	Los Angeles	★★★1/2
	3-way vs. Bam Bam Bigelow vs. Konnan (elimination match/World Wrestling Peace Festival)		
L		CROWD: 5,000	PAYOFF: $300

MATCH NOTES #566

I was looking for a way to break into the States after three years of working in Japan and Mexico only, so when I heard about this show, I went on the prowl. I called everybody I knew in L.A. from the small shows I had recently been working between Japanese tours, and I finally got a contact who was able to book me on the show. I don't think I even got paid, and I know for sure I used my points to fly to L.A., but I felt it was worth the shot. And it was! Somehow I got put into a three-way match with Mexican legend and my good friend Konnan and WrestleMania headliner Bam Bam Bigelow. And even better, Bam Bam decided for whatever reason that he wanted to put ME over! Me ... the only guy on the show who was not under contract to any company. Top that off with the fact that I met Eric Bischoff that night, who told me he wanted to sign me to a WCW contract on the spot — and then promptly left the building before my match.

567	June 02	Tijuana, Mexico	★★
	6-man with Leon Negro & Angel Mensajero vs. Halloween, Viernes 13 & Enfermero Jr.		
W	pinned Halloween/tiger suplex	CROWD: 4,300	PAYOFF: $300

568	June 06	Portage la Prairie, Manitoba	★★★
W	**Lance Storm**		
	superplex	CROWD: 400	PAYOFF: $150

569	June 07	Selkirk, Manitoba	★★★
L	**Big Titan**		
	DQ	CROWD: 300	PAYOFF: $150

570	June 10	Imabari, Japan	★★
	Tag with Big Titan vs. Koki Kitahara & Osamu Tachihikari		
L	pinned by Tachihikari/Thesz press	CROWD: 400	PAYOFF: $650

Got the figure-four locked in on Shane Douglas in the ECW Arena in 1996. Shane was great to me during my short time in the territory and we had a handful of very good straight wrestling matches, that weren't in the "hardcore style" that the company was known for.

571	June 11	Ehime, Japan	★★1/2
W	**6-man with Jado & Big Titan vs. Masaaki Mochizuki, Nobutaka Araya & Arashi**		
	pinned Mochizuki/lionsault	CROWD: 2,000	PAYOFF: $650

572	June 12	Kumamoto, Japan	★★★
L	**Ultimo Dragon**		
	magistral cradle	CROWD: 300	PAYOFF: $650

573	June 15	Fukaoka, Japan	★★★
L	**Tag with Big Titan vs. Ultimo Dragon & Genichiro Tenryu**		
	pinned by Tenryu/powerbomb	CROWD: 2,000	PAYOFF: $650

574	June 21	Plymouth Meeting, PA	★★★1/2
L	**Rob Van Dam**		
	top-rope crane kick	CROWD: 350	PAYOFF: $250

575	June 22	Philadelphia		★★★★1/2

Pitbull #2 (won ECW world television title/Hardcore Heaven)

W top-rope Frankensteiner   **CROWD:** 1,200   **PAYOFF:** $250

576	June 29	Middletown, NY		★★

Pitbull #2

W top-rope Frankensteiner   **CROWD:** 800   **PAYOFF:** $225

577	June 30	Deer Park, NY		★★★

Tag with Mikey Whipwreck vs. The Eliminators

L Saturn pinned Whipwreck   **CROWD:** 350   **PAYOFF:** $225

JULY 1996

578	July 12	Allentown, PA		★★1/2

Shane Douglas

DR 15 minutes   **CROWD:** 1,000   **PAYOFF:** $250

579	July 13	Philadelphia		★★★★1/2

4-way vs. Too Cold Scorpio vs. Shane Douglas vs. Pitbull #2 (lost ECW world television title/Heat Wave)

L pinned by Scorpio/tumbleweed   **CROWD:** 1,700   **PAYOFF:** $250

580	July 20	Tokyo		★★1/2

Tag with Big Titan vs. Ultimo Dragon & Nobukazu Hirai

L pinned by Dragon/running power bomb   **CROWD:** 11,000   **PAYOFF:** $1,300

581	July 21	Tokyo		★★★1/2

8-man with Gedo, Jushin Liger & Juventud Guerrera vs. Ultimo Dragon, Yuji Yasuraoka, Lance Storm & Rey Mytserio Jr.

L Juventud pinned   **CROWD:** 9,000   **PAYOFF:** $1,300

582	July 26	Jim Thorpe, PA		★★

Tag with Mikey Whipwreck vs. The Eliminators

L pinned by Kronus/total elimination   **CROWD:** 400   **PAYOFF:** $225

583	July 27	Warwick, PA		★★★

Shane Douglas

L small package   **CROWD:** 900   **PAYOFF:** $225

584	Aug. 02	Plymouth Meeting, PA		★★★1/2
	Sabu			
L	Sabusault		CROWD: 600	PAYOFF: $250

585	Aug. 03	Philadelphia		★★★★
	Too Cold Scorpio (The Doctor Is In)			
L	shooting star press		CROWD: 1,600	PAYOFF: $250

SECTION THREE

WCW

AUG. 20, 1996 - JULY 30, 1999

MATCHES 586 - 999

586 Aug. 20   Dalton, GA   ★

Mr. JL (Jerry Lynn)

W   lionsault   **CROWD:** 3,000   **PAYOFF:** $271

IN THEIR WORDS: **MR. JL (JERRY LYNN)**

Chris and I have talked about this. We went out there and thought we had a good match. Afterward, he took heat from the office for it — and he didn't have to — because I think they wanted more of a squash, but no one told us a thing or what they wanted at all. So, we just tried to have the best match we could and ended up getting heat for it.

---

587 Aug. 23   Orlando, FL   ★★1/2

The Gambler

W   lionsault   **CROWD:** 600   **PAYOFF:** $271

---

588 Aug. 24   Orlando, FL   ★★1/2

Manny Fernandez

W   lionsault   **CROWD:** 600   **PAYOFF:** $271

---

589 Aug. 24   Orlando, FL   ★★★

Dean Malenko

L   roll-up   **CROWD:** 600   **PAYOFF:** $271

---

590 Aug. 24   Orlando, FL   ★★

Mark Starr

W   lionsault   **CROWD:** 600   **PAYOFF:** $271

---

591 Aug. 25   Orlando, FL   ★★★1/2

Chris Benoit

L   roll-up   **CROWD:** 600   **PAYOFF:** $271

---

592 Aug. 26   Palmetto, FL   ★★1/2

Alex Wright

NC   NO CONTEST   **CROWD:** 3,000   **PAYOFF:** $271

---

593 Aug. 27   Orlando, FL   ★★1/2

Jerry Flynn

W   lionsault   **CROWD:** 600   **PAYOFF:** $272

---

594 Aug. 28   Orlando, FL   ★★★

Dean Malenko

L   cross-body rollover   **CROWD:** 600   **PAYOFF:** $272

595	Aug. 28	Orlando, FL		★★1/2
W	**Manny Fernandez**			
	lionsault		CROWD: 600	PAYOFF: $272

596	Aug. 29	Orlando, FL		★★
W	**Randy Starr**			
	lionsault		CROWD: 400	PAYOFF: $272

597	Aug. 30	Orlando, FL		★★1/2
W	**Prince Iaukea**			
	lionsault		CROWD: 400	PAYOFF: $272

598	Aug. 30	Orlando, FL		★★★
L	**Chris Benoit**			
	top-rope headbutt		CROWD: 400	PAYOFF: $272

599	Aug. 31	Utica, NY		★★
W	**Dean Malenko**			
	roll-up		CROWD: 2,000	PAYOFF: $271

SEPTEMBER 1996

600	Sept. 02	Chattanooga, TN		★★★1/2
W	**Dean Malenko**			
	roll-up		CROWD: 7,000	PAYOFF: $1,477

601	Sept. 04	Gainesville, GA		★★
W	**Billy Kidman**			
	lionsault		CROWD: 700	PAYOFF: $1,477

602	Sept. 15	Winston-Salem, NC		★★★1/2
L	**Chris Benoit (Fall Brawl)**			
	top-rope belly-to-back suplex		CROWD: 12,000	PAYOFF: $1,477

603	Sept. 16	Asheville, NC		★★★
L	**Tag with Marcus Bagwell vs. Ric Flair & Arn Anderson**			
	Bagwell submit to Flair		CROWD: 3,000	PAYOFF: $1,107

604	Sept. 23	Birmingham, AL		★★★
W	**Mike Enos**			
	small package		CROWD: 6,000	PAYOFF: $1,107

605	Sept. 25	Montgomery, AL		★★
W	**Konnan**			
	DQ		CROWD: 2,000	PAYOFF: $1,107

606	Sept. 25	Montgomery, AL	★★

Tag with Jim Powers vs. Dick Slater & Mike Enos

L Powers pinned by Enos   **CROWD:** 2,000   **PAYOFF:** $1,107

607	Sept. 30	Cleveland	★★★

Arn Anderson

L DDT   **CROWD:** 4,000   **PAYOFF:** $1,476

OCTOBER 1996

608	Oct. 08	Greenwood, SC	★★1/2

Steve Armstrong

W lionsault   **CROWD:** 2,500   **PAYOFF:** $1,476

609	Oct. 13	Tupelo, MS	★★★

Disco Inferno

W top-rope elbow   **CROWD:** 3,500   **PAYOFF:** $1,476

610	Oct. 16	Anderson, SC	★★★

Marcus Bagwell

W cross-body block   **CROWD:** 1,500   **PAYOFF:** $553

611	Oct. 18	Minneapolis	★★

Mr. JL (Jerry Lynn)

L DQ   **CROWD:** 8,000   **PAYOFF:** $553

612	Oct. 18	Minneapolis	★★★

Syxx

DC DOUBLE COUNTOUT   **CROWD:** 8,000   **PAYOFF:** $553

613	Oct. 19	La Crosse, WI	★★

Mr. JL (Jerry Lynn)

W top-rope elbow   **CROWD:** 1,800   **PAYOFF:** $553

614	Oct. 20	Sioux Falls, SD	★★1/2

Mr. JL (Jerry Lynn)

W top-rope elbow   **CROWD:** 2,500   **PAYOFF:** $554

615	Oct. 21	Mankato, MN	★★★

Bobby Eaton

W top-rope dropkick   **CROWD:** 2,800   **PAYOFF:** $554

616	Oct. 22	Rochester, MN	★★1/2

Jimmy Graffiti

W top-rope dropkick   **CROWD:** 2,500   **PAYOFF:** $554

BRYAN ALVAREZ'S TOP 5 STANDOUT CHRIS JERICHO PERFORMANCES

Bryan Alvarez is one of the industry's leading journalists and the host of Wrestling Observer Live.

In pro wrestling, many "standout moments" are scripted by company officials — a title win, a long-awaited victory over an adversary. But other standout moments are real, moments that were bigger perhaps than they were ever intended to be, or which inadvertently resulted in a turning point in a person's career. Here are five of Chris Jericho's.

5. INAUGURAL AEW WORLD HEAVYWEIGHT CHAMPIONSHIP RUN

Jericho beat Adam Page at the 2019 AEW All Out PPV to become the company's first-ever champion (#2693), a title he held until Feb. 29, 2020, when he lost it to Jon Moxley (#2705). As the company's biggest mainstream star, his championship reign helped cement AEW as a solid No. 2 promotion in the U.S., with a weekly prime-time television show on TNT that ended up being renewed years early because of its success in the prime 18-49 demographic — a fact that led Jericho to dub himself the "Demo God."

4. NEW JAPAN FEUD WITH KENNY OMEGA

Jericho once said he would only ever work for WWE. But in 2017, after a suggestion from his friend Don Callis, Jericho agreed to a deal with New Japan Pro-Wrestling, where he worked as a heel, the Painmaker, versus NJPW's top foreign star, Kenny Omega (#2685). It was probably the single biggest turning point of his career as it ultimately signaled his split from WWE, ushered in a new and creatively explosive stage of his career, and led to him becoming one of the cornerstones of AEW, WWE's first large-scale competition since the death of WCW in 2001.

3. HIS 2008 WRESTLING OBSERVER FEUD OF THE YEAR WITH SHAWN MICHAELS

You could write a book about this feud, easily one of the best of the 21st century in WWE. From managing to get himself over as a heel despite telling the truth about a babyface who had lied, to accidentally punching Michaels' wife, Rebecca, for real and inadvertently adding a whole new level of heat to the angle, to the great matches that followed, it was a career standout for both men.

2. HIS 1999 DEBUT AGAINST THE ROCK ON RAW

While it was not his greatest promo, it was among his most famous. For months, a mysterious countdown clock had appeared on *Raw*, and finally, on August 9, it struck zero — with the WWF debut of Chris Jericho. He interrupted an interview segment with The Rock and their byplay, which felt like a WWF vs. WCW inter-promotional moment, was among the more memorable segments of the Monday Night Wars. While he was presented as a tippy-top main eventer on night one, his WWF journey ended up being a rocky one for several years. But ultimately, he ended up being what they teased he'd be that first night in, one of the greatest stars in company history.

1. HIS FEUD THAT NEVER WAS WITH BILL GOLDBERG

Although it seems odd to list a standout performance as something that never happened, that's particularly why it stood out. While booked solidly as a mid-carder in WCW, Jericho did such a great job building up a feud with top star Bill Goldberg that it seemed impossible to believe the company wouldn't do SOMETHING with it — even if that something was a match where Goldberg destroyed him. But Jericho had been slotted by management, Goldberg wasn't interested in working with him, all of the great build went nowhere, and the entire debacle helped seal the deal on his departure and eventual jump to the competition.

617	Oct. 27	Las Vegas		★★★
L	**Syxx (Halloween Havoc)** spin-kick		CROWD: 11,000	PAYOFF: $554
618	Oct. 30	Rome, GA		★★★
L	**Chris Benoit** backslam		CROWD: 2,000	PAYOFF: $369
619	Oct. 30	Rome, GA		★★
W	**Bobby Eaton** missile kick		CROWD: 2,000	PAYOFF: $369
		NOVEMBER 1996		
620	Nov. 01	Hammond, IN		★★
L	**Dean Malenko** roll-up		CROWD: 3,800	PAYOFF: $369
621	Nov. 02	Battle Creek, MI		★★1/2
L	**Dean Malenko** roll-up		CROWD: 3,500	PAYOFF: $369
622	Nov. 03	Saginaw, MI		★★★
L	**Dean Malenko** roll-up		CROWD: 3,200	PAYOFF: $369
623	Nov. 04	Grand Rapids, MI		★★★
W	**Michael Wallstreet**		CROWD: 10,000	PAYOFF: $369

624	Nov. 05	Gainesville, GA		★★★
W	**Bunkhouse Buck**			
	missile kick		CROWD: 1,500	PAYOFF: $369

625	Nov. 07	Orlando, FL		★★★
W	**Jimmy Graffiti**			
	missile kick		CROWD: 400	PAYOFF: $369

626	Nov. 07	Orlando, FL		★★1/2
W	**Butch Long**			
	missile kick		CROWD: 400	PAYOFF: $369

627	Nov. 09	Orlando, FL		★★1/2
W	**Jack Boot**			
	missile kick		CROWD: 400	PAYOFF: $369

628	Nov. 09	Orlando, FL		★★
W	**Mr. JL (Jerry Lynn)**			
	missile kick		CROWD: 400	PAYOFF: $369

629	Nov. 10	Orlando, FL		★★1/2
W	**Scott Armstrong**			
	missile kick		CROWD: 400	PAYOFF: $369

630	Nov. 11	St. Petersburg, FL		★★
L	**Konnan**			
	DQ		CROWD: 4,000	PAYOFF: $492

631	Nov. 12	Orlando, FL		★★★
W	**Craig Pittman**			
	missile kick		CROWD: 400	PAYOFF: $492

632	Nov. 12	Orlando, FL		★★1/2
W	**La Parka**			
	crucifix		CROWD: 400	PAYOFF: $492

633	Nov. 13	Orlando, FL		★★★
W	**Jerry Flynn**			
	missile kick		CROWD: 400	PAYOFF: $492

634	Nov. 14	Orlando, FL		★★1/2
W	**The Gambler**			
	missile kick		CROWD: 400	PAYOFF: $492

635	Nov. 15	Orlando, FL		★★1/2
W	**Billy Kidman**			
	missile kick		CROWD: 400	PAYOFF: $492

636	Nov. 18	Florence, SC		★★1/2
W	**Johnny Grunge**			
	missile kick		CROWD: 4,500	PAYOFF: $492

637	Nov. 19	Fayetteville, NC		★★1/2
W	**Bobby Eaton**			
	missile kick		CROWD: 4,000	PAYOFF: $492

638	Nov. 24	Norfolk, WV		★★★
W	**Nick Patrick (One hand tied behind my back/World War 3)**			
	superkick		CROWD: 9,000	PAYOFF: $246

MATCH NOTES #638

This was basically my first big angle in WCW, against referee Nick Patrick, while I was being managed by Teddy Long, who at the time boasted Jimmy Powers, "Hardwork" Bobby Walker, and Ice Train on his roster. It was a dead-end push in a dead-end angle, but Teddy and Nick were great guys and we did our best. Nick actually had a ton of heat as the crooked NWO referee, so the one-arm-tied-behind-my-back match should've gotten a good reaction. And it did — until the rope holding my arm behind my back became untied about two minutes into the match. I had to work for another 10 minutes, pretending that I was still tied up and holding my arm behind my back like an idiot.

639	Nov. 24	Norfolk, WV		★★1/4
L	**3-ring 60-man battle royal (World War 3)**			
	Giant won		CROWD: 9,000	PAYOFF: $246

640	Nov. 30	Charleston, WV		★★
W	**David Taylor**			
	missile kick		CROWD: 3,000	PAYOFF: $1,476

| DECEMBER 1996 | | | | |

641	Dec. 01	Wheeling, WV		★★1/2
W	**David Taylor**			
	crucifix		CROWD: 2,000	PAYOFF: $1,476

642	Dec. 04	Gainesville, GA		★★★
W	**Sgt. Buddy Lee Parker**			
	missile kick		CROWD: 1,500	PAYOFF: $1,476

643	Dec. 09	Charlotte, NC		★★★
Bobby Eaton				
W	missile kick		CROWD: 6,000	PAYOFF: $1,476

644	Dec. 16	Pensacola, FL		★★
Masa Chono				
W	DQ/foot in ropes		CROWD: 5,500	PAYOFF: $1,476

645	Dec. 18	Montgomery, AL		★★★
Jimmy Graffiti				
W	missile kick		CROWD: 1,000	PAYOFF: $1,476

646	Dec. 30	Knoxville, TN		★★★
Chris Benoit				
L	top-rope belly-to-back suplex		CROWD: 5,000	PAYOFF: $2,214

JANUARY 1997

647	Jan. 04	Tokyo		★★
Koji Kanemoto				
W	tiger suplex		CROWD: 62,500	PAYOFF: $2,214

648	Jan. 13	New Orleans		★★1/2
Craig Pittman				
W	missile kick		CROWD: 11,000	PAYOFF: $4,428

649	Jan. 20	Chicago		★1/2
Alex Wright				
W	roll-up		CROWD: 18,000	PAYOFF: $553

650	Jan. 21	Milwaukee		★★★1/2
6-man with Chavo Guerrero Jr. & Super Calo vs. Konnan, La Parka & Mr. JL				
W	lion spike		CROWD: 6,000	PAYOFF: $553

651	Jan. 22	Green Bay, WI		★★1/2
Super Calo				
W	missile kick		CROWD: 4,000	PAYOFF: $553

652	Jan. 25	Cedar Rapids, IA		★★★1/2
Masa Chono (NWO Souled Out)				
L	Yakuza kick		CROWD: 7,000	PAYOFF: $553

653	Jan. 29	Fukushima, Japan		★★★
Tag with Koji Kanemoto vs. Jushin Liger & El Samurai				
L	pinned by Liger/top-rope fisherman buster		CROWD: 300	PAYOFF: $554

654	Jan. 30	Tsuruoka, Japan	★★1/2

Tag with Scotty Riggs vs. Black Cat & El Samurai

W pinned Cat/lionsault   **CROWD:** 3,500   **PAYOFF:** $554

655	Jan. 31	Sendai, Japan	★★1/2

6-man with Shinjiro Otani & Koji Kanemoto vs. El Samurai, Jushin Liger & Norio Honaga

W pinned Honaga/tiger suplex   **CROWD:** 4,500   **PAYOFF:** $554

FEBRUARY 1997

656	Feb. 02	Tokyo	★★1/2

Tag with Scotty Riggs vs. Akira Nogami & Kuniaki Kobayashi

W pinned Kobayashi/tiger roll   **CROWD:** 2,000   **PAYOFF:** $554

657	Feb. 06	Hakodate, Japan	★★★

6-man with Shinjiro Otani & Koji Kanemoto vs. El Samurai, Jushin Liger & Norio Honaga

L pinned by Liger/roll-up   **CROWD:** 1,500   **PAYOFF:** $492

658	Feb. 07	Muroran, Japan	★★★

Tag with Koji Kanemoto vs. Jushin Liger & Norio Honaga

W pinned Honaga/lionsault   **CROWD:** 1,000   **PAYOFF:** $492

659	Feb. 08	Sapporo, Japan	★★★

Tag with Scotty Riggs vs. Osamu Nishimura & Norio Honaga

L Riggs pinned   **CROWD:** 7,000   **PAYOFF:** $492

660	Feb. 09	Sapporo, Japan	★★★

Tag with Black Cat vs. Norio Honaga & Tatsuhito Takaiwa

L Cat pinned   **CROWD:** 7,000   **PAYOFF:** $492

661	Feb. 11	Osaka, Japan	★★★

Tag with Scotty Riggs vs. Akira Nogami & Kuniaki Kobayashi

L pinned by Nogami/German suplex   **CROWD:** 3,000   **PAYOFF:** $492

662	Feb. 13	Gifu, Japan	★★★1/2

Tag with Koji Kanemoto vs. Jushin Liger & El Samurai

L pinned by Samurai/roll-up   **CROWD:** 2,500   **PAYOFF:** $492

663	Feb. 14	Shizuoka, Japan	★★1/2

Tag with Scotty Riggs vs. Jushin Liger & El Samurai

W Riggs pinned Samurai   **CROWD:** 2,000   **PAYOFF:** $492

664	Feb. 15	Yamato, Japan	★★1/2

Tag with Scotty Riggs vs. Black Cat & Norio Honaga

W pinned Cat/lionsault   **CROWD:** 1,500   **PAYOFF:** $492

665	Feb. 16	Tokyo		★★★1/2

Tag with Scotty Riggs vs. El Samurai & Norio Honaga

W pinned Honaga/lionsault   **CROWD:** 11,500   **PAYOFF:** $492

666	Feb. 17	Tampa, FL		★★1/2

Jeff Jarrett

W roll-up   **CROWD:** 5,000   **PAYOFF:** $1,107

667	Feb. 18	Pensacola, FL		★★1/2

Bunkhouse Buck

W missile kick   **CROWD:** 3,000   **PAYOFF:** $1,107

668	Feb. 23	San Francisco		★★★

Eddy Guerrero (SuperBrawl VII)

L sunset flip   **CROWD:** 15,000   **PAYOFF:** $1,107

669	Feb. 24	Sacramento, CA		★★★★

Tag with Eddy Guerrero vs. Meng & The Barbarian

L Guerrero pinned   **CROWD:** 15,000   **PAYOFF:** $1,107

MARCH 1997

670	Mar. 04	Rome, GA		★★1/4

Mark Starr

W missile kick   **CROWD:** 2,000   **PAYOFF:** $1,476

671	Mar. 04	Rome, GA		★★

Pat Tanaka

W roll-up   **CROWD:** 2,000   **PAYOFF:** $1,476

672	Mar. 10	Panama City, FL		★★1/2

Scotty Riggs

L DQ   **CROWD:** 500   **PAYOFF:** $1,476

673	Mar. 19	Dalton, GA		★★★

Super Calo

W lion spike   **CROWD:** 1,500   **PAYOFF:** $865

674	Mar. 22	Minneapolis		★★★

Dean Malenko

L roll-up   **CROWD:** 9,000   **PAYOFF:** $865

675	Mar. 27	Baltimore		★★★

Dean Malenko

L roll-up   **CROWD:** 9,000   **PAYOFF:** $866

676	Mar. 28	Johnstown, PA		★★★★
	Dean Malenko			
L	roll-up		CROWD: 3,500	PAYOFF: $866

677	Mar. 29	Charleston, WV		★★1/2
	Dean Malenko			
L	roll-up		CROWD: 4,000	PAYOFF: $866

678	Mar. 31	Roanoke, VA		★★★
	Steven Regal			
W	roll-up		CROWD: 7,000	PAYOFF: $844

APRIL 1997

679	Apr. 01	Johnson City, TN		★★1/2
	Mr. JL			
W	missile kick		CROWD: 5,000	PAYOFF: $844

680	Apr. 07	Huntsville, AL		★★1/2
	Dean Malenko			
L	kick to head		CROWD: 5,000	PAYOFF: $844

681	Apr. 11	Montreal		★★1/2
	Jeff Jarrett			
L	roll-up		CROWD: 12,000	PAYOFF: $844

682	Apr. 12	Pittsburgh		★★★
	Jeff Jarrett			
L	roll-up		CROWD: 7,000	PAYOFF: $845

683	Apr. 16	Gainesville, GA		★★1/2
	Super Calo			
W	missile kick		CROWD: 1,100	PAYOFF: $703

684	Apr. 18	Dayton, OH		★★★
	Jeff Jarrett			
L	roll-up		CROWD: 8,000	PAYOFF: $703

685	Apr. 19	Grand Rapids, MI		★★★1/2
	Jeff Jarrett			
L	roll-up		CROWD: 10,000	PAYOFF: $704

686	Apr. 20	Kalamazoo, MI		★★1/2
	Jeff Jarrett			
L	roll-up		CROWD: 4,500	PAYOFF: $704

MY TOP 10 WCW OPPONENTS

• DEAN MALENKO

One of my all-time biggest and best rivalries was with Deano Machino, and the pop he got when he unmasked at Slamboree 1998 as Ciclope (#860) was one of the loudest I've ever been in the ring to hear. Dean was always the consummate ring general: he called the majority of our matches and was able to put together incredible finishes in mere minutes.

• JUVENTUD GUERRERA

I loved working with Juvie, and my best WCW match was the mask vs. title match I had with him at SuperBrawl VIII (#813).

• BOOKER T

Book was the first "main event" guy I worked with regularly in WCW, especially at house shows.

• EDDY GUERRERO

I rarely worked with Eddy in WWE, but we had some excellent matches in WCW, including my favorite (#754) at Fall Brawl 1997.

• MENG

What a super-underrated worker and the sweetest guy! Tonga had excellent psychology, and he and The Barbarian tore it up with Eddy and me on *Nitro* in 1997 (#669).

• LORD STEVEN REGAL

I learned a lot about how to feed a comeback from Regal, and also how to carry myself backstage at a show.

• PRINCE IAUKEA

Prince Nakamaki, as I called him, was a good worker whom I wrestled many times on house shows and TV. He apparently left the business after he won the lottery.

• PERRY SATURN

I've known Perry since 1995 and worked with him in WAR, ECW, WCW, and WWE. Our most famous encounter was a "loser wears a dress" match (#954) — which I won at Perry's request.

• DISCO INFERNO

A great house-show opponent. Disco knew exactly who he was in the ring, and we always had fun.

• CHAVO GUERRERO JR.

I think I beat Chavo 20 times in a row in WCW, which lead to us hiding a baseball bat under the ring at a *Thunder* taping, which he used to beat me up after the match (#895) — with no knowledge or permission given from anybody in the office. And nobody ever said a word about it after the show.

687	Apr. 21	Saginaw, MI	★
L	**Meng** choke	**CROWD:** 7,000	**PAYOFF:** $704
688	Apr. 27	Fayetteville, MI	★★
L	**Dean Malenko** roll-up	**CROWD:** 3,500	**PAYOFF:** $703
689	Apr. 29	Palmetto, FL	★★1/2
W	**La Parka** missile kick	**CROWD:** 3,000	**PAYOFF:** $324

MAY 1997

690	May 01	Orlando, FL	★★★
W	**Prince Iaukea** roll-up	**CROWD:** 400	**PAYOFF:** $324
691	May 03	Orlando, FL	★★★1/4
W	**Dave Heath** missile kick	**CROWD:** 400	**PAYOFF:** $324
692	May 03	Orlando, FL	★★3/4
W	**Psicosis** missile kick	**CROWD:** 400	**PAYOFF:** $324
693	May 04	Orlando, FL	★★★1/2
W	**Michael Wallstreet** sunset flip	**CROWD:** 400	**PAYOFF:** $324
694	May 06	Orlando, FL	★★★
W	**La Parka** missile kick	**CROWD:** 400	**PAYOFF:** $325
695	May 06	Orlando, FL	★★★
L	**Steven Regal** roll-up	**CROWD:** 400	**PAYOFF:** $325

696	May 07	Orlando, FL		★★★1/4
Dean Malenko				
L	small package		CROWD: 400	PAYOFF: $325

697	May 08	Orlando, FL		★★★1/4
Konnan				
DC	DOUBLE COUNTOUT		CROWD: 400	PAYOFF: $325

698	May 08	Orlando, FL		★★3/4
La Parka				
W	missile kick		CROWD: 400	PAYOFF: $325

699	May 08	Orlando, FL		★★★
Jeff Jarrett				
L	roll-up		CROWD: 400	PAYOFF: $325

700	May 09	Orlando, FL		★★★
Psicosis				
W	missile kick		CROWD: 400	PAYOFF: $324

701	May 09	Orlando, FL		★★1/2
Rick Fuller				
W	missile kick		CROWD: 400	PAYOFF: $325

702	May 13	Salisbury, MD		★★1/4
Pat Tanaka				
W	missile kick		CROWD: 2,000	PAYOFF: $432

703	May 16	Gunma, Japan		★★1/2
Takashi Iizuka				
L	blizzard suplex		CROWD: 1,100	PAYOFF: $432

704	May 17	Veda, Japan		★★3/4
8-man with Chavo Guerrero Jr., Koji Kanemoto & Scorpio Jr. vs. Jushin Liger, Robbie Brookside, Doc Dean & Gran Naniwa				
L	Scorpio pinned		CROWD: 2,000	PAYOFF: $432

705	May 18	Nagano, Japan		★★1/2
Scorpio Jr. (Best of the Super Juniors)				
W	lionsault		CROWD: 1,700	PAYOFF: $432

706	May 19	Tochigi, Japan		★★1/2
Hanzo Nakajima (Best of the Super Juniors)				
W	lionsault		CROWD: 2,000	PAYOFF: $432

707	May 20	Tokyo		★★★

Tag wth Hanzo Nakajima vs. Gran Naniwa & El Samurai

L pinned by Samurai/broken magistral cradle

CROWD: 2,200   PAYOFF: $432

708	May 21	Fukushima, Japan		★★

Tag with Robbie Brookside vs. Koji Kanemoto & Hanzo Nakajima

L Brookside pinned

CROWD: 2,000   PAYOFF: $432

709	May 23	Mie, Japan		★★★

8-man with Black Cat, Chavo Guerrero Jr. & Tatsuhito Takaiwa vs. Jushin Liger, El Samurai, Doc Dean & Gran Naniwa

W Dean pinned

CROWD: 2,500   PAYOFF: $432

710	May 24	Okayama, Japan		★★★1/2

Yoshihiro Tajiri (Best of the Super Juniors)

W lionsault

CROWD: 3,500   PAYOFF: $432

711	May 25	Tottori, Japan		★★★

El Samurai (Best of the Super Juniors)

W lion spike

CROWD: 3,500   PAYOFF: $432

712	May 26	Takamatsu, Japan		★★1/2

6-man with Chavo Guerrero Jr. & Shinjiro Otani vs. El Samurai, Gran Naniwa & Kendo Kashin

L Otani submitted

CROWD: 2,000   PAYOFF: $541

713	May 27	Otsu, Japan		★★★

6-man with Dr. Wagner Jr. & Hanzo Nakajima vs. Jushin Liger, El Samurai & Black Cat

L Wagner pinned

CROWD: 2,000   PAYOFF: $541

714	May 29	Uwajima, Japan		★★1/2

Robbie Brookside (Best of the Super Juniors)

L backslide

CROWD: 1,000   PAYOFF: $541

715	May 30	Kure, Japan		★★★

Yutaka Yoshie

W Boston crab

CROWD: 2,000   PAYOFF: $541

716	May 31	Himeji, Japan		★★★1/2

Shinjiro Otani (Best of the Super Juniors)

L springboard DDT

CROWD: 3,000   PAYOFF: $541

JUNE 1997

717	June 01	Odawara, Japan		★★1/2

6-man with El Samurai & Kendo Kashin vs. Robbie Brookside, Doc Dean & Shinjiro Otani

W Kashin pinned Brookside

CROWD: 4,000   PAYOFF: $541

718	June 03	Yamagata, Japan	★★★

8-man with Jushin Liger, Gran Naniwa & Kendo Kashin vs. Chavo Guerrero Jr., Koji Kanemoto, Tatsuhito Takaiwa & Hanzo Nakajima

W Kashin pinned Guerrero   **CROWD:** 2,700   **PAYOFF:** $541

719	June 05	Tokyo	★★1/2

8-man with Jushin Liger, Gran Naniwa & Dr. Wagner Jr. vs. Shinjiro Otani, Tatsuhito Takaiwa, Hanzo Nakajima & Yoshihiro Tajiri

W Liger pinned Takaiwa   **CROWD:** 14,000   **PAYOFF:** $541

720	June 09	Boston	★1/4

Alex Wright

L roll-up   **CROWD:** 18,000   **PAYOFF:** $1,082

MY TOP 10 FAVORITE REFEREES

- Brian Hildebrand/Mark Curtis (SMW/WCW)
- Roberto Rangel (CMLL)
- Rod "Spider" Zapata [WWE]
- Red Shoes Unno (WAR/NJPW)
- Charles Robinson (WCW/WWE)
- Mike Chioda (WWE)
- Chad Patton (WWE)
- Aubrey Edwards (AEW)
- Ed Langley (CNWA)
- Outside Enforcer Shaquille O'Neal (WWE, July 27, 2009 #2148)

721	June 11	Birmingham, AL	★★1/2

Johnny Swinger

W missile kick   **CROWD:** 3,000   **PAYOFF:** $1,082

722	June 11	Birmingham, AL	★★

Syxx

L buzzkill   **CROWD:** 3,000   **PAYOFF:** $1,082

723	June 16	Chicago	★★★

Ultimo Dragon

L tiger suplex   **CROWD:** 16,500   **PAYOFF:** $1,082

724	June 23	Macon, GA		★★★
W	**Alex Wright**			
	Boston crab		CROWD: 4,000	PAYOFF: $1,082

725	June 28	Los Angeles		★★
W	**Syxx (won WCW cruiserweight title)**			
	spin-kick		CROWD: 12,000	PAYOFF: $1,082

726	June 30	Las Vegas		★★★
W	**Juventud Guerrera**			
	liontamer		CROWD: 8,000	PAYOFF: $1,082

727	June 30	Las Vegas		★★★
W	**Syxx**			
	DQ		CROWD: 8,000	PAYOFF: $1,082

JULY 1997

728	July 08	Jackson, TN		★1/2
W	**Alex Wright**			
	liontamer		CROWD: 3,000	PAYOFF: $721

729	July 13	Daytona Beach, FL		★★★★
W	**Ultimo Dragon (Bash at the Beach)**			
	roll-up		CROWD: 8,500	PAYOFF: $721

730	July 15	Ft. Myers, FL		★★1/2
W	**Silver King**			
	liontamer		CROWD: 2,500	PAYOFF: $721

731	July 17	Orlando, FL		★★3/4
W	**Doc Dean**			
	liontamer		CROWD: 400	PAYOFF: $722

732	July 18	Orlando, FL		★★1/2
W	**Ciclope**			
	liontamer		CROWD: 400	PAYOFF: $722

733	July 18	Orlando, FL		★★★
W	**Johnny Swinger**			
	liontamer		CROWD: 400	PAYOFF: $722

734	July 26	Philadelphia		★★★
W	**Alex Wright**			
	liontamer		CROWD: 9,000	PAYOFF: $721

735	July 27	Johnstown, PA		★★3/4
	Alex Wright			
W	liontamer		CROWD: 3,000	PAYOFF: $721

736	July 28	Charleston, WV		★★★
	Alex Wright (lost WCW cruiserweight title)			
L	German suplex		CROWD: 4,500	PAYOFF: $721

737	July 30	Painesville, PA		★★★
	Psicosis			
W	liontamer		CROWD: 1,000	PAYOFF: $722

AUGUST 1997

738	Aug. 02	Battle Creek, MI		★★★1/2
	Eddy Guerrero			
W	hurricanrana		CROWD: 2,200	PAYOFF: $722

739	Aug. 03	Grand Rapids, MI		★★★
	Alex Wright			
L	side suplex		CROWD: 6,000	PAYOFF: $722

740	Aug. 09	Sturgis, SD		★★★1/4
	Alex Wright (Road Wild)			
L	roll-up		CROWD: 10,000	PAYOFF: $861

741	Aug. 11	Denver		★★★1/2
	Eddy Guerrero			
L	frog splash		CROWD: 7,000	PAYOFF: $861

742	Aug. 12	Colorado Springs, CO		★★3/4
	Alex Wright (won WCW cruiserweight title/2nd time)			
W	liontamer		CROWD: 2,500	PAYOFF: $861

743	Aug. 16	Huntsville, AL		★★1/2
	Alex Wright			
W	liontamer		CROWD: 3,000	PAYOFF: $862

744	Aug. 17	Tupelo, MS		★★★
	Alex Wright			
W	liontamer		CROWD: 2,500	PAYOFF: $862

745	Aug. 21	Nashville, TN		★★3/4
	Eddy Guerrero			
W	roll-up		CROWD: 2,500	PAYOFF: $1,082

746	Aug. 25	Columbia, SC		★★
W	**Yuji Nagata**			
	liontamer		CROWD: 4,000	PAYOFF: $1,082

747	Aug. 26	Augusta, GA		★★1/2
W	**Hector Guerrero**			
	liontamer		CROWD: 3,000	PAYOFF: $1,082

748	Aug. 31	Mobile, AL		★★★
W	**Alex Wright**			
	liontamer		CROWD: 2,500	PAYOFF: $1,082

SEPTEMBER 1997

749	Sept. 04	Springfield, IL		★★★
W	**Eddy Guerrero**			
	liontamer		CROWD: 3,000	PAYOFF: $721

750	Sept. 05	Peoria, IL		★★★
W	**Eddy Guerrero**			
	liontamer		CROWD: 3,000	PAYOFF: $721

751	Sept. 06	Indianapolis		★★★
W	**Ultimo Dragon**			
	liontamer		CROWD: 10,000	PAYOFF: $721

752	Sept. 07	Chicago		★★★
W	**Ultimo Dragon**			
	liontamer		CROWD: 8,000	PAYOFF: $722

753	Sept. 08	Milwaukee		★★1/2
W	**Brad Armstrong**			
	DQ		CROWD: 6,000	PAYOFF: $722

754	Sept. 14	Winston-Salem, NC		★★★★1/4
L	**Eddy Guerrero (lost WCW cruiserweight title/Fall Brawl)**			
	frog splash		CROWD: 8,500	PAYOFF: $722

755	Sept. 17	Osaka, Japan		★★★
W	**Yutaka Yoshie**			
	lionsault		CROWD: 6,000	PAYOFF: $481

756	Sept. 18	Tokuyama, Japan		★★3/4
L	**Tag with Tatsuhito Takaiwa vs. Wild Pegasus & Norio Honaga**			
	pinned by Honaga/magistral cradle		CROWD: 6,000	PAYOFF: $481

September, 1997
Live Events Calendar

NAVIGATION
EVENTS/PPVs ▼ Go

Sunday	Monday	Tuesday	Wednesday	Thursday	Friday	Saturday
	1 — Pensacola, FL Civic Center 7:30PM *TNT*	2	3	4 — Springfield, Prarie Capital Conv. 7:30PM	5 — Peoria, IL Civic Center 7:30PM	6 — Indianapolis, IN Market Square Arenea 7:30PM
7 — Chicago, IL United Center 7:30PM	8 — Milwaukee, WI Wisconsin Center 6:30PM *TNT*	9 — Madison, WI Dane CO. Expo Center 7:00PM	⑩	11 — *Terry Funk's shows ① Amarillo, TX ② Plainview, TX*	12 — *Party with old timers*	13
14 — *Terry's ranch* Winston-Salem NC Lawrence Joel Coliseum 6:30PM Pay-Per-View	15 — Charlotte, NC Independence Arena 7:30PM *TNT*	16 — Anderson, SC Civic Center 7:00PM TV Taping	17	18 — Spokane, WA Spokane Arena 7:30PM	19 — Seattle, WA Key Arena 7:30PM	⑳ — San Fancisco, CA Cow Palace 7:30PM *maybe go to Atlanta* — *go home*
21	22 — Salt Lake City, UT "E" Arena 5:30PM *TNT*	23	24	25	26 — Fairfax, VA Patriot Center 7:30PM	27 — Baltimore, MD Baltimore Arena 7:30PM
28	29 — Worcester, MA Coliseum 7:30PM *TNT*	30				

Stay in Greenville, SC →

[News | Hotline | Events and PPVs | Chat | Darkroom | Soundboard | Merchandise | Feedback]

If you think you've got a hectic schedule, check this out — I was on the road 22 out of 30 days in September of 1997 with WCW. But the crazy thing is my schedule was pretty much like this every month! At least I got to "party with old timers."

EXCALIBUR'S TOP 10 CHRIS JERICHO MATCHES

(IN CHRONOLOGICAL ORDER)

Excalibur is on the AEW Dynamite *broadcast team.*

10. #2716, ORANGE CASSIDY, AEW DYNAMITE, AUG. 12, 2020, JACKSONVILLE, FL

When you look back at WCW in the Monday Night Wars era, it was a period when, at best, it was about preserving the egos of the top stars, and at worst, inflating them. In this Wednesday Night Wars era we find ourselves in, it would have been very easy for Jericho to say, "Hey, I'm the top star. Everything has to revolve around me." Instead, Jericho has gone in the completely opposite direction and said, "Hey, I'm the top star. How can I build other guys into stars?" Orange Cassidy was one of the breakout stars during the first year of AEW *Dynamite*, someone the live audiences lost their minds for, but an unknown in terms of how the television audience would receive him. Then, because of the pandemic, there were no live audiences. Over the course of their trilogy, Jericho made sure the fans at home would react to Orange Cassidy the same way the live crowd did. And I'm not just saying that just because it's his book.

9. #2710, STADIUM STAMPEDE, MAY 23, 2020, JACKSONVILLE, FL

By the time you read this, I hope the COVID-19 pandemic will be on the way out. In early 2020, the pandemic completely disrupted the entire world, professional wrestling included, and required some creative thinking in terms of how to put on a wrestling pay-per-view with no fans in attendance. Enter the Stadium Stampede. Ostensibly it was a 5-on-5, no disqualification, falls count anywhere match. But the ring was on the 50-yard line of a football stadium. And there was a bar fight. And a golf cart. And a horse. And Chris Jericho beat up an NFL mascot. And it was glorious.

8. #2700, SCORPIO SKY, AEW DYNAMITE, NOV. 27, 2019, CHICAGO

This was a really meaningful match for me to be able to call because I've known Sky since more or less the beginning of his career, and I knew how much he looked up to Chris. This match was also important because even though *Dynamite* had been on the air for less than two months it established Sky, a relative newcomer to most of our audience despite his years of experience, as someone that could believably stand toe-to-toe with Jericho. Chris used his stature and star power to elevate one of our younger competitors, and it wouldn't be the last time.

7. #2685, KENNY OMEGA, NJPW WRESTLE KINGDOM 12, JAN. 4, 2018, TOKYO

When it's all said and done, this may be the most important match of its decade. For the first time in nearly 20 years, Chris Jericho wrestled outside of WWE, and he did so against someone considered to be the best wrestler in the world at that time: Kenny Omega. While the match itself was great — a wild, bloody brawl spilling out of the ring and into the crowd of the Tokyo Dome — even greater was the new world of possibilities it opened in helping to lay the groundwork for All Elite Wrestling.

6. #2514, KEVIN OWENS, WWE HOUSE SHOW, JULY 31, 2015, SAN DIEGO

This was the first time I had the privilege of seeing Jericho wrestle in person, and it happened to be against one of my good friends in the business. On top of that, this was the first time that Jericho and Kevin had ever wrestled, which led to one of the most memorable friendships/rivalries in recent memory in WWE. In one of our early conversations, Jericho insisted this was a steel cage match despite my having photographic evidence of it not being in a cage. Their match the next night was in a steel cage, but it is somewhat rewarding to be able to be proven right in Chris' own book, even if he will still call me a "stupid idiot" and tell me to "go shut [my] ass."

5. #1383, STONE COLD STEVE AUSTIN, WWF VENGEANCE, DEC. 9, 2001, SAN DIEGO

Though Jericho was largely stuck in the middle of the card during his WCW tenure, Y2J made an immediate impact when he appeared in WWF and rose to heights I don't think anyone (save Chris) thought he was capable of. Vengeance was the ultimate proof of that fact, where in a single night, Jericho defeated The Rock to win the WCW World title, and immediately went on to defeat "Stone Cold" Steve Austin to win the WWF Championship, unify the titles, and go down in history as the first-ever Undisputed WWF Champion. Hell of a night.

4. #754, EDDY GUERRERO, WCW FALL BRAWL, SEPT. 14, 1997, WINSTON-SALEM, NC

I was always more of a *Nitro* guy because of the cruiserweight division, which meant I could see favorites like Jericho and Eddy Guerrero wrestle every week without having to seek out third-generation VHS tapes from some dude on the internet. This match had everything I love about pro wrestling: two young, hungry competitors with mind-boggling chemistry (sense a pattern?) determined to steal the show and doing exactly that. While this match opened the pay-per-view, it really was the main event for me.

3. #585, 2 COLD SCORPIO, ECW THE DOCTOR IS IN, AUG. 3, 1996, PHILADELPHIA

Jericho spent only six months in ECW, but during that time he had so many memorable matches, I could have sworn his run was longer. I felt like 2 Cold Scorpio was one of his best opponents during that time and this match exemplified why — fast-paced and hard-hitting, Jericho utilizing his experience in Mexico and Japan, but ultimately at the end of the day being outclassed by perhaps the best high-flyer in the world at that time.

2. #517, WILD PEGASUS (CHRIS BENOIT), SUPER J-CUP 2ND STAGE, DEC. 13, 1995, TOKYO

The first two Super J-Cup tournaments were among the most influential shows that made me fall back in love with pro wrestling and ultimately want to become a wrestler. After winning the first Super J-Cup, Wild Pegasus was granted a first-round bye, whereas Jericho had to defeat Hanzo Nakajima in the first round. Despite the fact Jericho had wrestled a tough match previously, he hung with Pegasus until the very end (and I'd like to think softened Pegasus up for Gedo, who shockingly eliminated him in the following round).

1. #468, ULTIMO DRAGON, WAR THIRD ANNIVERSARY SHOW, JULY 7, 1995, TOKYO

The chemistry between Chris and Ultimo Dragon was like nothing I had ever seen to that point. You had a Canadian guy and a Japanese guy with a lucha libre-influenced persona and yet, somehow it was like they were born to wrestle each other. It was truly an eye-opening match that broadened my horizons in terms of what professional wrestling could be: two people from completely different parts of the world, united by pro wrestling, that could make magic together.

757	Sept. 19	Okayama, Japan		★★★1/4	
W	**Dr. Wagner Jr.**				
	lionsault		CROWD: 3,000	PAYOFF: $481	

758	Sept. 20	Nagoya, Japan		★★3/4	
L	**Jushin Liger**				
	super brain-buster		CROWD: 10,000	PAYOFF: $480	

759	Sept. 21	Hamamatsu, Japan		★★★1/2	
W	**Tag with Black Cat vs. Dr. Wagner Jr. & Wild Pegasus**				
	Cat pinned Pegasus		CROWD: 3,000	PAYOFF: $480	

760	Sept. 22	Niigata, Japan		★★★★	
W	**8-man with Tatsuhito Takaiwa, Shinjiro Otani & Koji Kanemoto vs. Jushin Liger, El Samurai, Wild Pegasus & Kendo Kashin**				
	Takaiwa pinned Samurai		CROWD: 3,500	PAYOFF: $480	

761	Sept. 23	Tokyo		★★★	
L	**6-man with Dr. Wagner Jr. & Koji Kanemoto vs. Jushin Liger, El Samurai & Wild Pegasus**				
	Liger pinned Wagner		CROWD: 14,000	PAYOFF: $480	

762	Sept. 26	Fairfax, VA		★★3/4
W	**Alex Wright**			
	liontamer		CROWD: 5,000	PAYOFF: $481

763	Sept. 27	Baltimore		★★3/4
L	**Eddy Guerrero**			
	frog splash		CROWD: 8,000	PAYOFF: $481

764	Sept. 29	Worcester, MA		★★3/4
W	**Syxx**			
	DQ		CROWD: 6,000	PAYOFF: $865

OCTOBER 1997

765	Oct. 01	Dalton, GA		★★1/2
W	**Denny Brown**			
	liontamer		CROWD: 2,000	PAYOFF: $865

766	Oct. 04	Duluth, MN		★★1/2
L	**Eddy Guerrero**			
	frog splash		CROWD: 2,000	PAYOFF: $866

767	Oct. 05	Mankato, MN		★★3/4
L	**Eddy Guerrero**			
	frog splash		CROWD: 2,500	PAYOFF: $866

768	Oct. 11	Orlando, FL		★★3/4
W	**Sgt. Buddy Lee Parker**			
	liontamer		CROWD: 400	PAYOFF: $866

769	Oct. 13	Tampa, FL		★★★
L	**Yuji Nagata**			
	reverse figure-four		CROWD: 12,000	PAYOFF: $866

770	Oct. 14	Ft. Myers, FL		★★★
W	**Rick Fuller**			
	liontamer		CROWD: 2,000	PAYOFF: $866

771	Oct. 15	Orlando, FL		★★1/2
W	**Johnny Attitude**			
	liontamer		CROWD: 400	PAYOFF: $866

772	Oct. 16	Orlando, FL		★★★
L	**Eddy Guerrero**			
	frog splash		CROWD: 400	PAYOFF: $865

773	Oct. 26	Las Vegas		★★3/4
W	**Gedo (Halloween Havoc)**			
	liontamer		CROWD: 13,000	PAYOFF: $865

774	Oct. 27	San Diego		★★★
L	**Eddy Guerrero**			
	frog splash		CROWD: 6,000	PAYOFF: $865

NOVEMBER 1997

775	Nov. 01	Salem, VA		★★3/4
W	**Steven Regal**			
	liontamer		CROWD: 3,000	PAYOFF: $865

776	Nov. 02	Norfolk, VA		★★★
W	**Steven Regal**			
	liontamer		CROWD: 6,000	PAYOFF: $866

777	Nov. 03	Philadelphia		★★★
W	**Scott Hall**			
	small package		CROWD: 12,000	PAYOFF: $866

778	Nov. 04	Bethlehem, PA		★★★
L	**Eddy Guerrero**			
	frog splash		CROWD: 6,000	PAYOFF: $866

779	Nov. 10	Memphis, TN		★★★
W	**Disco Inferno**			
	liontamer		CROWD: 6,000	PAYOFF: $1,082

780	Nov. 16	Dayton, OH		★★★
W	**Alex Wright**			
	liontamer		CROWD: 5,000	PAYOFF: $1,082

781	Nov. 17	Cincinnati		★★★★
L	**Rey Mysterio Jr.**			
	hurricanrana		CROWD: 9,000	PAYOFF: $1,082

782	Nov. 22	Kalamazoo, MI		★★1/2
L	**Perry Saturn**			
	submission		CROWD: 2,500	PAYOFF: $1,082

783	Nov. 23	Auburn Hills, MI		★
L	**3-ring 60-man Battle Royal (World War 3)**			
	Scott Hall won		CROWD: 17,000	PAYOFF: $1,082

784	Nov. 24	Saginaw, MI		★★3/4
L	**Marcus Bagwell**			
	blockbuster		CROWD: 5,000	PAYOFF: $2,164

785	Nov. 25	Toledo, OH		★★★
W	**Brad Armstrong**			
	liontamer		CROWD: 2,000	PAYOFF: $2,164

DECEMBER 1997

786	Dec. 09	Erie, PA		★★1/4
L	**Perry Saturn**			
	submission		CROWD: 2,000	PAYOFF: $1,442

787	Dec. 15	Charlotte, NC		★★1/4
L	**Scott Hall**			
	razor's edge		CROWD: 8,000	PAYOFF: $1,443

788	Dec. 16	Gainesville, GA		★★★
W	**Evan Karagias**			
	liontamer		CROWD: 1,500	PAYOFF: $1,443

Eddy, Chavo and I stare intently into what seems to be Marsellus Wallace's briefcase, in a Georgia parking lot in 1997.

789	Dec. 22	Macon, GA	★★3/4
L	**Marcus Bagwell** blockbuster	CROWD: 5,000	PAYOFF: $7,256

790	Dec. 29	Baltimore	★★★
L	**Curt Hennig** Perfect-plex	CROWD: 8,500	PAYOFF: $7,256

JANUARY 1998

791	Jan. 05	Atlanta	★★1/2
L	**Diamond Dallas Page** diamond cutter	CROWD: 30,000	PAYOFF: $639

792	Jan. 06	Rome, GA	★★3/4
L	**Diamond Dallas Page** diamond cutter	CROWD: 2,000	PAYOFF: $639

793	Jan. 08	Daytona Beach, FL	★★★1/4
L	**Ric Flair** figure-four	CROWD: 5,500	PAYOFF: $639

794	Jan. 10	Orlando, FL	★★
W	**Evan Karagias** liontamer	CROWD: 400	PAYOFF: $639

795	Jan. 11	Orlando, FL	★★★★
W	**Rey Mysterio Jr.** liontamer	CROWD: 400	PAYOFF: $640

796	Jan. 12	Jacksonville, FL	★★1/2
L	**Steve McMichael** piledriver	CROWD: 5,000	PAYOFF: $640

797	Jan. 15	Lakeland, FL	★★1/2
W	**Eddy Guerrero** liontamer	CROWD: 5,000	PAYOFF: $640

798	Jan. 18	Shreveport, LA	★★★
W	**Juventud Guerrera** liontamer	CROWD: 7,000	PAYOFF: $640

799	Jan. 19	New Orleans	★★★
W	**Juventud Guerrera** liontamer	CROWD: 21,000	PAYOFF: $1,022

800	Jan. 22	Huntsville, AL		★★★1/2
L	**Chris Benoit**			
	cross-face		CROWD: 5,000	PAYOFF: $1,022

801	Jan. 24	Dayton, OH		★★★
W	**Rey Mysterio Jr. (won WCW cruiserweight title/3rd time – Souled Out)**			
	liontamer		CROWD: 5,000	PAYOFF: $1,022

802	Jan. 29	Memphis, TN		★★★★
L	**Tag with Eddy Guerrero vs. Dean Malenko & Chris Benoit**			
	cross-face		CROWD: 8,000	PAYOFF: $1,023

803	Jan. 31	Boston		★★★★
W	**Dean Malenko**			
	liontamer		CROWD: 18,132	PAYOFF: $1,023

FEBRUARY 1998

804	Feb. 02	San Antonio		★★★
W	**Super Calo**			
	liontamer		CROWD: 30,000	PAYOFF: $730

805	Feb. 03	Corpus Christi, TX		★★★★
W	**Chavo Guerrero Jr.**			
	liontamer		CROWD: 3,000	PAYOFF: $730

806	Feb. 06	Huntsville, AL		★★★
W	**Eddy Guerrero**			
	liontamer		CROWD: 2,000	PAYOFF: $731

807	Feb. 07	Abilene, TX		★★★1/4
W	**Eddy Guerrero**			
	liontamer		CROWD: 8,000	PAYOFF: $731

808	Feb. 08	Midland, TX		★★3/4
W	**Eddy Guerrero**			
	liontamer		CROWD: 6,000	PAYOFF: $730

809	Feb. 09	El Paso, TX		★★★★
W	**Tag with Eddy Guerrero vs. Dean Malenko & Chavo Guerrero Jr.**			
	submitted Chavo/liontamer		CROWD: 6,000	PAYOFF: $731

810	Feb. 12	Oklahoma City		★★1/2
W	**Chavo Guerrero Jr.**			
	liontamer		CROWD: 5,000	PAYOFF: $730

811	Feb. 16	Tampa, FL	★★★	
L	**Tag with Eddy Guerrero vs. Dean Malenko & Chris Benoit**			
	submitted by Malenko/cloverleaf		CROWD: 4,000	PAYOFF: $730

812	Feb. 19	Birmingham, AL	★★★1/2	
W	**Dean Malenko**			
	liontamer		CROWD: 6,000	PAYOFF: $730

813	Feb. 22	San Francisco	★★★★	
W	**Juventud Guerrera (WCW cruiserweight title vs. mask/SuperBrawl VIII)**			
	liontamer		CROWD: 10,000	PAYOFF: $730

814	Feb. 23	Sacramento, CA	★★★	
W	**Lenny Lane**			
	liontamer		CROWD: 6,000	PAYOFF: $731

815	Feb. 26	Cedar Rapids, IA	★★★	
W	**Tag with Eddy Guerrero vs. Dean Malenko & Booker T**			
	Eddy pins Booker		CROWD: 6,000	PAYOFF: $731

816	Feb. 27	Lincoln, NE	★★★★	
W	**Eddy Guerrero**			
	liontamer		CROWD: 8,000	PAYOFF: $731

817	Feb. 28	Sioux City, IA	★★★1/4	
W	**Eddy Guerrero**			
	liontamer		CROWD: 4,000	PAYOFF: $731

MARCH 1998

818	Mar. 02	Philadelphia	★★★1/2	
L	**Tag with Eddy Guerrero vs. Dean Malenko & Booker T**			
	submitted by Malenko/cloverleaf		CROWD: 12,000	PAYOFF: $1,022

819	Mar. 03	Johnstown, PA	★★★	
L	**Tag with Chavo Guerrero vs. Dean Malenko & Chris Benoit**			
	Malenko submitted Guerrero		CROWD: 2,000	PAYOFF: $1,022

820	Mar. 05	Columbus, OH	★1/2	
W	**Ciclope**			
	liontamer		CROWD: 5,000	PAYOFF: $1,023

821	Mar. 09	Winston-Salem, NC	★★★	
W	**Disco Inferno**			
	liontamer		CROWD: 7,000	PAYOFF: $1,023

Trying to make Deano Machino submit in order to retain my Cruiserweight Championship at WCW Uncensored 1998. After the match, Dean "quit" and went home for a few months, i.e. his wife had a baby.

822	Mar. 15	Mobile, AL	★★★
	Dean Malenko (Uncensored)		
W	liontamer	CROWD: 8,000	PAYOFF: $1,023

823	Mar. 16	Panama City, FL	★★★1/4
	Juventud Guerrera		
L	DQ	CROWD: 2,000	PAYOFF: $457

824	Mar. 17	Ozark, AL	★★3/4
	Psicosis		
W	liontamer	CROWD: 2,000	PAYOFF: $457

825	Mar. 19	Terre Haute, IN	★★3/4
	Super Calo		
W	liontamer	CROWD: 5,000	PAYOFF: $457

826	Mar. 20	Troy, OH		★★1/2
W	**Prince Iaukea**			
	liontamer		CROWD: 3,000	PAYOFF: $457

827	Mar. 21	Hammond, IN		★★1/2
W	**Prince Iaukea**			
	liontamer		CROWD: 3,000	PAYOFF: $457

JUSTIN ROBERTS' TOP 11 MOMENTS OF JERICHO

Justin Roberts has served as ring announcer for more Chris Jericho matches than anyone else in pro wrestling history.

I was beyond honored to compile a top 10 list, though limiting any highlight list for Chris to anything under 100 is difficult — therefore we settled at 11. Chris stood out to me on TV when I was watching WCW in high school. He had a unique style in the ring, but the words he used, the way he pronounced them, and the random things he said and did made him stand out. The first time I got to see him live was March 21, 1998, in Hammond, Indiana, against Prince Iaukea (match #827). He was a bad guy, but my friends and I liked him so much that he was the one we wanted to cheer. Prince got "A.C. Slater" chants from us, and Chris got "Walls of Jericho" and the titles from his website that we used to visit — at a time where maybe he and Eddy Guerrero were the only two to have their own sites. We thought we were "inside" and he would appreciate our chants, but no. He yelled at us to shut the hell up. Exactly what I'd hope for and expect from one of the very best ever — the hard-working, always innovating, entertaining, creative, knowledgeable, finger-on-the-pulse wrestling star, rockstar, actor, best-selling author, game show host, podcast host, cruise director Chris Jericho. I never could have guessed that 12 years later I would be walking along the beach in Honolulu with Chris and we'd get on a boat with Rocky Iaukea! No, not his opponent from that night, Prince Iaukea — which would make for a better story — but close enough. I also couldn't have imagined one day being able to call him a friend, colleague, or mentor — but certainly an icon. I'd also be in the ring with him when he nearly incited a glow stick riot and angered a man so much that he tried to jump in the ring. I was also there for some of his biggest returns ever. So here is just a partial list of my favorite Moments of Jericho:

11. THE INTERACTIONS WITH MJF, 2019

As I write this, there have only been a few — however something seems to be brewing between Chris and the despicable Maxwell Jacob Friedman. Two of the best talkers going back and forth has been extremely entertaining, and I believe this is just the beginning and can ultimately lead to the No. 1 spot in his next 30-year book.

10. RALPHUS, 1998

Chris knew early on that he should be in the main-event picture. While he may not have been booked there at the time, he did whatever he could to construct his own path toward Bill Goldberg. In a situation where there weren't two to tango, Chris had to build the feud on his own or by borrowing a WCW truck driver and making him into one of the greatest sidekicks ever — his personal bodyguard, one of my favorite *Nitro* attractions.

9. "JUDAS" SING-ALONG, 2020

The star of his own cruise arrived during *Dynamite* not to a chorus of boos, but rather to the chorus of his own entrance music, "Judas." The fans appreciated the cruise(s) he put together and organically decided on the spot to celebrate and sing along. As I write this, the tradition still continues, and the fans love to sing along to the killer tune every time Jericho makes an entrance.

8. "YOU JUST MADE THE LIST!," 2016

Only Chris could get something like this over with the audience. A simple click of a pen and pad of paper where he would write someone's name down for any silly reason he wanted as a severe form of punishment! Was this partially funny because his reasonings were so similar to wrongdoings he would playfully accuse us of backstage? Yes. And now he was able to make those antagonizing antics part of his character. His "list" interactions were, no doubt, the highlight of the shows for a long stretch of time.

7. THE CODY VIDEO, 2019

Leading up to their big match at AEW Full Gear, the always excellent AEW production team put together a video capturing all of the emotions of the American Nightmare, Cody, as he prepared to face Chris. In return, Chris produced a ridiculously funny parody featuring the members of his Inner Circle as well as the former Virgil, Soul Train Jones, that stole the show.

6. "THE MAN OF 1,004 HOLDS," 1998

An unforgettable segment that captured Jericho's personality early on in WCW. While his rival Dean Malenko was known as the Man of 1,000 Holds, Chris had to one- (or four-) up him and boast himself as the Man of 1,004 Holds. While Dean was more than capable of applying 1,000 holds, it was Chris who actually had a list that named all of them, and he read it during the episode of *Nitro* that he made classic.

5. COUNTDOWN TO THE MILLENNIUM, 1999

I still get chills thinking about this moment. As I mentioned, Chris knew he belonged on a higher level, and on the night where the big countdown reached 0, he was revealed as the newest WWE superstar. I was in Chicago at the Allstate Arena and was so excited to see him break the proverbial walls down!

4. CHRIS MAKES HIS MARK — AGAIN — IN NEW JAPAN PRO-WRESTLING, 2018

While it seemed like the only place we would ever get to see Chris perform was WWE, in 2018 he shocked the world by showing up for Japan's NJPW promotion. Seeing Chris reinvent himself over the years was always fun, but the idea of a fresh start in a new promotion was huge. The Painmaker, the "Clockwork Orange"-inspired psychopath, was so special to watch. The idea that Chris could work outside of WWE started to rattle the industry.

3. ALL IN, 2018

September 1, 2018 was one of the greatest nights of my career and life. A potentially giant show that had all of the eyes on the industry watching. While it was known that Chris would only perform in international shows outside WWE, he shocked the world by attacking Kenny Omega before unmasking to reveal his identity to the sold-out crowd of 11,000 independent wrestling fans. His appearance would make my night even greater and that giant show even bigger — and finally shift the wrestling world.

2. CHRIS JERICHO ANNOUNCES HE IS ALL ELITE, 2019

The formation of AEW was the biggest thing to happen to pro wrestling in decades. In order for a new promotion to be a success in 2019, it would take the perfect storm. Tony Khan wanting to take the chance, Cody/Young Bucks/Kenny/Hangman building up momentum, and a star like Chris Jericho would be that storm to garner a spot on TNT. When Chris showed up at the end of the introductory press conference to announce that he was on board, it was off to the races. A ginormous moment in Chris' career and for the future of the business.

1. DISCOVERING AND ELEVATING OTHERS, ONGOING

It's not one moment — it's ongoing, too common, and my favorite moment. It's Chris spotting something in a talent and wanting to work with them, to elevate them. I have seen this unselfish and generous act so many times throughout the years — but now more than ever in AEW. He wants to help everyone become the best that they can be and his promotion, AEW, become the best that IT can be (I found a way to get IT in here). From Darby Allin, to Jungle Boy, to Sammy Guevara, to Orange Cassidy, to Sonny Kiss, to Marko Stunt ... my favorite moment is seeing Chris work to help them, the company, and the industry itself.

828	Mar. 22	Cincinnati	★★★
W	**Prince Iaukea** liontamer	**CROWD:** 13,000	**PAYOFF:** $457

829	Mar. 23	Louisville, KY	★★1/2
W	**Lenny Lane** liontamer	**CROWD:** 6,000	**PAYOFF:** $457

830	Mar. 25	Baltimore	★★★
L	**Booker T** kick	**CROWD:** 10,000	**PAYOFF:** $457

831	Mar. 26	Fairfax, VA	★★★
W	**Disco Inferno** liontamer	**CROWD:** 5,000	**PAYOFF:** $457

832	Mar. 27	Charlotesville, VA	★★
W	**Prince Iaukea** liontamer	**CROWD:** 6,000	**PAYOFF:** $457

833	Mar. 28	Detroit	★★3/4
L	**Booker T** kick	**CROWD:** 18,000	**PAYOFF:** $457

834	Mar. 29	Milwaukee	★★★1/4
L	**Booker T** kick	**CROWD:** 8,000	**PAYOFF:** $457

835	Mar. 30	Chicago	★★
W	**Marty Jannety** liontamer	**CROWD:** 15,000	**PAYOFF:** $612

836	Mar. 31	Madison, WI	★★1/2
W	**Lenny Lane** liontamer	**CROWD:** 3,000	**PAYOFF:** $612

APRIL 1998

837	Apr. 03	Orlando, FL	★★3/4
W	**Prince Iaukea** liontamer	**CROWD:** 400	**PAYOFF:** $612

838	Apr. 04	Orlando, FL	★★★1/2
W	**Juventud Guerrera** liontamer	**CROWD:** 400	**PAYOFF:** $612

Juventud hits me with a dive in 1998. At this point in WCW, Juvie and Rey Mysterio Jr. were neck-and-neck in talent and match quality.

839	Apr. 05	Orlando, FL		★★★3/4
W	**Silver King** liontamer		**CROWD:** 400	**PAYOFF:** $613
840	Apr. 06	Miami		★★★
W	**Juventud Guerrera** liontamer		**CROWD:** 10,000	**PAYOFF:** $613
841	Apr. 07	Ft. Myers, FL		★★★
W	**Prince Iaukea** liontamer		**CROWD:** 2,000	**PAYOFF:** $613
842	Apr. 08	Ft. Pierce, FL		★★★
W	**Prince Iaukea** liontamer		**CROWD:** 2,000	**PAYOFF:** $613
843	Apr. 09	Tallahassee, FL		★★★1/2
L	**Booker T** DQ		**CROWD:** 5,000	**PAYOFF:** $613
844	Apr. 13	Minneapolis		★★1/2
W	**Super Calo** liontamer		**CROWD:** 13,000	**PAYOFF:** $1,022

845	Apr. 14	Mankato, MN		★★★1/2
W	**Prince Iaukea**			
	liontamer		CROWD: 3,000	PAYOFF: $1,022

846	Apr. 16	Fargo, ND		★★1/2
W	**Chavo Guerrero Jr.**			
	liontamer		CROWD: 10,000	PAYOFF: $1,023

847	Apr. 19	Denver		★★★1/4
W	**Prince Iaukea (Spring Stampede)**			
	liontamer		CROWD: 12,000	PAYOFF: $1,023

848	Apr. 20	Colorado Springs, CO		★★★1/2
W	**Juventud Guerrera**			
	liontamer		CROWD: 5,000	PAYOFF: $1,023

849	Apr. 27	Norfolk, VA		★★★
W	**Chavo Guerrero Jr.**			
	liontamer		CROWD: 8,000	PAYOFF: $466

850	Apr. 27	Norfolk, VA		★★1/2
W	**Psicosis**			
	liontamer		CROWD: 8,000	PAYOFF: $466

851	Apr. 28	Salisbury, MD		★★
L	**Juventud Guerrera**			
	COUNTOUT		CROWD: 1,000	PAYOFF: $466

852	Apr. 29	Cincinnati		★★★1/2
L	**Chris Benoit (Brian Pillman Memorial Show)**			
	cross-face		CROWD: 1,100	PAYOFF: $466

MATCH NOTES #852

I only met Brian once in ECW, but it was a meeting that left a big impression on me. So when I was asked to work with Benoit on this show, I felt I owed it to Pillman and the legacy of Stampede Wrestling to do it. I remember Chris split me open with a headbutt in the first few minutes of the match. This night was also the first time I ever met one of my biggest future rivals: Stone Cold Steve Austin.

MAY 1998

853	May 04	Indianapolis		★★
W	**Bore Us Malenko (Johnny Boone)**			
	liontamer		CROWD: 9,000	PAYOFF: $466

854	May 05	Springfield, IL		★★★
NC	**Juventud Guerrera** NO CONTEST		CROWD: 2,000	PAYOFF: $466

855	May 06	Des Moines, IA		★★★
W	**Disco Inferno** liontamer		CROWD: 5,000	PAYOFF: $466

856	May 07	Omaha, NE		★★★
W	**Disco Inferno** liontamer		CROWD: 6,000	PAYOFF: $467

857	May 08	Salina, KS		★★★
W	**Disco Inferno** liontamer		CROWD: 5,000	PAYOFF: $466

858	May 09	Wichita, KS		★★★
W	**Disco Inferno** liontamer		CROWD: 4,000	PAYOFF: $466

859	May 10	Topeka, KS		★★★
W	**Disco Inferno** liontamer		CROWD: 5,000	PAYOFF: $466

860	May 17	Worcester, MA		★★★★
L	**Dean Malenko (lost WCW cruiserweight title/Slamboree)** cloverleaf		CROWD: 9,000	PAYOFF: $1,275

861	May 18	Providence, RI		★
W	**Ciclope** liontamer		CROWD: 8,000	PAYOFF: $1,275

862	May 20	Youngstown, OH		★★★1/2
W	**Disco Inferno** liontamer		CROWD: 2,000	PAYOFF: $1,276

863	May 21	Cleveland		★★
W	**Super Calo** liontamer		CROWD: 6,000	PAYOFF: $1,275

864	May 25	Evansville, IN		★★
W	**El Dandy** liontamer		CROWD: 3,000	PAYOFF: $1,040

MAXWELL JACOB FRIEDMAN'S TOP 5 JERICHO MATCHES

1. #1582, SHAWN MICHAELS, WRESTLEMANIA 19, MAR. 30, 2003, SEATTLE

It was a beautifully told story bell to bell that showcased not just how great an athlete Chris is, but also how smart he is when constructing a match.

2. #1227, CHRIS BENOIT, ROYAL RUMBLE, JAN. 21, 2001, NEW ORLEANS

The image of Benoit being put in the Walls of Jericho on top of a ladder will never escape my mind.

3. #1152, TRIPLE H, LAST MAN STANDING MATCH, FULLY LOADED, JULY 23, 2000, DALLAS

A very fun, hard-hitting, smash-mouth wrestling brawl that is super-timeless.

4. #1879, LANCE STORM, JUNE 12, 1995, NEW YORK CITY

ECW One Night Stand was a really cool moment to watch two guys who started from the very bottom in Canada and were best friends be given the opportunity to wrestle each other for god-knows-what-number-match-it-was. Their chemistry is insane.

5. #860, DEAN MALENKO, SLAMBOREE, MAY 17, 1998, WORCESTER, MA

The amount of heat Chris got for talking about Dean's late father before this match proves that if you get the crowd going, it makes everything else mean so much more. Plus, Dean wrestling the whole match in that outlandish Lucha outfit was just epic.

		JUNE 1998		
865	June 01	Washington, D.C.		★★1/2
W	**Juventud Guerrera** pinfall		CROWD: 11,000	PAYOFF: $1,040
866	June 05	Muncie, IN		★★1/2
L	**Dean Malenko** cloverleaf		CROWD: 3,000	PAYOFF: $1,040
867	June 06	Fort Wayne, IN		★★★
L	**Dean Malenko** cloverleaf		CROWD: 4,000	PAYOFF: $1,040

868	June 07	Grand Rapids, MI		★★3/4
	Dean Malenko			
L	cloverleaf		CROWD: 5,000	PAYOFF: $1,040

869	June 09	Saginaw, MI		★★
	Chavo Guerrero Jr.			
W	lionsault		CROWD: 4,000	PAYOFF: $1,282

870	June 12	Erie, PA		★★★
	Dean Malenko			
L	cloverleaf		CROWD: 2,000	PAYOFF: $1,282

871	June 13	Pittsburgh		★★★
	Dean Malenko			
L	cloverleaf		CROWD: 3,500	PAYOFF: $1,282

872	June 14	Baltimore		★★★
	Dean Malenko (won WCW cruiserweight title/4th time – Great American Bash)			
W	DQ		CROWD: 15,000	PAYOFF: $1,282

873	June 24	Orlando, FL		★★★1/2
	Ultimo Dragon			
W	DQ		CROWD: 11,000	PAYOFF: $1,266

Another amazing random group party shot, this one at 8 Trax in Downtown Disney Orlando in 1998. Colorado Kid, Benoit, Regal, Scott Armstrong, Doc Dean, Nancy and I are all off our rockers here. Later that night, Scott pinned me for the three count as I was lying on the floor of the bar. "You gotta take the wins when you can!" he proclaimed.

874	June 26	Orlando, FL		★★★
L	**Dean Malenko** cloverleaf		**CROWD:** 400	**PAYOFF:** $1,266

875	June 27	Orlando, FL		★
L	**Julio Sanchez** COUNTOUT		**CROWD:** 400	**PAYOFF:** $1,267

JULY 1998

876	July 02	Columbus, GA		★★
L	**"Ray Mystery"** self-inflicted cover		**CROWD:** 7,000	**PAYOFF:** $1,267

877	July 06	Atlanta		★★
W	**Ultimo Dragon** DQ		**CROWD:** 40,000	**PAYOFF:** $751

878	July 07	Macon, GA		★★
W	**Barry Houston** liontamer		**CROWD:** 2,000	**PAYOFF:** $751

879	July 08	Birmingham, AL		★★★★
W	**Ultimo Dragon** liontamer		**CROWD:** 6,000	**PAYOFF:** $751

880	July 10	Los Angeles		★★★
W	**Rey Mysterio Jr.** DQ		**CROWD:** 15,000	**PAYOFF:** $751

881	July 12	San Diego		★★
L	**Rey Mysterio Jr. (Bash at the Beach)** pinfall		**CROWD:** 8,000	**PAYOFF:** $751

882	July 14	Reno, NV		★★★
W	**Dean Malenko** pinfall		**CROWD:** 5,000	**PAYOFF:** $752

883	July 15	Stockton, CA		★★
W	**Dean Malenko** pinfall		**CROWD:** 1,000	**PAYOFF:** $752

884	July 26	New York City		★★★1/4
L	**Dean Malenko** submission		**CROWD:** 700	**PAYOFF:** $898

| 885 | July 27 | San Antonio | ★★★★ |

L   DQ   **CROWD:** 20,000   **PAYOFF:** $898

IN THEIR WORDS: **DEAN MALENKO**

It was our proverbial "last match ever" in front of 20,000-21,000 people. The things that made it memorable were that it was one of the biggest crowds we had ever worked in front of, and this was the second time I had ever done a DDT off the top rope. I think we had such good chemistry because a number of us who became very close had the same kind of mentality about the business. There were guys coming in from a lot of different places like Europe and Mexico. We all had the same work ethic and drive with what we wanted to accomplish.

| 886 | July 28 | Baton Rouge, LA | ★★★ |

L   cloverleaf   **CROWD:** 6,000   **PAYOFF:** $898

Dean Malenko (for 886)

| 887 | July 29 | Alexandria, LA | ★★ |

Dean Malenko

L   submission   **CROWD:** 6,000   **PAYOFF:** $898

| 888 | July 30 | Shreveport, LA | ★★1/2 |

Dean Malenko

L   submission   **CROWD:** 6,000   **PAYOFF:** $898

AUGUST 1998

| 889 | Aug. 01 | Little Rock, AR | ★★★ |

Brad Armstrong

L   pinfall   **CROWD:** 7,000   **PAYOFF:** $898

| 890 | Aug. 03 | Denver | ★★★1/2 |

Rey Mysterio Jr.

L   DQ   **CROWD:** 10,000   **PAYOFF:** $824

| 891 | Aug. 05 | Casper, WY | ★★★1/2 |

Rey Mysterio Jr.

L   pinfall   **CROWD:** 6,000   **PAYOFF:** $824

| 892 | Aug. 08 | Sturgis, SD | ★★★1/2 |

Juventud Guerrera (lost WCW cruiserweight title/Dean Malenko referee – Road Wild)

L   top-rope Frankensteiner   **CROWD:** 10,000   **PAYOFF:** $824

| 893 | Aug. 10 | Rapid City, SD | ★★★1/2 |

Stevie Ray (won WCW television title)

W   liontamer   **CROWD:** 6,000   **PAYOFF:** $824

Malenko displays one of his 1,000 moves on me in 1998. One of my all-time favorite opponents, he was just so easy and smooth to work with.

894	Aug. 11	Sioux Falls, SD		★★	
	Chavo Guerrero Jr.				
W	liontamer		**CROWD:** 3,000	**PAYOFF:** $824	

895	Aug. 13	Fargo, ND		★★★★1/2	
	Chavo Guerrero Jr.				
W	DQ		**CROWD:** 10,000	**PAYOFF:** $824	

896	Aug. 16	Providence, RI		★★	
	Dean Malenko				
L	cloverleaf		**CROWD:** 5,000	**PAYOFF:** $824	

897	Aug. 17	Hartford, CT		★★1/2	
	3-way vs. Stevie Ray vs. Chavo Guerrero Jr.				
W	COUNTOUT		**CROWD:** 10,000	**PAYOFF:** $1,211	

898	Aug. 23	Rockford, IL		★★★1/2	
	Dean Malenko				
L	cloverleaf		**CROWD:** 2,000	**PAYOFF:** $1,211	

899	Aug. 24	Chicago		★★★1/4	
	Curt Hennig				
DR	10 minutes		**CROWD:** 10,000	**PAYOFF:** $1,211	

900	Aug. 25	Peoria, IL	★★★
	Stevie Ray		
W	DQ	CROWD: 3,000	PAYOFF: $1,211

901	Aug. 26	Terre Haute, IN	★★★
	Alex Wright		
W	liontamer	CROWD: 6,000	PAYOFF: $1,211

902	Aug. 31	Miami	★★★
	Disco Inferno		
W	liontamer	CROWD: 8,000	PAYOFF: $757

SEPTEMBER 1998

903	Sept. 04	Tupelo, MS	★★1/2
	Chavo Guerrero Jr.		
W	liontamer	CROWD: 5,000	PAYOFF: $757

904	Sept. 05	Jackson, MS	★★
	Juventud Guerrera		
W	liontamer	CROWD: 6,000	PAYOFF: $757

905	Sept. 06	Biloxi, MS	★★★
	Juventud Guerrera		
W	liontamer	CROWD: 6,000	PAYOFF: $758

906	Sept. 07	Pensacola, FL	★★1/2
	Jim Neidhart		
W	liontamer	CROWD: 6,000	PAYOFF: $758

907	Sept. 08	Mobile, AL	★★★
	Scott Putski		
W	liontamer	CROWD: 5,000	PAYOFF: $757

908	Sept. 09	Evansville, IN	★★★
	Juventud Guerrera		
L	Juvi-driver	CROWD: 2,000	PAYOFF: $758

909	Sept. 13	Winston-Salem, NC	★★
	Goldberg Jr. (Fall Brawl)		
W	liontamer	CROWD: 10,000	PAYOFF: $757

910	Sept. 23	Yokohama, Japan	★★★
	Tag with Black Tiger vs. Shinjiro Otani & Tatsuhio Takaiwa		
L	Tiger pinned	CROWD: 14,000	PAYOFF: $5,769

911	Oct. 02	Florence, SC		★★★
	Juventud Guerrera			
W	liontamer		CROWD: 3,000	PAYOFF: $1,153

912	Oct. 03	Charleston, SC		★★★
	Juventud Guerrera			
W	liontamer		CROWD: 3,000	PAYOFF: $1,153

913	Oct. 04	Savannah, GA		★★1/2
	Juventud Guerrera			
W	liontamer		CROWD: 3,000	PAYOFF: $1,153

914	Oct. 06	Gainesville, GA		★★★★
	Fit Finlay			
DR	15 minutes		CROWD: 1,500	PAYOFF: $1,153

915	Oct. 07	Huntsville, AL		★★★1/4
	Billy Kidman			
L	roll-up		CROWD: 4,000	PAYOFF: $1,153

916	Oct. 12	Chicago		★★
	Raven			
W	liontamer		CROWD: 15,000	PAYOFF: $721

917	Oct. 19	Minneapolis		★★★1/2
	Diamond Dallas Page			
W	DQ		CROWD: 12,000	PAYOFF: $721

918	Oct. 20	Mankato, MN		★★★
	Psicosis			
W	liontamer		CROWD: 3,000	PAYOFF: $721

919	Oct. 20	Mankato, MN		★★★
	Eddy Guerrero			
W	DQ		CROWD: 3,000	PAYOFF: $721

920	Oct. 21	Duluth, MN		★★
	Juventud Guerrera			
W	liontamer		CROWD: 2,000	PAYOFF: $721

921	Oct. 22	Albuquerque, NM		★★★1/4
	Kanyon			
W	liontamer		CROWD: 6,000	PAYOFF: $721

Most definitely the best father a man could ask for. Teddy and I in Las Vegas, 1998.

922	Oct. 22	Albuquerque, NM		★★★
W	**Disco Inferno**			
	liontamer		**CROWD:** 6,000	**PAYOFF:** $721

923	Oct. 25	Las Vegas		★★★★
W	**Raven (Halloween Havoc)**			
	liontamer		**CROWD:** 13,000	**PAYOFF:** $721

NOVEMBER 1998

924	Nov. 02	Fort Lauderdale, FL		★★3/4
DR	**Billy Kidman**			
	10 minutes		**CROWD:** 10,000	**PAYOFF:** $1,442

925	Nov. 03	Ft. Myers, FL		★★★
W	**Disco Inferno**			
	liontamer		**CROWD:** 2,000	**PAYOFF:** $1,442

926	Nov. 04	Sarasota, FL		★★1/2
W	**Juventud Guerrera**			
	liontamer		**CROWD:** 1,200	**PAYOFF:** $1,442

927	Nov. 05	Roanoke, VA		★★1/2
W	**Prince Iaukea**			
	liontamer		**CROWD:** 6,000	**PAYOFF:** $1,442

928	Nov. 16	Wichita, KS		★★★
L	**Bobby Duncam Jr.**			
	COUNTOUT		**CROWD:** 6,000	**PAYOFF:** $1,153

After being told about some particularly bad creative for that night's WCW show, I vigorously ran my hands through my hair and messed it up in frustration. When I looked in the mirror and saw the rat's nest resembling a 1987 glam metal coif that my hair had become, I thought to myself, "I'm going to go to the ring looking as stupid as I feel right now." And I did.

929	Nov. 17	Salina, KS		★★
W	**Kendall Windham**			
	liontamer		CROWD: 2,000	PAYOFF: $1,153

930	Nov. 18	Topeka, KS		★★★
W	**Rey Mysterio Jr.**			
	liontamer		CROWD: 3,000	PAYOFF: $1,153

931	Nov. 20	Toledo, OH		★★★
L	**Scott Hall**			
	powerbomb		CROWD: 5,000	PAYOFF: $1,153

932	Nov. 22	Detroit		★★3/4
W	**Bobby Duncam Jr. (World War 3)**			
	pinfall		CROWD: 12,000	PAYOFF: $576.50

933	Nov. 22	Detroit		★★1/4
L	**3-ring 60-man Battle Royal (World War 3)**			
	Kevin Nash won		CROWD: 12,000	PAYOFF: $577

934	Nov. 27	Augusta, GA		★★★
L	**Bobby Duncam Jr.**			
	DDT		CROWD: 4,000	PAYOFF: $1,153

935	Nov. 28	Johnson City, TN		★★
L	**Bobby Duncam Jr.**			
	DDT		CROWD: 4,000	PAYOFF: $1,153

| 936 | Nov. 29 | Knoxville, TN | ★★★★ |

Tag with Eddy Guerrero vs. Chris Benoit & Dean Malenko

L submitted by Benoit   **CROWD:** 4,500   **PAYOFF:** $1,153

MATCH NOTES #936, BRIAN HILDEBRAND APPRECIATION

Brian was a good friend of me and my gang's, and when we found out he had cancer in 1997, we were all really bummed. I first met Brian in 1994 when he was Jim Cornette's right-hand man and we hit it off. He was a tape trader and talked to me often about my early matches (he referred to Bret Como as "Cuomo," like the governor), so when he arrived in WCW I made sure to put him over to my bros. He fit right in with us, and when the idea of a tribute show came up, the four of us embraced it wholeheartedly. We had an amazing match that ended with a ref bump, which, of course, caused Brian to slide in and make the final three count. It was an awesome night that ended with us eating pot brownies in Brian's kitchen because the THC helped ease his pain.

| 937 | Nov. 30 | Chattanooga, TN | ★★★★ |

Konnan (lost WCW television title)

L pinfall   **CROWD:** 10,000   **PAYOFF:** $1,153

IN THEIR WORDS: KONNAN

Editor's note: Jericho and Charles "Konnan" Ashenoff became friends while wrestling for rival promotions in Mexico during the early 1990s. Their paths inside the ring finally crossed in 1996, leading to the two squaring off in WCW.

I remember Chris had told [WCW president Eric] Bischoff he was going to WWE, and Eric said, "OK, you are losing the [TV title] to Konnan" to fuck with him. Jericho didn't care because we were boys. I remember telling him that it reminded me of that scene during the Vietnam War where the U.S. had helicopters on top of the U.S. embassy taking people back to the U.S. and they had a ladder hanging down as the copter was taking off, and all these people were left behind. I told Chris, "Make sure you come back for us and don't leave us behind," meaning me, Rey [Mysterio Jr.], Disco [Inferno], etc.

Anyway, we never really had a program or matches in WCW or Mexico because we worked in different companies, but it's always cool wrestling your friends. I was really looking forward to it. He put the match together. The crowd was really hot, in Chattanooga at the University of Tennessee campus. College crowds were always hot and this was no exception.

When I won, the place really popped. After the match, I told him, "Everyone talks about what a great worker you are, but what you are is a young ring general." He basically called most of the match in the ring.

I was happy I won but was sad to see him go because we were always clowning around backstage and busting each other's balls and sharing hot news. It's funny — the first week he got to WWE, he called me and said, "You owe it to yourself to come to WWE." How times change.

Straight up, he is one of the greatest performers I have ever been around in our industry. Keep shining, my friend.

Note from Jericho: "His finish at the time was a submission called the Tequila Sunrise. But whenever he applied it, it always looked lame, like it could never actually hurt somebody. So before the match I told him, 'If you're gonna use that hold to beat me, you better tighten that shit up and make me submit for real!' So he did ..."

This was at the Box Y Lucha awards in Mexico City, December of 1993 – the night I first met Konnan. We are still close friends to this day.

DECEMBER 1998

938	Dec. 03	Memphis, TN		★★
Bobby Duncam Jr.				
L	roll-up		CROWD: 8,000	PAYOFF: $1,153

939	Dec. 07	Houston		★★★★
Bobby Duncam Jr.				
W	Toyota roll		CROWD: 30,000	PAYOFF: $960

940	Dec. 15	Palmetto, FL		★★★
Booker T				
W	DQ		CROWD: 1,100	PAYOFF: $960

941	Dec. 17	Charlotte, NC		★★1/2
Perry Saturn				
W	liontamer		CROWD: 10,000	PAYOFF: $960

942	Dec. 18	Tulsa, OK		★★3/4
Booker T				
L	kick		CROWD: 6,000	PAYOFF: $961

943	Dec. 19	Springfield, MO		★★3/4
Booker T				
L	kick		CROWD: 5,000	PAYOFF: $961

944	Dec. 20	Kansas City, MO	★★1/2

Tag with Eddy Guerrero vs. Chris Benoit & Dean Malenko

L submitted · CROWD: 19,000 · PAYOFF: $961

945	Dec. 27	Washington, D.C.	★★1/2

Konnan (Starrcade)

L submitted · CROWD: 10,000 · PAYOFF: $684

946	Dec. 29	New York City	★★★

Tag with Eddy Guerrero vs. Chris Benoit & Dean Malenko

L submitted · CROWD: 17,000 · PAYOFF: $684

947	Dec. 30	Philadelphia	★★★

Tag with Eddy Guerrero vs. Chris Benoit & Dean Malenko

L submitted · CROWD: 15,000 · PAYOFF: $684

JANUARY 1999

948	Jan. 02	Macon, GA	★★★1/2

Tag with Juventud Guerrera vs. Dean Malenko & Chris Benoit

L Guerrera pinned · CROWD: 2,000 · PAYOFF: $684

949	Jan. 03	Columbus, GA	★★1/2

Tag with Juventud Guerrera vs. Dean Malenko & Chris Benoit

L Guerrera pinned · CROWD: 3,000 · PAYOFF: $684

950	Jan. 04	Atlanta	★★★

Perry Saturn

W liontamer · CROWD: 40,000 · PAYOFF: $684

951	Jan. 06	Mobile, AL	★★★

Booker T

L kick · CROWD: 3,000 · PAYOFF: $684

952	Jan. 07	Richmond, VA	★★★

Van Hammer

W liontamer · CROWD: 4,500 · PAYOFF: $684

953	Jan. 07	Richmond, VA	★★★

Konnan

L facebuster · CROWD: 4,500 · PAYOFF: $684

954	Jan. 17	Charleston, WV	★★

Perry Saturn (loser wears a dress/Souled Out)

W small package · CROWD: 6,000

JESSICA IRVINE'S TOP 11 JERICHO MOMENTS

Jessica Irvine is Chris's lovely wife of over 20 years

11. "Release the Hounds" AEW promo
10. "Man of 1,004 Holds" promo
9. Jericho's Personal Security, Ralphus
8. "Save Us, Y2J" Second Coming vignettes
7. Jericho vs. The Rock in Hawaii, with Bruce Willis in the crowd (#1464)
6. Jericho and The Rock burying Stephanie McMahon's boob job
5. Beating The Rock and Stone Cold Steve Austin to become
   the first-ever Undisputed Champion (#1382 and #1383)
4. Jericho returns to WWE with light-up jacket
3. WWE debut with The Rock
2. Fans singing "Judas" on the Jericho Cruise
1. Winning the AEW Championship and becoming "Le Champion"

955	Jan. 18	Columbus, OH	★★★★
W	**Booker T**		
	top-rope dropkick	CROWD: 10,000	

956	Jan. 19	Dayton, OH	★★★
W	**Manny Fernandez**		
	liontamer	CROWD: 3,000	

957	Jan. 20	Frankfort, KY	★★★
L	**Booker T**		
	spin-kick	CROWD: 1,000	

958	Jan. 21	Indianapolis	★★★
W	**Silver King**		
	liontamer	CROWD: 10,000	

FEBRUARY 1999

961	Feb. 01	Minneapolis	★★★
L	**Scott Steiner**		
	camel clutch	CROWD: 12,000	

962	Feb. 02	La Crosse, WI	★★★
W	**Damian**		
	liontamer	CROWD: 3,000	

963	Feb. 03	Madison, WI	★★★★
L	**Booker T** kick	CROWD: 4,000	

964	Feb. 04	Providence, RI	★★★1/2
W	**Scotty Riggs** liontamer	CROWD: 8,000	

965	Feb. 16	Lakeland, FL	★★★1/4
L	**Booker T** DQ	CROWD: 2,000	

966	Feb. 18	Salt Lake City	★★★
W	**Juventud Guerrera** liontamer	CROWD: 10,000	

967	Feb. 19	San Francisco	★★1/2
L	**Booker T** kick	CROWD: 6,000	

968	Feb. 21	Oakland, CA	★★3/4
W	**Perry Saturn (SuperBrawl IX)** DQ	CROWD: 10,000	

969	Feb. 22	Sacramento, CA	★★1/2
L	**Hugh Morrus** moonsault	CROWD: 8,000	

970	Feb. 26	San Antonio	★★3/4
L	**6-man with Barry Windham & Curt Hennig vs. Ric Flair, Chris Benoit & Dean Malenko** pinned by Flair/small-package	CROWD: 20,000	

971	Feb. 28	Greenville, SC	★★1/2
L	**6-man with Barry Windham & Curt Hennig vs. Ric Flair, Chris Benoit & Dean Malenko** pinned by Benoit/headbutt	CROWD: 12,000	

MARCH 1999

972	Mar. 02	Rock Hill, SC	★★★
W	**Billy Kidman** DQ	CROWD: 2,000	

973	Mar. 03	Cullowhee, NC	★
L	**Perry Saturn** DVD	CROWD: 1,000	

Showing my disdain for the audience somewhere in America in 1998, my peak year for WCW.

974	Mar. 05	Florence, SC	★★
Perry Saturn			
L	DVD		**CROWD:** 1,000

975	Mar. 06	Bethlehem, PA	★★★
Perry Saturn			
L	DVD		**CROWD:** 2,000

976	Mar. 07	Rochester, NY	★★1/2
Perry Saturn			
L	DVD		**CROWD:** 3,000

977	Mar. 08	Worcester, MA	★1/2
Lizmark Jr. (dog collar match)			
W	liontamer		**CROWD:** 5,000

978	Mar. 14	Louisville, KY	★★1/4
Perry Saturn (dog collar match/Uncensored)			
L	DVD		**CROWD:** 10,000

979	Mar. 15	Cincinnati	★★★1/2
	Booker T		
L	DQ		**CROWD:** 10,000

980	Mar. 16	Toledo, OH	★★★
	Perry Saturn		
W	DQ		**CROWD:** 2,000

981	Mar. 17	Dayton, OH	★★★
	Perry Saturn		
L	DVD		**CROWD:** 3,000

982	Mar. 22	Panama City, FL	★★★1/4
	Scott Steiner		
L	Steiner recliner		**CROWD:** 1,500

983	Mar. 26	Port Huron, MI	★★★
	Perry Saturn		
L	DVD		**CROWD:** 4,000

984	Mar. 27	Auburn Hills, MI	★★3/4
	Perry Saturn		
L	DVD		**CROWD:** 13,000

985	Mar. 28	Kalamazoo, MI	★★★
	Perry Saturn		
L	DVD		**CROWD:** 3,000

986	Mar. 29	Toronto	★★
	Jerry Flynn		
W	liontamer		**CROWD:** 18,000

987	Mar. 30	Kitchner, Ontario	★★★
	Kaz Hayashi		
W	liontamer		**CROWD:** 3,000

APRIL 1999

988	Apr. 01	Richmond, VA	★★1/4
	Chris Adams		
W	liontamer		**CROWD:** 4,000

989	Apr. 01	Richmond, VA	★★★1/2
	Booker T		
L	pin		**CROWD:** 4,000

| 990 | Apr. 05 | Las Vegas | ★★1/2 |

Booker T

L DQ   CROWD: 12,000

JUNE 1999

| 991 | June 04 | Cincinnati | ★★★★ |

Rey Mysterio Jr.

L pin   CROWD: 4,200

| 992 | June 05 | Columbus, OH | ★★1/2 |

Tag with Chris Benoit vs. Rey Mysterio Jr. & Konnan

L pin   CROWD: 3,000

| 993 | June 06 | Athens, OH | ★★★★ |

Tag with Chris Benoit vs. Rey Mysterio Jr. & Konnan

L pin   CROWD: 2,500

| 994 | June 25 | Detroit | ★★1/2 |

Marcus Bagwell

L pin   CROWD: 4,900

| 995 | June 26 | Fort Wayne, IN | ★★3/4 |

Marcus Bagwell

L pin   CROWD: 2,600

| 996 | June 27 | Milwaukee | ★★1/2 |

Marcus Bagwell

L pin   CROWD: 3,500

JULY 1999

| 997 | July 07 | Montgomery, AL | ★★3/4 |

Tag with Eddy Guerrero vs. Konnan & Rey Mysterio Jr.

L pin   CROWD: 3,000

| 998 | July 21 | Peoria, IL | ★★★★ |

Tag with Eddy Guerrero vs. Konnan & Rey Mysterio Jr.

L pin   CROWD: 2,500

| 999 | July 30 | Pittsburgh | ★★ |

Terry Taylor (Curtis Comes Home fundraiser for Brian Hildebrand)

W liontamer   CROWD: 1,500

WWE ACT 1

AUG. 21, 1999 - AUG. 22, 2005

MATCHES 1000 - 1895

1000	Aug. 21	Winnipeg, Manitoba	★★

Big Bossman (nightstick match)

W pin · CROWD: 12,500

1001	Aug. 24	Kansas City, MO	★★★

Road Dogg

L DQ · CROWD: 10,000

1002	Aug. 31	Worcester, MA	★★★1/4

X-Pac

L DQ · CROWD: 8,000

JIM ROSS TIDBITS

Chris' debut on *Raw* in Chicago was a creative thing of beauty, as Chris had the "audacity" to interrupt The Rock, who was in the ring doing a live promo. The crowd confirmed what I felt since first meeting with Chris in Tampa, along with Jerry Brisco, at the Bombay Bicycle Club for lunch, and that was we were acquiring an underutilized, main-event star.

Chris accepted less money from WWE than he was going to be guaranteed at WCW but, as promised, Jericho blew away his downside guarantee to consistently top the seven-figure number.

1003	Sept. 12	San Diego	★★1/4

Ken Shamrock

L ankle lock · CROWD: 10,000

1004	Sept. 13	Anaheim, CA	DUD

Gotch Gracie (Curtis Hughes)

W · CROWD: 11,000

1005	Sept. 20	Houston	★★★

Billy Gunn (Dr. Tom Pritchard referee)

W DQ · CROWD: 10,000

1006	Sept. 21	Dallas	★★

Ken Shamrock (first-blood match)

W splash · CROWD: 12,000

1007	Sept. 25	Augusta, GA	★★1/4

Rock

L People's elbow · CROWD: 4,000

DR. BRITT BAKER'S TOP 8
JERICHO MOMENTS

8. #2718, ORANGE CASSIDY, MIMOSA MAYHEM, SEPT. 5, 2020, JACKSONVILLE, FL

This concept was just about as ridiculous as it sounds yet one of my favorite match stipulations I've ever seen. During his feud with Orange Cassidy, the forces of Bubbly and OJ were combined, and the Mimosa Mayhem match came to life. The match could be won by pinfall, submission — or by throwing your opponent in a giant tub of mimosa. The image of Chris Jericho plummeting into a swimming pool of orange juice and champagne is one we will cherish forever.

7. THE LIGHT-UP JACKET

My favorite piece of wrestling gear that has ever existed was Chris' Y2J light-up jacket. I had never seen anything like it and thought it was the greatest entrance gear to ever grace a wrestling ring. This is a prime example of how innovative and a step ahead of the game he always is.

6. "JUDAS" ON THE JERICHO CRUISE, JAN. 21, 2020

On our very special edition of *Dynamite* that took place at sea on the Jericho Cruise, we saw the true rockstar energy radiating off Le Champion. As he made his grand entrance, the entire ship sang the words to HIS song during HIS walk to the ring on HIS boat. It catapulted him to almost an unobtainable level of legendary status. I had chills and couldn't help but join in and hum along! "Judas" by Fozzy would never be the same. From that moment on, every fan in attendance has made their very entertaining attempts at singing every lyric during Chris's entrance.

5. #2710, STADIUM STAMPEDE, MAY 23, 2020, JACKSONVILLE, FL

This was one of my favorite projects to be able to witness the behind-the-scenes of. Stadium Stampede was a creative masterpiece that few will truly appreciate for how much hard work went into the making of it. Chris was very instrumental in helping tell the story of the match and in the fine-tuning that goes on off camera. I was lucky enough to witness this whole process be filmed, which didn't end until almost 6 a.m.! Only in a Stadium Stampede can you challenge the referee's call and review the play! Tremendous performance by the Inner Circle and the Elite.

4. CONSPIRACY VICTIM (WCW, SPRING 1998)

Chris insisted that he lost the Cruiserweight title to Dean Malenko because of a heinous conspiracy within WCW. He went to great lengths to make his case, including trying to speak to the president of the U.S. and walking around Washington, D.C., holding a "conspiracy victim" sign in true brilliantly hilarious Chris Jericho fashion. Tony Schiavone had the privilege of holding the famous "conspiracy victim" sign in WCW, but little did he know he would go on to hold the microphone for another victim of conspiracy in AEW in yours truly.

3. ROLE MODEL (WCW MARCH 1998)

The self-proclaimed role model and delusional hero of WCW would go on to inspire a character in AEW over two decades later — ME! Watching these promos consisting of Chris explaining to his fans and fellow wrestlers that they should admire him for all his accomplishments and idolize him as a role model was so obnoxious and condescending. I wanted to channel that same nature and apply it to my own story of being a dentist and a wrestler. What better way to annoy my fans than shoving down their throats over and over again that I am an accomplished dentist and a wrestler that they should admire? It's incredible to have the motivation behind your character as someone who just so happens to be backstage and always willing to help as a mentor.

2. JERICHO DEBUTS ON MONDAY NIGHT RAW, AUG. 9, 1999

Who could forget this epic debut, with his arms stretched wide and his back to the fans announcing, "Welcome to *Raw is Jericho*!" The deafening roar of the crowd when "JERICHO" appeared on the Titan-Tron, made for one of my favorite debuts in wrestling history. His half-ponytail hair style still remains my go-to on a regular basis.

1. AEW'S FIRST JACKSONVILLE PEP RALLY, JAN. 8, 2019

This will forever be a memorable moment to me. I had just finished my own speech to the fans that had gathered announcing myself as the first female signed to AEW. Next thing I knew, the sky was lit up with pyro as Chris Jericho made his way to the podium to announce he, too, was ALL ELITE. This gave me chills knowing I would be working alongside one of my all-time favorite wrestlers.

1008	Sept. 26	Charlotte, NC		★★1/4
L	**X-Pac (Unforgiven)**			
	DQ		CROWD: 8,000	
1009	Sept. 27	Greensboro, NC		★★
L	**Big Show**			
	DQ		CROWD: 8,000	
1010	Sept. 28	Richmond, VA		★★1/4
L	**Road Dogg**			
	DQ		CROWD: 8,000	

1011	Oct. 02	Birmingham, England	★★★1/2
	Road Dogg (Rebellion)		
W	low blow	**CROWD:** 10,000	

1012	Oct. 04	Newark, NJ	★★1/2
	Rock		
L	People's elbow	**CROWD:** 9,000	

1013	Oct. 05	Uniondale, NY	★★
	Tag with Curtis Hughes vs. The Dudley Boyz		
L	Hughes pinned	**CROWD:** 9,000	

1014	Oct. 10	Miami	★★1/2
	Road Dogg		
L	pin	**CROWD:** 10,000	

1015	Oct. 11	Atlanta	★★1/2
	Tag with Curtis Hughes vs. The Headbangers		
L	Hughes pinned	**CROWD:** 35,000	

1016	Oct. 12	Birmingham, AL	★
	Curtis Hughes		
W	pin	**CROWD:** 8,000	

1017	Oct. 16	Dayton, OH	★★★
	Road Dogg		
L	pump-handle slam	**CROWD:** 4,000	

1018	Oct. 19	Louisville, KY	★★★
	D'Lo Brown		
L	top-rope bomb	**CROWD:** 8,000	

1019	Oct. 23	Chicago	★★1/2
	Mankind		
W	pin	**CROWD:** 12,000	

1020	Oct. 24	St. Louis	★★1/4
	Mankind		
W	pin	**CROWD:** 8,000	

1021	Oct. 25	Providence, RI	★★1/2
	Tag with Stevie Richards vs. Chyna & D'Lo Brown		
L	Richards pinned	**CROWD:** 8,000	

Suplexing my first WWE rival Chyna in 1999. I learned a lot about the politics of that company from this feud, lessons that I carry with me to this day.

1022	Oct. 26	Springfield, MA	★★
L	**Stevie Richards**		
	pin	CROWD: 5,000	

1023	Oct. 30	New York City	★★★
L	**Rock**		
	People's elbow	CROWD: 20,000	

1024	Oct. 31	New Haven, CT	★★★
L	**Chyna**		
	roll-up	CROWD: 7,000	

NOVEMBER 1999

1025	Nov. 02	Philadelphia	★★1/2
L	**Godfather**		
	ho-train	CROWD: 15,000	

1026	Nov. 14	Detroit	★★★1/2
L	**Chyna (Survivor Series)**		
	top-rope pedigree	CROWD: 14,000	

1027	Nov. 15	Pittsburgh	★★★
L	**Gangrel**		
	Northern lights suplex	CROWD: 10,000	

Tapping out Gangrel in 1999.

1028	Nov. 16	Cincinnati	★★1/2
Mark Henry			
W lionsault		CROWD: 10,000	

1029	Nov. 20	Toronto	★★
3-on-2 with Too Cool vs. Edge & Christian			
L Scott Taylor pinned		CROWD: 20,000	

1030	Nov. 21	Montreal	★★3/4
3-on-2 with Too Cool vs. Edge & Christian			
L Scott Taylor pinned		CROWD: 14,000	

1031	Nov. 22	Buffalo, NY	★★★
Godfather			
W lionsault		CROWD: 14,000	

1032	Nov. 23	Rochester, NY	★★★
Big Show			
L chokeslam		CROWD: 10,000	

1033	Nov. 26	San Jose, CA	★★★1/4
	3-on-2 with Too Cool vs. Edge & Christian		
L	Scott Taylor pinned		CROWD: 10,000

1034	Nov. 27	Sacramento, CA	★★
	3-on-2 with Too Cool vs. Edge & Christian		
L	Scott Taylor pinned		CROWD: 10,000

1035	Nov. 30	Anaheim, CA	★★★
	Mankind		
W	roll-up		CROWD: 12,000

DECEMBER 1999

1036	Dec. 04	New York City	★★3/4
	3-on-2 with Too Cool vs. Edge & Christian		
L	Scott Taylor pinned		CROWD: 20,000

1037	Dec. 06	Worcester, MA	★★3/4
	Tag with Al Snow vs. Rock & Mankind		
NC	NO CONTEST		CROWD: 10,000

1038	Dec. 07	Boston	★★★
	Road Dogg		
L	pump-handle slam		CROWD: 12,000

1039	Dec. 12	Fort Lauderdale, FL	★★★1/2
	Chyna (won WWF Intercontinental title/Armageddon)		
W	Walls of Jericho		CROWD: 13,000

1040	Dec. 13	Tampa, FL	★★3/4
	X-Pac		
W	DQ		CROWD: 14,000

1041	Dec. 14	Tallahassee, FL	★★★
	Prince Albert		
W	lionsault		CROWD: 10,000

1042	Dec. 20	Houston	★★★
	Godfather		
W	roll-up		CROWD: 15,000

1043	Dec. 21	Dallas	★★3/4
	Hardcore Holly		
W	DQ		CROWD: 10,000

1044	Dec. 26	Charlotte, NC	★★
W	**Al Snow**		
	Walls of Jericho		CROWD: 9,000

1045	Dec. 27	Greensboro, NC	★★★
W	**Al Snow**		
	DQ		CROWD: 8,000

1046	Dec. 28	Richmond, VA	★★★1/4
NC	**Chyna (WWF Intercontinental title vacated)**		
	NO CONTEST/DOUBLE PIN		CROWD: 10,000

1047	Dec. 29	Nashville, TN	★★1/2
W	**Al Snow**		
	Walls of Jericho		CROWD: 10,000

1048	Dec. 30	Memphis, TN	★★★
W	**Al Snow**		
	Walls of Jericho		CROWD: 18,000

JANUARY 2000

1049	Jan. 04	Orlando, FL	★★★
L	**Tag with Chyna vs. Hardcore Holly & Crash Holly**		
	Orange bomb		CROWD: 10,000

1050	Jan. 08	Minneapolis	★★★
W	**Al Snow**		
	Walls of Jericho		CROWD: 10,000

1051	Jan. 09	Kansas City, MO	★★1/2
W	**Al Snow**		
	Walls of Jericho		CROWD: 12,000

1052	Jan. 10	St. Louis	★★3/4
L	**Tag with Chyna vs. Hardcore Holly & Crash Holly**		
	Chyna pinned		CROWD: 8,000

1053	Jan. 11	Chicago	★★★
L	**Kane**		
	tombstone		CROWD: 10,000

1054	Jan. 12	Grand Rapids, MI	★★★1/4
W	**Al Snow**		
	Walls of Jericho		CROWD: 8,000

1055	Jan. 16	Newark, NJ	★★★1/2
W	**Hardcore Holly** lionsault		CROWD: 15,000

1056	Jan. 17	New Haven, CT	★★1/2
L	**Rikishi** DQ		CROWD: 8,000

1057	Jan. 18	Providence, RI	★★★
L	**6-man with Hardcore Holly & Chyna vs. Too Cool & Rikishi** DQ		CROWD: 8,000

1058	Jan. 23	New York City	★★★
W	**3-way vs. Chyna vs. Hardcore Holly** **(won vacated WWF Intercontinental title/2nd time — Royal Rumble)** pinned Chyna/lionsault		CROWD: 18,000

1059	Jan. 23	New York City	★★
L	**Royal Rumble** Eliminated by Chyna after 3:47		CROWD: 18,000

1060	Jan. 24	Philadelphia	★★★
W	**Hardcore Holly** lionsault		CROWD: 15,000

1061	Jan. 25	Baltimore	★★★
W	**Crash Holly** Walls of Jericho		CROWD: 11,000

1062	Jan. 31	Pittsburgh	★★★
L	**X-Pac** X-factor		CROWD: 12,000

FEBRUARY 2000

1063	Feb. 01	Detroit	★★1/4
W	**Gangrel** Walls of Jericho		CROWD: 12,000

1064	Feb. 07	Dallas	★★
W	**Viscera** DQ		CROWD: 10,000

1065	Feb. 08	Austin, TX	★★1/2
W	**2-on-1 handicap vs. Bob Holly & Crash Holly** pinfall		CROWD: 10,000

1066	Feb. 11	Denver	★★
W	**Bob Holly**		
	Walls of Jericho	CROWD: 8,000	

1067	Feb. 12	San Diego	★★★
W	**3-way vs. X-Pac vs. Bob Holly**		
	pinned Holly/lionsault	CROWD: 10,000	

1068	Feb. 13	Davis, CA	★★3/4
W	**Bob Holly**		
	lionsault	CROWD: 5,000	

1069	Feb. 15	Fresno, CA	★★★★
W	**Jeff Hardy**		
	lionsault	CROWD: 8,000	

1070	Feb. 20	Augusta, GA	★★★
W	**3-way vs. Bob Holly vs. Chris Benoit**		
	pinned Holly/lionsault	CROWD: 4,000	

1071	Feb. 21	Atlanta	★★3/4
L	**Tag with Chyna vs. Kurt Angle & Davey Boy Smith**		
	Angle	CROWD: 27,000	

1072	Feb. 22	Nashville, TN	★★★
L	**Tag with Rock vs. Big Show & Kurt Angle**		
	DQ	CROWD: 10,000	

1073	Feb. 23	Little Rock, AR	★★★1/2
L	**Kurt Angle**		
	DQ	CROWD: 10,000	

1074	Feb. 27	Hartford, CT	★★★★
L	**Kurt Angle (lost WWF Intercontinental title/No Way Out)**		
		CROWD: 10,000	

1075	Feb. 28	New York City	★★1/4
W	**Perry Saturn**		
	lionsault	CROWD: 15,000	

1076	Feb. 29	Trenton, NJ	★★★1/4
L	**6-man with Too Cool vs. Dean Malenko, Perry Saturn & Chris Benoit**		
	Too Cool	CROWD: 10,000	

1077	Mar. 03	Toronto	★★★
	Kurt Angle		
L	pin	CROWD: 22,000	

1078	Mar. 04	Ottawa, Ontario	★★★1/4
	3-way vs. Kurt Angle vs. Chris Benoit		
L	pinned by Angle	CROWD: 10,000	

1079	Mar. 05	Montreal	★★★
	Kurt Angle		
L	pinned	CROWD: 12,000	

1080	Mar. 06	Springfield, MA	★★3/4
	Kurt Angle		
W	DQ	CROWD: 10,000	

1081	Mar. 07	Boston	★★★1/4
	Dean Malenko		
W	lionsault	CROWD: 15,000	

1082	Mar. 13	East Rutherford, NJ	★★★★
	3-way vs. Taz vs. Kurt Angle		
L	pinned by Angle	CROWD: 15,000	

1083	Mar. 14	Uniondale, NY	★★★
	Tag with Taz vs. Bob Backlund vs. Kurt Angle		
W	DQ	CROWD: 14,000	

1084	Mar. 18	Cedar Falls, IA	★★★1/4
	3-way vs. Kurt Angle vs. Chris Benoit		
L	pinned	CROWD: 14,000	

1085	Mar. 19	Moline, IL	★★★
	3-way vs. Kurt Angle vs. Chris Benoit		
L	pinned	CROWD: 10,000	

1086	Mar. 20	Chicago	★★★1/2
	Chris Benoit		
W	lionsault	CROWD: 11,000	

1087	Mar. 21	Milwaukee	★★★★
	Tag with Taz vs. Edge & Christian		
W	lionsault	CROWD: 10,000	

1088	Mar. 22	Champaign, IL		★★★
	3-way vs. Kurt Angle vs. Chris Benoit			
L	pinned		**CROWD:** 8,000	

1089	Mar. 27	Houston		★★1/2
	Tag with Chyna vs. Chris Benoit & Eddy Guerrero			
L	pinned by Benoit		**CROWD:** 11,000	

1090	Mar. 28	San Antonio		★★1/2
	Eddy Guerrero			
W	DQ		**CROWD:** 7,000	

APRIL 2000

1091	Apr. 02	Anaheim, CA		★★★
	2-fall 3-way vs. Kurt Angle vs. Chris Benoit (WrestleMania 2000)			
L	Fall One pinned by Benoit/headbutt		**CROWD:** 16,000	

1092	Apr. 02	Anaheim, CA		★★★
	2-fall 3-way vs. Kurt Angle vs. Chris Benoit (won WWF European title/ WrestleMania 2000)			
W	Fall Two pinned Benoit/lionsault		**CROWD:** 16,000	

1093	Apr. 03	Los Angeles		★★★
	Eddy Guerrero (lost WWF European title)			
L	pinned		**CROWD:** 14,000	

1094	Apr. 04	San Jose, CA		★★★1/2
	Viscera			
L	splash		**CROWD:** 10,000	

1095	Apr. 10	Fort Lauderdale, FL		★★1/2
	Eddy Guerrero			
L	pinned		**CROWD:** 12,000	

1096	Apr. 11	Tampa, FL		★★★
	2-on-1 handicap vs. Road Dogg & X-Pac			
L	pinned		**CROWD:** 14,000	

1097	Apr. 15	New York City		★★★
	Chris Benoit			
L	pinned		**CROWD:** 18,000	

1098	Apr. 16	Pittsburgh		★★1/2
	Chris Benoit			
L	pinned		**CROWD:** 15,000	

1099	Apr. 17	State College, PA	★★★★★
	Triple H (won WWF World Heavyweight title/later reversed)		
W	lionsault	**CROWD:** 8,000	

1100	Apr. 17	State College, PA	★★
	6-man with Acolytes vs. Triple H, Road Dogg & X-Pac		
L	pinned by Triple H/pedigree	**CROWD:** 8,000	

1101	Apr. 18	Philadelphia	★★★
	Rock (lumberjack match)		
W	pin	**CROWD:** 12,000	

1102	Apr. 19	Allentown, PA	★★★
	Eddy Guerrero (Gary Albright memorial show)		
W	Walls of Jericho	**CROWD:** 500	

1103	Apr. 23	Greensboro, NC	★★★1/2
	Tag with Rock vs. Chris Benoit & Triple H		
W	Rock pinned Benoit	**CROWD:** 8,000	

1104	Apr. 24	Raleigh, NC	★★★★
	Tag with Rock vs. Chris Benoit & Triple H		
L		**CROWD:** 12,000	

1105	Apr. 25	Charlotte, NC	★★1/2
	Tag with Taz vs. Perry Saturn & Chris Benoit		
W	lionsault	**CROWD:** 10,000	

1106	Apr. 29	Hershey, PA	★★★1/4
	Chris Benoit		
L	DQ	**CROWD:** 5,000	

1107	Apr. 30	Washington, D.C.	★★★★
	Chris Benoit (Backlash)		
L	DQ	**CROWD:** 15,000	

MAY 2000

1108	May 01	Baltimore	★★★1/4
	X-Pac		
W	DQ	**CROWD:** 12,000	

1109	May 02	Richmond, VA	★★★★
	Chris Benoit (won WWF Intercontinental title/3rd time)		
W	lionsault	**CROWD:** 8,000	

I love looking at a picture like this that I've never seen before and have zero memory of. Big Show goozles me as I have Regal in the Walls, I'd guess sometime in 2000.

1110	May 06	London	★★★
L	**Eddy Guerrero (Insurrextion)** pin		**CROWD:** 18,000

1111	May 08	Uniondale, NY	★★★1/4
W	**Kurt Angle** Walls of Jericho		**CROWD:** 11,000

1112	May 08	Uniondale, NY	★★3/4
W	**Big Show** COUNTOUT		**CROWD:** 11,000

1113	May 08	Uniondale, NY	★★★★
L	**Chris Benoit (lost WWF Intercontinental title)** bell		**CROWD:** 11,000

1114	May 09	New Haven, CT	★★1/2
L	**6-man with Matt & Jeff Hardy vs. Edge, Christian & Kurt Angle** Hardy pinned		**CROWD:** 8,000

1115	May 14	Columbus, OH	★★1/2
L	**3-way vs. Hardcore Holly vs. Chris Benoit** Holly pinned by Benoit		**CROWD:** 10,000

1116	May 15	Cleveland	★★★1/4
L	**Hardcore Holly**		
	chair		**CROWD:** 12,000

1117	May 16	Detroit	★★1/2
W	**Tag with Val Venis vs. Chris Benoit & Hardcore Holly (hardcore match)**		
	DQ		**CROWD:** 12,000

1118	May 21	Louisville, KY	★★★1/2
L	**Chris Benoit (submission match/Judgment Day)**		
			CROWD: 10,000

1119	May 23	Evansville, IN	★★1/2
W	**2-on-1 handicap vs. Test & Prince Albert**		
	lionsault		**CROWD:** 8,000

1120	May 23	Evansville, IN	★★1/4
L	**3-way vs. Val Venis vs. Hardcore Holly**		
	Venis pinned by Holly		**CROWD:** 8,000

1121	May 27	Calgary, Alberta	★★★★
L	**Chris Benoit**		
	small package		**CROWD:** 13,000

1122	May 28	Edmonton, Alberta	★★★★
L	**Chris Benoit**		
	headbutt		**CROWD:** 15,000

1123	May 29	Vancouver, British Columbia	★★1/2
L	**6-man with Matt & Jeff Hardy vs. Test, Prince Albert & Val Venis**		
	Matt Hardy pinned		**CROWD:** 18,000

1124	May 30	Tacoma, WA	★★★
W	**Bob Holly**		
	lionsault		**CROWD:** 10,000

JUNE 2000

1125	June 04	Toronto	★★
L	**Four-way vs. Val Venis, Chris Benoit & Hardcore Holly**		
	Benoit pinned Holly		**CROWD:** 17,000

1126	June 05	Rochester, NY	★★1/2
L	**6-man with The Dudley Boyz vs. Edge, Christian & Kurt Angle**		
	Bubba Ray pinned		**CROWD:** 8,000

| 1127 | June 06 | Buffalo, NY | ★★★ |
| L | **Four-way vs. Val Venis, Chris Benoit & Hardcore Holly,** Benoit pinned Holly | | |

| 1128 | June 06 | Buffalo, NY | ★★3/4 |
| W | **Test,** lionsault | | |

| 1129 | June 09 | Las Cruces, NM | ★★1/4 |
| L | **Chris Benoit,** pin | | |

| 1130 | June 10 | Albuquerque, NM | ★★★ |
| L | **Chris Benoit,** pin | | |

MY TOP 10 STRANGEST MERCH ITEMS

• Y2J BOWLING BALL

I'm not sure how many of these sold, or why they were even made, but I can envision Homer Simpson rolling turkeys with this bad boy on a consistent basis. After not being able to find one for years, I now have one proudly displayed in my office.

• JERICHO EYEGLASSES

Ray-Ban. Philippe Chevallier. Jericho. Eyewear made and designed for only the most serious of fashion plates ... obviously.

• JERICHO ACTUAL SMACKDOWN STOCK CAR

This was unveiled during a stock car race somewhere in Delaware, I believe. I had to wave the flag to start the race, and I couldn't believe how loud — and smelly — it was on the track. My car finished in last place.

• JERICHO HALLOWEEN MASK

This is one of the creepiest things I've ever seen. Cross my face with Kurt Cobain and add Carol Channing's hair, and you might get a sense of what this monstrosity resembles.

• JERICHO DORITOS

I was surprised when I walked into a convenience store in Sherwood Park, Alberta, and saw an endcap display of "Official WWE Doritos." However, the only WWE Superstar on the bag was me. And why not? When I think Jericho, I think ZESTY! Total amount of royalties received from said bags? About 83 cents ... Canadian.

• JERICHO PIZZA

My all-time favorite pizza place is D-Jay's Pizza in Winnipeg. I've been eating there all my life and even worked there for a short period of time when I was 14. My pie of choice has always been their amazing pepperoni and ground beef combo, and about 15 years ago, they made it official by naming it and adding "The Jericho" to their menu. Next time you're in Winnipeg, stop by and try one out!

• JERICHO WOMEN'S SPANDEX LEGGINGS

Not sure where the idea for this came from, but, ladies, if you wanna wear multiple designs of my wrestling tights out on the town and look sexy at the same time, this spectacular spandex is for you!

• JERICHO OFFICIAL COLORING BOOK

I had no idea this even existed until a fan brought it to a signing. They could have at least clued me in and sent me a free copy!

• AUSTIN/ROCK/JERICHO BEACH TOWEL

The fact I was featured on a merch item with the two biggest stars maybe in company history shows how high up on the WWE planning food chain I was in the year 2000. Also hammers home the fact that I was the George Harrison of the WWE at the time.

RUNNER-UP TOWEL: There was a weird towel sold by WAR in 1995 that featured the entire roster as cartoons, playing in a symphony orchestra. Doesn't make sense to me either. (I was on French horn.)

• JERICHO CHRISTMAS TREE ORNAMENT

There have been many different designs to hang on your tree, from a Y2J logo to a Painmaker globe, to an actual little Jericho with arms outstretched. Any and all of them are sure to enhance your joyous season and always look great next to Marilyn Monroe and Greedo on my Douglas fir.

1131 L	June 11	Columbia, MO	★★1/2
	Four-way vs. Chris Benoit, Hardcore Holly & Al Snow, Benoit pinned Snow		

1132 L	June 12	St. Louis	★★★★★
	Triple H, pedigree		

1133 L	June 13	Chicago	★★1/2
	Bull Buchanan, kick		

1134 L	June 17	Minneapolis	★★★
	Four-way vs. Bob Holly, Chris Benoit & Val Venis, Benoit pinned Holly		

| 1135 | June 18 | Huntsville, AL | ★★★1/4 |
| **L** | **Four-way vs. Bob Holly, Chris Benoit & Val Venis,** Benoit pinned Holly | | |

| 1136 | June 19 | Nashville, TN | ★★★ |
| **W** | **Edge,** Walls of Jericho | | |

| 1137 | June 20 | Memphis, TN | ★★★1/4 |
| **W** | **Bob Holly,** lionsault | | |

| 1138 | June 24 | New York City | ★★1/2 |
| **L** | **Four-way vs. Bob Holly, Chris Benoit & Val Venis,** Benoit | | |

| 1139 | June 25 | Boston | ★★★★ |
| **L** | **Kurt Angle (King of the Ring),** Angle slam | | |

| 1140 | June 26 | Worcester, MA | ★★★ |
| **L** | **X-Pac,** pinned | | |

| 1141 | June 27 | Hartford, CT | ★★1/2 |
| **L** | **6-man with The Dudley Boyz vs. Triple H, Road Dogg & X-Pac** | | |

JULY 2000

| 1142 | July 01 | Houston | ★★★★ |
| **W** | **Kurt Angle,** DQ | | |

| 1143 | July 02 | Tampa, FL | ★★1/2 |
| **W** | **Kurt Angle,** DQ | | |

| 1144 | July 03 | Orlando, FL | ★★★ |
| **W** | **3-on-2 with The Acolytes vs. Road Dogg & X-Pac,** pinned X-Pac/lionsault | | |

| 1145 | July 04 | Fort Lauderdale, FL | ★★1/2 |
| **L** | **Kurt Angle,** Angle slam | | |

| 1146 | July 08 | Anaheim, CA | ★★1/2 |
| **L** | **3-way vs. Chris Benoit vs. Kurt Angle,** Benoit | | |

| 1147 | July 09 | Sacramento, CA | ★★★★ |
| **W** | **Chris Benoit,** DQ | | |

| 1148 | July 10 | San Jose, CA | ★★3/4 |
| **W** | **Road Dogg,** lionsault | | |

| 1149 | July 15 | Kansas City, MO | ★★★ |
| **W** | **Chris Benoit,** DQ | | |

| 1150 | July 16 | Trenton, NJ | ★★1/2 |
| **L** | **Chris Benoit,** pin | | |

| 1151 | July 18 | Uniondale, NY | ★★★ |
| **L** | **Tag with Rock vs. Triple H & Chris Benoit,** DQ | | |

| 1152 | July 23 | Dallas | ★★★★★ |
| **L** | **Triple H (last man standing/Fully Loaded),** COUNTOUT | | |

| 1153 | July 25 | San Antonio | ★★3/4 |
| **W** | **Mixed tag with Lita vs. Chris Benoit & Trish Stratus,** lionsault | | |

AUGUST 2000

| 1154 | Aug. 07 | New York City | ★★★ |
| **L** | **3-way vs. Triple H vs. Kurt Angle,** double pin | | |

| 1155 | Aug. 08 | Meadowlands, NJ | ★★3/4 |
| **L** | **Tag with Eddy Guerrero vs. Val Venis & Chris Benoit,** Guerrero | | |

| 1156 | Aug. 13 | New Haven, CT | ★★★1/4 |
| **W** | **Chris Benoit,** lionsault | | |

| 1157 | Aug. 14 | Providence, RI | ★★★ |
| **W** | **Val Venis,** DQ | | |

| 1158 | Aug. 19 | Greenville, NC | ★★★★ |
| **L** | **Val Venis,** roll-up | | |

| 1159 | Aug. 20 | Mobile, AL | ★★★ |
| **L** | **Chris Benoit,** roll-up | | |

| 1160 | Aug. 21 | Lafayette, LA | ★★ |
| **W** | **Perry Saturn,** DQ | | |

| 1161 | Aug. 22 | New Orleans | ★★★ |
| **W** | **6-man with The Hardy Boyz vs. Edge, Christian & Chris Benoit,** pinned Edge/lionsault | | |

| 1162 | Aug. 27 | Raleigh, NC | ★★★ |
| **L** | **Chris Benoit (2-out-of-3 falls/Summer Slam),** roll-up | | |

| 1163 | Aug. 28 | Greensboro, NC | ★★3/4 |
| **W** | **6-man with The Acolytes vs. Test, Prince Albert & Chris Benoit,** pinned Albert/lionsault | | |

| 1164 | Aug. 29 | Fayetteville, NC | ★★★ |
| **W** | **Taz,** lionsault | | |

1165	Sept. 02	Boston	★★★
L	**3-way vs. Triple H vs. Rock,** Rock pinned Triple H		

1166	Sept. 03	Knoxville, TN	★★3/4
L	**3-way vs. Triple H vs. Rock,** Rock pinned Triple H		

1167	Sept. 04	Lexington, KY	★★
W	**Tag with Jerry Lawler vs. Taz & Mideon,** Lawler pinned Taz		

1168	Sept. 05	Louisville, KY	★★★
L	**X-Pac,** backslide		

1169	Sept. 09	Seattle	★★3/4
L	**Triple H,** pedigree		

1170	Sept. 10	Denver	★★★1/2
L	**Triple H,** pedigree		

1171	Sept. 11	Phoenix	★★★
W	**Triple H,** DQ		

1172	Sept. 12	Phoenix	★★★
L	**Tag with The Hardy Boyz vs. X-Pac, Edge & Christian,** X-Pac pinned Jeff Hardy		

1173	Sept. 19	Milwaukee	★★★
L	**Tag with Jerry Lawler vs. Taz & X-Pac,** X-Pac pinned Lawler		

1174	Sept. 23	New York City	★★3/4
W	**Tag with Rikishi vs. X-Pac & Eddy Guerrero,** pinned Guerrero/roll-up		

1175	Sept. 24	Philadelphia	★★★1/4
W	**X-Pac (Unforgiven),** Walls of Jericho		

1176	Sept. 25	State College, PA	★★★
L	**X-Pac (first-blood match),** glass		

1177	Sept. 26	Pittsburgh	★★3/4
L	**Tag with Jerry Lawler vs. Taz & Raven,** pinned by Raven/DDT		

1178	Sept. 30	San Juan, Puerto Rico	★★★
L	**Chris Benoit,** cross-face		

1179	Oct. 01	Hershey, PA	★★3/4
L	**Kurt Angle,** pin		

1180	Oct. 02	Washington, D.C.	★★3/4
W	**6-man with The Dudley Boyz vs. X-Pac, Taz & Raven,** pinned Raven/lionsault		

1181	Oct. 03	Baltimore	★★★
L	**Chris Benoit,** DQ		

1182	Oct. 07	San Jose, CA	★★★
W	**X-Pac,** pin		

1183	Oct. 08	Fresno, CA	★★★1/2
W	**X-Pac,** Walls of Jericho		

1184	Oct. 09	Anaheim, CA	★★★1/4
L	**Tag with Triple H vs. Chris Benoit & X-Pac,** Triple H pinned		

1185	Oct. 10	Los Angeles	★★★★
W	**William Regal,** lionsault		

1186	Oct. 10	Los Angeles	★★★
L	**3-way vs. Eddy Guerrero vs. X-Pac,** pinned by Guerrero		

1187	Oct. 15	Toledo, OH	★★★
W	**3-way vs. X-Pac vs. Chris Benoit,** pinned X-Pac		

1188	Oct. 16	Detroit	N/A
NC	**Eddy Guerrero,** NO CONTEST		

1189	Oct. 17	Cleveland	★★★
NC	**6-man with The Hardy Boyz vs. X-Pac, Edge & Christian,** NO CONTEST		

1190	Oct. 22	Albany, NY	★★★
W	**X-Pac (cage match/No Mercy),** escaped		

1191	Oct. 23	Hartford, CT	★
W	**William Regal,** DQ		

1192	Oct. 24	Uniondale, NY	★★★
W	**Kurt Angle,** DQ		

1193	Oct. 28	Toronto	★★★
L	**Kane,** chokeslam		

1194	Oct. 30	Boston	★★★★
L	**Rock,** rock bottom		

1195	Oct. 31	Rochester, NY	★★★
W	**Rikishi,** DQ		

NOVEMBER 2000

1196	Nov. 04	Las Cruces, NM	★★1/2
W	**Tag with Steve Austin vs. Rikishi & Val Venis,** Austin		

Dropkicking Austin from the top rope. Every night Steve stepped in the ring, he gave it his all. EVERY night.

| 1197 | Nov. 05 | Lubbock, TX | ★★★ |
| W | **Tag with Steve Austin vs. Rikishi & Val Venis,** Austin | | |

| 1198 | Nov. 07 | Dallas | ★★★ |
| L | **4-way with Undertaker vs. Kane vs. Chris Benoit,** pinned by Undertaker/powerbomb | | |

| 1199 | Nov. 11 | Cincinnati | ★★1/2 |
| L | **Kurt Angle,** pin | | |

| 1200 | Nov. 12 | Huntington, WV | ★★★1/2 |
| W | **Chris Benoit,** lionsault | | |

| 1201 | Nov. 13 | Columbus, OH | ★★★ |
| W | **Tag with Steve Blackman vs. Kane & Test,** pinned Kane/lionsault | | |

| 1202 | Nov. 14 | Indianapolis | ★★3/4 |
| L | **Tag with Undertaker vs. Kane & Test,** Undertaker | | |

| 1203 | Nov. 19 | Tampa, FL | ★★1/2 |
| L | **Kane (Survivor Series),** chokeslam | | |

| 1204 | Nov. 20 | Orlando, FL | ★★★ |
| W | **Tag with Rock vs. Kane & Rikishi,** Rock | | |

| 1205 | Nov. 21 | Fort Lauderdale, FL | ★★3/4 |
| L | **Tag with Steve Austin vs. Kane & Chris Benoit,** DQ | | |

| 1206 | Nov. 25 | Chicago | ★★★ |
| L | **Kurt Angle,** Angle slam | | |

| 1207 | Nov. 26 | Omaha, NE | ★★★1/2 |
| L | **Kurt Angle,** Angle slam | | |

| 1208 | Nov. 27 | Amos, IA | ★★★ |
| W | **6-man with The Hardy Boyz vs. Chris Benoit, Perry Saturn & Dean Malenko,** Walls of Jericho | | |

| 1209 | Nov. 28 | Minneapolis | ★★★ |
| L | **Tag with Billy Gunn vs. Chris Benoit & Kane,** Gunn | | |

DECEMBER 2000

| 1210 | Dec. 02 | Sheffield, England | ★★1/2 |
| L | **Kane (Rebellion),** chokeslam | | |

| 1211 | Dec. 04 | East Rutherford, NJ | ★★★★ |
| L | **Kurt Angle,** Angle slam | | |

PETER THOMAS "BOOM BOOM" FORNATALE'S TOP 10 CHRIS JERICHO MATCHES

Peter Thomas Fornatale has co-written three books with Chris Jericho and edited two others, including this magnificent tome.

10. #1363, THE ROCK, NO MERCY, WCW HEAVYWEIGHT TITLE MATCH, OCTOBER 21, 2001, ST. LOUIS

You always remember your first. This was Jericho's first world title win, and it came against the biggest star in the wrestling business. There was a point with Chris where all his fans wanted was to see him bust through the glass ceiling. I know everyone points to the night where he became undisputed champion, but this is the match that made that moment a reality.

9. #811, TAG MATCH WITH EDDY GUERRERO VS. CHRIS BENOIT AND DEAN MALENKO, NITRO, FEB. 16, 1998, TAMPA

A forgotten classic featuring four of the best wrestlers in the world in an incredibly well-paced TV match. Chris and Eddy made an amazing team, both of their heel antics playing so well off of each other versus the no-nonsense duo of Dean and Benoit.

8. #860, CICLOPE (DEAN MALENKO), SLAMBOREE, CRUISERWEIGHT TITLE MATCH, MAY 17, 1998, WORCESTER, MA

I'm going to cheat a bit here and also consider the preceding Battle Royal as part of the match, as Chris did a hilarious job of announcing all the cruiserweight entrants to build up an insane pop once the winner, Ciclope, unmasked to reveal he was Dean Malenko. Just a masterclass in storytelling and action, this entire segment is a must-watch for any Jerichoholic.

7. #517, WILD PEGASUS (CHRIS BENOIT), 1995 SUPER J-CUP, DEC. 13, 1995, TOKYO

In the early '90s, Chris Benoit was quite possibly the world's greatest wrestler. There was just one problem: most of his matches were impossible to see unless you were into the tape trading scene and had a hookup (yes, kids, there was once a world without YouTube). I can't tell you how many times I re-watched my tape of the '94 Super J-Cup and, specifically, Benoit's classic match with the Great Sasuke in the Finals. A year later, Benoit was back in the tournament, and wrestled a guy named "Lionheart" in the quarter-finals. This was my first time seeing Chris Jericho wrestle, and I was blown away by the chemistry between him and Benoit. As for the match, it's still as fun to watch today as it was back in 1995. I'd love to go back in time and tell 1996 me that I'd one day get the chance to collaborate on books with Chris just to see the look on my face.

6. #2698, CODY, FULL GEAR, AEW TITLE MATCH, NOV. 9, 2019, BALTIMORE

Probably my favorite AEW match so far, Chris and Cody put together a masterpiece that made everyone take notice. The match stipulation added to the drama, as this would be Cody's last title shot ever if he couldn't bring home the gold. But in typical Jericho fashion, they zigged when everyone expected a zag, and Cody ended up getting the short end of the stick.

5. #1284, TAG MATCH WITH CHRIS BENOIT VS. TRIPLE H AND STEVE AUSTIN, RAW, TAG TITLE MATCH, MAY 21, 2001, SAN JOSE, CA

The greatest WWF/WWE tag match of all time. This match was a spectacle that people still talk about almost 20 years later. Jericho and Benoit made amazing opponents, but they made even better tag partners. This match tore the house down (as well as Triple H's quad). A must-watch for any wrestling fan.

4. #1152, TRIPLE H, LAST MAN STANDING MATCH, FULLY LOADED, JULY 23, 2000, DALLAS

Welcome to the main event, Chris Jericho. I have long felt that despite his loss, this is the match that truly cemented Chris' headliner status. The build to this match included a bait-and-switch on *Raw* where Jericho had won the WWF Title from Triple H, only to be forced to give it back after the commercial break. The crowd was on fire for the LMS match as Triple H bled like a stuck pig, making each 10 count from the ref even more dramatic. Despite their higher profile consecutive PPV main events two years later, this will forever be my favorite Jericho/Triple H match.

3. #1227, CHRIS BENOIT, LADDER MATCH, ROYAL RUMBLE, WWF INTERCONTINENTAL TITLE MATCH, JAN. 21, 2001, NEW ORLEANS

My favorite Jericho/Benoit match ever in peak Attitude Era. Jericho had been in multiple ladder matches, but this was his first in the WWF. The creativity was off the charts, and they put together some of the best ladder sequences we had ever seen. Nothing can top the visual of Jericho locking Benoit in the Walls of Jericho while they were atop the ladder.

2. #2685, KENNY OMEGA, WRESTLE KINGDOM 12, IWGP U.S. HEAVYWEIGHT TITLE, JAN. 4, 2018, TOKYO

I'm still in shock that this match ever happened. Kenny Omega had become a megastar in New Japan following his classics against Okada. Chris Jericho was still a WWE guy, but he shocked the wrestling world (while racking up YouTube views) with his attack on Kenny. Their match at WK12 was an absolute classic, a rare no-DQ affair that saw Chris do some of his best work ever. It proved that there was a lot more to what made him special besides writing names down on his List.

1. #2003, SHAWN MICHAELS, LADDER MATCH, NO MERCY, WWE WORLD HEAVYWEIGHT TITLE MATCH, OCT. 5, 2008, PORTLAND, OR

The setup for this match is as great as the match itself. Shawn and Chris had worked together before, but this one was born from the fallout of HBK retiring Ric Flair at WrestleMania six months earlier. In the months that followed, Chris bloodied HBK numerous times and even punched Shawn's wife in the face at SummerSlam. Their match at No Mercy was a brutal spectacle: It focused less on spots falling off a ladder and more on using the ladder as weapon. In the end, Chris retained his World Heavyweight Championship, but the visual of his bloodied face and broken tooth helped make this match unforgettable.

1212	Dec. 05	New York City	★★★
W	**Tag with Hardcore Holly vs. Kane & William Regal,** Holly		

1213	Dec. 10	Birmingham, AL	★★★
W	**Kane (Armageddon),** COUNTOUT		

1214	Dec. 12	Little Rock, AR	★★1/2
L	**Dean Malenko,** pin		

1215	Dec. 18	Greenville, NC	★★
W	**Saturn,** Walls of Jericho		

1216	Dec. 19	Charlotte, NC	★★★
W	**6-man with The Hardy Boyz vs. Perry Saturn, Dean Malenko & Chris Benoit,** lionsault		

1217	Dec. 22	Chattanooga, TN	★★★
L	**6-man with The Dudley Boyz vs. Edge, Christian & Kurt Angle,** pinned by Angle/ Angle slam		

1218	Dec. 23	Nashville, TN	★★★
L	**2-on-1 vs. Edge & Christian,** pinned		

1219	Dec. 28	Amarillo, TX	★★★
W	**Tag with Undertaker vs. Kane & Kurt Angle,** Undertaker pinned Angle		

1220	Dec. 29	Austin, TX	★★★1/2
W	**6-man with The Dudley Boyz vs. Edge, Christian & Kurt Angle (tables match),** Dudley pinned Edge		

1221	Dec. 30	San Antonio	★★★
W	**Chris Benoit,** DQ		

1222	Jan. 06	Anaheim, CA	★★★

W **Perry Saturn,** Walls of Jericho

1223	Jan. 08	San Jose, CA	★★★

W **6-man with The Hardy Boyz vs. Perry Saturn, Dean Malenko & Chris Benoit,** pinned Benoit/
backslide

1224	Jan. 09	Oakland, CA	★★

NC **6-man with The Dudley Boyz vs. Edge, Christian & Chris Benoit,** NO CONTEST

1225	Jan. 13	Detroit	★★★

L **Kurt Angle,** small package

1226	Jan. 14	Green Bay, WI	★★★★

L **Kurt Angle,** small package

1227	Jan. 21	New Orleans	★★★★

W **Chris Benoit (won WWF Intercontinental title/4th time – ladder match/
Royal Rumble)**

1228	Jan. 22	Lafayette, LA	★★★

W **Tag with Rock vs. Chris Benoit & Big Show,** Rock pinned Benoit

---

1229	Jan. 23	Mobile, AL	★★1/4

L **Big Show,** DQ

1230	Jan. 27	New York City	★★★

L **Kurt Angle,** Angle slam

1231	Jan. 28	Philadelphia	★★★1/2

L **Kurt Angle,** Angle slam

1232	Jan. 29	Pittsburgh	★★1/2

L **4-way with Big Show vs. Rock vs. Chris Benoit,** rock bottom

---

1233	Jan. 30	Columbus, OH	★★★

W **Taz,** lionsault

1234	Feb. 04	Columbus, GA	★★★1/2

L **Kurt Angle,** Angle slam

| 1235 | Feb. 05 | Atlanta | ★★3/4 |
| **W** | **Matt Hardy,** lionsault | | |

| 1236 | Feb. 06 | North Charleston, SC | ★★★ |
| **L** | **Triple H,** pedigree | | |

| 1237 | Feb. 11 | Boston | ★★★ |
| **L** | **Kurt Angle,** Angle slam | | |

| 1238 | Feb. 12 | East Rutherford, NJ | ★★3/4 |
| **W** | **Eddy Guerrero,** DQ | | |

| 1239 | Feb. 13 | Uniondale, NY | ★★1/2 |
| **L** | **X-Pac,** DQ | | |

| 1240 | Feb. 17 | Cedar Rapids, IA | ★★★ |
| **L** | **Kurt Angle,** Angle slam | | |

| 1241 | Feb. 18 | Cape Girardeau, MO | ★★★1/4 |
| **L** | **Kurt Angle,** Angle slam | | |

| 1242 | Feb. 20 | Kansas City, MO | ★★1/2 |
| **L** | **Tag with X-Pac vs. Eddy Guerrero & Chris Benoit,** submitted by Benoit/crossface | | |

| 1243 | Feb. 25 | Las Vegas | ★★★★ |
| **W** | **Tag with X-Pac vs. Eddy Guerrero & Chris Benoit (No Way Out),** roll-up | | |

| 1244 | Feb. 26 | Phoenix | ★ |
| **W** | **Raven,** lionsault | | |

| 1245 | Feb. 27 | Tuscon, AZ | ★★★ |
| **W** | **Perry Saturn,** lionsault | | |

MARCH 2001

| 1246 | Mar. 03 | Springfield, MA | ★★1/2 |
| **W** | **Kurt Angle,** pin | | |

| 1247 | Mar. 04 | Wilkes-Barre, PA | ★★★1/2 |
| **W** | **Kurt Angle,** roll-up | | |

| 1248 | Mar. 05 | Washington, D.C. | ★★★ |
| **W** | **Eddy Guerrero,** pin | | |

| 1249 | Mar. 06 | Washington, D.C. | ★★3/4 |
| **W** | **Val Venis,** lionsault | | |

| 1250 | Mar. 10 | El Paso, TX | ★★★1/4 |
| **W** | **Kurt Angle,** roll-up | | |

| 1251 | Mar. 11 | Bakersfield, CA | ★★★★ |
| **W** | **Kurt Angle,** roll-up | | |

| 1252 | Mar. 12 | Los Angeles | ★★★ |
| **L** | **4-on-1 handicap vs. Godfather, Val Venis, Steven Richards & Bull Buchanan,** pinned by Venis/Val bomb | | |

| 1253 | Mar. 13 | Anaheim, CA | ★★1/2 |
| **L** | **2-on-1 vs. The Dudley Boyz (tables match),** 3-D | | |

| 1254 | Mar. 17 | Toronto | ★★ |
| **W** | **Eddy Guerrero,** Walls of Jericho | | |

| 1255 | Mar. 18 | Montreal | ★★1/4 |
| **W** | **Eddy Guerrero,** Walls of Jericho | | |

| 1256 | Mar. 19 | Albany, NY | ★★1/2 |
| **L** | **3-on-2 handicap with Rock vs. Kurt Angle, William Regal & Chris Benoit,** pinned by Regal | | |

| 1257 | Mar. 20 | Providence, RI | ★★★ |
| **NC** | **Raven,** NO CONTEST | | |

| 1258 | Mar. 24 | New York City | ★★★1/4 |
| **W** | **Eddy Guerrero,** Walls of Jericho | | |

| 1259 | Mar. 25 | Worcester, MA | ★★★1/4 |
| **W** | **Haku,** Walls of Jericho | | |

| 1260 | Mar. 26 | Cleveland | ★★★ |
| **L** | **Big Show,** pin | | |

| 1261 | Mar. 27 | Detroit | ★★★ |
| **L** | **Tag with Kane vs. Big Show & William Regal,** Regal stretch | | |

APRIL 2001

| 1262 | Apr. 01 | Houston | ★★1/2 |
| **W** | **William Regal (WrestleMania 17),** lionsault | | |

| 1263 | Apr. 02 | Ft. Worth, TX | ★★★ |
| **L** | **3-way vs. William Regal vs. Kurt Angle,** pinned by Regal | | |

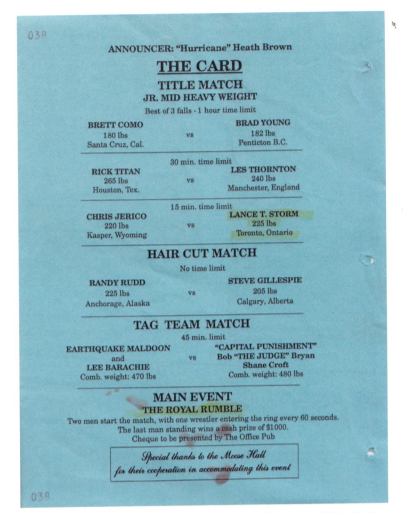

ANNOUNCER: "Hurricane" Heath Brown

THE CARD

TITLE MATCH
JR. MID HEAVY WEIGHT
Best of 3 falls - 1 hour time limit

BRETT COMO		BRAD YOUNG
180 lbs	vs	182 lbs
Santa Cruz, Cal.		Penticton B.C.

30 min. time limit

RICK TITAN		LES THORNTON
265 lbs	vs	240 lbs
Houston, Tex.		Manchester, England

15 min. time limit

CHRIS JERICO		LANCE T. STORM
220 lbs	vs	225 lbs
Kasper, Wyoming		Toronto, Ontario

HAIR CUT MATCH
No time limit

RANDY RUDD		STEVE GILLESPIE
225 lbs	vs	205 lbs
Anchorage, Alaska		Calgary, Alberta

TAG TEAM MATCH
45 min. limit

EARTHQUAKE MALDOON		"CAPITAL PUNISHMENT"
and	vs	Bob "THE JUDGE" Bryan
LEE BARACHIE		Shane Croft
Comb. weight: 470 lbs		Comb. weight: 480 lbs

MAIN EVENT
THE ROYAL RUMBLE
Two men start the match, with one wrestler entering the ring every 60 seconds.
The last man standing wins a cash prize of $1000.
Cheque to be presented by The Office Pub

Special thanks to the Moose Hall
for their cooperation in accommodating this event

The program from my very first match in Ponoka, AB on Oct 2, 1990 with the Canadian Wrestling Connection. Both my name and my supposed birth place are spelled wrong.

Your new ECW television champion! Im covered in pure sweat as the ECW Arena was a total sweatbox. It has obtained legendary status over the years, but it essentially was nothing more than a converted warehouse with little ventilation and no showers.

More fringe? Why YES! Dr Luther's mom Karen made this ensemble and it's still one of my favorite ring jackets ever. If Sgt Pepper and Puff the Magic Dragon's vomit had a baby, it might look something like this.

Photo shoot in the middle of Mexico, with a fancy pants new zebra striped outfit.

Using the cocky pin that I stole from Fuyuki (and still use to this day) on Benoit in the Super J-Cup classic.

Eddy raises my hand in victory. I'm not sure when this was was, but it's a great pic and brings a smile to my face. Eddy was such a great, yet complex person.

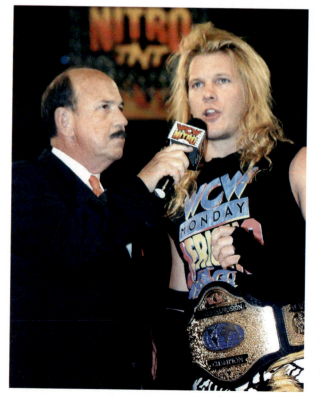

Being led through a promo by the legendary Mean Gene Okerlund. Anybody who thinks I'm good on the mic can thank Gene for helping me get there. The guy was an absolute genius at quarterbacking an interview and got the best out of everybody he worked with. He also bought me a lap dance the first time I met him at the Cheetah in Atlanta, which made him ok by me.

Steve Austin was another guy I loved going toe to toe with on the mic. We had so much fun trying to make each other laugh in the ring, especially on live events and when we did a whole summer of highlight reels in 2003 with Steve as my guest. Talk about an easy night ... improv comedy, only one bump (the Stunner of course) and a ton of laughs. The only bad thing was my ring gear reeked of beer from having a half dozen of them dumped on me nightly.

I was the first ever Undisputed Champion in WWE history, after beating The Rock and Steve Austin in the same night in 2001. It wasn't the best work of my career by any stretch, but it sure looks good on my résumé! I still think that this WWF "Eagle" title is the best looking one in company history.

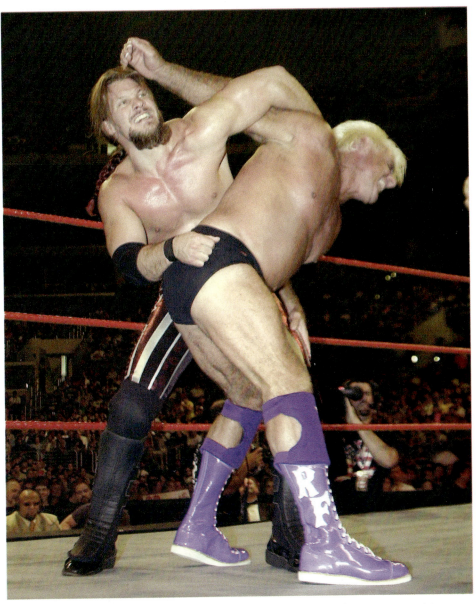

Putting the all-time greatest champ in an old-school abdominal stretch seems appropriate, doesn't it? Flair has been nothing but a total gentleman to me and my family from the moment I met him, even to this day. He's the epitome of what a top guy should be, for all the right (and wrong) reasons! I'm proud to call him my friend and I still talk to him regularly.

The famous 2008 cage match with John Cena in Madison Square Garden that drew the biggest WWE gate in MSG history at the time AND "was the best cage match I've ever seen" according to Howard Finkel ... the man who had pretty much seen them all.

The only match I ever had with Roddy Piper and it was a big one at Wrestlemania 25 in 2009. It was a three-on-one with me vs. Piper, Steamboat & Snuka and I ended up pinning Hot Rod with an enzuigiri ... the only time I ever won with that move.

What do you do when it's WrestleMania 33, but you're bored with light-up jackets AND scarves? Well you make a LIGHT-UP SCARF!

The third version of the jacket, made with digital lights. It only worked about 25% of the time and currently resides in my closet, probably never to be worn again.

I honestly believe this is one of the greatest factions in pro wrestling history. From co-workers, to friends, to brothers for life ... the Inner Circle FOREVER!

This was taken at Shad Khan's high rise apartment in Chicago in 2019. I love the big fight feel Tony Khan created for the inaugural AEW championship match between Hangman and me.

Slapping hands on the sold-out first Rock 'N' Wrestling Rager at Sea. It took me three years to get the cruise up and running and now it's a bonafide success that will take place for years to come.

With Don Callis and Kenny in the Tokyo Dome on the day we changed the business. Don was integral in putting together Alpha vs Omega, which was a huge financial success worldwide and the match that convinced Tony Khan he could start AEW.

When we had the Celebrashon for Le Champion, I wanted to make it special. So I had my dad hiding in a box, Hager dragging the JeriGoat to the ring, Puerto Rican gift baskets and the coup de grâce ... a coupon for 50 cents off Jericho merch hidden under everybody's chair.

The Painmaker hits the stage somewhere in Japan.

A good old crossbody from the top rope still always gets a great reaction. If you look closely, you can see the quarter-sized bald patch on the top of my head, caused by Naito's piledriver on the ramp only minutes earlier.

Out of all my accomplishments over the last 30 years, my most prized possession is my beautiful family. Thanks to Jessica, Ash, Cheyenne and Sierra for helping me become a better man. I love you guys!

| 1264 | Apr. 03 | Oklahoma City | ★★★★ |

L   **Triple H (lost WWF Intercontinental title),** pedigree

| 1265 | Apr. 09 | Boston | ★★★ |

NC   **Chris Benoit (William Regal guest referee),** NO CONTEST double hold on Regal

| 1266 | Apr. 10 | Philadelphia | ★★★ |

L   **4-on-2 handicap with Chris Benoit vs. William Regal, Kurt Angle, Edge & Christian,** pinned by Angle/Angle slam

| 1267 | Apr. 11 | Tallahassee, FL | ★★1/2 |

W   **6-man with Kane & Undertaker vs. Steve Austin, Triple H and William Regal,** pinned Regal/lionsault

| 1268 | Apr. 12 | Ft. Myers, FL | ★★★1/2 |

W   **Kurt Angle,** lionsault

| 1269 | Apr. 16 | Knoxville, TN | ★★★ |

W   **Kurt Angle,** DQ

| 1270 | Apr. 17 | Nashville, TN | ★★ |

L   **Tag with Chris Benoit vs. The Dudley Boyz (tables match),** Benoit through a table

| 1271 | Apr. 21 | Tyler, TX | ★★★ |

L   **Kurt Angle,** Angle slam

| 1272 | Apr. 22 | Albuquerque, NM | ★★★ |

W   **6-man with Kane & Undertaker vs. Steve Austin, Triple H and William Regal,** pinned Regal/lionsault

| 1273 | Apr. 23 | Denver | ★★ |

W   **Tag with Chris Benoit vs. Kurt Angle & William Regal (submission match),** Benoit submitted Regal

| 1274 | Apr. 24 | Denver | ★★★★ |

L   **Tag with Chris Benoit vs. Kurt Angle & William Regal ,** double submission

| 1275 | Apr. 29 | Chicago | ★★★ |

L   **William Regal (Duchess of Queensbury rules/Backlash),** pin

| 1276 | Apr. 30 | Milwaukee | ★★★ |

L   **Rhyno,** gore

1277	May 01	Indianapolis	★★3/4

W 3-on-2 with Matt Hardy vs. Edge, Christian & Rhyno, Hardy

1278	May 05	London	★★★1/4

W William Regal (Queens Cup/Insurrextion), Walls of Jericho

1279	May 07	Uniondale, NY	★★★

W William Regal (cage match), escaped

1280	May 08	Hartford, CT	★★★

L Christian, roll-up

1281	May 14	Cincinnati	★★★1/4

W Tag with Chris Benoit vs. Edge & Christian, pinned Edge/lionsault

1282	May 15	Louisville, KY	★★★

L Edge, pin

1283	May 20	Sacramento, CA	★★★1/4

W Elimination tag with Chris Benoit vs. Edge & Christian vs. X-Pac & Justin Credible
vs. APA (Ron Simmons & John Layfield) vs. The Dudley Boyz vs. The Hardy Boyz
vs. Dean Malenko & Perry Saturn (Judgment Day), Benoit submitted Christian

1284	May 21	San Jose, CA	★★★★★

W Tag with Chris Benoit vs. Triple H & Steve Austin (won WWF tag team titles), pinned
Austin/Lionsault

1285	May 22	Anaheim, CA	★★★★★

W Tag with Chris Benoit vs. The Dudley Boyz vs. The Hardy Boyz vs. Edge & Christian
(tables, ladders & chairs), Benoit got the belts

1286	May 26	Salt Lake City	★★1/2

W Tag with Chris Benoit vs. Steve Austin & William Regal, Benoit pinned Austin

1287	Mar. 27	Vancouver, British Columbia	★★3/4

W Tag with Chris Benoit vs. Steve Austin & William Regal, Benoit pinned Austin

1288	May 28	Calgary, Alberta	★★★

W Big Show (won WWF Hardcore title), lionsault

1289	May 28	Calgary, Alberta	★★★

L Rhyno (lost WWF Hardcore title)

Look at the strength of The Big Show ... he's gorilla pressing me and I'm not holding on or posting myself in the least. That's scary strong.

1290	May 29	Edmonton, Alberta	★★★
W	**Kurt Angle,** lionsault		

JUNE 2001

1291	June 03	Winnipeg, Manitoba	★★★★
L	**Steve Austin,** pin		
1292	June 04	Minneapolis	★★★1/4
L	**Steve Austin,** stunner		
1293	June 05	Grand Forks, ND	★★★
W	**Tag with Chris Benoit vs. APA,** pinned Farooq/lionsault		
1294	June 05	Grand Forks, ND	★★★
W	**Tag with Chris Benoit vs. Rhyno & Big Show,** DQ		
1295	June 05	Grand Forks, ND	★★★
W	**Tag with Chris Benoit vs. Steve Austin & Vince McMahon,** Benoit pinned Austin		

MY TOP 10 TAG TEAM PARTNERS

• SAMMY GUEVARA

I brought Sammy to AEW's attention after seeing him on an NWA show. The moment I saw him I knew he would be a star, but what I didn't expect was how quick of a study he is. Any advice I give him, he takes and makes it his own within days. He's gonna be a massive star, and it's been a blast to work with him during the early stages of his career. The Jericho/Guevara hug and his performances in both the Stadium Stampede (#2710) AND the preceding street fight versus Matt Hardy and Kenny Omega (#2708) are my favorite moments working with him.

• JAKE HAGER

I suggested that Jack Swagger be my suit-wearing silent killer bodyguard in WWE in 2010. It never happened there, but nine years later my vision came to life when I suggested him for the same position in AEW. I could never figure out how a 6-foot-6, good-looking, legit credentialed fighter who can talk slipped through the McMahon cracks, but their mistake was our gain. Jake has totally reinvented and reinvigorated his career and become the legit, believable headliner I always knew he could be. His Flim-Flam dance is an all-time highlight for me.

• CHRISTIAN

Underrated in so many ways, Jay Reso is the prototype of how to become successful as a smaller wrestler. The guy is so smart in putting together his matches, and even though his backstage demeanor can be serious, he has no problem being the butt of the joke in the ring. One of my favorite bits we did was when the Dudleys stole our clothes on *RAW* and we spent the rest of the show wearing towels around our waists trying to find them. Finally, Spike Dudley ran up behind us and stripped off our towels leaving us near nude in the middle of the arena. FYI — Vince's original idea was for us to LITERALLY be left naked in front of 10,000 fans on live TV.

• CHRIS BENOIT

We were very similar in our wrestling styles and backgrounds, and Chris always brought out the best in me. As far as a Chris and Chris highlight? Well, it's hard to top the 1-2 punch of beating HHH & Austin on a Monday in San Jose (#1284) and then winning the forgotten TLC in Anaheim the very next night (#1285).

• MIKE LOZANSKI

I met Mike before I had my very first match and he served as a sort-of mentor to me in those early years. He had achieved success in Mexico as Tigre Canadiense at the time and eventually brought me into Monterrey to be his tag team partner. Since I was known as Lionheart, we called ourselves Los Gatos Salvaje (The Wild Cats) and proceeded to work together, live together, and spend pretty much every waking moment together for the next six months. We eventually went our own separate ways, but Mike was integral in getting me hired in the country where I first became a huge star. My favorite memory was our going to a "massage parlor" in Monterrey with Hector and Humberto Garza and finding out that there were more than just massages on the menu ...

• KEVIN OWENS

Kevin and I were randomly thrown together as a team on a *RAW* in London. At the end of the show as we were walking up the ramp I yelled, "I'm the GOAT!" In retort Kevin screamed, "Yeah ... and I'm the donkey!" (#2564) At that moment I knew we could do some great things together, and we did. The Jericho-Owens "Best Friends" story line was one of my career favorites and THE best angle of 2016-17. We should've headlined WrestleMania, made a buddy cop WWE movie (we pitched it and were flatly turned down by the WWE Studios head) and been tag team champions. None of those things happened, but we had so much fun and left a major mark on the business anyway. One of my favorite moments was getting Superman punched by Roman Reigns as I was hanging on a shark cage containing KO six feet off the ground (#2660). Top entertainment!

• LANCE STORM

I trained with Lance, worked against him in my first match and spent most of the first five years of my career tagging with him. We were Ying and Yang as people but meshed perfectly in the ring. I'll never forget the day he told me he wanted to break up our team and go his own way. I felt like I was getting dumped by my girlfriend! We eventually tagged again in SMW and wrestled on and off until he stopped working full-time. We always had great matches because we pushed each other, which is the sign of a great partnership. My most obscure memory is the night we got into the only fight we ever had, in the dressing room at an FMW show in 1991. We rolled around on the floor for a bit in anger, until we were eventually broken up. I'd call it a draw.

• DR. LUTHER

We only tagged once in Japan in Korakuen Hall for WAR, but it was a match we had been looking forward to the whole tour (#552). We called ourselves The Lovely Lads (Nigel & David's first band in *Spinal Tap*) and had a pretty kick-ass match with our Japanese opponents before losing and then violently breaking up in the end. I remember screaming "You're bullshit, you're really bullshit Luther," to which he responded, "You're drunk!" ... like Ned Braden arguing with his wife in *Slapshot*.

• EDDY GUERRERO

I always say we were the best tag team that never really was because WCW only put us together sporadically (we barely crossed paths in WWE either, which is another travesty), but when we did team together, it was pure magic! And you might think I'm only talking about the two of us as heels, but we were a great babyface team as well. Our match against Meng & Barbarian on *Nitro* in 1997 (#669) is a standout example of that and one of the best I had in the company. *¡Viva Los Eh And Whey!*

• BIG SHOW

Show was handpicked by Vince to replace Edge (my choice was Kane) when he tore his Achilles in 2009. I agreed, but only if we could rebuild Show into the "Giant Destroyer" that he is. We succeeded in doing that and thus began an amazing six-month partnership that was both hard-hitting and serious yet completely hilarious at times. We were around each other so much that we started acting like an old married couple backstage.

"Where are we on the card?"

"You can read, put on your glasses, Show!"

"I can't find them!!"

"They're on your head!"

Highlights are too many to mention, but facing off with DX in a TLC match for the tag titles left us both beaten and bruised (#2209) and our Rom-Com breakup ("Will I ever see you again, Show?" "Maybe Chris, but you'll always be with me no matter what.") on *RAW* in Rhode Island still makes me smile to this day.

1296	June 09	Greenville, SC	★★★1/2
W	**Elimination tag with Chris Benoit vs. Edge & Christian vs. X-Pac & Justin Credible,** double submission on Edge & Christian		

1297	June 10	Hampton, VA	★★★★
W	**Tag with Chris Benoit vs. Steve Austin & William Regal,** Benoit		

1298	June 11	Richmond, VA	★★★
L	**2-on-1 handicap vs. Rhyno & Big Show,** chokeslam		

1299	June 12	Baltimore	★★★1/2
W	**Tag with Chris Benoit vs. Edge & Christian,** pinned Edge/lionsault		

1300	June 16	Toronto	★★★★
L	**Steve Austin (cage match)**		

1301	June 17	Fort Lauderdale, FL	★★
W	**Tag with Chris Benoit vs. Rhyno & Steve Austin (cage match),** submission		

1302	June 18	Tampa, FL	★★★1/4
W	**6-man with Chris Benoit & Spike Dudley vs. The Dudley Boyz & Steve Austin,** submitted Austin		

| 1303 | June 19 | Orlando, FL | ★★★ |

L   **Tag with Chris Benoit vs. The Dudley Boyz (lost WWF tag-team titles),** Benoit pinned

| 1304 | June 24 | East Rutherford, NJ | ★★3/4 |

L   **3-way vs. Steve Austin vs. Chris Benoit (King of the Ring),** Austin pinned Benoit

| 1305 | June 25 | New York City | ★★★★ |

W   **Tajiri,** lionsault

| 1306 | June 26 | New York City | ★★★ |

W   **Tag with Scotty 2 Hotty vs. William Regal & Tajiri,** Scotty

| 1307 | June 27 | Louisville, KY | ★★★1/4 |

L   **Flash Flanigan (Last Dance),** roll-up

JULY 2001

| 1308 | July 01 | Spokane, WA | ★★★1/2 |

W   **William Regal,** Walls of Jericho

| 1309 | July 02 | Tacoma, WA | ★★1/2 |

W   **2-on-1 handicap vs. The Dudley Boyz,** lionsault

| 1310 | July 03 | Tacoma, WA | ★★★ |

L   **Tag with Spike Dudley vs. The Dudley Boyz,** Spike pinned

| 1311 | July 09 | Atlanta | ★★★ |

W   **Tag with Kane vs. Lance Storm & Mike Awesome,** DQ

| 1312 | July 10 | Birmingham, AL | ★★★ |

W   **Lance Storm,** Walls of Jericho

| 1313 | July 14 | Albany, NY | ★★★ |

W   **Sean Stasiak,** Walls of Jericho

| 1314 | July 15 | New Haven, CT | ★★★1/4 |

W   **Sean Stasiak,** Walls of Jericho

| 1315 | July 16 | Providence, RI | ★★★★ |

L   **Booker T,** roll-up

| 1316 | July 17 | Boston | ★★1/2 |

L   **Diamond Dallas Page,** DQ

| 1317 | July 22 | Cleveland | ★★3/4 |

L 5-on-5 with Steve Austin, Undertaker, Angle & Kane vs. Diamond Dallas Page, Booker T, Rhyno & The Dudley Boyz (WCW-ECW Inaugural Brawl/Invasion), Angle

---

| 1318 | July 23 | Buffalo, NY | ★★★ |

W Kanyon, Walls of Jericho

| 1319 | July 24 | Pittsburgh | ★★3/4 |

L Tag with Tajiri vs. Kanyon & Rob Van Dam, Tajiri

| 1320 | July 28 | Syracuse, NY | ★★3/4 |

L 8-man with Tajiri, William Regal & Kane vs. Rob Van Dam, Taz, Mike Awesome & Rhyno

---

| 1321 | July 29 | Wilkes-Barre, PA | ★★1/2 |

L 6-man with Tajiri & William Regal vs. Rob Van Dam, Taz & Mike Awesome

---

| 1322 | July 30 | Philadelphia | ★★★ |

W Taz, lionsault

| 1323 | July 31 | Washington, D.C. | ★★★ |

L 6-man with Edge & Christian vs. Rhyno & The Dudley Boyz, pin

---

AUGUST 2001

| 1324 | Aug. 06 | Anaheim, CA | ★★★ |

W Tag with Kurt Angle vs. The Dudley Boyz, Angle

| 1325 | Aug. 07 | Los Angeles | ★★3/4 |

W Hugh Morrus, Walls of Jericho

| 1326 | Aug. 11 | Uniondale, NY | ★★★ |

W Rhyno, Walls of Jericho

| 1327 | Aug. 12 | Rockford, IL | ★★★ |

W Rhyno, Walls of Jericho

| 1328 | Aug. 13 | Chicago | ★★★ |

L Tag with Rock vs. Rhyno & Booker T, roll-up

| 1329 | Aug. 14 | Salt Lake City | ★★★ |

L Tag with Jeff Hardy vs. Rob Van Dam & Rhyno, Hardy

| 1330 | Aug. 17 | Las Vegas | ★★★ |

W Rhyno, Walls of Jericho

1331	Aug. 18	Fresno, CA	★★★
W	**Rhyno,** Walls of Jericho		

1332	Aug. 19	San Jose, CA	★
W	**Rhyno (Summer Slam),** Walls of Jericho		

1333	Aug. 20	Sacramento, CA	★★★
L	**Test,** boot		

1334	Aug. 21	Denver	★★★3/4
L	**Steve Austin,** roll-up		

1335	Aug. 24	Wichita, KS	★★★
W	**Rob Van Dam,** breakdown		

1336	Aug. 25	Des Moines, IA	★★3/4
W	**Rob Van Dam,** lionsault		

1337	Aug. 26	Fort Wayne, IN	★★★
W	**Rob Van Dam,** lionsault		

1338	Aug. 27	Grand Rapids, MI	★★1/2
W	**Tag with Kurt Angle vs. Rob Van Dam & Taz,** Angle		

1339	Aug. 28	Detroit	★★★★
L	**Tag with Rock vs. Rhyno & Rob Van Dam,** Rhyno pinned Rock		

SEPTEMBER 2001

1340	Sept. 01	Worcester, MA	★★★1/2
W	**Rob Van Dam,** lionsault		

1341	Sept. 02	Halifax, Nova Scotia	★★★
W	**Rob Van Dam,** lionsault		

1342	Sept. 03	Toronto	★★★
W	**Tag with Jeff Hardy vs. Rob Van Dam & Rhyno,** pinned Van Dam/roll-up		

1343	Sept. 04	Toronto	★★3/4
L	**8-man with Rock & APA vs. The Dudley Boyz, Booker T & Rhyno,** pinned by Booker T		

1344	Sept. 10	San Antonio	★★★
W	**6-man with APA vs. Rhyno & The Dudley Boyz,** lionsault		

1345	Sept. 13	Houston	★★
W	**Christian,** school boy cradle		

1346	Sept. 17	Nashville, TN	★★★

W **Tag with Kurt Angle vs. Steve Austin & Rob Van Dam,** Angle pinned Austin

1347	Sept. 22	Reading, PA	★★★

W **Rob Van Dam,** lionsault

1348	Sept. 23	Pittsburgh	★★★

L **Rob Van Dam (Unforgiven),** splash

1349	Sept. 24	Columbus, OH	★★1/2

W **Christian,** DQ

1350	Sept. 25	Dayton, OH	★★★★

L **Rob Van Dam,** Vandaminator

1351	Sept. 29	Jacksonville, FL	★★★

W **Raven,** Walls of Jericho

1352	Sept. 30	Biloxi, MS	★★1/2

W **Raven,** Walls of Jericho

OCTOBER 2001

1353	Oct. 01	Baton Rouge, LA	★★

L **6-man with Undertaker & Kane vs. Test, Booker T & Rob Van Dam,** kick

1354	Oct. 02	Mobile, AL	★★★1/2

W **6-man with Rock & Mike Chioda vs. The Dudley Boyz & Nick Patrick,** Chioda

MATCH NOTES #1354

I totally forgot about this match until Chioda reminded me of it on *Talk Is Jericho*. (It's funny to think I would forget a match where I teamed with The Rock, but we worked together a TON back in the early 2000s). WWE used to do fun matches like this from time to time, and with the right build and characters, they always got INSANE reactions. Which this one did.

1355	Oct. 06	Winnipeg, Manitoba	★★★1/4

W **Lance Storm,** Walls of Jericho

1356	Oct. 07	St. Paul, MN	★★★

W **Lance Storm,** Walls of Jericho

1357	Oct. 08	Indianapolis	★★★1/4

L **Tag with Rock vs. Rob Van Dam & Shane McMahon,** Rock

| 1358 | Oct. 09 | Moline, IL | ★★★ |
| **W** | **Rob Van Dam,** pin | | |

| 1359 | Oct. 13 | Saginaw, MI | ★★★ |
| **L** | **Rhyno,** DQ | | |

| 1360 | Oct. 14 | Toledo, OH | ★★★1/2 |
| **L** | **Rhyno,** DQ | | |

| 1361 | Oct. 15 | Ottawa, Ontario | ★★1/2 |
| **W** | **Rhyno,** DQ | | |

| 1362 | Oct. 16 | Montreal | ★★★ |
| **NC** | **Tag with Rock vs. Raven & Justin Credible,** NO CONTEST | | |

| 1363 | Oct. 21 | St. Louis | ★★★★★ |
| **W** | **Rock (won WCW world title/No Mercy),** breakdown | | |

| 1364 | Oct. 22 | Kansas City, MO | ★★1/2 |
| **W** | **Tag with Rock vs. The Dudley Boyz (won WWF tag-team titles/2nd time)** | | |

| 1365 | Oct. 23 | Omaha, NE | ★★3/4 |
| **W** | **Booker T,** roll-up | | |

| 1366 | Oct. 29 | Louisville, KY | ★★★ |
| **W** | **Tag with Rock vs. Booker T & Test,** Walls of Jericho | | |

| 1367 | Oct. 30 | Cincinnati | ★★★ |
| **L** | **Tag with Rock vs. Booker T & Test (lost WWF world tag team titles),** Rock | | |

NOVEMBER 2001

| 1368 | Nov. 03 | Manchester, England | ★★★3/4 |
| **W** | **Kurt Angle (Rebellion),** roll-up | | |

| 1369 | Nov. 05 | Uniondale, NY | ★★★ |
| **L** | **Rock (lost WCW world title),** roll-up | | |

| 1370 | Nov. 10 | Cleveland | ★★1/2 |
| **L** | **Kurt Angle,** Angle slam | | |

| 1371 | Nov. 11 | Hartford, CT | ★★★ |
| **L** | **Kurt Angle,** Angle slam | | |

| 1372 | Nov. 13 | Albany, NY | ★★★★ |
| **W** | **Tag with Rock vs. Steve Austin & Kurt Angle,** DQ | | |

| 1373 | Nov. 18 | Greenville, NC | ★★★1/4 |

W **10-man tag with Rock, Big Show, Kane & Undertaker vs. Steve Austin, Kurt Angle, Rob Van Dam, Booker T & Shane McMahon (Team WWF vs. Team Alliance/ Survivor Series),** Rock

| 1374 | Nov. 19 | Charlotte, NC | ★ |

L **Kane,** DQ

| 1375 | Nov. 20 | Fayetteville, NC | ★★★ |

W **3-on-2 handicap with The Dudley Boyz vs. Rock & Rob Van Dam,** pinned Rock/rock bottom

| 1376 | Nov. 26 | Oklahoma City | ★★★1/4 |

L **Tag with Kurt Angle vs. Rock & Kane,** DDT

DECEMBER 2001

| 1377 | Dec. 01 | Detroit | ★★★★ |

L **Rock,** rock bottom

| 1378 | Dec. 02 | Champaign, IL | ★★1/2 |

L **Rock,** rock bottom

| 1379 | Dec. 03 | Milwaukee | ★★★ |

L **Steve Austin,** stunner

| 1380 | Dec. 04 | Chicago | ★★★ |

L **Tag with Kurt Angle vs. Steve Austin & Rock,** sharpshooter

| 1381 | Dec. 08 | San Jose, CA | ★★★★ |

L **Tag with Kurt Angle vs. Steve Austin & Rock (tornado match),** rock bottom

| 1382 | Dec. 09 | San Diego | ★★★1/2 |

W **Rock (won WCW world title/Vengeance),** rock bottom

| 1383 | Dec. 09 | San Diego | ★★★ |

W **Steve Austin (won WWF world championship – unified WWF & WCW titles into the Undisputed WWF world championship/Vengeance),** pin/Booker T belt shot

| 1384 | Dec. 10 | Anaheim, CA | ★★1/2 |

W **Steve Austin (cage match),** escaped

| 1385 | Dec. 11 | Bakersfield, CA | ★★★1/2 |

L **Tag with Undertaker vs. Rock & Rob Van Dam,** Vandaminator

| 1386 | Dec. 17 | Lafayette, LA | ★★1/2 |

L **Rob Van Dam (Ric Flair referee),** DQ

TONY SCHIAVONE'S TOP 10 JERICHO MOMENTS

Tony Schiavone is a legendary commentator currently working with AEW.

10. JERICHO VS. KENNY OMEGA AT WRESTLE KINGDOM 12 (#2685, JAN. 4, 2018)

My apologies to all the wrestling purists out there who are mad that I put this great match at number 10. But I can remember seeing a recording of a press conference where Omega attacked Jericho and thinking, "Damn, I need to see this match!" Well, I did. It got five stars from the Wrestling Observer and is one of my favorite matches of all time.

9. JERICHO BRINGS IN RALPHUS (1998)

Another Chris Jericho gem was the introduction of his "Personal Security" guard, Ralphus. This was all Chris. He was the WCW TV champ, and by using poor old John Riker (who drove one of the trucks for WCW), he made the angle with Goldberg very entertaining. And who could forget the "hair" of Jericho as he walked out that night with Ralphus for the first time. It was all over the place.

8. JERICHO'S LETTER FROM UNCLE TED ON WCW MONDAY NITRO (JUNE 8, 1998)

I was all too happy to be holding the microphone for this classic. After weeks of claiming a conspiracy as a result of Slamboree, Jericho read a letter from Ted Turner. It was hilarious and shows the true genius of Jericho. Do you think anyone else had a hand in that bit? Hell, no. It was all Chris Jericho. From the moment where he was thrilled about all the nice things "Uncle Ted" and "Jane" said about him, to the end where he cried. It was classic.

7. JERICHO'S TELEVISED DEBUT ON WCW MONDAY NITRO (#592, AUG. 26, 1996)

I did not call his first televised match; Eric Bischoff and Bobby Heenan did. However, did I know he was something special the first time I saw him wrestle? Damn right. He was smooth and confident and his chops were stiff. He beat Alex Wright via countout but would not take the win. The referee declared it a no contest. Jericho did a fine interview ringside with "Mean" Gene Okerlund explaining his reasons. It was a great first-time interview. He left Alex no time to talk. No one complained.

6. JERICHO ADDS SOMETHING SPECIAL TO WILLIAM REGAL'S CUP OF TEA ON RAW IS WAR (MAR. 19, 2001)

I did not see this when it happened because we were at the end of a bitter, emotional run at WCW. However, the skit was played perfectly by Jericho (who snuck behind the curtain to take a tinkle) and by Regal (whose reaction upon tasting the concoction was priceless). I literally fell out when I saw it. Only talents like Jericho and Regal could have pulled it off.

5. JERICHO SHOWS HIS LEADERSHIP ON AN AEW ZOOM CALL (APRIL 2020)

This is really some behind-the-scenes stuff, but here goes. Tony Khan and the members of the AEW corporate team held the first of many "team" meetings via Zoom during the pandemic of 2020. This was done to let everyone know that Tony and the company really and truly cared and that the health of all performers and staff members came first. Everyone had a chance to speak up, and many did. But it was Chris Jericho's comments that rang true to me. He encouraged the talent to make the most of the down-time by video recording something that could possibly be used in the upcoming shows. "Let the creative juices flow," I think I remember him saying. It was there that I realized how he was leading by example among the talent. It was also then I realized he was worth every penny both in and out of the ring.

4. JERICHO BECOMES FIRST WWF UNDISPUTED WORLD CHAMPION AT WWF VENGEANCE (#1383, DEC. 9, 2001)

Sure, this was all part of an angle involving Mr. McMahon, but here's the plain-cold fact. Chris Jericho picked up wins over BOTH The Rock and Stone Cold Steve Austin on the same night to become the FIRST-EVER undisputed champion. It's something that lives in the "record books" forever and a feat that will never again be accomplished.

3. STADIUM STAMPEDE (#2710, MAY 23, 2020)

I have done so many matches that it's troubling trying to remember many of the big moments, but this night I will NEVER forget, and for all the zany things that were done and tried, my favorite memory? Chris Jericho getting a stripe painted right down the middle — crotch to face — with field marking paint, courtesy of Hangman Adam Page. The best!

2. JERICHO BECOMES THE FIRST-EVER AEW WORLD CHAMPION (#2693, AUG. 31, 2019)

Chris completed his transformation as not only did he become the first-ever AEW Champion, but he also began the formation of the Inner Circle and made "A Little Bit of the Bubbly" a household phrase among wrestling fans.

1. APPEARANCE AT AEW'S LAUNCH ANNOUNCEMENT (JAN. 8, 2019)

The fact that Jericho interrupted the Jacksonville press conference to announce AEW — complete with his music blaring and pyro — while the WWE was performing across the street — solidified the fact that he was reinventing himself yet again.

1387	Dec. 18	New Orleans	★★★
W	**Big Show,** pin/belt shot		

1388	Dec. 21	Miami	★★★★
W	**3-way vs. Rock vs. Kurt Angle**		

JANUARY 2002

1389	Jan. 03	Washington, D.C.	★★★1/4
W	**Tag with Kurt Angle vs. Rob Van Dam & Edge**		

1390	Jan. 04	Binghamton, NY	★★1/2
L	**Tag with Kurt Angle vs. Triple H & Kane,** pinned by Triple H/pedigree		

1391	Jan. 05	Springfield, MA	★★3/4
L	**Tag with Kurt Angle vs. Triple H & Kane,** pinned by Triple H/pedigree		

1392	Jan. 06	Trenton, NJ	★★★1/2
L	**Tag with Kurt Angle vs. Triple H & Kane,** pinned by Triple H/pedigree		

Throwing hands with The Rock in Madison Square Garden ... a match I have no recollection of, which is insane when you think of the factors involved! If you look closely you can see Curtis Hughes, my bodyguard (who I was bigger than) for about a month, standing ringside.

1393	Jan. 07	New York City	★★★
W	**Rikishi,** belt shot		

1394	Jan. 08	New York City	★★★3/4
L	**Tag with Test vs. Rock & Rob Van Dam,** sharpshooter		

1395	Jan. 12	Lubbock, TX	★★3/4
L	**Triple H,** DQ		

1396	Jan. 13	Houston	★★★
L	**Triple H,** DQ		

1397	Jan. 14	Dallas	★★★
W	**6-man with Lance Storm & Christian vs. APA & Rikishi,** pinned Farooq/breakdown		

1398	Jan. 20	Atlanta	★★★★1/4
W	**Rock (Royal Rumble),** school boy cradle		

1399	Jan. 21	Greenville, SC	★★★
L	**Tag with Kurt Angle vs. Rock & Triple H,** pinned by Rock/rock bottom		

1400	Jan. 26	Pittsburgh	★★3/4
W	**Triple H,** DQ		

1401	Jan. 27	Hershey, PA	★★★1/4
W	**Triple H,** DQ		

1402	Jan. 28	Richmond, VA	★★★1/2
W	**Maven,** Walls of Jericho		

1403	Jan. 29	Norfolk, VA	★★★
W	**Taz,** breakdown		

FEBRUARY 2002

1404	Feb. 02	Vancouver, British Columbia	★★★1/4
W	**Triple H,** DQ		

1405	Feb. 03	Seattle	★★★3/4
W	**Triple H,** DQ		

1406	Feb. 04	Las Vegas	★★★★
W	**Tag with Undertaker vs. Rock & Steve Austin,** pinned Rock		

1407	Feb. 05	Los Angeles	★★
W	**2-on-1 handicap with Kurt Angle vs. Triple H,** Angle		

| 1408 | Feb. 09 | Albuquerque, NM | ★★★1/4 |
| **L** | **Steve Austin,** DQ | | |

| 1409 | Feb. 10 | El Paso, TX | ★★★1/2 |
| **L** | **Steve Austin,** DQ | | |

| 1410 | Feb. 11 | Jonesboro, AR | ★★★ |
| **W** | **Edge,** breakdown | | |

| 1411 | Feb. 12 | Little Rock, AR | ★★★ |
| **L** | **Kane,** DQ | | |

| 1412 | Feb. 17 | Milwaukee | ★★★ |
| **W** | **Steve Austin (No Way Out),** pin | | |

| 1413 | Feb. 25 | Providence, RI | ★★★1/4 |
| **W** | **Kurt Angle,** breakdown | | |

| 1414 | Feb. 26 | Boston | ★★★1/2 |
| **L** | **Tag with Kurt Angle vs. Kane & Triple H,** Angle | | |

MARCH 2002

| 1415 | Mar. 01 | Yokohama, Japan | ★★★★1/2 |
| **W** | **Rock,** roll-up | | |

| 1416 | Mar. 03 | Singapore | ★★★★ |
| **W** | **Rock,** roll-up | | |

The Rock and I had a great rivalry, as not only did we have excellent chemistry in the ring (people forget how good of a worker he was), but I could match him on the mic, which was very difficult. It was the ultimate heel vs. the ultimate babyface, and had he not left the WWE for Hollywood so early in his career, I feel we would have had dozens of other classic matches.

| 1417 | Mar. 04 | Kuala Lumpur, Malaysia | ★★★★1/4 |
| **W** | **Rock,** roll-up | | |

| 1418 | Mar. 07 | San Antonio | ★★★ |
| **W** | **Kane,** lionsault | | |

| 1419 | Mar. 10 | Fort Wayne, IN | ★★★ |
| **W** | **Triple H,** roll-up | | |

| 1420 | Mar. 17 | Toronto | ★★★1/2 |
| **L** | **Triple H (lost WWF heavyweight title/WrestleMania 18),** pedigree | | |

JIM ROSS MEMORY

Having to close WrestleMania 18 in Toronto and having to follow Hulk vs. Rock was the ultimate challenge. Nonetheless, mission accomplished with Triple H, and they got the job done. Most talents would have essentially phoned it in, but not Chris — who was also "doing the honors" and who performed his assignment like the true pro that he is.

| 1421 | Mar. 25 | State College, PA | ★★★ |
| **L** | **3-way vs. Triple H vs. Stephanie McMahon,** Stephanie pinned | | |

| 1422 | Mar. 26 | Philadelphia | ★★★1/4 |
| **W** | **Matt Hardy,** Walls of Jericho | | |

| 1423 | Mar. 27 | Gainesville, FL | ★★★★ |
| **W** | **Edge,** breakdown | | |

| 1424 | Mar. 28 | Jacksonville, FL | ★★★★ |
| **W** | **Edge,** breakdown | | |

APRIL 2002

| 1425 | Apr. 02 | Rochester, NY | ★★★★ |
| **L** | **Rock,** rock bottom | | |

| 1426 | Apr. 06 | Davis, CA | ★★★ |
| **L** | **Triple H,** pedigree | | |

| 1427 | Apr. 07 | Fresno, CA | ★★★1/4 |
| **L** | **Triple H,** pedigree | | |

| 1428 | Apr. 08 | Yuma, AZ | ★★★1/2 |
| **W** | **Rikishi,** roll-up | | |

1429	Apr. 09	Tuscon, AZ	★★★1/2
W	**Edge,** roll-up		

1430	Apr. 13	Montgomery, AL	★★★1/4
L	**Triple H**		

1431	Apr. 14	Huntsville, AL	★★★1/2
L	**Triple H**		

1432	Apr. 15	Denton, TX	★★★
W	**Rikishi,** roll-up		

1433	Apr. 16	Houston	★★★★
NC	**Tag with Kurt Angle vs. Triple H & Hulk Hogan,** NO CONTEST		

1434	Apr. 22	Valparaiso, IN	★★★1/4
W	**Rikishi,** roll-up		

1435	Apr. 23	Peoria, IL	★★★1/4
W	**Triple H,** roll-up		

1436	Apr. 27	Baltimore	★★★1/2
L	**Triple H,** pedigree		

1437	Apr. 28	Syracuse, NY	★★★1/4
W	**Rikishi,** roll-up		

1438	Apr. 29	Erie, PA	★★1/2
W	**Rikishi,** roll-up		

1439	Apr. 30	Pittsburgh	★★★★
L	**Hulk Hogan (no DQ),** roll-up		

MATCH NOTES #1439, MY FIRST SINGLES MATCH WITH HULK HOGAN (BROTHER)

Working with Hulk was a young Chris Irvine's dream come true. But the best part of wrestling with him regularly was that we had actual chemistry and never had a bad match. Hulk would show up at the venue for a live event with a case of beer and say, "You got this, brother?" I would nod and then tell him my ideas for the match, and he would go with all of them. He trusted my instincts implicitly and even worked outside of his box. He took a lionsault, gave me a second-rope superplex, and even let me sweep his legs and put him in the Walls when he went for his famous leg-drop finish. I loved working with the Hulkster, and I still contend that this was his last GREAT match.

I always enjoyed working with Hulk. No surprise that he's one of the best babyfaces I ever wrestled who always had the crowd in the palm of his hand. After we worked together a few times, he would show up at the building and say, "You got me brother?" which was his code for, "Put the match together and tell me what you want me to do."

MAY 2002

| 1440 | May 04 | Fort Lauderdale, FL | ★★★ |
| **L** | **Tag with Kurt Angle vs. Hulk Hogan & Rock,** People's elbow | | |

| 1441 | May 05 | Worcester, MA | ★★★1/2 |
| **L** | **Hulk Hogan,** leg-drop | | |

| 1442 | May 06 | Lowell, MA | ★★1/2 |
| **L** | **Tag with Kurt Angle vs. Taz & Edge,** Angle pinned | | |

| 1443 | May 07 | Bridgeport, CT | ★★★ |
| **NC** | **Tag with Kurt Angle vs. Edge & Hulk Hogan,** NO CONTEST | | |

| 1444 | May 11 | Quebec City | ★★★★ |
| **W** | **Rikishi,** roll-up | | |

| 1445 | May 12 | Halifax, Nova Scotia | ★★★ |
| **W** | **Rikishi,** roll-up | | |

| 1446 | May 13 | Cornwall, Ontario | ★★1/2 |
| **W** | **Rikishi,** roll-up | | |

| 1447 | May 14 | Montreal | ★★★ |
| **W** | **Tag with Kurt Angle vs. Triple H & Edge,** Angle | | |

| 1448 | May 18 | Macon, GA | ★★★ |
| **W** | **Rikishi,** roll-up | | |

1449	May 19	Nashville, TN	★★★★
L	**Triple H (Hell in a Cell/Judgment Day)**, pedigree		

1450	May 20	Birmingham, AL	★★★
L	**Hulk Hogan,** leg-drop		

1451	May 21	Tupelo, MS	★★1/2
W	**Mark Henry,** chair shot		

1452	May 25	Saskatoon, Saskatchewan	★★★1/4
W	**Edge,** fall out		

1453	May 26	Regina, Saskatchewan	★★1/2
W	**Edge,** breakdown		

1454	May 27	Lethridge, Alberta	★★★
W	**Edge,** breakdown		

1455	May 28	Calgary, Alberta	★★★
W	**Farooq,** fall out		

JUNE 2002

1456	June 01	Pensacola, FL	★★★
L	**Bob Holly,** Alabama slam		

1457	June 02	Jackson, MS	★★3/4
L	**Bob Holly,** Alabama slam		

1458	June 03	Tulsa, OK	★★★1/4
L	**Bob Holly,** Alabama slam		

1459	June 04	Oklahoma City	★★
L	**No. 1 contender Battle Royal,** Eliminated by Hulk Hogan		

1460	June 08	Albany, GA	★★1/2
W	**Big Valbowski,** Walls of Jericho		

1461	June 09	Augusta, GA	★★★
W	**Big Valbowski,** Walls of Jericho		

1462	June 10	Florence, SC	★★★1/2
W	**Big Valbowski,** Walls of Jericho		

1463	June 11	Greenville, SC	★★★
L	**Tag with Lance Storm vs. Big Valbowski & Billy Kidman,** Storm/double pin		

| 1464 | June 15 | Honolulu | ★★★★★ |
| **L** | **Rock,** People's elbow | | |

| 1465 | June 16 | Anaheim, CA | ★★3/4 |
| **L** | **Triple H (cage match),** pedigree | | |

| 1466 | June 17 | Fresno, CA | ★★★ |
| **W** | **Val Venis,** Walls of Jericho | | |

| 1467 | June 18 | Sacramento, CA | ★★★1/2 |
| **W** | **Val Venis,** Walls of Jericho | | |

| 1468 | June 22 | Huntington, WV | ★★★1/2 |
| **L** | **Triple H (cage match),** pedigree | | |

| 1469 | June 23 | Columbus, OH | ★★★★1/2 |
| **L** | **Rob Van Dam (King of the Ring),** frog splash | | |

| 1470 | June 24 | Moline, IL | ★★★ |
| **L** | **Val Venis,** splash | | |

| 1471 | June 25 | Chicago | ★★★★ |
| **L** | **Hulk Hogan,** DQ | | |

JULY 2002

| 1472 | July 02 | Boston | ★★★ |
| **W** | **John Cena,** flashback | | |

| 1473 | July 06 | Mobile, AL | ★★3/4 |
| **L** | **Edge,** spear | | |

| 1474 | July 07 | Savannah, GA | ★★★ |
| **L** | **Edge,** spear | | |

| 1475 | July 08 | Salisbury, MD | ★★★1/4 |
| **L** | **Edge,** spear | | |

| 1476 | July 09 | Atlantic City, NJ | ★★1/2 |
| **L** | **Tag with Kurt Angle vs. Undertaker & John Cena,** roll-up | | |

| 1477 | July 15 | Binghamton, NY | ★★★1/4 |
| **W** | **John Cena,** Walls of Jericho | | |

| 1478 | July 16 | Wilkes-Barre, PA | ★★1/2 |
| **L** | **John Cena,** DQ | | |

1479	July 20	Sarnia, Ontario	★★★
L	**John Cena,** pin		

1480	July 21	Detroit	★★★1/4
L	**John Cena (Vengeance),** roll-up		

1481	July 22	Flint, MI	★★3/4
L	**Edge,** spear		

1482	July 23	Indianapolis	★★★★1/2
L	**Edge,** spear		

1483	July 27	Jonesboro, AR	★★★
L	**Tag with Kurt Angle vs. John Cena & Edge,** DDT		

1484	July 28	Little Rock, AR	★★★
L	**Edge,** spear		

AUGUST 2002

1485	Aug. 04	Pittsburgh	★★★1/4
L	**Rob Van Dam,** splash		

1486	Aug. 05	Baltimore	★★★1/2
L	**Rob Van Dam,** splash		

1487	Aug. 10	Melbourne, Australia	★★★★
L	**Edge,** roll-up		

1488	Aug. 12	Seattle	★★★
W	**Tag with Big Show vs. Ric Flair & Bubba Ray Dudley,** Walls of Jericho		

1489	Aug. 24	Trenton, NJ	★★★1/2
L	**Rob Van Dam,** splash		

1490	Aug. 25	Uniondale, NY	★★★
L	**Ric Flair (Summer Slam),** figure-four		

1491	Aug. 26	New York City	★★3/4
L	**Jeff Hardy,** DQ		

1492	Aug. 30	Lincoln, NE	★★★★
W	**Bubba Ray Dudley,** Walls of Jericho		

1493	Aug. 31	Springfield, IL	★★★
W	**Bubba Ray Dudley,** Walls of Jericho		

1494	Sept. 01	Chicago	★★1/2
W	**Bubba Ray Dudley,** Walls of Jericho		

1495	Sept. 02	Milwaukee	★★1/2
L	**Tag with Triple H vs. Ric Flair & Rob Van Dam,** Triple H		

1496	Sept. 07	Rapid City, SD	★★★
L	**Rob Van Dam,** splash		

1497	Sept. 08	Cedar Rapids, IA	★★★
W	**Bubba Ray Dudley,** Walls of Jericho		

1498	Sept. 09	Ames, IA	★★★
L	**4-way elimination vs. Jeff Hardy vs. Big Show vs. Rob Van Dam,** splash		

1499	Sept. 13	St. Louis	★★1/2
W	**Ric Flair (street fight),** Walls of Jericho		

1500	Sept. 14	Casper, WY	★★★
W	**Ric Flair (street fight),** Walls of Jericho		

1501	Sept. 15	Laramie, WY	★★
W	**Ric Flair,** Walls of Jericho		

1502	Sept. 16	Denver	★★★1/2
W	**Rob Van Dam (won WWE Intercontinental title/5th time),** Walls of Jericho		

1503	Sept. 21	Fresno, CA	★★3/4
W	**Rob Van Dam,** Walls of Jericho		

1504	Sept. 22	Los Angeles	★★3/4
W	**Ric Flair (Unforgiven),** Walls of Jericho		

1505	Sept. 23	Anaheim, CA	★★3/4
W	**Goldust,** Walls of Jericho		

1506	Sept. 29	Beaumont, TX	★★★
W	**Booker T,** belt shot		

1507	Sept. 30	Houston	★★★★
L	**Kane (lost WWE Intercontinental title),** chokeslam		

1508	Oct. 05	Sacramento, CA	★★★
W	**Jeff Hardy,** Walls of Jericho		

1509	Oct. 06	Reno, NV	★★★1/4
W	**Jeff Hardy,** Walls of Jericho		

1510	Oct. 07	Las Vegas	★★★★★
L	**4-way with Christian vs. Bubba Ray & Spike Dudley vs. Jeff Hardy & Rob Van Dam vs. Kane (no partner/Tables, Ladders & Chairs),** Kane		

1511	Oct. 12	Edmonton, Alberta	★★★
W	**Matt Hardy,** Walls of Jericho		

1512	Oct. 13	Calgary, Alberta	★★★★
L	**Brock Lesnar,** F-5		

1513	Oct. 14	Montreal	★★★
W	**Tag with Christian vs. Kane & Hurricane Helms (won WWE tag-team titles/3rd time),** roll-up		

IN THEIR WORDS: SHANE HELMS (AKA THE HURRICANE)

The highest-profile match that involved Chris Jericho and The Hurricane was proba-bly when Jericho and Christian (that sumbitch) won the WWE World Tag Team Cham-pionship by defeating myself and the "Big Red Machine" Kane (#1513). However, the Hurricane/Jericho encounter that stands out the most to me was a match on WWE's Sunday Night Heat (#1593). These TV tapings were being held in Halifax, Nova Scotia, and therein lies the trickery. Canadian fans are the most fiercely loyal fans in the entire world. Anytime a Canadian wrestler performs on a show, the Canadian audience is gen-erally fully behind this wrestler (yes, even Christian) and it doesn't matter if that wrestler is a babyface or a heel.

This gets tricky for TV because if you see a character that is supposed to be loved and admired and now they're being booed out of the building, that makes it hard to tell the story you're trying to tell. You would see some of the most popular names in the history of our industry get vilified in Canada. Guys like "Stone Cold" Steve Austin, The Rock, and The Undertaker all felt the nationalistic heat of going against a Canadian while on location in the Great White North.

WWE Creative LOVED to put The Hurricane against a Canadian whenever we were in Canada. I know they loved it because they did it A LOT. This wasn't easy for me because there isn't a babyface character in the business that needs a villain more than a super-hero. If I don't have a villain as a foil, who am I? Typically, in these situations, most guys simply resign themselves to the fact that the American babyface is gonna get booed, and the Canadian heel is gonna get cheered (even Christian). They either switch roles or just ignore the crowd reaction. But on this night, Chris and I were convinced that we could turn the crowd.

We were wrong.

Chris was the first Canadian to perform on this show that night. To say that the deck was stacked against The Hurricane would be to imply that there was a deck. There was no deck. This was a fiery Chris Jericho performance and The Hurricane was caught in the flames!

But we still tried. Oh, how hard we tried! And to be fair, the fans were kinder to me than they would have been to any other babyface in that position. But they effing LOVED Chris Jericho! They cheered every teeny-tiny thing he did. He told them to "shut up," they cheered. He poked my eyes, pulled my hair, and hit me in the balls, and they cheered. He even went so far as to choke me with his wrist tape, something so old-school that I don't recall it ever happening in a WWE ring before or since! And what did these Halifax natives do? You guessed it — they cheered him on even more!

The finish was my favorite part. Chris, being the professional that he is, wanted his baby-face to look great, even in defeat. He was meant to get me in the Walls of Jericho, and I, the valiant superhero, would struggle bravely to crawl to the ropes. But just as I got centimeters away from the ropes, he would foil that escape attempt and drag me back to the middle of the ring. We were going to do that twice, and finally, once the Walls were sunk in deep on that third application, the mighty Hurricane would tap to his dastardly foe.

And I know what's going through your head right now; you're thinking that we turned that crowd around, right? Nope! That shit wasn't happening and we knew it. I knew it, Chris knew it, the referee knew it. Even Christian knew it and he wasn't even watching, that sumbitch. Chris got me in the Walls, and before he even had that shit on for two seconds, I said "Fuck this" and tapped! Chris giggled and said, "Good call." That crowd wanted to see Chris Jericho make me submit. That night Jericho was the hero, and Shane Helms was caught in the path of a Y2J hurricane.

| 1514 | Oct. 19 | Texarkana, AR | ★★3/4 |

W   **Tag with Christian vs. Booker T & Goldust,** belt shot

| 1515 | Oct. 20 | Little Rock, AR | ★★★ |

W   **Tag with Christian vs. Booker T & Goldust (No Mercy),** moonsault

IN THEIR WORDS: **DUSTIN RHODES**
MATCH 1515 (OCT. 20, 2002)

The middle rope broke, so we kind of just went through the motions and continued, but it was a really good match and people were going crazy. Jericho is one of the greatest wrestlers as far as his technical abilities in the ring, and I've loved to watch him grow and change characters and evolve over the years — kind of like myself. It's very impressive to see what he has become after 30 years of being in the business and doing so much and now giving back and teaching these kids how he was taught and them actually listening and learning and utilizing the information in their matches. They're following what he's saying and accomplishing these great things. The older generation like Chris and me, that's the payoff for us. We enjoy that when you teach the kids something, they go out and do it and see how it goes over. It makes us feel good.

1516	Oct. 21	Nashville, TN	★★★1/4
W	**6-person with Victoria & Christian vs. Goldust, Booker T & Trish Stratus,** Walls of Jericho		

1517	Oct. 25	Topeka, KS	★★1/2
W	**Tag with Christian vs. Bubba Ray Dudley & Jeff Hardy,** lionsault		

1518	Oct. 26	Wichita, KS	★★★
W	**Tag with Christian vs. Bubba Ray Dudley & Jeff Hardy,** lionsault		

1519	Oct. 27	Toledo, OH	★★★1/4
W	**Tag with Christian vs. Bubba Ray Dudley & Jeff Hardy,** lionsault		

1520	Oct. 28	Detroit	★★★3/4
W	**Tag with Christian vs. Bubba Ray Dudley & Jeff Hardy,** lionsault		

NOVEMBER 2002

1521	Nov. 01	Springfield, MA	★★
W	**Tag with Christian vs. Bubba Ray Dudley & Jeff Hardy,** bulldog		

1522	Nov. 02	Halifax, Nova Scotia	★★★
W	**Tag with Christian vs. Bubba Ray Dudley & Jeff Hardy,** lionsault		

1523	Nov. 03	Moncton, New Brunswick	★★
W	**Tag with Christian vs. Bubba Ray Dudley & Jeff Hardy,** pin		

1524	Nov. 04	Boston	★★1/4
L	**Tag with Triple H vs. Kane & Booker T,** Triple H		

1525	Nov. 04	Boston	★1/2
W	**10-man with Christian, Triple H, Rosey & Jamal vs. Bubba Ray Dudley, Jeff Hardy, Kane, Booker T & Rob Van Dam,** Triple H		

1526	Nov. 09	Philadelphia	★★3/4
W	**Tag with Christian vs. Bubba Ray Dudley & Booker T,** pinned Bubba/lionsault		

1527	Nov. 10	Hershey, PA	★★1/2
W	**Tag with Christian vs. Bubba Ray Dudley & Booker T,** Walls of Jericho		

| 1528 | Nov. 11 | Cincinnati | ★★★★ |

L   **Tag with Christian vs. Kane & Rob Van Dam,** DQ

| 1529 | Nov. 16 | Reading, PA | ★★★ |

W   **Tag with Christian vs. Booker T & Goldust,** lionsault

| 1530 | Nov. 17 | New York City | ★★★1/2 |

L   **6-way vs. Shawn Michaels vs. Triple H vs. Booker T vs. Rob Van Dam vs. Kane (Elimination Chamber/Survivor Series),** Michaels/superkick

| 1531 | Nov. 18 | Bridgeport, CT | ★★★ |

L   **3-way vs. Booker T vs. Rob Van Dam (no DQ),** pinned by Van Dam/splash

| 1532 | Nov. 21 | New Dehli, India | ★★★ |

W   **Tag with Christian vs. Booker T & Goldust,** lionsault

| 1533 | Nov. 22 | Mumbai, India | ★★★1/4 |

W   **Tag with Christian vs. Rob Van Dam & Jeff Hardy,** lionsault

| 1534 | Nov. 23 | Bangalore, India | ★★★ |

L   **Kane,** chokeslam

| 1535 | Nov. 25 | Charleston, SC | ★★★1/4 |

W   **Tag with Christian vs. The Dudley Boyz,** submitted Bubba Ray/Walls of Jericho

| 1536 | Nov. 30 | Amarillo, TX | ★★★1/2 |

W   **Tag with Christian vs. The Dudley Boyz,** lionsault

DECEMBER 2002

| 1537 | Dec. 01 | Laredo, TX | ★★★★ |

W   **Tag with Christian vs. Booker T & Goldust,** lionsault

| 1538 | Dec. 02 | Austin, TX | ★★★1/2 |

NC   **Booker T,** NO CONTEST

| 1539 | Dec. 02 | Austin, TX | ★★★★ |

W   **Tag with Christian vs. Booker T & Goldust,** pinned Booker T/lionsault

| 1540 | Dec. 08 | Chattanooga, TN | ★★3/4 |

L   **Tag with Christian vs. Test & Booker T,** book-end

| 1541 | Dec. 09 | Knoxville, TN | ★★3/4 |

L   **6-person tag with Christian & Victoria vs. The Dudley Boyz & Trish Stratus,** Victoria pinned/ table

| 1542 | Dec. 13 | Norfolk, VA | ★★★★ |

W **Test,** breakdown

| 1543 | Dec. 14 | Ft. Myers, FL | ★★3/4 |

W **Test,** breakdown

| 1544 | Dec. 15 | Fort Lauderdale, FL | ★★★1/4 |

L **4-way with Christian vs. Booker T & Goldust vs. The Dudley Boyz vs. Lance Storm & William Regal (lost WWE tag-team titles/Armageddon),** book-end

| 1545 | Dec. 16 | Orlando, FL | ★★3/4 |

NC **Booker T,** NO CONTEST

| 1546 | Dec. 21 | Oklahoma City | ★★★1/2 |

L **Tag with Christian vs. Booker T & Goldust,** pinned by Goldust/roll-up

JANUARY 2003

| 1547 | Jan. 02 | Honolulu | ★★3/4 |

L **Tag with Christian vs. Booker T & Goldust,** Christian pinned

| 1548 | Jan. 03 | Honolulu | ★★★ |

L **Booker T,** book-end

| 1549 | Jan. 04 | Anaheim, CA | ★★★ |

L **Booker T,** roll-up

| 1550 | Jan. 05 | Colorado Springs, CO | ★★3/4 |

L **Booker T,** roll-up

| 1551 | Jan. 06 | Phoenix | ★★3/4 |

L **Tag with Christian vs. Rob Van Dam & Kane,** Christian pinned

| 1552 | Jan. 07 | El Paso, TX | ★★★ |

L **Tag with Christian vs. Kane & Booker T,** Christian pinned

| 1553 | Jan. 13 | Uncasville, CT | ★★1/2 |

W **4-way vs. Rob Van Dam vs. Kane vs. Batista (over-the-top-rope challenge),** Van Dam

| 1554 | Jan. 19 | Boston | ★★★1/2 |

L **Royal Rumble,** Eliminated by Test after 39:00

| 1555 | Jan. 20 | Providence, RI | ★★★ |

NC **Test (hit Stacy Keibler with a chair),** NO CONTEST

| 1556 | Jan. 23 | Seoul, South Korea | ★★★1/4 |

W **Tajiri,** Walls of Jericho

| 1557 | Jan. 24 | Tokyo | ★★★★ |

L **Tajiri,** kick

| 1558 | Jan. 25 | Tokyo | ★★★★ |

W **Rob Van Dam,** Walls of Jericho

| 1559 | Jan. 31 | Minneapolis | ★★3/4 |

W **Test,** breakdown

FEBRUARY 2003

| 1560 | Feb. 01 | New York City | ★★★ |

W **Test,** breakdown

| 1561 | Feb. 02 | Binghamton, NY | ★★★1/4 |

W **Test,** breakdown

| 1562 | Feb. 03 | Washington, D.C. | ★★ |

L **Scott Steiner,** second-rope fall-away slam

| 1563 | Feb. 07 | Houston | ★★1/2 |

W **Test,** breakdown

| 1564 | Feb. 08 | Fresno, CA | ★★1/2 |

W **Test,** breakdown

| 1565 | Feb. 09 | San Diego | ★★★1/2 |

W **Test,** breakdown

| 1566 | Feb. 10 | Los Angeles | ★★★ |

W **Jeff Hardy,** roll-up

| 1567 | Feb. 15 | Winnipeg, Manitoba | ★★★★ |

L **Kurt Angle,** roll-up

| 1568 | Feb. 16 | Detroit | ★★★ |

L **Tag with Christian vs. Rikishi & Rey Mysterio Jr.,** Christian pinned

| 1569 | Feb. 17 | Columbus, OH | ★★★ |

L **Tag with Christian vs. Shawn Michaels & Jeff Hardy (no DQ),** pinned by Hardy/swanton

| 1570 | Feb. 23 | Montreal | ★★★1/2 |

W **Jeff Hardy (No Way Out),** Walls of Jericho

| 1571 | Feb. 24 | Toronto | ★★1/2 |
| **L** | **Mixed tag with Christian vs. Test & Stacy Keibler,** DQ | | |

| 1572 | Feb. 24 | Toronto | ★★ |
| **L** | **No. 1 contender Battle Royal,** Booker T | | |

MARCH 2003

| 1573 | Mar. 01 | Reading, PA | ★★1/2 |
| **W** | **Test,** roll-up | | |

| 1574 | Mar. 02 | Rochester, NY | ★★★ |
| **W** | **Test,** roll-up | | |

| 1575 | Mar. 03 | Uniondale, NY | ★★★ |
| **W** | **Test,** breakdown | | |

| 1576 | Mar. 08 | East Lansing, MI | ★★★1/2 |
| **L** | **Test,** boot | | |

| 1577 | Mar. 09 | Dayton, OH | ★★★ |
| **W** | **Test,** breakdown | | |

| 1578 | Mar. 10 | Cleveland | ★★★ |
| **W** | **Tag with Christian vs. Kane & Rob Van Dam,** lionsault | | |

| 1579 | Mar. 15 | Lincoln, NE | ★★3/4 |
| **W** | **Test,** Walls of Jericho | | |

| 1580 | Mar. 16 | Columbia, MO | ★★★★ |
| **W** | **Test,** Walls of Jericho | | |

| 1581 | Mar. 17 | St. Louis | ★★★1/2 |
| **W** | **Tag with Christian vs. Scott Steiner & Test,** roll-up | | |

| 1582 | Mar. 30 | Seattle | ★★★★★ |
| **L** | **Shawn Michaels (WrestleMania 19),** roll-up | | |

MATCH NOTES #1582

This match did something that had only been done 18 times before: stole the show at WrestleMania. This was the first time HBK and I had ever stepped in the ring, and it was magic. Best part was we put the whole thing together in only about 30 minutes. Shawn showed up with the idea for the start of the match and I showed up with the idea for the end. The rest is history.

| 1583 | Mar. 31 | Seattle | ★★★ |

L **Booker T,** DQ

| 1584 | Apr. 07 | Milwaukee | ★★1/2 |

L **Tag with Triple H vs. Shawn Michaels & Booker T,** Triple H

| 1585 | Apr. 12 | Roanoke, VA | ★★★ |

L **6-man with Triple H & Ric Flair vs. Shawn Michaels, Booker T & Kevin Nash,** Triple H

| 1586 | Apr. 13 | Charlottesville, VA | ★★1/2 |

L **6-man with Triple H & Ric Flair vs. Shawn Michaels, Booker T & Kevin Nash,** Triple H

| 1587 | Apr. 14 | Richmond, VA | ★★★ |

W **Test,** lionsault

| 1588 | Apr. 21 | Atlanta | ★★★1/4 |

W **Hurricane Helms,** Walls of Jericho

| 1589 | Apr. 26 | Portland, ME | ★★★1/4 |

W **Test,** Walls of Jericho

| 1590 | Apr. 27 | Worcester, MA | ★ |

L **6-man with Triple H & Ric Flair vs. Shawn Michaels, Booker T & Kevin Nash
(Backlash),** Triple H

| 1591 | May 03 | Kitchener, Ontario | ★★★3/4 |

L **Test (street fight),** boot

| 1592 | May 04 | Ottawa, Ontario | ★★★1/2 |

W **Test (street fight),** Walls of Jericho

| 1593 | May 05 | Halifax, Nova Scotia | ★★★ |

W **Hurricane Helms,** Walls of Jericho

| 1594 | May 10 | Newark, NJ | ★★★ |

L **Hurricane Helms,** chokeslam

| 1595 | May 12 | Philadelphia | ★★3/4 |

L **Kevin Nash,** DQ

| 1596 | May 18 | Charlotte, NC | ★★ |

L **Intercontinental title battle royal (Judgment Day),** Eliminated by Christian/Christian won

| 1597 | May 19 | Greenville, SC | ★★★ |

L   Tag with Christian vs. Kane & Rob Van Dam, DQ

| 1598 | June 02 | San Diego | ★★ |

L   Tag with Christian vs. Booker T & Goldust, Christian pinned

| 1599 | June 06 | Nottingham, England | ★★ |

L   Tag with Triple H vs. Kevin Nash & Scott Steiner, Triple H pinned

| 1600 | June 15 | Houston | ★★★ |

L   Goldberg (Bad Blood), jackhammer

JIM ROSS MEMORY

Walking in on a locker room dustup between Chris and Bill Goldberg in 2003 was eye-opening to say the least. Chris' relentless front face lock held his much bigger and stronger adversary at bay until we were able to separate the two. Chris earned significant respect from his peers after standing up to the formidable Goldberg.

| 1601 | June 16 | Dallas | ★★★1/4 |

L   Tag with Christian vs. Goldberg & Booker T, Christian pinned

| 1602 | June 21 | Hartford, CT | ★★★ |

W   Val Venis, Walls of Jericho

| 1603 | June 23 | New York City | ★★★1/4 |

L   Tag with Lance Storm vs. The Dudley Boyz, Storm

| 1604 | June 30 | Buffalo, NY | ★★3/4 |

W   Mixed tag with Test vs. Scott Steiner & Stacy Keibler (no DQ), Test

| 1605 | July 07 | Montreal | ★★1/2 |

W   Mark Jindrak, Walls of Jericho

| 1606 | July 21 | Los Angeles | ★★★★1/2 |

W   Shawn Michaels, Walls of Jericho

| 1607 | July 25 | Louisville, KY | ★★★★ |

W   Johnny Jeter, Walls of Jericho

| 1608 | July 28 | Colorado Springs, CO | ★★1/2 |

L   Kevin Nash, DQ

| 1609 | July 31 | Melbourne, Australia | ★★★ |

L   **Tag with Randy Orton vs. Shawn Michaels & Kevin Nash,** pinned by Michaels/superkick

AUGUST 2003

| 1610 | Aug. 01 | Sydney | ★★★ |

W   **Tag with Christian vs. Booker T & Goldust,** pinned Booker T/belt shot

| 1611 | Aug. 02 | Sydney | ★★★1/2 |

L   **Booker T,** book-end

| 1612 | Aug. 04 | Vancouver, British Columbia | ★★★★ |

L   **Rob Van Dam,** split-legged moonsault

| 1613 | Aug. 18 | Grand Rapids, MI | ★★★★ |

W   **Kevin Nash (hair vs. hair),** brass knuckles

| 1614 | Aug. 24 | Phoenix | ★★★1/2 |

L   **6-way vs. Shawn Michaels vs. Goldberg vs. Triple H vs. Kevin Nash vs. Randy Orton (Elimination Chamber/Summer Slam),** Goldberg/spear

| 1615 | Aug. 25 | Tuscon, AZ | ★★1/2 |

NC   **Shane McMahon,** NO CONTEST

SEPTEMBER 2003

| 1616 | Sept. 01 | Lafayette, LA | ★★★ |

L   **Christian,** roll-up

| 1617 | Sept. 05 | Tallahassee, FL | ★★★1/2 |

W   **Ric Flair,** Walls of Jericho

| 1618 | Sept. 06 | Savannah, GA | ★★★ |

W   **Ric Flair,** Walls of Jericho

| 1619 | Sept. 07 | Chattanooga, TN | ★★★1/4 |

L   **3-way vs. Christian vs. Maven,** Maven

| 1620 | Sept. 12 | Nashville, TN | ★★★1/4 |

L   **3-way vs. Christian vs. Val Venis,** Venis pinned

| 1621 | Sept. 13 | Knoxville, TN | ★★★ |

L   **3-way vs. Christian vs. Val Venis,** Venis pinned

| 1622 | Sept. 14 | Asheville, NC | ★★★ |

L   **3-way vs. Christian vs. Val Venis,** Venis pinned

| 1623 | Sept. 15 | Columbia, SC | ★★1/2 |

NC **Rob Van Dam,** NO CONTEST

| 1624 | Sept. 21 | Hershey, PA | ★★★ |

L **3-way vs. Christian vs. Rob Van Dam (Unforgiven),** Van Dam

| 1625 | Sept. 22 | Washington, D.C. | ★★★★ |

L **Goldberg,** spear

OCTOBER 2003

| 1626 | Oct. 06 | Uncasville, CT | ★★★1/2 |

L **Tag with Christian vs. Rob Van Dam & Lance Storm,** pinned by Storm/springboard dropkick

| 1627 | Oct. 10 | Louisville, KY | ★★1/2 |

L **6-man with Christian & Test vs. Rob Van Dam, Shane McMahon & Lance Storm (street fight),** Test

| 1628 | Oct. 11 | Norfolk, VA | ★★★1/2 |

L **8-man with Christian & La Resistance vs. The Dudley Boyz, Shane McMahon & Booker T (table match),** Rob Conway pinned

| 1629 | Oct. 12 | Wheeling, WV | ★★1/2 |

L **8-man with Christian & La Resistance vs. The Dudley Boyz, Shane McMahon & Booker T (table match),** Rob Conway pinned

| 1630 | Oct. 13 | Pittsburgh | ★★★ |

L **8-man with Christian & La Resistance vs. The Dudley Boyz, Shane McMahon & Booker T (table match),** Rob Conway pinned

| 1631 | Oct. 19 | Portland, ME | ★★★1/4 |

L **Tag with Scott Steiner vs. Booker T & Maven,** Booker pinned Steiner

| 1632 | Oct. 20 | Wilkes-Barre, PA | ★★★ |

W **Tag with Scott Steiner vs. Lance Storm & Rob Van Dam,** Van Dam

| 1633 | Oct. 26 | Columbia, SC | ★★★ |

L **Rob Van Dam**

| 1634 | Oct. 27 | Fayetteville, NC | ★★1/2 |

W **Rob Van Dam (won WWE Intercontinental title/6th time),** Walls of Jericho

| 1635 | Oct. 27 | Fayetteville, NC | ★★★ |

L **Rob Van Dam (lost WWE Intercontinental title/cage match),** escape

| 1636 | Nov. 01 | Toledo, OH | ★★★ |

L   **Rob Van Dam,** splash

| 1637 | Nov. 02 | Columbus, OH | ★★★ |

L   **Rob Van Dam,** splash

| 1638 | Nov. 03 | Cleveland | ★★★ |

W   **Tag with Christian vs. Booker T & Rob Van Dam,** breakdown

| 1639 | Nov. 07 | Toronto | ★★★ |

L   **6-man with Christian & Mark Henry vs. The Dudley Boyz & Rob Van Dam,** 3-D

IN THEIR WORDS: ALLIE

Back before I started wrestling training, I waited in line for two hours to meet Chris at a signing in the Toronto area. I was 17 at the time, and I remember wanting to tell him that I was going to start wrestling training after my 18th birthday but I was far too nervous. I wish I had the picture!! It's pretty fucking cool that I work with him now. I don't think 17-year-old me would have believed me if I told her.

| 1640 | Nov. 08 | Springfield, MA | ★★ |

L   **8-man with Christian, Scott Steiner & Mark Henry vs. The Dudley Boyz, Booker T & Rob Van Dam,** Booker pinned Christian

| 1641 | Nov. 09 | Burlington, VT | ★★★1/2 |

L   **8-man with Christian, Scott Steiner & Mark Henry vs. The Dudley Boyz, Booker T & Rob Van Dam,** Booker pinned Christian

| 1642 | Nov. 10 | Boston | ★1/2 |

L   **Booker T,** roll-up

| 1643 | Nov. 16 | Dallas | ★★★★ |

W   **10-man tag with Christian, Scott Steiner, Mark Henry & Randy Orton vs. Shawn Michaels, The Dudley Boyz, Rob Van Dam & Booker T (elimination match/Survivor Series),** Orton

| 1644 | Nov. 21 | Detroit | ★★1/2 |

W   **Maven,** Walls of Jericho

| 1645 | Nov. 22 | Tacoma, WA | ★★★ |

L   **Tag with Christian vs. The Dudley Boyz,** 3-D

| 1646 | Nov. 23 | Yakima, WA | ★★★ |

W   **Maven,** Walls of Jericho

1647	Nov. 24	Salt Lake City	★★

W   **Tag with Triple H vs. Ric Flair & Batista,** Michaels

1648	Nov. 28	Las Vegas	★★1/2

L   **3-way vs. Christian vs. Rob Van Dam,** Van Dam pinned Christian

1649	Nov. 29	San Francisco	★★★

L   **3-way vs. Christian vs. Rob Van Dam,** Van Dam pinned Christian

1650	Nov. 30	Bakersfield, CA	★★★1/2

L   **4-way vs. Christian vs. Rob Van Dam vs. Randy Orton,** Van Dam

DECEMBER 2003

1651	Dec. 01	Sacramento, CA	★★★1/4

W   **Mixed tag with Trish Stratus vs. Rico Constantino & Jackie Gayda,** Stratus

1652	Dec. 02	Las Vegas	★★★

NC   **Rey Mysterio Jr.,** NO CONTEST

1653	Dec. 04	Las Vegas	★★★

L   **Mixed tag with Victoria vs. Rey Mysterio Jr. & Trish Stratus (Spike TV video game award show)**

1654	Dec. 07	Fresno, CA	★★

L   **Tag with Christian vs. The Dudley Boyz (tables match),** table

1655	Dec. 08	Anaheim, CA	★★★

L   **Tag with Christian vs. The Dudley Boyz,** 3-D

1656	Dec. 12	New York City	★★★

L   **Tag with Christian vs. The Dudley Boyz (tables match),** table

1657	Dec. 13	West Palm Beach, FL	★★★

L   **Tag with Christian vs. The Dudley Boyz,** 3-D

1658	Dec. 14	Orlando, FL	★★★1/2

W   **Mixed tag with Christian vs. Trish Stratus & Lita (Armageddon),** roll-up

1659	Dec. 15	Tampa, FL	★★★

NC   **Mixed tag with Christian vs. Trish Stratus & Lita,** NO CONTEST

1660	Dec. 15	Tampa, FL	★★3/4

L   **Kane,** DQ

| 1661 | Jan. 03 | Jackson, MS | ★★★ |
| **L** | **Kane,** chokeslam | | |

| 1662 | Jan. 04 | Tupelo, MS | ★★★ |
| **L** | **Kane,** DQ | | |

| 1663 | Jan. 05 | Memphis, TN | ★★1/2 |
| **W** | **Tag with Christian vs. Rosey & Hurricane Helms,** Christian | | |

| 1664 | Jan. 09 | Oshawa, Ontario | ★★★ |
| **W** | **Kane,** roll-up | | |

| 1665 | Jan. 10 | Halifax, Nova Scotia | ★★★1/4 |
| **W** | **Kane,** roll-up | | |

| 1666 | Jan. 11 | St. John's, Newfoundland | ★★★ |
| **W** | **Kane,** roll-up | | |

| 1667 | Jan. 12 | Uniondale, NY | ★★★ |
| **L** | **Mark Henry,** slam | | |

| 1668 | Jan. 16 | Des Moines, IA | ★★1/2 |
| **W** | **Mark Henry,** roll-up | | |

| 1669 | Jan. 17 | Madison, WI | ★★★ |
| **W** | **Mark Henry,** roll-up | | |

| 1670 | Jan. 18 | Milwaukee | ★★★ |
| **W** | **Mixed tag with Trish Stratus vs. Mark Henry & Jazz,** roll-up | | |

| 1671 | Jan. 19 | Green Bay, WI | ★★★ |
| **W** | **Rene Dupree,** Walls of Jericho | | |

| 1672 | Jan. 19 | Green Bay, WI | ★★1/2 |
| **L** | **Over-the-top-rope challenge,** Orton/Henry | | |

| 1673 | Jan. 25 | Philadelphia | ★★1/2 |
| **L** | **Royal Rumble,** Eliminated by Big Show after 14:58 | | |

| 1674 | Jan. 26 | Hershey, PA | ★★1/2 |
| **L** | **3-on-2 handicap with Rob Van Dam vs. Randy Orton, Batista & Ric Flair,** pinned by Batista | | |

| 1675 | Jan. 31 | Dayton, OH | ★★★ |
| **W** | **Kane,** roll-up | | |

1676	Feb. 01	Youngstown, OH	★★★
W	**Christian,** Walls of Jericho		

1677	Feb. 02	State College, PA	★★
L	**Tag with Christian vs. Ric Flair & Batista,** figure-four		

1678	Feb. 05	Hiroshima, Japan	★★★1/2
W	**Christian,** Walls of Jericho		

1679	Feb. 06	Osaka, Japan	★★★★
L	**Randy Orton,** RKO		

1680	Feb. 07	Tokyo	★★★★1/2
L	**Chris Benoit,** cross-face		

1681	Feb. 09	Portland, OR	★★★
W	**Mixed tag with Trish Stratus vs. Matt Hardy & Molly Holly,** Stratus		

1682	Feb. 16	Bakersfield, CA	★★
NC	**Kane,** NO CONTEST		

1683	Feb. 21	Springfield, IL	★★★
L	**Kane,** DQ		

1684	Feb. 22	Valparaiso, IN	★★
W	**Kane,** DQ		

1685	Feb. 28	Birmingham, AL	★★★
W	**Christian,** Walls of Jericho		

1686	Feb. 29	Chattanooga, TN	★★★
W	**Christian,** small package		

MARCH 2004

1687	Mar. 05	Syracuse, NY	★★★
W	**Christian,** Walls of Jericho		

1688	Mar. 06	Elmira, NY	★★★
W	**Christian,** Walls of Jericho		

1689	Mar. 07	Baltimore	★★★
W	**Christian,** Walls of Jericho		

1690	Mar. 08	Bridgeport, CT	★★
L	**Stevie Richards,** small package		

1691	Mar. 14	New York City	★★★★
L	**Christian (WrestleMania 20),** roll-up		

1692	Mar. 15	East Rutherford, NJ	★★
L	**Matt Hardy,** DQ		

1693	Mar. 21	Fort Wayne, IN	★★★1/2
L	**Christian,** roll-up		

1694	Mar. 22	Detroit	★★
W	**Rene Dupree,** enziguri		

1695	Mar. 27	Cape Girardeau, MO	★★★
L	**Christian,** roll-up		

1696	Mar. 28	St. Louis	★★★1/2
L	**Christian,** roll-up		

APRIL 2004

1697	Apr. 02	Hidalgo, TX	★★★1/4
L	**Christian,** roll-up		

1698	Apr. 03	Monterrey, Mexico	★★★
W	**Christian,** Walls of Jericho		

1699	Apr. 04	Laredo, TX	★★★
W	**Christian,** Walls of Jericho		

1700	Apr. 05	Houston	★★★
W	**Matt Hardy,** Walls of Jericho		

1701	Apr. 10	Saginaw, MI	★★★
W	**Christian,** Walls of Jericho		

1702	Apr. 11	Peoria, IL	★★★
W	**Christian,** Walls of Jericho		

1703	Apr. 18	Edmonton, Alberta	★★★1/2
W	**2-on-1 handicap vs. Christian & Trish Stratus (Backlash),** enziguri		

1704	Apr. 19	Calgary, Alberta	★★★★
L	**Christian,** pin		

| 1705 | Apr. 23 | St. Paul, MN | ★★★ |
| **W** | **Christian (no DQ),** Walls of Jericho | | |

| 1706 | Apr. 24 | Kansas City, MO | ★★1/2 |
| **L** | **Christian,** pin | | |

| 1707 | Apr. 25 | Wichita, KS | ★★1/2 |
| **L** | **Christian (no DQ),** pin | | |

MAY 2004

| 1708 | May 01 | Lubbock, TX | ★★★ |
| **W** | **Christian,** Walls of Jericho | | |

| 1709 | May 02 | Yuma, AZ | ★★★1/4 |
| **W** | **Christian,** Walls of Jericho | | |

| 1710 | May 09 | Fresno, CA | ★★1/2 |
| **W** | **Christian (cage match),** escaped | | |

| 1711 | May 10 | San Jose, CA | ★★1/2 |
| **W** | **Christian (cage match),** Walls of Jericho | | |

| 1712 | May 15 | Spokane, WA | ★★★1/4 |
| **W** | **Tyson Tomko (cage match),** escaped | | |

| 1713 | May 16 | Everett, WA | ★★1/2 |
| **W** | **Tyson Tomko (cage match),** escaped | | |

| 1714 | May 17 | San Diego | ★★ |
| **L** | **18-man battle royal,** eliminated | | |

| 1715 | May 22 | Philadelphia | ★★ |
| **W** | **Tyson Tomko (cage match),** escaped | | |

| 1716 | May 23 | Moline, IL | ★★1/2 |
| **W** | **Tyson Tomko (cage match),** escaped | | |

| 1717 | May 24 | Rockford, IL | ★★★ |
| **W** | **Tag with Shelton Benjamin vs. Randy Orton & Batista,** Benjamin | | |

| 1718 | May 26 | Dublin | ★★1/2 |
| **W** | **Tyson Tomko (no DQ),** enziguri | | |

| 1719 | May 27 | Dublin | ★★★★ |
| **W** | **6-man with Edge & Shawn Michaels vs. Batista, Randy Orton & Ric Flair,** Michaels pinned Orton | | |

| 1720 | May 28 | Manchester, England | DUD |
| **W** | **Tyson Tomko (no DQ),** enziguri | | |

| 1721 | May 29 | Birmingham, England | ★★★ |
| **W** | **Tag with Eugene vs. Lance Cade & Johnny Nitro,** Walls of Jericho | | |

JUNE 2004

| 1722 | June 05 | Boston | ★★★ |
| **W** | **Tyson Tomko (no holds barred),** Walls of Jericho | | |

| 1723 | June 06 | Rochester, NY | ★★1/2 |
| **W** | **Tyson Tomko (no DQ),** Walls of Jericho | | |

| 1724 | June 07 | Albany, NY | ★★1/2 |
| **W** | **A-Train,** Walls of Jericho | | |

| 1725 | June 13 | Columbus, OH | ★★★ |
| **W** | **Tyson Tomko (Bad Blood),** enziguri | | |

| 1726 | June 14 | Dayton, OH | ★★★1/4 |
| **W** | **6-man with Edge & Chris Benoit vs. Batista, Randy Orton & Ric Flair (elimination match)** | | |

| 1727 | June 18 | Spartanburg, SC | ★★★★ |
| **W** | **Batista,** enziguri | | |

| 1728 | June 19 | Charleston, SC | ★★★ |
| **W** | **Batista,** enziguri | | |

| 1729 | June 20 | Ft. Myers, FL | ★★3/4 |
| **W** | **Batista,** enziguri | | |

| 1730 | June 21 | Miami | ★★★ |
| **L** | **Tag with Edge vs. Batista & Randy Orton,** Batista | | |

| 1731 | June 24 | New York City | ★★★1/2 |
| **W** | **Batista,** roll-up | | |

| 1732 | June 25 | Salisbury, MD | ★★1/2 |
| **W** | **Batista,** roll-up | | |

| 1733 | June 26 | Richmond, VA | ★★★ |
| W | **Tag with Edge vs. Batista & Randy Orton,** lionsault | | |

| 1734 | July 05 | Winnipeg, Manitoba | ★★★★ |
| L | **Randy Orton,** roll-up | | |

| 1735 | July 11 | Hartford, CT | ★★ |
| L | **Batista (Vengeance),** powerbomb | | |

| 1736 | July 12 | Manchester, England | ★★1/2 |
| W | **Kane,** DQ | | |

| 1737 | July 16 | Wilkes-Barre, PA | ★★★ |
| W | **Kane,** roll-up | | |

| 1738 | July 17 | Reading, PA | ★★★ |
| W | **Kane,** roll-up | | |

MY TOP 13 FAVORITE ARENAS

- MGM Grand, Las Vegas
- O2 Arena, London
- Madison Square Garden, New York City
- Tokyo Dome, Tokyo
- Korakuen Hall, Tokyo
- ECW Arena (now 2300 Arena), Philadelphia
- Arena México, Mexico City
- Arena Coliseo, Mexico City
- Rod Laver Arena, Melbourne, Australia
- Winnipeg Arena, Winnipeg, Manitoba
- Scottrade Center (now Enterprise Center), St. Louis
- (tie) Rosemont Horizon (now Allstate Arena)
  and Sears Centre (now NOW Arena), Chicago

| 1739 | July 18 | Frederick, VA | ★★ |
| W | **Batista,** roll-up | | |

| 1740 | July 19 | Washington, D.C. | ★★★1/4 |
| L | **Kane (falls count anywhere),** pinned | | |

1741	July 24	Erie, PA	★★★
W	**Kane,** roll-up		

1742	July 25	Wheeling, WV	★★
W	**Kane,** roll-up		

1743	July 26	Pittsburgh	★★★1/2
L	**No. 1 contender Battle Royal,** Orton		

1744	July 30	Albuquerque, NM	★1/2
L	**3-way vs. Edge vs. Batista,** Edge/spear		

1745	July 31	Austin, TX	★★★1/2
W	**Batista,** roll-up		

AUGUST 2004

1746	Aug. 01	Corpus Christi, TX	★★
L	**3-way vs. Edge vs. Batista,** Edge/spear		

1747	Aug. 02	San Antonio	★★★1/4
L	**6-man with Edge & Chris Benoit vs. Batista, Randy Orton & Ric Flair,** Orton pinned Benoit		

1748	Aug. 07	Trenton, NJ	★★1/2
L	**3-way vs. Edge vs. Batista,** Edge/spear		

1749	Aug. 08	Toledo, OH	★★1/2
L	**3-way vs. Edge vs. Batista,** Edge/spear		

1750	Aug. 09	Cleveland	★★★★
W	**Edge,** roll-up		

1751	Aug. 15	Toronto	★★★
L	**3-way vs. Edge vs. Batista (Summer Slam),** Edge/spear		

1752	Aug. 16	London, Ontario	★★★1/2
W	**Batista,** DQ		

1753	Aug. 20	Bismark, ND	★★★
L	**Edge,** roll-up		

1754	Aug. 21	Fargo, ND	★★★
L	**Edge,** roll-up		

1755	Aug. 22	Palm Springs, CA	★★★
L	**Edge,** roll-up		

| 1756 | Aug. 23 | Anaheim, CA | ★★1/2 |
| **W** | **Edge,** DQ | | |

| 1757 | Aug. 28 | Salt Lake City | ★ |
| **W** | **Edge,** countout | | |

| 1758 | Aug. 29 | Stockton, CA | ★★★★ |
| **W** | **Kane,** roll-up | | |

| 1759 | Aug. 30 | San Francisco | ★★★1/2 |
| **W** | **Stevie Richards,** Walls of Jericho | | |

SEPTEMBER 2004

| 1760 | Sept. 06 | Wichita Falls, TX | ★1/2 |
| **L** | **Tyson Tomko,** problem solver | | |

| 1761 | Sept. 12 | Portland, OR | ★★★1/2 |
| **W** | **Christian (won WWE Intercontinental title/7th time – ladder match/Unforgiven)** | | |

| 1762 | Sept. 13 | Seattle | ★★★★ |
| **W** | **Tag with Shawn Michaels vs. Christian & Tyson Tomko,** Michaels pinned Tomko | | |

| 1763 | Sept. 17 | Bossier City, LA | ★★★ |
| **W** | **Christian,** DQ | | |

Talking shit ringside, complete with the Intercontinental Title and Eddie Van Halen tights.

1764	Sept. 17	Bossier City, LA	★★★

W   **Tag with Hurricane Helms vs. Christian & Tyson Tomko,** submitted Tomko/Walls of Jericho

1765	Sept. 18	Waco, TX	★★★

W   **Christian,** Walls of Jericho

1766	Sept. 19	Tyler, TX	★★★1/2

W   **Christian,** Walls of Jericho

1767	Sept. 20	Tuscon, AZ	★★★1/2

NC   **Shawn Michaels,** NO CONTEST

1768	Sept. 27	Kansas City, MO	★★1/2

W   **Tag with Shawn Michaels vs. Christian & Tyson Tomko,** Michaels pinned Tomko

OCTOBER 2004

1769	Oct. 01	Portland, ME	★★★

W   **Christian,** Walls of Jericho

1770	Oct. 02	Burlington, VT	★★★1/2

W   **Christian,** Walls of Jericho

1771	Oct. 03	Binghamton, NY	★★★

W   **Christian,** Walls of Jericho

1772	Oct. 04	New York City	★★★1/4

L   **Triple H (lumberjack match)**

1773	Oct. 06	Helsinki	★★★

W   **3-way vs. Edge vs. Christian**

1774	Oct. 07	Sheffield, England	★★

W   **Tag with Triple H vs. Christian & Tyson Tomko**

1775	Oct. 08	London	★★★★

W   **3-way vs. Edge vs. Christian**

1776	Oct. 09	Frankfurt, Germany	★★★

W   **Tag with Triple H vs. Christian & Tyson Tomko**

1777	Oct. 10	Cardiff, Wales	★★★1/2

W   **3-way vs. Edge vs. Christian**

1778	Oct. 11	Manchester, England	★★1/2

NC   **Rhyno,** NO CONTEST

One word to describe this picture: intensity.

| 1779 | Oct. 11 | Manchester, England | ★★★ |

W   **Tag with Rhyno vs. Christian & Tyson Tomko**

| 1780 | Oct. 18 | Chicago | ★★★ |

L   **Tag with Randy Orton vs. Ric Flair & Batista**

| 1781 | Oct. 19 | Milwaukee | ★★★★ |

L   **Shelton Benjamin (lost WWE Intercontinental title/Taboo Tuesday),** T-bone suplex

---

| 1782 | Oct. 22 | Green Bay, WI | ★★★ |

W   **6-man with Randy Orton & Chris Benoit vs. Ric Flair, Triple H & Batista**
W   Orton

| 1783 | Oct. 23 | Madison, WI | ★★★ |

W   **6-man with Randy Orton & Chris Benoit vs. Ric Flair, Triple H & Batista,** Orton

---

| 1784 | Oct. 24 | Cedar Rapids, IA | ★★★ |

W   **6-man with Randy Orton & Chris Benoit vs. Ric Flair, Triple H & Batista,** Orton

---

| 1785 | Oct. 25 | Des Moines, IA | ★★★1/2 |

L   **Shelton Benjamin,** roll-up

| 1786 | Nov. 01 | Peoria, IL | ★★★ |

W   **6-man with Maven & Randy Orton vs. Batista & Ric Flair & Triple H (Triple H no-showed),** Orton pinned Batista

| 1787 | Nov. 05 | Laredo, TX | ★★★ |

W   **Tag with Randy Orton vs. Triple H & Batista (cage match),** Orton

| 1788 | Nov. 06 | Monterrey, Mexico | ★★3/4 |

W   **Tag with Randy Orton vs. Triple H & Batista (cage match),** Orton

| 1789 | Nov. 07 | Hidalgo, TX | ★★★1/4 |

W   **Tag with Randy Orton vs. Triple H & Batista (cage match),** Orton

| 1790 | Nov. 14 | Cleveland | ★★★ |

W   **8-man with Randy Orton, Chris Benoit & Maven vs. Triple H, Batitsa, Edge & Snitsky (elimination match/Survivor Series),** Orton

| 1791 | Nov. 15 | Indianapolis | ★★1/2 |

W   **Stevie Richards,** DQ

| 1792 | Nov. 19 | Detroit | ★★1/2 |

W   **Tag with Randy Orton vs. Triple H & Batista,** Orton

| 1793 | Nov. 20 | Kingston, Ontario | ★ |

W   **Tag with Randy Orton vs. Triple H & Batista,** Orton

| 1794 | Nov. 21 | Barrie, Ontario | ★★★ |

W   **Tag with Randy Orton vs. Triple H & Batista,** Orton

| 1795 | Nov. 22 | Buffalo, NY | ★★★ |

W   **Batista,** DQ

| 1796 | Nov. 26 | Hershey, PA | ★★ |

W   **6-man with Randy Orton & Chris Benoit vs. Edge, Triple H & Batista,** Orton

| 1797 | Nov. 27 | Philadelphia | ★★★ |

W   **Tag with Randy Orton vs. Triple H & Batista,** Orton

| 1798 | Nov. 28 | Bethlehem, PA | ★★★ |

W   **Tag with Randy Orton vs. Triple H & Batista,** Orton

1799	Nov. 29	Baltimore	★★★1/4
L	**No. 1 contenders Battle Royal,** Edge-Chris Benoit		

DECEMBER 2004

1800	Dec. 03	Augusta, GA	★★★
W	**Tag with Randy Orton vs. Triple H & Batista,** Orton		

1801	Dec. 04	Savannah, GA	★★1/2
W	**Tag with Randy Orton vs. Triple H & Batista,** Orton		

1802	Dec. 05	Asheville, NC	★★★
W	**Tag with Randy Orton vs. Triple H & Batista,** Orton		

1803	Dec. 06	Charlotte, NC	★★★
W	**Tag with Randy Orton vs. Triple H & Batista,** DQ		

1804	Dec. 10	Columbus, GA	★★1/2
L	**Snitsky**		

1805	Dec. 11	Macon, GA	★★3/4
L	**Snitsky**		

1806	Dec. 12	Chattanooga, TN	★★★
L	**Snitsky**		

1807	Dec. 13	Huntsville, AL	★★★1/4
L	**Tag with Chris Benoit vs. Triple H & Batista,** Batista pinned Benoit		

1808	Dec. 27	Biloxi, MS	★★★1/2
W	**Christian (beat the clock challenge),** Walls of Jericho		

1809	Dec. 28	Phoenix	★★★
L	**Batista (last man standing)**		

1810	Dec. 29	El Paso, TX	★★★
L	**Batista (last man standing)**		

JANUARY 2005

1811	Jan. 03	Uniondale, NY	★★★
L	**Edge**		

1812	Jan. 04	Poughkeepsie, NY	★★★
L	**Batista (knockout match)**		

| 1813 | Jan. 05 | Wilkes-Barre, PA | ★★★ |
| **L** | **Batista (last man standing)** | | |

1814	Jan. 09	San Juan, Puerto Rico	★★★★
	6-way vs. Edge vs. Chris Benoit vs. Triple H vs. Randy Orton vs. Batista (Elimination		
	Chamber/New Year's Revolution)		
L	Triple H		

| 1815 | Jan. 10 | Fort Lauderdale, FL | ★★★ |
| **W** | **Tag with Chris Benoit vs. Christian & Tyson Tomko,** Walls of Jericho | | |

| 1816 | Jan. 10 | Fort Lauderdale, FL | ★ |
| **L** | **6-man with Chris Benoit & Randy Orton vs. Triple H, Batista & Edge,** Batista | | |

| 1817 | Jan. 14 | Minneapolis | ★★★ |
| **L** | **Muhammad Hassan,** roll-up | | |

| 1818 | Jan. 15 | Grand Forks, ND | ★★ |
| **L** | **Muhammad Hassan,** roll-up | | |

Matching beards and matching attitudes about the business. From one of the last times we worked together in 2005. I never had a bad match against Chris ... ever.

1819	Jan. 16	Winnipeg, Manitoba	★★★★

W   **Muhammad Hassan,** Walls of Jericho

1820	Jan. 17	Toronto	★★★1/2

W   **Chris Benoit,** roll-up

1821	Jan. 17	Toronto	★★1/2

W   **6-man with Chris Benoit & Randy Orton vs. Triple H, Batista & Edge,** Orton

1822	Jan. 22	Tyler, TX	★★★

L   **Batista (last man standing)**

1823	Jan. 23	Tulsa, OK	★★3/4

L   **Batista**

1824	Jan. 24	Oklahoma City	★★1/2

W   **6-man with Chris Benoit & Shawn Michaels vs. Edge, Christian & Tyson Tomko,** Benoit
beat Tomko

1825	Jan. 24	Oklahoma City	★★1/2

W   **6-man with Chris Benoit & Randy Orton vs. Triple H, Batista & Edge,** Orton

1826	Jan. 30	Fresno, CA	★★★

L   **Royal Rumble,** Eliminated by Batista after 28:22

1827	Jan. 31	San Jose, CA	★

NC   **Tag with Chris Benoit vs. La Resistance,** NO CONTEST

FEBRUARY 2005

1828	Feb. 01	Honolulu	★★★1/2

L   **Battle Royal,** Benoit

1829	Feb. 04	Saitama, Japan	★★★1/2

L   **Chris Benoit (submission match),** cross-face

1830	Feb. 05	Seoul, South Korea	★★★★

L   **Muhammad Hassan,** roll-up

1831	Feb. 06	Anchorage, AK	★★★

L   **Battle Royal,** Benoit

1832	Feb. 14	Cincinnati	★★★

L   **Muhammad Hassan**

| 1833 | Feb. 18 | Cadillac, MI | ★★★ |
| **L** | **Muhammad Hassan** | | |

| 1834 | Feb. 19 | Kalamazoo, MI | ★★★ |
| **L** | **Muhammad Hassan** | | |

| 1835 | Feb. 20 | Erie, PA | ★★1/2 |
| **L** | **Muhammad Hassan** | | |

| 1836 | Feb. 21 | State College, PA | ★★1/2 |
| **W** | **Simon Dean,** Walls of Jericho | | |

| 1837 | Feb. 25 | New York City | ★★★★ |
| **L** | **Chris Benoit (submission match),** cross-face | | |

| 1838 | Feb. 26 | Springfield, MA | ★★★ |
| **L** | **Chris Benoit (submission match),** cross-face | | |

| 1839 | Feb. 28 | Providence, RI | ★★★ |
| **W** | **Maven,** Walls of Jericho | | |

MARCH 2005

| 1840 | Mar. 04 | Corpus Christi, TX | ★★★ |
| **W** | **Christian,** Walls of Jericho | | |

| 1841 | Mar. 05 | Greensboro, NC | ★★★ |
| **W** | **Christian,** Walls of Jericho | | |

| 1842 | Mar. 06 | Norfolk, VA | ★★★1/2 |
| **W** | **Christian,** Walls of Jericho | | |

| 1843 | Mar. 07 | Raleigh, NC | ★★★1/4 |
| **L** | **Edge,** DDT | | |

| 1844 | Mar. 12 | Mobile, AL | ★★★ |
| **W** | **Christian,** Walls of Jericho | | |

| 1845 | Mar. 13 | Dotham, AL | ★★★ |
| **W** | **Christian,** Walls of Jericho | | |

| 1846 | Mar. 19 | Greenville, SC | ★★3/4 |
| **L** | **Muhammad Hassan,** roll-up | | |

| 1847 | Mar. 20 | Columbia, SC | ★★★1/2 |
| **W** | **Edge,** Walls of Jericho | | |

| 1848 | Mar. 21 | Birmingham, AL | ★★★1/2 |

L **Tag with Shelton Benjamin vs. Edge & Christian,** Benjamin

| 1849 | Mar. 28 | Ft. Worth, TX | ★★★★ |

W **6-man with Shelton Benjamin & Chris Benoit vs. Edge, Christian & Tyson Tomko,**
Walls of Jericho

APRIL 2005

| 1850 | Apr. 03 | Los Angeles | ★★★★ |

L **6-way match vs. Edge vs. Chris Benoit vs. Christian vs. Kane vs.**
Shelton Benjamin (Money In the Bank ladder match/WrestleMania 21), Edge

| 1851 | Apr. 04 | Los Angeles | ★★★1/2 |

L **3-way vs. Christian vs. Shelton Benjamin,** Benjamin

| 1852 | Apr. 07 | Melbourne, Australia | ★★★ |

L **Muhammad Hassan,** roll-up

| 1853 | Apr. 08 | Newcastle, Australia | ★★3/4 |

W **6-man with Chris Benoit & Batista vs. Edge, Triple H & Ric Flair,** Batista

| 1854 | Apr. 09 | Sydney | ★★★1/4 |

L **Muhammad Hassan,** roll-up

| 1855 | Apr. 20 | Berlin | ★★★ |

L **3-way vs. Christian vs. Shelton Benjamin,** Benjamin

| 1856 | Apr. 21 | Aberdeen, Scotland | ★★★ |

W **Tyson Tomko,** Walls of Jericho

| 1857 | Apr. 22 | Edinburgh, Scotland | ★★★★ |

L **3-way vs. Christian vs. Shelton Benjamin,** Benjamin

| 1858 | Apr. 23 | Newcastle, England | ★★★1/4 |

W **Tyson Tomko,** Walls of Jericho

| 1859 | Apr. 24 | Hull, England | ★★★ |

L **Shelton Benjamin,** T-bone suplex

| 1860 | Apr. 25 | Birmingham, England | ★★1/2 |

W **Sylvain Grenier,** Walls of Jericho

| 1861 | May 01 | Manchester, NH | ★★★★ |

L **Shelton Benjamin (Backlash),** roll-up

| 1862 | May 02 | Boston | ★★ |

L **Edge,** spear

| 1863 | May 09 | Wilkes-Barre, PA | ★★3/4 |

W **Daivari,** Walls of Jericho

| 1864 | May 13 | Evansville, IN | ★★1/2 |

W **Tag with Shelton Benjamin vs. Muhammad Hassan & Daivari,** Walls of Jericho

| 1865 | May 14 | Terre Haute, IN | ★★ |

W **Tag with Shelton Benjamin vs. Muhammad Hassan & Daivari,** Walls of Jericho

| 1866 | May 15 | Ft. Wayne, IN | ★★★ |

W **Tag with Shelton Benjamin vs. Muhammad Hassan & Daivari,** Walls of Jericho

| 1867 | May 16 | Omaha, NE | ★★★ |

L **Tag with Shelton Benjamin vs. Muhammad Hassan & Daivari,** pinned by Hassan/spiral

| 1868 | May 20 | Albuquerque, NM | ★★★ |

W **Muhammad Hassan,** Walls of Jericho

| 1869 | May 21 | Loveland, CO | ★★★1/2 |

L **Muhammad Hassan,** spiral

| 1870 | May 22 | Colorado Springs, CO | ★★3/4 |

W **Christian,** Walls of Jericho

| 1871 | May 23 | Green Bay, WI | ★★1/4 |

W **Sylvain Grenier,** Walls of Jericho

| 1872 | May 27 | Tacoma, WA | ★★★1/2 |

W **Muhammad Hassan (Roddy Piper in corner),** Walls of Jericho

| 1873 | May 28 | Vancouver, British Columbia | ★★1/2 |

W **Muhammad Hassan (Roddy Piper in corner),** Walls of Jericho

| 1874 | May 29 | Victoria, British Columbia | ★★★ |

W **Muhammad Hassan (Roddy Piper in corner),** Walls of Jericho

| 1875 | May 30 | Calgary, Alberta | ★★★ |

W **Simon Dean,** Walls of Jericho

| 1876 | June 03 | Huntington, WV | ★★1/2 |
| **L** | **Muhammad Hassan,** pinfall | | |

| 1877 | June 04 | Dayton, OH | ★★★ |
| **L** | **Muhammad Hassan,** pinfall | | |

| 1878 | June 05 | Rockford, IL | ★★★ |
| **L** | **Muhammad Hassan,** pinfall | | |

| 1879 | June 12 | New York City | ★★★1/2 |
| **L** | **Lance Storm (One Night Stand),** pinfall | | |

Pancaking Lance off the top rope at ECW One Night Only in 2005. It was the last match we ever had and one of our best, even though I've never watched it back. That's because I'm still sulking that they only gave us seven minutes. What an insult!

| 1880 | June 13 | Binghamton, NY | ★ |
| **W** | **Tag with John Cena vs. Christian & Tyson Tomko,** Cena | | |

| 1881 | June 17 | Portland, OR | ★★★★ |
| **L** | **3-way vs. Christian vs. Shelton Benjamin,** Benjamin | | |

| 1882 | June 18 | Boise, ID | ★★★ |

L   **3-way vs. Christian vs. Shelton Benjamin,** Benjamin

| 1883 | June 26 | Las Vegas | ★★★★ |

L   **3-way vs. John Cena vs. Christian (Vengeance),** Cena

| 1884 | June 27 | Anaheim, CA | ★★★ |

L   **6-man with Tyson Tomko & Christian vs. Hulk Hogan, Shawn Michaels & John Cena,** Hogan
pinned Tomko

| 1885 | June 30 | Seoul, South Korea | ★★★ |

W   **Shelton Benjamin,** Walls of Jericho

Summer Slam 2005 vs. Cena, the last match before my two-and-a-half year sabbatical from
the business. At least it was supposed to be, until Vince decided last minute that he wanted a
rematch "Loser Gets Fired" the next night on RAW, even though my contract expired that day.
After a 20-minute telephone argument with him, I finally agreed ... for a double payoff. Just
another day at the office.

1886	July 01	Tokyo	★★★★
W	**Shelton Benjamin,** Walls of Jericho		

1887	July 02	Tokyo	★★★★1/2
L	**Shawn Michaels,** superkick		

1888	July 23	Utica, NY	★★★
L	**John Cena,** FU		

1889	July 24	Watertown, NY	★★★
L	**John Cena,** FU		

1890	Aug. 08	Pittsburgh	★★
W	**Chad Patton,** Walls of Jericho		

1891	Aug. 13	Kingston, Ontario	★★★
W	**Snitsky,** Walls of Jericho		

1892	Aug. 14	Ottawa, Ontario	★★★1/4
W	**Snitsky,** Walls of Jericho		

1893	Aug. 15	Montreal	★★★1/4
L	**2-on-1 handicap with Carlito vs. John Cena,** Carlito		

1894	Aug. 21	Washington, D.C.	★★★★1/4
L	**John Cena (Summer Slam),** FU		

1895	Aug. 22	Hampton, VA	★★★★
L	**John Cena (loser leaves town),** FU		

WWE ACT 2

NOV. 26, 2007 - SEP. 20, 2010

MATCHES 1896 - 2324

| 1896 | Nov. 26 | Charlotte, NC | ★★★ |

W Santino Marella (first match in 823 days — 2 years, 3 months, 1 day), codebreaker

MATCH NOTES #1896

This was a strange match for me. I literally hadn't worked in years, wasn't sure who I was as a character, and was in the ring against Santino — who, even though he is one of my all-time favorite WWE characters, wasn't known for his prowess in the ring. But the match was fine, preceded by a super-entertaining promo (Santana? Sandusky? San Luis Obispo?) and ended with the debut of my new Codebreaker finish, so it served its purpose.

DECEMBER 2007

| 1897 | Dec. 03 | Charleston, SC | ★★★ |

W Umaga, DQ

| 1898 | Dec. 07 | Camp Speicher, Iraq | ★★★1/2 |

W Randy Orton (Tribute to the Troops), DQ

| 1899 | Dec. 16 | Pittsburgh | ★★★3/4 |

W Randy Orton (Armageddon), DQ

| 1900 | Dec. 17 | Buffalo, NY | ★★★ |

W Randy Orton, DQ

| 1901 | Dec. 26 | Nashville, TN | ★★★1/2 |

W Randy Orton, DQ

| 1902 | Dec. 27 | Chattanooga, TN | ★★★1/2 |

W Randy Orton, DQ

| 1903 | Dec. 28 | Atlanta | ★★★★ |

W Randy Orton, DQ

| 1904 | Dec. 29 | Greensboro, NC | ★★★ |

W Tag with Jeff Hardy vs. Randy Orton & JBL, Hardy

JANUARY 2008

| 1905 | Jan. 07 | Uncasville, CT | ★★ |

W Snitsky, DQ

| 1906 | Jan. 20 | Binghamton, NY | ★★1/2 |

W JBL, countout

| 1907 | Jan. 26 | Providence, RI | ★★★1/4 |

W   **Tag with Jeff Hardy vs. Randy Orton & JBL,** Hardy

| 1908 | Jan. 27 | New York City | ★★3/4 |

L   **JBL (Royal Rumble),** DQ

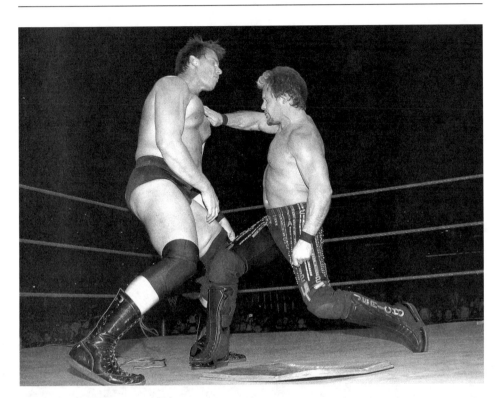

Chopping meat with JBL at the Royal Rumble 2007 in MSG. Not a great match, but I ended up covered in blood, which enabled me to freak out a bunch of fans backstage afterward.

| 1909 | Jan. 28 | Philadelphia | ★★★ |

L   **Tag with Jeff Hardy vs. Randy Orton & JBL,** pinned by Orton/RKO

FEBRUARY 2008

| 1910 | Feb. 04 | Austin, TX | ★★★ |

W   **6-man with Jeff Hardy & Shawn Michaels vs. JBL, Umaga & Snitsky,** Hardy

| 1911 | Feb. 04 | Austin, TX | ★★3/4 |

W   **JBL,** codebreaker

1912	Feb. 06	Fairbanks, AK	★★★

W **Tag with John Cena vs. Randy Orton & Umaga,** Cena

1913	Feb. 07	Anchorage, AK	★★

W **Kennedy,** Walls of Jericho

1914	Feb. 07	Anchorage, AK	★★

L **Battle Royal,** John Cena

With JBL in Japan in 1995. John and I became friends when he came to WAR as "Death Mask" and thankfully that relationship spared me his razzing and wrath when I came to WWE in 1999.

1915	Feb. 09	Seoul, South Korea	★★★

W **Tag with Shawn Michaels vs. Randy Orton & Umaga,** Michaels

1916	Feb. 10	Tokyo	★★★★1/2

L **Randy Orton,** RKO

1917	Feb. 11	Tokyo	★★★★

W **Kennedy,** Walls of Jericho

| 1918 | Feb. 11 | Tokyo | ★★ |
| **L** | **Battle Royal,** Jeff Hardy | | |

| 1919 | Feb. 13 | Honolulu | ★★★3/4 |
| **L** | **Randy Orton,** RKO | | |

| 1920 | Feb. 16 | Los Angeles | ★★★ |
| **W** | **JBL (street fight),** codebreaker | | |

| 1921 | Feb. 17 | Las Vegas | ★★★★ |
| **L** | **6-way vs. Triple H vs. Shawn Michaels vs. JBL vs. Umaga vs. Jeff Hardy (Elimination Chamber/No Way Out),** Hardy | | |

| 1922 | Feb. 25 | Phoenix | ★★★★ |
| **W** | **Jeff Hardy,** roll-up | | |

| 1923 | Feb. 29 | Cape Girardeau, MO | ★1/2 |
| **W** | **Kennedy,** Walls of Jericho | | |

MARCH 2008

| 1924 | Mar. 01 | Louisville, KY | ★★1/2 |
| **W** | **Kennedy,** Walls of Jericho | | |

| 1925 | Mar. 02 | Danville, IL | ★★1/2 |
| **W** | **Kennedy,** Walls of Jericho | | |

| 1926 | Mar. 08 | Madison, WI | ★★★ |
| **L** | **Randy Orton (street fight),** RKO | | |

| 1927 | Mar. 09 | Green Bay, WI | ★★★1/2 |
| **L** | **Randy Orton (street fight),** RKO | | |

| 1928 | Mar. 10 | Milwaukee | ★★★★1/4 |
| **W** | **Jeff Hardy (won WWE Intercontinental title/8th time),** codebreaker | | |

| 1929 | Mar. 17 | Lafayette, LA | ★★★★ |
| **L** | **Big Show,** DQ | | |

| 1930 | Mar. 24 | Columbia, SC | ★★ |
| **L** | **Tag with CM Punk vs. MVP & Carlito,** Punk | | |

| 1931 | Mar. 25 | Fayetteville, NC | ★★★1/2 |
| **NC** | **MVP,** NO CONTEST | | |

MY TOP 10 FINISHING MOVES

• WALLS OF JERICHO
Triple H wanted me to call this the Standing Torture Device — or the STD — when I first arrived in WWE.

• CODEBREAKER
Such a perfect and timely name for a finish, as I started using it after I did the "Can You Break the Code?" vignettes for my 2007 WWE comeback.

• JUDAS EFFECT
When I started in AEW, I wanted a finish I could use on everybody that nobody would ever, or hadn't ever, kicked out of. I came up with this during a kickboxing workout.

• LIONSAULT
Luther came up with this idea, and I started practicing it in an empty Arena México on a bag of dirty laundry.

• BREAKDOWN
I beat The Rock for the WCW World title with this move — I should use it again!

• TOP-ROPE DROPKICK
My original finish in WCW.

• CLOTHESLINE
I used it only once in WAR in Japan with an opponent named Okamura, who I didn't like (#510).

• FRONT FLIP OFF THE TOP ROPE
Trust me, it was inventive and daring in 1992!

• THE DREADED KICK TO THE BALLS/HEAD INTO THE EXPOSED TURNBUCKLE/ROLL-UP WITH THE FEET ON THE ROPES
When I was trying to think of a way to cheat to beat The Rock and retain the Undisputed Title at Royal Rumble 2002 (#1398), I decided to combine all three of these dastardly moves to win.

• SHAWN MICHAELS SUPERKICK
I won my sixth WWE World title from The Undertaker by pinning him directly after an HBK run-in (#2235).

| 1932 | Mar. 30 | Orlando, FL | ★★★★1/2 |

L 7-way vs. Carlito vs. MVP vs. John Morrison vs. CM Punk vs. Shelton Benjamin vs. Kennedy (Money In the Bank ladder match/WrestleMania 24), Punk

| 1933 | Mar. 31 | Orlando, FL | ★★★★ |

W CM Punk, codebreaker

APRIL 2008

| 1934 | Apr. 10 | Belfast, Ireland | ★★★1/2 |

W Umaga, codebreaker

| 1935 | Apr. 11 | Liverpool, England | ★★3/4 |

W Tag with Triple H vs. Umaga & Snitsky, Triple H

| 1936 | Apr. 12 | Cardiff, Wales | ★★★★ |

W Tag with Triple H vs. Randy Orton & Umaga, Triple H

| 1937 | Apr. 13 | Nottingham, England | ★★★1/2 |

W Tag with CM Punk vs. Umaga & Snitsky, pinned Snitsky/codebreaker

| 1938 | Apr. 14 | London | ★★★1/2 |

W Umaga, roll-up

| 1939 | Apr. 16 | Vienna | ★★★1/2 |

W JBL, codebreaker

| 1940 | Apr. 17 | Granada, Spain | ★★★1/2 |

W JBL, codebreaker

| 1941 | Apr. 18 | A Coruna, Spain | ★★★★1/2 |

W Tag with Triple H vs. Randy Orton & Umaga

| 1942 | Apr. 19 | Lisbon, Portugal | ★★★3/4 |

W Tag with Triple H vs. Randy Orton & Umaga

| 1943 | Apr. 21 | Greenville, SC | ★★★ |

W MVP, Walls of Jericho

| 1944 | Apr. 21 | Greenville, SC | ★★★1/4 |

L CM Punk, GTS

MAY 2008

| 1945 | May 02 | Montreal | ★★★ |

W Snitsky, codebreaker

1946	May 03	Hamilton, Ontario	★★1/2
W	**Tag with Kennedy vs. William Regal & Snitsky,** codebreaker		

1947	May 04	London, Ontario	★★★1/2
W	**Tag with Triple H vs. Randy Orton & Snitsky,** Triple H		

1948	May 05	Toronto	★★1/2
W	**Tag with Shawn Michaels vs. Miz & John Morrison,** pinned Morrison/lionsault		

1949	May 05	Toronto	★★★
W	**Randy Orton,** codebreaker		

1950	May 09	Saginaw, MI	★★★
W	**Tag with Shawn Michaels vs. JBL & William Regal,** codebreaker		

1951	May 10	Kalamazoo, MI	★★★1/4
W	**Tag with Shawn Mchaels vs. JBL & Umaga,** codebreaker		

1952	May 18	Omaha, NE	★★★★1/2
L	**Shawn Michaels (Judgment Day),** roll-up		

1953	May 19	Kansas City, MO	★★★★
L	**Batista,** powerbomb		

1954	May 21	Monterrey, Mexico	★★1/2
W	**Jeff Hardy,** codebreaker		

1955	May 22	Queretaro, Mexico	★★★★
L	**Shawn Michaels**		

1956	May 23	Mexico City	★★★★
L	**Shawn Michaels**		

1957	May 24	Mexico City	★★3/4
W	**Lance Cade,** Walls of Jericho		

1958	May 26	Denver	★★★1/2
DC	**Shawn Michaels,** DOUBLE COUNTOUT		

JUNE 2008

1959	June 02	Bakersfield, CA	★★
W	**JBL,** DQ		

1960	June 08	Stockton, CA	★★★★
W	**Jeff Hardy,** codebreaker		

MY TOP 10 WWE OPPONENTS

• THE ROCK

I was one of the few who could go toe to toe with Rock on the mic, and our matches were always built up perfectly because of it. My favorite backstage bit saw us creating our own "special handshake," that included Rock quacking like a duck and then shooting my "bird" out of the sky.

• EDGE

Working with him was always a pleasure, and he was one of the only rivals I've had who thought pretty much like me when putting together matches. Our contest at Wrestle-Mania 26 (#2248) is a forgotten classic.

• CHRISTIAN

Let me put it like this: at WWE Taboo Tuesday 2004, I had to wrestle one out of a 15 possible opponents depending on fan voting. I walked through the locker room asking everybody what their finish was and what moves they do, as I had no idea who was going to win the vote (it ended up being Shelton Benjamin #1781), and I wanted to have a basic plan for all the contenders. When I got to Christian, I said, "If you get voted in, let's just call it out there." Nothing but respect for Jay Reso.

• TRIPLE H

We didn't like each other much in the early 2000s, but that animosity led to some very intense matches.

• CHRIS BENOIT

Hard-hitting, physical, intense, Benoit always gave his all in every match he was in, and we had excellent chemistry.

• ROMAN REIGNS

My favorite in-ring rival during my last WWE run in 2016 and 2017. My favorite high spot was when he used his Superman Punch to knock me off the cage I was hanging on — which contained my best friend, Kevin Owens — as it rose in the air (#2660).

• REY MYSTERIO JR.

Rey and I finally had the classic rivalry I knew we were capable of in WWE in 2009. The finish at Extreme Rules that year (#2118), when I pulled off his mask during his 619 is one of my all-time favorites.

• STEVE AUSTIN

Steve had a very unorthodox style, but as long as you could hang on to the tail of the dragon, he was a great opponent.

• THE UNDERTAKER

We didn't have a ton of matches, but the ones we did (including our 4-star classic [#2191] on a *SmackDown* taping in Sheffield, England, that I was super-hungover for) were everything I could've asked for from the best big-man worker in wrestling history.

• SHAWN MICHAELS

Still the greatest of all time in my opinion, and I think my story line with him in 2008 is one of the best told and most intricate in WWE history.

1961 **L**	June 16 Triple H, DQ	Salt Lake City	★★★1/2
1962 **W**	June 21 Shawn Michaels, roll-up	Albuquerque, NM	★★★1/4
1963 **W**	June 22 Shawn Michaels, roll-up	Amarillo, TX	★★★
1964 **W**	June 27 Jeff Hardy, roll-up	Lubbock, TX	★★1/2
1965 **W**	June 28 Jeff Hardy, roll-up	Abilene, TX	★★★
1966 **L**	June 29 Kofi Kingston (lost WWE Intercontinental title/Night of Champions), double spin-kick	Dallas	★★3/4
1967 **L**	June 30 Kofi Kingston, DQ	Oklahoma City	★★
JULY 2008			
1968 **L**	July 02 Shawn Michaels	Santiago, Chile	★★★1/2
1969 **L**	July 03 Shawn Michaels	Lima, Peru	★★3/4
1970 **L**	July 04 Shawn Michaels	Panama City	★★★1/4

1971	July 05	San Salvador, El Salvador	★★★
L	**Shawn Michaels**		

1972	July 14	Raleigh, NC	★★1/2
W	**Paul London,** Walls of Jericho		

1973	July 20	Uniondale, NY	★★★★1/2
W	**Shawn Michaels (Great American Bash),** TKO		

1974	July 25	Youngstown, OH	★★1/2
L	**6-man with Ted DiBiase Jr. & Cody Rhodes vs. Cryme Time & John Cena,** Cena pinned DiBiase		

1975	July 26	Wheeling, WV	★★★★
L	**6-man with Ted DiBiase Jr. & Cody Rhodes vs. Cryme Time & John Cena,** Cena pinned DiBiase		

1976	July 27	Altoona, PA	★★★
L	**6-man with Ted DiBiase Jr. & Cody Rhodes vs. Cryme Time & John Cena,** Cena pinned DiBiase		

AUGUST 2008

1977	Aug. 01	Springfield, IL	★★1/2
L	**CM Punk,** GTS		

1978	Aug. 02	Evansville, IN	★★★3/4
L	**CM Punk,** GTS		

1979	Aug. 03	Bowling Green, KY	★★★
L	**CM Punk,** GTS		

1980	Aug. 04	Knoxville, TN	★★★★
W	**2-on-1 with JBL vs. CM Punk,** JBL pinned Punk		

1981	Aug. 08	Wildwood, NJ	★★★1/2
L	**6-man with Ted DiBiase Jr. & Cody Rhodes vs. Cryme Time & John Cena,** Cena pinned DiBiase		

1982	Aug. 09	Newark, DE	★★★
L	**6-man with Ted DiBiase Jr. & Cody Rhodes vs. Cryme Time & John Cena,** Cena pinned DiBiase		

1983	Aug. 10	Salisbury, MD	★★★
L	**CM Punk (no DQ),** GTS		

1984	Aug. 11	Richmond, VA	★★1/2
W	**Kane,** codebreaker		

1985	Aug. 18	Chicago	★★★
W	**CM Punk,** codebreaker		

1986	Aug. 22	Bridgeport, CT	★★1/2
L	**Tag with Kane vs. John Cena & Batista,** Kane		

1987	Aug. 23	New York City	★★★★1/2
L	**Tag with Kane vs. John Cena & Batista,** Kane		

1988	Aug. 24	Bethlehem, PA	★★★
L	**Tag with Kane vs. John Cena & Batista,** Kane		

SEPTEMBER 2008

1989	Sept. 07	Cleveland	★★★★1/2
L	**Shawn Michaels (unsanctioned match/Unforgiven),** KO		

1990	Sept. 07	Cleveland	★★1/2
W	**5-way vs. Batista vs. Kane vs. JBL vs. Rey Mysterio Jr. (won World Heavyweight Championship - scramble match/Unforgiven),** pinned Kane		

The last days of Y2J with the "Save Us" gimmick in 2007. The crowd still liked me, but their tolerance was wearing thin.

| 1991 | Sept. 08 | Ft. Wayne, IN | ★★1/2 |

W **2-on-1 handicap with JBL vs. Batista,** JBL

| 1992 | Sept. 12 | Texarkana, AR | ★★ |

W **3-way vs. JBL vs. Rey Mysterio Jr.,** JBL

| 1993 | Sept. 13 | Little Rock, AR | ★★1/2 |

W **3-way vs. JBL vs. Batista,** JBL

| 1994 | Sept. 14 | Jackson, TN | ★★1/2 |

W **3-way vs. JBL vs. Batista,** JBL

| 1995 | Sept. 15 | Memphis, TN | ★★★★ |

W **CM Punk (cage match)**

| 1996 | Sept. 22 | Cincinnati | ★★1/2 |

W **3-on-2 handicap with JBL & Lance Cade vs. Shawn Michaels & Batista,** Cade pinned Michaels

| 1997 | Sept. 24 | Bilbao, Spain | ★★3/4 |

L **Tag with Lance Cade vs. Shawn Michaels & CM Punk**

| 1998 | Sept. 25 | Madrid | ★★★ |

L **Tag with Lance Cade vs. Shawn Michaels & CM Punk**

| 1999 | Sept. 26 | Barcelona, Spain | ★★★1/4 |

L **Tag with Lance Cade vs. Shawn Michaels & CM Punk**

| 2000 | Sept. 27 | Paris | ★★★1/2 |

L **Tag with Lance Cade vs. Shawn Michaels & CM Punk**

| 2001 | Sept. 29 | Minneapolis | ★★★ |

L **Tag with Lance Cade vs. Shawn Michaels & Triple H,** Cade

| 2002 | Sept. 30 | Green Bay, WI | ★★★ |

L **3-way vs. Triple H vs. Matt Hardy**

IN THEIR WORDS: **MATT HARDY**

For me, this was really cool, and it was a big deal. It was a match with all three WWE brand champions. I don't want to say it was weird going in. Chris and I were friends and he was always the guy cool with everyone from top to bottom everywhere he worked so it was comfortable working with him. But Hunter was different. He was a little intimidating because he was such an important person of power. But Chris just made that match and night so easy and so fun.

2003   Oct. 05   Portland, OR   ★★★★★

W   **Shawn Michaels (ladder match/No Mercy)**

With Shawn Michaels after recording Talk Is Jericho in 2017. Both story lines I did with HBK in 2003 and 2008 are textbook examples of how to tell a riveting tale. As great as Shawn is inside the ring, he could be even better at putting together the details behind and the reasons for the matches. I loved collaborating with him!

2004   Oct. 06   Seattle   ★★★

L   **Tag with Kane vs. Rey Mysterio Jr. & Batista**

2005   Oct. 11   Reno, NV   ★★★

W   **Batista,** codebreaker

2006   Oct. 12   San Bernardino, CA   ★★★

W   **Batista,** codebreaker

2007   Oct. 13   Anaheim, CA   ★★★

L   **CM Punk (Batista referee)**

2008   Oct. 13   Anaheim, CA   ★★★

L   **Tag with Kane vs. Rey Mysterio Jr. & Batista**

2009   Oct. 16   Arecibo, Puerto Rico   ★★1/2

L   **Tag with JBL vs. Shawn Michaels & Batista**

2010   Oct. 17   Ponce, Puerto Rico   ★★★1/4

L   **Tag with JBL vs. Shawn Michaels & Batista**

2011	Oct. 18	San Juan, Puerto Rico	★★★★
W	**Shawn Michaels (no DQ)**		

2012	Oct. 20	Corpus Christi, TX	★★
W	**William Regal (gauntlet match),** codebreaker		

2013	Oct. 20	Corpus Christi, TX	★★
L	**Mark Henry (gauntlet match),** DQ		

2014	Oct. 20	Corpus Christi, TX	★★1/2
L	**Kane (gauntlet match),** big boot		

2015	Oct. 26	Phoenix	★★★1/4
L	**Batista (lost World Heavyweight Championship – Steve Austin guest referee/Cyber Sunday)**		

2016	Oct. 27	Tuscon, AZ	★★★
L	**Tag with JBL vs. Shawn Michaels & Batista,** JBL		

2017	Oct. 27	Tuscon, AZ	★★★
L	**Batista (cage match)**		

NOVEMBER 2008

2018	Nov. 03	Tampa, FL	★★★★1/4
W	**Batista (won World Heavyweight Championship/2nd time – cage match)**		

2019	Nov. 05	Mannheim, Germany	★★1/2
W	**Batista**		

2020	Nov. 06	Milan	★★3/4
L	**Tag with Randy Orton vs. Batista & CM Punk**		

2021	Nov. 07	Rome	★★★
L	**Tag with Randy Orton vs. Batista & CM Punk**		

2022	Nov. 08	Minehead, England	★★★
L	**Tag with Randy Orton vs. Batista & CM Punk**		

2023	Nov. 09	Sheffield, England	★★★★
W	**Batista**		

2024	Nov. 10	Manchester, England	★★★1/2
W	**Shawn Michaels (last man standing)**		

| 2025 | Nov. 11 | Birmingham, England | ★★★ |
| **W** | **Batista** | | |

| 2026 | Nov. 12 | Newcastle, England | ★★★ |
| **L** | **Tag with Randy Orton vs. Batista & Rey Mysterio Jr.** | | |

| 2027 | Nov. 13 | Belfast, Ireland | ★★★★ |
| **L** | **Tag with Randy Orton vs. Batista & Rey Mysterio Jr.** | | |

| 2028 | Nov. 14 | Glasgow, Scotland | ★★★1/2 |
| **L** | **Tag with Randy Orton vs. Batista & Rey Mysterio Jr.** | | |

| 2029 | Nov. 15 | Aberdeen, Scotland | ★★ |
| **W** | **3-way vs. JBL vs. Batista** | | |

| 2030 | Nov. 17 | Atlanta | ★★ |
| **W** | **3-way vs. JBL vs. Batista** | | |

| 2031 | Nov. 23 | Boston | ★★★1/2 |
| **L** | **John Cena (lost World Heavyweight Championship/Survivor Series)** | | |

| 2032 | Nov. 24 | Providence, RI | ★★★1/2 |
| **W** | **3-way vs. Randy Orton vs. Batista** | | |

| 2033 | Nov. 24 | Providence, RI | ★★★ |
| **L** | **John Cena** | | |

| 2034 | Nov. 30 | Reading, PA | ★★★1/4 |
| **L** | **John Cena** | | |

DECEMBER 2008

| 2035 | Dec. 01 | Washington, D.C. | ★★ |
| **L** | **Batista** | | |

| 2036 | Dec. 05 | Baghdad | ★★★★ |
| **L** | **6-man with Randy Orton & Big Show vs. John Cena, Rey Mysterio Jr. & Batista (Tribute to the Troops)** | | |

| 2037 | Dec. 08 | Philadelphia | ★★★1/2 |
| **W** | **Jeff Hardy** | | |

| 2038 | Dec. 13 | Hamilton, Ontario | ★★★1/2 |
| **L** | **John Cena** | | |

| 2039 | Dec. 14 | Buffalo, NY | ★★★★ |
| **L** | **John Cena (Armageddon)** | | |

The chicken wire cage gets stretched to the limit by Cena's fat head in MSG.

| 2040 | Dec. 15 | Pittsburgh | ★★★ |
| **L** | **John Cena (street fight)** | | |

| 2041 | Dec. 22 | Toronto | ★★★★1/4 |
| **W** | **CM Punk** | | |

| 2042 | Dec. 22 | Toronto | ★★★1/2 |
| **L** | **John Cena (street fight)** | | |

| 2043 | Dec. 26 | Hershey, PA | ★★★ |
| **L** | **John Cena** | | |

| 2044 | Dec. 27 | Trenton, NJ | ★★★1/2 |
| **L** | **John Cena** | | |

| 2045 | Dec. 28 | New York City | ★★★★★ |
| **L** | **John Cena (cage match)** | | |

| 2046 | Dec. 29 | Manchester, NH | ★★ |

L   **4-way vs. JBL vs. Shawn Michaels vs. Randy Orton**

| 2047 | Dec. 29 | Manchester, NH | ★★★1/2 |

L   **John Cena (street fight)**

JANUARY 2009

| 2048 | Jan. 05 | New Orleans | ★★★ |

L   **Tag with Randy Orton vs. John Cena & Shawn Michaels**

| 2049 | Jan. 05 | New Orleans | ★★★ |

L   **John Cena (street fight)**

| 2050 | Jan. 09 | Winnipeg, Manitoba | ★★★★★ |

L   **John Cena**

| 2051 | Jan. 10 | Rochester, MN | ★★★ |

L   **John Cena**

| 2052 | Jan. 11 | Des Moines, IA | ★★★1/2 |

L   **John Cena**

| 2053 | Jan. 19 | Chicago | ★★★3/4 |

L   **John Cena (street fight)**

| 2054 | Jan. 25 | Detroit | ★★★ |

L   **Royal Rumble,** Eliminated by Undertaker after 37:17

| 2055 | Jan. 26 | Cleveland | ★★ |

L   **CM Punk (street fight)**

| 2056 | Jan. 26 | Cleveland | ★★★1/2 |

L   **John Cena**

| 2057 | Jan. 30 | Champaign, IL | ★★1/2 |

L   **Shawn Michaels**

| 2058 | Jan. 31 | Hammond, IN | ★★★ |

L   **Shawn Michaels**

FEBRUARY 2009

| 2059 | Feb. 01 | Cape Girardeau, MO | ★★★1/2 |

L   **Shawn Michaels**

MY TOP 10 GIMMICK MATCHES

- **HELL IN A CELL VS. TRIPLE H** (#1449, MAY 19, 2002)
A very important step for the HIAC, as it was the first to not feature a crazy stunt bump. It was the bridge to a safer style of HIAC matches, and Hunter and I are quite proud of that to this day.

- **BARBED WIRE MATCH VS. BIFF WELLINGTON** (#106, JAN. 29, 1993)
This was the first of its kind in Canadian history and drew a lot of attention (and flak) from the national media — even though we clipped most of the wires before the match.

- **PENALTY BOX MATCHES WITH LANCE STORM VS. WELL DUNN** (#344-347 & #350-352, JULY 1994)
A unique, and kind of confusing, Jim Cornette idea where if you were caught breaking the rules, the ref would make you sit in a makeshift ringside "penalty box" for a minute, causing your partner to face a two-on-one situation for the duration of the penalty.

- **AMBROSE ASYLUM MATCH VS. DEAN AMBROSE** (#2574, MAY 22, 2016)
Most critics hated it, but I loved it … save for the thumbtack bump, after which I had to pull 69 tacks out of my body.

- **ELIMINATION CHAMBER MATCH**
I've been in the most chamber matches out of anybody in WWE history (8) and caused the most eliminations (10).

- **ROYAL RUMBLE**
I have the longest cumulative time in the Rumble in WWE history: a total of 4 hours, 59 minutes, and 33 seconds.

- **MONEY IN THE BANK**
Not only did I help create this gimmick with former WWE head writer Brian Gewirtz, I've appeared in five of them.

- **MIMOSA MAYHEM** (#2718, SEPT. 5, 2020)
I came up with this idea and drew a quick picture of the concept (that might as well have been on the napkin from *This Is Spinal Tap*), which Tony Khan instantly loved. He understood my vision and ran with it, and the rest is champagne-and-orange-juice history.

• LADDER MATCH

I still feel my ladder matches with Shawn Michaels (#2003) and Chris Benoit (#1227) rank among the best ever.

• TLC

My favorite is still TLC 3 from Anaheim (#1285) — aka the "Forgotten TLC." We only had a short time to put together the intricate encounter as we didn't find about it until we landed in Anaheim at around noon Pacific Time, and the live show was starting only hours later.

• STADIUM STAMPEDE (#2710, MAY 23, 2020)

For me, this is the epitome of what I love about pro wrestling: creativity, character, and concept. My favorite parts were the Hager/Hangman barroom brawl, Sammy being chased by the golf cart, me knocking out the stupid mascot Jaxson de Ville with the Judas Effect, and Ortiz literally getting his bell rung.

2060 **L**	Feb. 02	St. Louis	★★★★
	John Cena		
2061 **L**	Feb. 06	Vancouver, British Columbia	★★★
	3-way vs. Randy Orton vs. John Cena		
2062 **L**	Feb. 07	Victoria, British Columbia	★★1/2
	3-way vs. Randy Orton vs. John Cena		
2063 **L**	Feb. 08	Sacramento, CA	★★★1/2
	3-way vs. Randy Orton vs. John Cena		
2064 **W**	Feb. 09	Seattle	★★1/2
	6-man with Kane & Mike Knox vs. Kofi Kingston, Rey Mysterio Jr. & John Cena, pinned Kingston/codebreaker		
2065 **L**	Feb. 13	Los Angeles	★★★
	John Cena (cage match)		
2066 **L**	Feb. 15	Seattle	★★★★1/4
	6-way vs. Edge vs. Mike Knox vs. John Cena vs. Kane vs. Rey Mysterio Jr. (Elimination Chamber/No Way Out)		
2067 **W**	Feb. 20	Huntington, WV	★★★
	Kofi Kingston		
2068 **W**	Feb. 21	Bristol, TN	★★★1/2
	Kofi Kingston		

2069	Feb. 22	Asheville, NC	★★★
W	**Kofi Kingston**		

2070	Feb. 27	Uniondale, NY	★★★
L	**6-man with Randy Orton & Vladimir Kozlov vs. John Cena, Triple H & Shawn Michaels**		

2071	Feb. 28	Wilkes-Barre, PA	★★★
W	**Kofi Kingston**		

MARCH 2009

2072	Mar. 01	Poughkeepsie, NY	★★★
W	**Kofi Kingston**		

2073	Mar. 06	Albany, NY	★★★
L	**Tag with Edge vs. John Cena & Rey Mysterio Jr.**		

2074	Mar. 07	Tallahassee, FL	★★★
W	**Kofi Kingston**		

2075	Mar. 08	Savannah, GA	★★★1/2
L	**6-man with Edge & Ted DiBiase Jr. vs. John Cena, Rey Mysterio Jr. & Kofi Kingston**		

2076	Mar. 09	Jacksonville, FL	★★★
L	**Kofi Kingston**		

2077	Mar. 13	Midland, TX	★★★
L	**Tag with Kane vs. Shawn Michaels & Rey Mysterio Jr.**		

2078	Mar. 14	Lubbock, TX	★★★1/4
L	**Tag with Kane vs. Shawn Michaels & Rey Mysterio Jr.**		

2079	Mar. 15	San Antonio	★★★1/2
L	**Tag with Kane vs. Shawn Michaels & Rey Mysterio Jr.**		

2080	Mar. 20	Rolla, MO	★★★
L	**CM Punk**		

2081	Mar. 21	Topeka, KS	★★★1/4
L	**CM Punk**		

2082	Mar. 22	Wichita, KS	★★★
L	**CM Punk**		

2083	Mar. 30	Dallas	★★1/4
W	**Jerry Lawler**		

| 2084 | Apr. 05 | Houston | ★★1/2 |
| **W** | 3-on-1 handicap elimination vs. Ricky Steamboat, Jimmy Snuka & Roddy Piper (WrestleMania 25) | | |

| 2085 | Apr. 06 | Houston | ★★★★ |
| **L** | 5-on-5 with Kane, Matt Hardy, Big Show & Edge vs. Jeff Hardy, CM Punk, Rey Mysterio Jr., Ricky Steamboat & John Cena, Mysterio | | |

| 2086 | Apr. 13 | Atlanta | ★★★ |
| **W** | Tommy Dreamer, codebreaker | | |

| 2087 | Apr. 15 | Dublin | ★★★ |
| **L** | Rey Mysterio Jr. | | |

| 2088 | Apr. 16 | Dublin | ★★★★ |
| **L** | CM Punk | | |

| 2089 | Apr. 17 | Glasgow, Scotland | ★★★★ |
| **L** | CM Punk | | |

| 2090 | Apr. 18 | Aberdeen, Scotland | ★★★1/2 |
| **L** | Rey Mysterio Jr. | | |

| 2091 | Apr. 19 | Nottingham, England | ★★★1/2 |
| **L** | CM Punk | | |

| 2092 | Apr. 20 | London | ★★★★ |
| **L** | John Cena | | |

| 2093 | Apr. 21 | Cardiff, Wales | ★★★3/4 |
| **L** | John Cena | | |

| 2094 | Apr. 22 | Liverpool, England | ★★★★ |
| **L** | CM Punk | | |

| 2095 | Apr. 23 | Newcastle, England | ★★★★ |
| **L** | Rey Mysterio Jr. | | |

| 2096 | Apr. 24 | Belfast, Ireland | ★★★★1/4 |
| **L** | CM Punk | | |

| 2097 | Apr. 26 | Providence, RI | ★★★1/2 |
| **W** | Ricky Steamboat (Backlash), Walls of Jericho | | |

| 2098 | Apr. 28 | New York City | ★★★ |

L   4-way elimination vs. Kane vs. Rey Mysterio Jr. vs. Jeff Hardy, DQ

| 2099 | Apr. 28 | New York City | ★★★★ |

L   6-man with Edge & Randy Orton vs. Batista, Rey Mysterio Jr. & John Cena

MAY 2009

| 2100 | May 05 | Pittsburgh | ★★★3/4 |

L   Jeff Hardy

| 2101 | May 05 | Pittsburgh | ★★3/4 |

W   John Morrison

| 2102 | May 09 | Grand Rapids, MI | ★★★1/2 |

L   Rey Mysterio Jr.

| 2103 | May 10 | Fort Wayne, IN | ★★★ |

L   Rey Mysterio Jr.

| 2104 | May 11 | Evansville, IN | ★★★1/2 |

L   Rey Mysterio Jr.

| 2105 | May 12 | Dayton, OH | ★★★1/4 |

L   Edge

| 2106 | May 17 | Chicago | ★★★★ |

L   Rey Mysterio Jr. (Judgment Day)

| 2107 | May 18 | Louisville, KY | ★★★★ |

L   CM Punk

| 2108 | May 19 | Cincinnati | ★★★1/2 |

L   CM Punk

| 2109 | May 19 | Cincinnati | ★★★ |

L   Rey Mysterio Jr. (cage match)

| 2110 | May 24 | Las Cruces, NM | ★★★ |

L   Rey Mysterio Jr.

| 2111 | May 26 | Los Angeles | ★★ |

L   2-on-1 handicap with Edge vs. Jeff Hardy, countout

| 2112 | May 30 | Chattanooga, TN | ★★★ |

L   John Morrison, starship pain

2113	May 31	Bowling Green, KY	★★3/4

L   **John Morrison,** starship pain

JUNE 2009

2114	June 01	Birmingham, AL	★★

L   **Tag with Dolph Ziggler vs. Jeff Hardy & R-Truth**

2115	June 02	Memphis, TN	★★★★

W   **R-Truth,** codebreaker

2116	June 02	Memphis, TN	★★★1/2

L   **Tag with Edge vs. Jeff Hardy & CM Punk (Jerry Lawler referee)**

2117	June 06	Pensacola, FL	★★★★3/4

L   **6-man with Randy Orton & Edge vs. John Cena, Jeff Hardy & CM Punk,** pinned by Cena/FU

2118	June 07	New Orleans	★★★★

W   **Rey Mysterio Jr. (won WWE Intercontinental title/9th time – no holds barred/Extreme Rules),** codebreaker

2119	June 08	Lafayette, LA	★★★

W   **John Morrison,** roll-up

2120	June 09	Biloxi, MS	★★

L   **CM Punk,** GTS

2121	June 09	Biloxi, MS	★★

L   **Tag with Edge vs. CM Punk & Jeff Hardy (cage match)**

2122	June 14	Hershey, PA	★★

L   **Rey Mysterio Jr.**

2123	June 15	Charlotte, NC	★★★1/2

L   **Rey Mysterio Jr.**

2124	June 16	Roanoke, VA	★★

L   **Jeff Hardy,** countout

2125	June 16	Roanoke, VA	★★

L   **Tag with Edge vs. Jeff Hardy & Rey Mysterio Jr.**

2126	June 20	Saginaw, MI	★★★1/2

L   **John Morrison**

2127	June 21	Kalamazoo, MI	★★★

L John Morrison

2128	June 22	Green Bay, WI	★★1/2

L 6-man with Edge & Dolph Ziggler vs. The Great Khali, Rey Mysterio Jr. & Jeff Hardy

2129	June 23	Milwaukee	★★★

W Tag with Edge vs. Jeff Hardy & Rey Mysterio Jr. (CM Punk referee)

2130	June 28	Sacramento, CA	★★★★

L Rey Mysterio Jr. (lost WWE Intercontinental title – mask vs. title/The Bash)

MATCH NOTES #2130

This was another one of my all-time favorite feuds, and this match might have been the best out of the four or five excellent ones we had during this story line. The finish was one of my favorites ever, occurring when I pulled Rey's mask off midway through his 619 finishing move. When I explained the idea to Vince, he said we couldn't do it. I said, "We can't do it because you don't want us to, or because you don't think we physically can?" When he said he didn't think it was possible, I dragged him to the ring, and Rey and I performed it flawlessly. Vince asked us to do it again like a kid watching a magic trick and when we did, he said, "There's your finish," and walked back to his office.

2131	June 28	Sacramento, CA	★★★1/2

W 3-way with Edge vs. Carlito & Primo Colon vs. Cody Rhodes & Ted DiBiase Jr. (won WWE tag team titles/3rd time – The Bash)

2132	June 29	San Jose, CA	★★

W Tag with Edge vs. Carlito & Primo Colon

2133	June 30	Fresno, CA	★★★1/2

W Tag with Edge vs. CM Punk & Jeff Hardy

2134	June 30	Fresno, CA	★★★1/2

L Tag with Edge vs. Jeff Hardy & Rey Mysterio Jr. (cage match)

JULY 2009

2135	July 01	Bakersfield, CA	★★★★

L Rey Mysterio Jr.

2136	July 02	Palm Springs, CA	★★★1/2

L Rey Mysterio Jr.

2137	July 03	San Diego	★★★1/2
L	**John Morrison**		

2138	July 05	Honolulu	★★★★
L	**Rey Mysterio Jr. (Ricky Steamboat referee)**		

2139	July 07	Tokyo	★★★★1/2
L	**Rey Mysterio Jr.**		

2140	July 08	Tokyo	★★★1/4
W	**Ricky Steamboat**		

2141	July 10	Manila, Philippines	★★★1/2
L	**Rey Mysterio Jr. (Ricky Steamboat referee)**		

2142	July 13	Orlando, FL	★★1/2
L	**Mark Henry,** DQ		

2143	July 14	Miami	★★★1/2
L	**Tag with Dolph Ziggler vs. Jeff Hardy & Rey Mysterio Jr.**		

2144	July 19	Greenville, SC	★★★★
L	**Ricky Steamboat**		

2145	July 20	Raleigh, NC	★★
L	**Mark Henry,** countout		

2146	July 21	Richmond, VA	★★★3/4
L	**Jeff Hardy,** swanton		

2147	July 26	Philadelphia	★★
W	**Tag with Big Show vs. Cody Rhodes & Ted DiBiase Jr. (Night of Champions)**		

2148	July 27	Washington, D.C.	★★★
L	**Tag with Big Show vs. Cryme Time (JTG & Shad Gaspard) – Shaquille O'Neal special enforcer,** DQ		

AUGUST 2009

2149	Aug. 01	Manchester, NH	★★1/2
W	**Tag with Big Show vs. Cryme Time**		

2150	Aug. 02	Verona, NH	★★★
W	**Tag with Big Show vs. Cryme Time**		

With my all-time favorite tag team partner, holding the double tag team titles. Pictures like this remind me just how fucking MASSIVE The Big Show is!

2151	Aug. 04	Uniondale, NY	★★★★
L	**JTG,** roll-up		

2152	Aug. 08	Regina, Saskatchewan	★★★1/4
L	**CM Punk,** GTS		

2153	Aug. 09	Medicine Hat, Alberta	★★3/4
L	**CM Punk,** GTS		

2154	Aug. 10	Calgary, Alberta	★★★
L	**John Cena,** attitude adjustment		

2155	Aug. 17	St. Louis	★★★1/2
L	**Tag with Big Show vs. John Cena & Randy Orton (lumberjack match),** pinned by Cena/ attitude adjustment		

2156	Aug. 18	Kansas City, MO	★★★1/2
W	**6-man with Big Show & Dolph Ziggler vs. Rey Mysterio Jr. & Cryme Time**		

2157	Aug. 23	Los Angeles	★★★
W	**Tag with Big Show vs. Cryme Time (Summer Slam)**		

2158	Aug. 24	Las Vegas	★★★1/2
L	**Tag with Big Show vs. MVP & Mark Henry**		

2159	Aug. 25	Phoenix	★★
W	**Tag with Big Show vs. Cryme Time**		

2160	Aug. 31	Detroit	★★★
W	**MVP**		

SEPTEMBER 2009

2161	Sept. 04	San Juan, Puerto Rico	★★
W	**3-way with Big Show vs. The Hart Dynasty (Davey Boy Smith Jr. & Tyson Kidd) vs. Cryme Time**		

2162	Sept. 05	Arecibo, Puerto Rico	★★
L	**6-man with CM Punk & Big Show vs. Undertaker, Great Khali & Matt Hardy**		

2163	Sept. 06	Ponce, Puerto Rico	★★★★
W	**Tag with Big Show vs. Carlito & Primo Colon**		

2164	Sept. 07	Chicago	★★★★
L	**MVP**		

2165	Sept. 08	Rockford, IL	★★1/2
W	**Tag with Big Show vs. Cryme Time**		

2166	Sept. 13	Montreal	★★★
W	**Tag with Big Show vs. MVP & Mark Henry (Breaking Point)**		

2167	Sept. 14	Toronto	★★
L	**6-person tag with Big Show & Beth Phoenix vs. MVP, Mark Henry & Trish Stratus**		

2168	Sept. 15	Toronto	★★1/2
L	**Batista**		

2169	Sept. 21	Little Rock, AR	★★★
L	**6-man with Randy Orton & Big Show vs. John Cena, MVP & Mark Henry**		

2170	Sept. 24	Madrid	★★★1/2
L	**Batista**		

2171	Sept. 25	Nice, France	★★★★
L	**6-man with Big Show & CM Punk vs. Undertaker, Batista & Mark Henry**		

2172	Sept. 26	Paris	★★★1/2
L	**6-man with Big Show & CM Punk vs. Undertaker, Batista & Mark Henry**		

2173	Sept. 27	Paris	★★★★
L	**Batista**		

2174	Sept. 28	Albany, NY	★★
W	**Tag with Big Show vs. MVP & Mark Henry**		

OCTOBER 2009

2175	Oct. 04	Newark, NJ	★★★1/4
W	**Tag with Big Show vs. Rey Mysterio Jr. & Batista (Hell In a Cell)**		

2176	Oct. 05	Wilkes-Barre, PA	★★★
L	**Tag with Big Show vs. Triple H & Shawn Michaels**		

2177	Oct. 06	Trenton, NJ	★★★
L	**Rey Mysterio Jr.**		

2178	Oct. 12	Indianapolis	★★1/2
L	**Big Show,** countout		

2179	Oct. 15	Monterrey, Mexico	★★★★
L	**Tag with Kane vs. Rey Mysterio Jr. & Batista**		

2180	Oct. 16	Puebla, Mexico	★★★1/2
L	**Rey Mysterio Jr.**		

2181	Oct. 17	Mexico City	★★★★
L	**6-man with Kane & CM Punk vs. Undertaker, Rey Mysterio Jr. & Batista**		

2182	Oct. 20	Columbia, SC	★★★★
L	**Christian**		

2183	Oct. 20	Columbia, SC	★★★1/2
L	**Tag with Kane vs. Rey Mysterio Jr. & Batista**		

2184	Oct. 25	Pittsburgh	★★3/4
W	**7-on-7 tag with Kane, Matt Hardy, Finlay, R-Truth & Hart Dynasty vs. Shawn Michaels, Triple H, Mark Henry, Big Show, Kofi Kingston, Jack Swagger & Cody Rhodes (Bragging Rights/Team Smackdown vs. Team Raw)**		

| 2185 | Oct. 26 | Buffalo, NY | ★★★1/4 |
| **L** | **Kofi Kingston** | | |

| 2186 | Oct. 27 | Rochester, NY | ★★3/4 |
| **W** | **Kane,** codebreaker | | |

NOVEMBER 2009

| 2187 | Nov. 02 | Worcester, MA | ★★3/4 |
| **W** | **3-way vs. Big Show vs. John Cena,** beat Cena | | |

| 2188 | Nov. 03 | Providence, RI | ★★★1/2 |
| **W** | **Fit Finlay** | | |

| 2189 | Nov. 08 | Liverpool, England | ★1/2 |
| **W** | **Mark Henry** | | |

| 2190 | Nov. 09 | Sheffield, England | ★★1/2 |
| **L** | **Tag with Big Show vs. Triple H & Shawn Michaels** | | |

| 2191 | Nov. 10 | Sheffield, England | ★★★★1/2 |
| **L** | **Undertaker** | | |

| 2192 | Nov. 11 | London | ★★★ |
| **W** | **Battle Royal** | | |

| 2193 | Nov. 11 | London | ★★★★1/2 |
| **L** | **John Cena** | | |

| 2194 | Nov. 12 | Birmingham, England | ★★★ |
| **L** | **Battle Royal** | | |

| 2195 | Nov. 12 | Birmingham, England | ★★★★ |
| **W** | **Evan Bourne** | | |

IN THEIR WORDS: **MATT SYDAL (AKA EVAN BOURNE)**

The match in Birmingham really stood out because I had been doing a lot of shows and I had never really experienced the intense level of the crowd. I would be in the opening match with Chavo (Guerrero Jr.) and T.J. Wilson and have great classic pro wrestling matches. But the crowd was hot because we were the first match. It's a different feeling than when John Cena would take the ring. You would hear this roar from the crowd that I had never heard before in my life. Being in there with Chris, you could hear that sound and the pop.

We were like 12 minutes in. We had been digging and digging for my comeback, and then he took off to the ropes and nailed me with a clothesline. When he smashed me with that, it was the feeling I was always looking for — to hear the crowd deep in the match and be really with it. It was like they felt it when he hit me. He had all eyes in the building on him and made them feel bad. It felt like a real pro wrestling match to me and was one of the biggest accomplishments in my life.

| 2196 | Nov. 13 | Lyon, France | ★★★ |
| **L** | **Battle Royal** | | |

| 2197 | Nov. 13 | Lyon, France | ★★★ |
| **L** | **Tag with Big Show vs. Triple H & Shawn Michaels** | | |

| 2198 | Nov. 14 | Lyon, France | ★★★ |
| **L** | **6-man with Big Show & Randy Orton vs. Shawn Michaels, Triple H & John Cena** | | |

| 2199 | Nov. 16 | New York City | ★★★1/2 |
| **L** | **3-way with Big Show vs. Shawn Michaels & Triple H vs. John Cena & Undertaker** | | |

| 2200 | Nov. 17 | Philadelphia | ★★★ |
| **NC** | **Tag with Big Show vs. Undertaker & Kane,** NO CONTEST | | |

| 2201 | Nov. 22 | Washington, D.C. | ★★3/4 |
| **L** | **3-way vs. Big Show vs. Undertaker (Survivor Series),** Undertaker | | |

| 2202 | Nov. 24 | Bridgeport, CT | ★★★ |
| **L** | **Undertaker,** DQ | | |

| 2203 | Nov. 28 | Upper Marlboro, MD | ★★★1/2 |
| **L** | **Rey Mysterio Jr.** | | |

| 2204 | Nov. 29 | Hampton, VA | ★★★ |
| **W** | **Tag with Big Show vs. Cryme Time** | | |

| 2205 | Nov. 30 | Baltimore | ★★★★ |
| **L** | **Triple H** | | |

DECEMBER 2009

| 2206 | Dec. 04 | Baghdad | ★★1/2 |
| **L** | **John Cena (Tribute to the Troops)** | | |

| 2207 | Dec. 07 | Dallas | ★★1/2 |
| **NC** | **2-on-1 handicap vs. Shawn Michaels & Triple H,** NO CONTEST | | |

2208	Dec. 08	Houston	★★

W **2-on-1 handicap with Big Show vs. Eric Escobar,** Walls of Jericho

2209	Dec. 13	San Antonio	★★★

L **Tag with Big Show vs. Triple H & Shawn Michaels** (lost WWE tag-team titles – tables, ladders & chairs match/TLC)

2210	Dec. 14	Corpus Christi, TX	★★

L **Tag with Big Show vs. Triple H & Shawn Michaels,** DQ

2211	Dec. 15	Laredo, TX	★★1/2

L **Great Khali,** DQ

2212	Dec. 18	Miami	★★★1/2

W **Kane,** roll-up

IN THEIR WORDS: CODY RHODES
(WWE RAW/DEC. 21, 2009)

I spent way too long thinking of my favorite Chris Jericho segment. The lesson in that is Chris Jericho has one of the most sought-after attributes in our sport — staying power. I didn't choose the mat classic against Shawn Michaels and changing of the guard from WrestleMania 19 (#1582). I didn't choose him putting the Intercontinental title on Kofi Kingston in 2008 (#1966) and subsequently giving my whole developmental generation a reminder that there's hope. I didn't even choose standing across from him in a sold-out Royal Farms Arena in Baltimore at Full Gear in 2019 as I had finally entered my prime and earned the spot to genuinely draw with him on the marquee (#2698). And I didn't even pick a personal highlight of overlooking the water from his house with Tony Khan while we talked about our aspirations for future creative ideas within the premium brand that is AEW.

Instead, I chose a quaint moment. The moment that keeps playing frames in my mind: Chris Jericho pretending to be Santa Claus — rosy cheeks and all — while he sat on Big Show's lap. There was just something densely magical about him taking that material and telling that story. The twisted tale of how they had been banned from tagging together and Show's Christmas wish that they could do it again. I remember it being a "locker-room sell-out" and the genuine giggles it was receiving from the biggest marks of all — us, the boys themselves. Whether it's his ability to make something of hackneyed material or his steadfast commitment to making sure the fans enjoy themselves, Chris has never taken a segment and considered it anything other than the most important segment on the show. He's the rising tide. He's Chris Jericho.

2213	Dec. 27	Raleigh, NC	★★★

L **Tag with CM Punk vs. Kane & Rey Mysterio Jr.**

| 2214 | Dec. 29 | East Rutherford, NJ | ★★★★ |

L   **Rey Mysterio Jr.,** roll-up

| 2215 | Jan. 04 | Dayton, OH | ★★★ |

L   **Tag with Big Show vs. Triple H & Shawn Michaels**

| 2216 | Jan. 05 | Louisville, KY | ★★1/2 |

W   **6-man with Hart Dynasty vs. Cryme Time & R-Truth,** beat JTG/Walls of Jericho

| 2217 | Jan. 09 | Fargo, ND | ★★★ |

W   **Matt Hardy**

| 2218 | Jan. 10 | Duluth, MN | ★★★1/4 |

W   **Matt Hardy**

| 2219 | Jan. 11 | Minneapolis | ★★★ |

L   **Tag with Mike Tyson vs. Triple H & Shawn Michaels**

| 2220 | Jan. 12 | Green Bay, WI | ★★★1/4 |

W   **John Morrison,** codebreaker

| 2221 | Jan. 16 | Augusta, GA | ★★★1/4 |

L   **Six-man tag with CM Punk & Batista vs. Kane, Matt Hardy & Undertaker**

| 2222 | Jan. 17 | Florence, SC | ★★★1/2 |

L   **6-man with CM Punk & Batista vs. Kane, Matt Hardy & Undertaker**

| 2223 | Jan. 19 | Greenville, SC | ★★★1/2 |

L   **Kane,** countout

| 2224 | Jan. 19 | Greenville, SC | ★★3/4 |

L   **Tag with Drew McIntyre vs. Morrison & R-Truth**

| 2225 | Jan. 23 | Hammond, IN | ★★★1/2 |

L   **Tag with CM Punk vs. Rey Mysterio Jr. & Kane**

| 2226 | Jan. 24 | Cleveland | ★★★ |

L   **Triple H,** pedigree

| 2227 | Jan. 26 | Cincinnati | ★★★ |

L   **R-Truth,** roll-up

| 2228 | Jan. 31 | Atlanta | ★★★ |

L   **Royal Rumble,** Eliminated by Edge after 2:24

| 2229 | Feb. 02 | Memphis, TN | ★★★1/4 |
| **W** | **Matt Hardy,** codebreaker | | |

| 2230 | Feb. 09 | Baton Rouge, LA | ★★★3/4 |
| **W** | **Undertaker** (no DQ) | | |

| 2231 | Feb. 11 | Quito, Ecuador | ★★★1/2 |
| **L** | **Tag with Batista vs. Undertaker & Rey Mysterio Jr.** | | |

| 2232 | Feb. 12 | Guayaquil, Ecuador | ★★★★ |
| **L** | **Rey Mysterio Jr.** | | |

| 2233 | Feb. 13 | San Jose, Costa Rica | ★★★★ |
| **L** | **Rey Mysterio Jr.** | | |

| 2234 | Feb. 14 | Guadalajara, Mexico | ★★★1/2 |
| **L** | **Tag with CM Punk vs. Kane & Undertaker** | | |

| 2235 | Feb. 21 | St. Louis | ★★★★ |
| **W** | **6-way vs. Undertaker vs. John Morrison vs. Rey Mysterio Jr. vs. CM Punk vs. R-Truth (won WWE heavyweight title/3rd time – Elimination Chamber)** | | |

MATCH NOTES #2235

This was the sixth and last time I won a WWE World Title, when I pinned The Undertaker after a Shawn Michaels superkick. But the real story of this match was Taker getting second-degree burns over most of his torso after essentially being blown up by his own pyro. He was then trapped inside the chamber pod for 20 minutes, pouring water over his rapidly reddening skin. When he was finally let into the match, he did everything he needed to do to put me over strong and make it a great bout, even though he was in tremendous pain and missed the majority of the next month. What a TOUGH son of a bitch!

| 2236 | Feb. 23 | Milwaukee | ★★★★ |
| **W** | **Daniel Bryan,** Walls of Jericho | | |

| 2237 | Feb. 27 | Tyler, TX | ★★ |
| **L** | **Tag with CM Punk vs. Edge & John Morrison** | | |

| 2238 | Feb. 28 | Abilene, TX | ★ |
| **L** | **Tag with CM Punk vs. Edge & John Morrison** | | |

2239	Mar. 02	Wichita, KS	★★★
W	Goldust		

2240	Mar. 06	Pullman, WA	★★★
W	4-way vs. Rey Mysterio Jr. vs. CM Punk vs. Edge		

2241	Mar. 07	Yakima, WA	★★★1/2
W	Tag with CM Punk vs. Rey Mysterio Jr. & Edge		

2242	Mar. 09	Seattle	★★1/2
L	Edge, DQ		

2243	Mar. 13	Stockton, CA	★★3/4
L	6-man with CM Punk & Luke Gallows vs. Undertaker, Rey Mysterio Jr. & Edge		

2244	Mar. 14	San Francisco	★★★1/2
W	6-man with CM Punk & Luke Gallows vs. Undertaker, Rey Mysterio Jr. & Edge		

2245	Mar. 15	San Diego	★★3/4
L	Shawn Michaels, countout		

2246	Mar. 16	Los Angeles	★★
L	8-man with Batista, CM Punk & Sheamus vs. Edge, John Cena, Rey Mysterio Jr. & Triple H		

2247	Mar. 21	Sacramento, CA	★★★1/2
L	6-man with CM Punk & Luke Gallows vs. Undertaker, Rey Mysterio Jr. & Edge		

2248	Mar. 28	Phoenix	★★★1/2
W	Edge (WrestleMania 26), codebreaker		

2249	Mar. 29	Phoenix	★★★
L	Edge, DQ		

2250	Mar. 30	Las Vegas	★★★1/2
L	Jack Swagger (lost WWE heavyweight title)		

IN THEIR WORDS: JAKE HAGER (AKA JACK SWAGGER)

The first match that comes to mind is when I won the WWE championship. I got the call after Monday Night *RAW* from talent relations to come to Las Vegas the next day. I'm the Money in the Bank winner. Chris was champ and had defeated Edge just one day earlier at WrestleMania. I'm, of course, in the proverbial "outside in the hall in front of Vince [McMahon's] office." First, [WWE executive vice president] Johnny Ace goes in there. And then Edge goes in. And then Chris goes in. I'm thinking, "I want to go in there," and they shut the door in my face. Johnny is like, "Wait here for a second." They were probably just in there making the rookie sweat for 10 minutes. Chris then laid out what he wants and at the end of it turns to me — and I've known him for years at this point — and says deadpan to me, "You better not fuck this up. I'm going to make sure you don't fuck this up." I'm like, "Yes, sir! I just want to make you look good. I won't..." and then Chris interrupts and screams, "I know you won't!" So we go out there and it went great.

When you're in the ring with Chris, you don't have to worry about as many things because he's already got it handled and likely two steps ahead of you on how he wants it done. It's very reassuring being in there with him. At the same time, you get someone in your face screaming at you, your anxiety goes up. But it ended up being a fun moment.

2251	Mar. 30	Las Vegas	★★★1/2
W	**8-man with CM Punk, Matt Hardy & R-Truth vs. Christian, Carlito, William Regal & Miz**		

APRIL 2010

2252	Apr. 06	Chicago	★★★1/2
DC	**Edge,** DOUBLE COUNTOUT		

2253	Apr. 11	Manchester, England	★★★
L	**3-way vs. Jack Swagger vs. Edge (Bret Hart enforcer)**		

IN THEIR WORDS: JAKE HAGER (AKA JACK SWAGGER)

Edge, Chris, and I did a [three-way] match with Bret Hart as the referee. He's doing a 10-count during a triple-down, and Chris turns to me in the middle of the ring and says, "So you want to be a wrestler, huh, kid?"

They were always great matches. They were always hard-hitting. They were always entertaining.

2254	Apr. 12	Nottingham, England	★★★★
L	**Edge (street fight)**		

2255	Apr. 13	London	★★★★
L	**3-way vs. Jack Swagger vs. Edge**		

2256	Apr. 14	Oberhausen, Germany	★★★
L	**3-way vs. Jack Swagger vs. Edge (Bret Hart enforcer)**		

2257	Apr. 15	Hanover, Germany	★★★1/4
L	**3-way vs. Jack Swagger vs. Edge (Bret Hart enforcer)**		

2258	Apr. 16	Zurich	★★★1/4
L	**3-way vs. Jack Swagger vs. Edge**		

2259	Apr. 19	East Rutherford, NJ	★★★

L 6-man with CM Punk & Luke Gallows vs. Rey Mysterio Jr., Edge & Triple H

2260	Apr. 20	Uncasville, CT	★★★

L Heath Slater

2261	Apr. 20	Uncasville, CT	★★★1/4

L 3-way vs. Jack Swagger vs. Rey Mysterio Jr.

2262	Apr. 25	Baltimore	★★★1/4

L Edge (cage match/Extreme Rules)

2263	Apr. 26	Richmond, VA	★★★1/2

W Christian

2264	Apr. 27	Hershey, PA	★★★

W Tag with Wade Barrett vs. Christian & Heath Slater

2265	Apr. 27	Hershey, PA	★★

L 3-way vs. Jack Swagger vs. Big Show

2266	Apr. 27	Hershey, PA	★★1/2

L Kofi Kingston

MAY 2010

2267	May 01	Knoxville, TN	★★★1/2

L Kane

2268	May 02	Johnson City, TN	★★★1/4

L Kane

2269	May 06	Mexico City	★★3/4

L Tag with Edge vs. Hart Dynasty

2270	May 07	Queretaro, Mexico	★★3/4

L Tag with Edge vs. Undertaker & Kane

2271	May 08	Leon, Mexico	★★★

L Tag with Edge vs. Undertaker & Kane

2272	May 09	Monterrey, Mexico	★★★1/2

L Tag with Edge vs. Undertaker & Kane

2273	May 10	Pittsburgh	★★1/2

W Davey Boy Smith Jr.

| 2274 | May 23 | Detroit | ★★★ |
| **L** | **Tag with Miz vs. Hart Dynasty (Over the Limit)** | | |

| 2275 | May 24 | Toledo, OH | ★★★1/4 |
| **L** | **3-way vs. Edge vs. John Cena** | | |

| 2276 | May 28 | New Orleans | ★★★★ |
| **L** | **John Cena** | | |

| 2277 | May 29 | Monroe, LA | ★★★1/4 |
| **L** | **John Cena** | | |

| 2278 | May 30 | Memphis, TN | ★★★1/2 |
| **L** | **John Cena** | | |

| 2279 | May 31 | Austin, TX | ★★★ |
| **L** | **R-Truth** | | |

JUNE 2010

| 2280 | June 05 | Greenville, SC | ★★★ |
| **L** | **R-Truth** | | |

| 2281 | June 06 | Columbia, SC | ★★★ |
| **L** | **R-Truth** | | |

| 2282 | June 07 | Miami | ★★ |
| **L** | **Big Show (bodyslam challenge)** | | |

| 2283 | June 14 | Charlotte, NC | ★★ |
| **L** | **Evan Bourne** | | |

| 2284 | June 20 | Uniondale, NY | ★★★★ |
| **L** | **Evan Bourne (Fatal 4-Way pay-per-view)** | | |

IN THEIR WORDS: MATT SYDAL (AKA EVAN BOURNE)

I love our Fatal 4-Way match that was on pay-per-view because of the creative way we did it and because Chris went out on a limb to make me win and take the momentum we were feeling at that time and really try and catapult me forward. That was a huge moment in my career. We did really think it was going to keep going. It didn't after that, but we had that moment. I felt that was my first chance to break out. Chris is a starmaker and knows how to do it. It wasn't done in a way where he wanted to take credit. He just wanted to be a part of it and guide me and show me the right way. I really benefited a lot from that match.

2285	June 21	Bridgeport, CT	★★★
W	**Evan Bourne**		

2286	June 25	Erie, PA	★★★1/2
L	**Evan Bourne**		

2287	June 28	Philadelphia	★★1/2
L	**8-man with Edge, Miz & Ted DiBiase Jr. vs. Randy Orton, John Morrison, Evan Bourne & R-Truth**		

JULY 2010

2288	July 05	Nashville, TN	★★1/2
L	**Tag with Edge vs. Randy Orton & Evan Bourne**		

2289	July 11	Huntington, WV	★★★1/2
L	**Evan Bourne**		

2290	July 12	Louisville, KY	★★★
W	**Yoshi Tatsu**		

2291	July 17	Omaha, NE	★★★1/2
L	**8-man with Edge, Jack Swagger & Sheamus vs. John Cena, Randy Orton, Rey Mysterio Jr. & Big Show**		

2292	July 18	Kansas City, MO	★★★★1/4
L	**8-way vs. Edge vs. Miz vs. Randy Orton vs. Ted DiBiase Jr. vs. Evan Bourne vs. Mark Henry vs. John Morrison (ladder match/Money in the Bank),** Miz		

2293	July 19	Tulsa, OK	★★★★1/2
L	**3-way vs. Randy Orton vs. Edge**		

2294	July 23	Houston	★★★★
L	**Evan Bourne**		

2295	July 24	Shreveport, LA	★★★1/2
L	**Evan Bourne**		

2296	July 25	Beaumont, TX	★★★
L	**Evan Bourne**		

2297	July 26	San Antonio	★★★1/2
L	**John Cena**		

2298	July 26	San Antonio	★★1/4
L	**Tag with John Cena vs. Miz & Sheamus**		

| 2299 | July 30 | Tallahassee, FL | ★★1/2 |

W 6-man with John Cena & John Morrison vs. Wade Barrett, Skip Sheffield & David Otunga

| 2300 | July 31 | Daytona Beach, FL | ★★★ |

W 6-man with John Cena & John Morrison vs. Wade Barrett, Skip Sheffield & David Otunga

AUGUST 2010

| 2301 | Aug. 01 | Ft. Myers, FL | ★★3/4 |

W 6-man with John Cena & John Morrison vs. Wade Barrett, Skip Sheffield & David Otunga .

| 2302 | Aug. 09 | Sacramento, CA | ★★★★ |

NC Tag with Edge vs. John Cena & Bret Hart (lumberjack match), NO CONTEST

| 2303 | Aug. 15 | Los Angeles | ★★★3/4 |

W 14-man tag with John Cena, R-Truth, John Morrison, Edge, Daniel Bryan & Bret Hart vs. Darren Young, Heath Slater, David Otunga, Skip Sheffield, Michael Tarver, Wade Barrett & Justin Gabriel (elimination match/Summer Slam), Cena

| 2304 | Aug. 16 | Los Angeles | ★★ |

W 18-man 3-way battle royal with John Cena, R-Truth, John Morrison, Edge & Randy Orton vs. CM Punk, Cody Rhodes, Jack Swagger, Kofi Kingston, Rey Mysterio Jr. & Big Show vs. David Otunga, Heath Slater, Justin Gabriel, Michael Tarver, Skip Sheffield & Wade Barrett

| 2305 | Aug. 16 | Los Angeles | ★★ |

W Great Khali, Walls of Jericho

| 2306 | Aug. 16 | Los Angeles | ★★★ |

L Wade Barrett

| 2307 | Aug. 18 | Honolulu | ★★★ |

W Yoshi Tatsu, Walls of Jericho

| 2308 | Aug. 20 | Tokyo | ★★★★ |

W Yoshi Tatsu, Walls of Jericho

| 2309 | Aug. 21 | Tokyo | ★★★3/4 |

L Tag with Sheamus vs. Yoshi Tatsu & John Cena, pinned by Cena/attitude adjustment

| 2310 | Aug. 22 | Shanghai | ★★★★ |

L   Rey Mysterio Jr., 619

MATCH NOTES #2310, FIRST WWE SHOW IN CHINA

We had to fly to Shanghai from Haneda Airport in Tokyo dressed in suits (at the insistence of John Laurinaitis), even though it was hot, stuffy, and smoky … and I had a brutal hangover! When we got to China, I remember the architecture was completely incredible, and I was excited for the sold-out show — which ended up being about 15 percent full. The reason it was deemed "sold out" was because the Chinese government was worried that our "violent game" would incite the fans to follow suit and riot. So the entire lower bowl of the 10,000-seat venue was totally empty except for a few dignitaries sitting behind tables decorated in bunting, like villains in a James Bond movie. The upper deck was jam-packed with actual fans who were going nuts with every move. The only problem was they were so far away, they resembled ants scurrying over a giant elevated pile. We also weren't allowed to fight on the floor for any reason, so I think this was the only match I ever had with Rey with no dives.

| 2311 | Aug. 28 | Wildwood, NJ | ★★★ |

W   6-man with John Cena & Daniel Bryan vs. Wade Barrett, Michael Tarver & Justin Gabriel, Cena

| 2312 | Aug. 29 | Newark, NJ | ★★★ |

W   6-man with Randy Orton & Daniel Bryan vs. Wade Barrett, Michael Tarver & Justin Gabriel

| 2313 | Aug. 30 | Boston | ★★★ |

L   10-man elimination tag with Edge, John Cena, Randy Orton & Sheamus vs. David Otunga, Heath Slater, Justin Gabriel, Michael Tarver & Wade Barrett, Barrett

SEPTEMBER 2010

| 2314 | Sept. 02 | Arecibo, Puerto Rico | ★★1/2 |

W   Daniel Bryan, Walls of Jericho

| 2315 | Sept. 03 | Ponce, Puerto Rico | ★★★ |

L   Evan Bourne

| 2316 | Sept. 04 | San Juan, Puerto Rico | ★★★★ |

W   Primo Colon

| 2317 | Sept. 06 | Washington, D.C. | ★★★1/2 |

W   John Morrison

| 2318 | Sept. 10 | Toronto | ★★1/2 |

W **Tag with Edge vs. Michael Tarver & Wade Barrett**

| 2319 | Sept. 11 | Hamilton, Ontario | ★★1/2 |

W **8-man elimination with Edge & The Hart Dynasty vs. Michael Tarver, Wade Barrett, David Otunga & Heath Slater**

| 2320 | Sept. 12 | Peterborough, Ontario | ★★1/2 |

W **8-man elimination with Edge & The Hart Dynasty vs. Michael Tarver, Wade Barrett, David Otunga & Heath Slater**

| 2321 | Sept. 13 | Cincinnati | ★★1/2 |

W **2-on-1 handicap vs. The Hart Dynasty (cage match)**

| 2322 | Sept. 19 | Chicago | ★★ |

L **6-man vs. Wade Barrett vs. Sheamus vs. Edge vs. Randy Orton vs. Christian (Night of Champions)**

| 2323 | Sept. 20 | Indianapolis | ★★★ |

W **John Morrison**

| 2324 | Sept. 20 | Indianapolis | ★★★1/4 |

NC **Randy Orton,** NO CONTEST

ALL 45 WWE HALL OF FAME INDUCTEES THROUGH 2020 WHO HAVE WRESTLED OR TEAMED WITH CHRIS JERICHO

(43 INDIVIDUALS, 2 TAG TEAMS)

Arn Anderson

Kurt Angle

Steve Austin

Batista

Big Boss Man

Bob Backlund

Booker T

Chyna

The Dudley Boyz

Edge

Ric Flair

Mick Foley

Godfather

Goldberg

Eddy Guerrero

Billy Gunn

Scott Hall

Curt Hennig

Mark Henry

Hulk Hogan

Jeff Jarrett

Jerry Lawler

John Bradshaw Layfield

Jushin "Thunder" Liger

Lita

Mil Mascaras

Shawn Michaels

Kevin Nash

Jim Neidhart

Diamond Dallas Page

The Rock 'n' Roll Express

Beth Phoenix

Roddy Piper

Stevie Ray

Rikishi

Road Dogg

Ron Simmons

Jimmy Snuka

Ricky Steamboat

Trish Stratus

Triple H

Sean Waltman

Barry Windham

SECTION SIX
WWE ACT 3

JAN. 16, 2012 - JULY 25, 2017
MATCHES 2325 - 2684

2325   Jan. 16   Anaheim, CA   ★★★

NC **6-man with CM Punk & Daniel Bryan vs. Mark Henry, David Otunga & Dolph Ziggler,** NO CONTEST

2326   Jan. 29   St. Louis   ★★★1/2

L **Royal Rumble,** Eliminated by Sheamus after 11:34

2327   Feb. 06   Oklahoma City   ★★★

W **6-way vs. CM Punk vs. Kofi Kingston vs. Dolph Ziggler vs. Miz vs. R-Truth**

2328   Feb. 09   Abu Dhabi, United Arab Emirates   ★★★1/2

L **Kofi Kingston**

2329   Feb. 10   Abu Dhabi, United Arab Emirates   ★★★

W **Kofi Kingston**

2330   Feb. 11   Abu Dhabi, United Arab Emirates   ★★★

L **Tag with Miz vs. CM Punk & R-Truth**

The classic Jericho pose with light-up jacket, circa 2012. This jacket was a prototype and the only one of its kind, so it's probably worth more than the Shroud of Turin, right?

| 2331 | Feb. 13 | San Diego | ★★1/2 |
| **W** | **Kofi Kingston** | | |

| 2332 | Feb. 19 | Milwaukee | ★★★3/4 |
| **L** | **6-way vs. Kofi Kingston vs. Miz vs. CM Punk vs. Dolph Ziggler vs. R-Truth (Elimination Chamber)** | | |

| 2333 | Feb. 20 | Minneapolis | ★★★1/2 |
| **W** | **10-man No. 1 WWE heavyweight title contender battle royal,** Eliminated Cody Rhodes | | |

| 2334 | Feb. 24 | Los Angeles | ★★★★ |
| **W** | **Kofi Kingston** | | |

| 2335 | Feb. 25 | Ontario, CA | ★★★ |
| **W** | **Kofi Kingston** | | |

| 2336 | Feb. 26 | Eugene, OR | ★★★3/4 |
| **W** | **Kofi Kingston** | | |

MARCH 2012

| 2337 | Mar. 02 | Cornwall, Ontario | ★★★ |
| **W** | **Kofi Kingston** | | |

| 2338 | Mar. 03 | Ottawa, Ontario | ★★★ |
| **W** | **Kofi Kingston** | | |

| 2339 | Mar. 04 | Bangor, ME | ★★★1/2 |
| **W** | **Kofi Kingston** | | |

| 2340 | Mar. 05 | Boston | ★★1/2 |
| **W** | **Tag with Daniel Bryan vs. CM Punk & Sheamus** | | |

| 2341 | Mar. 09 | Toronto | ★★★ |
| **W** | **Kofi Kingston** | | |

| 2342 | Mar. 10 | London, Ontario | ★★★ |
| **W** | **Kofi Kingston** | | |

| 2343 | Mar. 10 | London, Ontario | ★★★ |
| **L** | **Tag with Dolph Ziggler vs. CM Punk & Kofi Kingston** | | |

| 2344 | Mar. 11 | Buffalo, NY | ★★★ |
| **W** | **Kofi Kingston** | | |

| 2345 | Mar. 13 | Columbus, OH | ★★★1/2 |
| **W** | **Sheamus,** countout | | |

| 2346 | Mar. 16 | Montreal | ★★★ |
| **W** | **Kofi Kingston** | | |

| 2347 | Mar. 17 | Providence, RI | ★★★ |
| **W** | **Kofi Kingston** | | |

| 2348 | Mar. 18 | New York City | ★★★1/2 |
| **L** | **6-man with Dolph Ziggler & Cody Rhodes vs. Triple H, Randy Orton & CM Punk** | | |

| 2349 | Mar. 24 | San Juan, Puerto Rico | ★★★1/2 |
| **W** | **Kofi Kingston** | | |

| 2350 | Mar. 25 | Charlotte, NC | ★★★ |
| **W** | **Kofi Kingston** | | |

| 2351 | Mar. 26 | Atlanta | ★★★ |
| **W** | **Kofi Kingston** | | |

APRIL 2012

| 2352 | Apr. 01 | Miami Gardens, FL | ★★★3/4 |
| **L** | **CM Punk (WrestleMania 28)** | | |

| 2353 | Apr. 13 | Stuttgart, Germany | ★★★ |
| **L** | **CM Punk (no DQ)** | | |

| 2354 | Apr. 14 | Berlin | ★★★ |
| **L** | **CM Punk (no DQ)** | | |

| 2355 | Apr. 15 | Nottingham, England | ★★★1/2 |
| **L** | **CM Punk (no DQ)** | | |

| 2356 | Apr. 16 | London | ★★ |
| **L** | **CM Punk,** DQ | | |

| 2357 | Apr. 17 | Rome | ★★★1/2 |
| **L** | **CM Punk (no DQ)** | | |

| 2358 | Apr. 18 | Milan | ★★★★ |
| **L** | **CM Punk (no DQ)** | | |

| 2359 | Apr. 19 | Toulouse, France | ★★★1/2 |
| **L** | **CM Punk (no DQ)** | | |

2360	Apr. 20	Paris	★★★★
L	**CM Punk (no DQ)**		

2361	Apr. 21	Merksem, Belgium	★★★
L	**CM Punk (no DQ)**		

2362	Apr. 23	Detroit	★★★
W	**Kofi Kingston**		

2363	Apr. 23	Detroit	★★
L	**Tag with Kane vs. CM Punk & John Cena**		

2364	Apr. 29	Chicago	★★★★
L	**CM Punk (Chicago street fight/Extreme Rules)**		

Hoisting Punk up during our underrated classic Chicago streetfight in 2012. I was pissed off afterward because nobody in the gorilla position really said much about it when we came through the curtain, yet gave Brock Lesnar a standing ovation 30 minutes later after his return beatdown of John Cena.

2365	Apr. 30	Dayton, OH	★★3/4
DR	**Big Show (beat the clock challenge)**		

| 2366 | May 05 | Knoxville, TN | ★★★1/2 |
| **L** | **CM Punk** | | |

| 2367 | May 06 | Chattanooga, TN | ★★★ |
| **L** | **CM Punk** | | |

| 2368 | May 07 | Greensboro, NC | ★★★ |
| **W** | **Tag with Alberto Del Rio vs. Sheamus & Randy Orton** | | |

| 2369 | May 08 | Roanoke, VA | ★★★ |
| **W** | **Sheamus**, DQ | | |

| 2370 | May 08 | Roanoke, VA | ★★★ |
| **DQ** | **Tag with Alberto Del Rio vs. Sheamus & Randy Orton**, DOUBLE DQ | | |

| 2371 | May 12 | Syracuse, NY | ★★★★ |
| **L** | **CM Punk** | | |

| 2372 | May 13 | Rochester, NY | ★★★ |
| **L** | **CM Punk** | | |

| 2373 | May 14 | Pittsburgh | ★★★1/2 |
| **W** | **Randy Orton**, DQ | | |

| 2374 | May 20 | Raleigh, NC | ★★★★ |
| **L** | **4-way vs. Sheamus vs. Alberto Del Rio vs. Randy Orton (Over the Limit)** | | |

| 2375 | May 24 | Sao Paulo | ★★★1/2 |
| **L** | **CM Punk**, DQ | | |

| 2376 | June 25 | Fort Wayne, IN | ★★★ |
| **L** | **John Cena**, DQ | | |

| 2377 | June 29 | Monroe, LA | ★★1/2 |
| **L** | **Kane** | | |

| 2378 | June 30 | Lafayette, LA | ★★1/2 |
| **L** | **Kane** | | |

| 2379 | July 01 | Hidalgo, TX | ★★★ |
| **L** | **Kane** | | |

2380	July 02	Laredo, TX	★★★
NC	**Tag with Daniel Bryan vs. CM Punk & John Cena,** NO CONTEST		

2381	July 07	El Paso, TX	★★★
L	**Kane**		

2382	July 08	Rio Rancho, NM	★★★1/2
L	**4-way vs. CM Punk vs. Daniel Bryan vs. Kane,** Punk		

2383	July 09	Denver	★★★★
L	**Sheamus**		

2384	July 09	Denver	★★★
L	**Tag with Big Show vs. John Cena & Kane,** DQ		

2385	July 15	Phoenix	★★★★
L	**5-way vs. John Cena vs. Big Show vs. Miz vs. Kane (ladder match/Money in the Bank),** Cena		

2386	July 23	St. Louis	★★★
L	**6-man with Dolph Ziggler & Alberto Del Rio vs. Sheamus, Rey Mysterio Jr. & Sin Cara**		

2387	July 28	Johnson City, TN	★★★
W	**Tag with Christian vs. Dolph Ziggler & Cody**		

2388	July 29	Pikeville, KY	★★★1/2
W	**Tag with Christian vs. Dolph Ziggler & Cody**		

2389	July 30	Cincinnati	★★★1/2
W	**Tag with Christian vs. Dolph Ziggler & Miz**		

2390	July 31	Indianapolis	★★★1/2
L	**6-man with Christian & Kane vs. Dolph Ziggler, Miz & Daniel Bryan**		

AUGUST 2012

2391	Aug. 03	Jacksonville, FL	★★★
W	**Tag with Zack Ryder vs. Dolph Ziggler & Miz**		

2392	Aug. 04	Albany, GA	★★★
W	**Tag with Zack Ryder vs. Dolph Ziggler & Miz**		

2393	Aug. 05	Dothan, AL	★★★
W	**Tag with Zack Ryder vs. Dolph Ziggler & Miz**		

| 2394 | Aug. 13 | Dallas | ★★★ |
| **L** | **3-way vs. Dolph Ziggler vs. Miz** | | |

| 2395 | Aug. 14 | Austin, TX | ★★★ |
| **L** | **Alberto Del Rio** | | |

| 2396 | Aug. 19 | Los Angeles | ★★★1/2 |
| **W** | **Dolph Ziggler (Summer Slam)** | | |

| 2397 | Aug. 20 | Fresno, CA | ★★★1/4 |
| **L** | **Dolph Ziggler** | | |

JANUARY 2013

| 2398 | Jan. 27 | Phoenix | ★★★★1/2 |
| **L** | **Royal Rumble,** Eliminated by Dolph Ziggler after 47:53 | | |

| 2399 | Jan. 28 | Las Vegas | ★★1/2 |
| **L** | **Tag with Dolph Ziggler vs. Kane & Daniel Bryan** | | |

FEBRUARY 2013

| 2400 | Feb. 04 | Atlanta | ★★★★1/2 |
| **L** | **CM Punk** | | |

| 2401 | Feb. 09 | Springfield, MO | ★★1/2 |
| **W** | **Dolph Ziggler (no DQ)** | | |

| 2402 | Feb. 10 | Cape Girardeau, MO | ★★3/4 |
| **W** | **Dolph Ziggler (no DQ)** | | |

| 2403 | Feb. 11 | Nashville, TN | ★★★★ |
| **W** | **Daniel Bryan** | | |

| 2404 | Feb. 12 | North Little Rock, AR | ★★★3/4 |
| **L** | **Big Show** | | |

| 2405 | Feb. 17 | New Orleans | ★★★★ |
| **L** | **6-way vs. Jack Swagger vs. Daniel Bryan vs. Kane vs. Mark Henry vs. Randy Orton (Elimination Chamber),** Swagger | | |

| 2406 | Feb. 18 | Lafayette, LA | ★★★3/4 |
| **L** | **Tag with Ryback & Sheamus vs. Dean Ambrose, Roman Reigns & Seth Rollins** | | |

Triangle dropkicking future WWE World Champion Drew McIntyre right out of the 2013 Royal Rumble.

| 2407 | Mar. 09 | Broomfield, CO | ★★★ |
| **W** | **Dolph Ziggler (no DQ)** | | |

| 2408 | Mar. 10 | Loveland, CO | ★★★ |
| **W** | **Dolph Ziggler (no DQ)** | | |

| 2409 | Mar. 11 | Indianapolis | ★★ |
| **NC** | **Miz,** NO CONTEST | | |

| 2410 | Mar. 12 | Ft. Wayne, IN | ★★★3/4 |
| **L** | **Jack Swagger** | | |

| 2411 | Mar. 16 | Providence, RI | ★★★3/4 |
| **W** | **Dolph Ziggler (no DQ)** | | |

| 2412 | Mar. 17 | Binghamton, NY | ★★★1/4 |
| **W** | **Dolph Ziggler (no DQ)** | | |

| 2413 | Mar. 18 | Pittsburgh | ★★★1/2 |
| **L** | **3-way vs. Wade Barrett vs. Miz** | | |

| 2414 | Mar. 19 | Cincinnati | ★★★1/2 |
| **L** | **Jack Swagger** | | |

| 2415 | Mar. 21 | Orlando, FL | ★★★1/2 |
| **W** | **Bray Wyatt** | | |

| 2416 | Mar. 23 | Fairfax, VA | ★★★ |
| **W** | **Dolph Ziggler** | | |

| 2417 | Mar. 24 | Salisbury, MD | ★★★ |
| **W** | **Dolph Ziggler** | | |

| 2418 | Mar. 25 | Philadelphia | ★★★1/4 |
| **W** | **Dolph Ziggler** | | |

| 2419 | Mar. 26 | Hershey, PA | ★★★ |
| **W** | **Wade Barrett** | | |

| 2420 | Mar. 30 | Atlantic City, NJ | ★★★ |
| **W** | **6-man with Alberto Del Rio & Miz vs. Fandango, Jack Swagger & Wade Barrett** | | |

| 2421 | Mar. 31 | White Plains, NY | ★★★1/4 |
| **W** | **6-man with Alberto Del Rio & Miz vs. Fandango, Jack Swagger & Wade Barrett** | | |

APRIL 2013

| 2422 | Apr. 01 | Washington, D.C. | ★★★ |
| **W** | **Antonio Cesaro** | | |

| 2423 | Apr. 07 | East Rutherford, NJ | ★★★1/4 |
| **L** | **Fandango (WrestleMania 29)** | | |

| 2424 | Apr. 09 | Boston | ★★★★ |
| **L** | **Dolph Ziggler** | | |

| 2425 | Apr. 22 | London | ★★★1/2 |
| **L** | **Dolph Ziggler** | | |

| 2426 | May 07 | Raleigh, NC | ★★★★1/4 |
| **W** | **Ryback** | | |

| 2427 | May 11 | Beaumont, TX | ★★1/2 |
| **L** | **Fandango** | | |

| 2428 | May 12 | Ft. Worth, TX | ★★★1/2 |
| **L** | **Fandango** | | |

| 2429 | May 14 | Wichita, KS | ★★★★ |
| **W** | **Antonio Cesaro** | | |

MY TOP 10 DUDS

(IN CHRONOLOGICAL ORDER)

#3, TAG MATCH WITH LANCE STORM VS. STEVE GILLESPIE AND ED LANGLEY, OCT. 16, 1990, STRATHMORE, ALBERTA

The first match of my career against Lance a week earlier couldn't have gone better. This one couldn't have gone worse. Watching it back with Lance during a *Talk Is Jericho* episode recently was equal parts hilarious and embarrassing. Steve and Ed were "vets" who knew nothing about how to put together a match, put over their babyfaces, or get any heat whatsoever. So what transpired was 15 minutes of Lance and me getting beaten up with no offense, me getting an "inner thigh shot" during my hot tag comeback ("You need to know the difference between an inner thigh shot and a ball shot," an incredulous Ed said afterward), and a screw-job finish where I literally got carried out after taking a punch.

#237, TAG MATCH WITH BOSTON BLACKIE VS. RENE LASARTESSE AND MOONDOG REX, OCT. 12, 1993, HAMBURG, GERMANY

Rene was about 65 years old at this point, stood around 6-foot-6 with flowing white hair, a big nose, and a full-length vampire cape that he wore to the ring. He didn't wrestle a lot, but when he did he thought he was still 50 and did all of his old moves … not that there were a lot of them. The highlight of the match was Rene going for a one-handed cartwheel where he would choke his opponent mid-roll. Except this time, when he went for the cartwheel, he just collapsed like a giant tree on top of me, muttering, "What the fuck," in a thick Swiss accent. Things went downhill from there.

#525, KAMIKAZE, FEB. 13, 1996, KISARAZU, JAPAN

Kamikaze was a Japanese indie worker who got on a WAR tour because Tenryu needed extra bodies. He wore a mask and a full-body suit and was completely red reels. We were working in the middle of February, and the building was fucking freezing. I chopped him, and it was like catching a football when it's cold out, it just killed my poor hands. He totally no-sold my offense, and I finally just shoot-punched him in the face and pinned him with a lionsault. We shan't work together again.

#586, MR. JL (JERRY LYNN), AUG. 20, 1996, DALTON, GA

This wasn't necessarily a bad match in the ring, but it sure was catastrophic out of it. With no direction or guidance from the office, Jerry and I went out and had the best possible back-and-forth match we could have in the seven or eight minutes they gave us. Problem was, I was used to taking my time and doing more of a back-and-forth Japanese style. Wrestling for seven minutes seemed like such a short time, and since I was winning, I wanted to make Mr. JL look as good as possible. Unfortunately, that's not what the WCW powers that be wanted, and after the match, booker Terry Taylor even said to me, "Well, that sucked. I thought you were supposed to be good?" Talk about lack of confidence from Jump Street!

#875, JULIO SANCHEZ, JUNE 27, 1998, ORLANDO, FL

Once again not so much of a bad match, just more of a horrible outcome. This is because I thought I separated my shoulder on a head-scissor bump from Julio. As wrestlers, we know when our body is really hurt, and I was in so much pain I walked out of the ring and straight to the back — the only time in my 30-year career I ever had to do that. Thankfully, the shoulder was only slightly separated and I was back in the ring a few days later.

#1244, RAVEN, FEB. 26, 2001, PHOENIX

I don't remember the exact details of why it was so bad, but Steve Austin was so disgusted by this match that he threw his proverbial hat (a gesture he would make when he thought something sucked, where he would snatch an imaginary baseball cap off his head and toss it in disgust) into the corner while the entire roster watched it again in catering the next day. I was in the back of the room as it aired and silently slipped out in shame when it mercifully ended.

#1332, RHYNO, AUG. 19, 2001, SAN JOSE, CA

This SummerSlam match wasn't bad in theory, but early on, I whacked my head on the floor something fierce, which caused me to botch a few moves and things just went downhill from there.

#1590 6-MAN WITH TRIPLE H AND RIC FLAIR VS. SHAWN MICHAELS, BOOKER T AND KEVIN NASH, APR. 27, 2003, WORCESTER, MA

I don't remember anything about this match, but how could a contest between six Hall Of Fame World Champions have been so bad? On a PPV no less? My guess is everybody was lazy and decided to just "call it in the ring," which obviously ended up with things being a slow, plodding and boring mess.

#1720, TYSON TOMKO, MAY 28, 2004, MANCHESTER, ENGLAND

Tyson and I had good matches, but this was not one of them. I remember I came backstage afterward, found an empty room, and completely flipped out — throwing chairs, screaming at the walls, the whole deal. It was also the match were I broke my right pinkie and never got it set properly, leaving me with a crooked appendage that makes it impossible to throw proper "Dio horns." As a result I'm forced to think about this match every day.

#1827, TAG MATCH WITH CHRIS BENOIT VS. LA RESISTANCE, JAN. 31, 2005, SAN JOSE, CA

I never saw Chris Benoit have a bad match ... with the exception of this one. I just remember waiting for Chris to take control and save this thing, but not even the genius of the Rabid Wolverine could turn this piece of shit around.

#2238, TAG MATCH WITH CM PUNK VS. EDGE AND JOHN MORRISON, FEB. 28, 2010, ABILENE, TX

This took place on a Sunday afternoon in a barn in front of about 1,000 people, but is worthy of making this list due to the fact that Punk refused to tag me in for the entire match. He was mad because Edge and I were too busy watching the Canada-USA Olympic gold medal hockey game beforehand to put together the match. It was obviously a monumental game for Canadians everywhere, and we were stoked when we scored the final goal to win the gold medal just as my ring music started playing. Edge and I had more than enough confidence and experience to know we could easily just call the matinee match in the ring, but Punk felt differently and decided to have a hissy fit in the middle of the bout. About five minutes in, I realized what he was doing and decided to let him hang himself. When the time was right, I ran into the ring on my own and Edge and I saved the match, but I was furious. When it was done I called him into the trainers' room and let him have it for being so unprofessional. He just looked at the floor and didn't say a word in his defense.

| 2430 | May 19 | St. Louis | ★★★ |

 W   Fandango (Extreme Rules)

| 2431 | May 20 | Kansas City, MO | ★★ |
| **W** | **Tag with Miz vs. Fandango & Wade Barrett** | | |

| 2432 | May 21 | Omaha, NE | ★★1/2 |
| **W** | **Big Show,** countout | | |

| 2433 | May 24 | Salt Lake City | ★★★ |
| **L** | **Ryback (no DQ)** | | |

| 2434 | May 25 | Red Deer, Alberta | ★★1/2 |
| **L** | **Ryback (no DQ)** | | |

| 2435 | May 26 | Lethbridge, Alberta | ★★★ |
| **L** | **Ryback (no DQ)** | | |

| 2436 | May 28 | Edmonton, Alberta | ★★★ |
| **W** | **Cody Rhodes,** Walls of Jericho | | |

JUNE 2013

| 2437 | June 01 | Manchester, NH | ★★★ |
| **W** | **Fandango (no DQ)** | | |

| 2438 | June 02 | Augusta, ME | ★★★ |
| **W** | **Fandango (no DQ)** | | |

| 2439 | June 04 | Uniondale, NY | ★★★ |
| **L** | **Curtis Axel** | | |

| 2440 | June 10 | Richmond, VA | ★★1/2 |
| **W** | **Big E. Langston** | | |

| 2441 | June 11 | Greensboro, NC | ★★★ |
| **W** | **Tag with Alberto Del Rio vs. Dolph Ziggler & Big E. Langston** | | |

| 2442 | June 15 | Bloomington, IL | ★★★ |
| **W** | **Six-man tag with Kane & Daniel Bryan vs. Dean Ambrose, Seth Rollins & Roman Reigns,** DQ | | |

| 2443 | June 16 | Chicago | ★★★★ |
| **L** | **CM Punk (Payback)** | | |

| 2444 | June 17 | Grand Rapids, MI | ★★ |
| **W** | **Heath Slater** | | |

One of the few matches I had with Cody Rhodes in WWE in 2013. Six years later, we would change the wrestling world together.

2445	June 18	Dayton, OH	★★★1/2
L	**Alberto Del Rio,** DQ		

2446	June 24	North Charleston, SC	★★★3/4
W	**Alberto Del Rio,** DQ		

2447	June 25	Columbia, SC	★★★
W	**Cody Rhodes**		

JULY 2013

2448	July 04	Tokyo	★★★★
W	**Antonio Cesaro (no DQ)**		

2449	July 05	Tokyo	★★★1/2
W	**Curtis Axel**		

2450	July 06	Taipei, Taiwan	★★★3/4
W	**Antonio Cesaro**		

2451	July 08	Baltimore	★★★
W	**Curtis Axel**		

Jericho – the suave and debonair years. I got the idea of the slow-talking, suit-wearing villain from Nick Bockwinkel.

| 2452 | July 09 | Hampton, VA | ★★★ |
| **W** | **Curtis Axel,** countout | | |

| 2453 | July 13 | Trenton, NJ | ★★★1/2 |
| **W** | **Tag with CM Punk vs. Cody Rhodes & Damien Sandow** | | |

| 2454 | July 14 | Philadelphia | ★★3/4 |
| **L** | **Ryback (Money In the Bank)** | | |

| 2455 | July 15 | New York City | ★★★★ |
| **L** | **Rob Van Dam** | | |

| 2456 | July 16 | Providence, RI | ★★★1/2 |
| **L** | **Curtis Axel** | | |

JULY 2014

| 2457 | July 06 | Toronto | ★★★ |
| **W** | **Miz** | | |

| 2458 | July 07 | Montreal | ★★1/2 |
| **W** | **Miz** | | |

2459	July 08	Ottawa, Ontario	★★★
L	**Randy Orton**		

2460	July 12	New York City	★★★1/2
W	**Randy Orton**		

2461	July 13	Wildwood, NJ	★★★1/2
W	**Tag with John Cena vs. Randy Orton & Bray Wyatt**		

2462	July 15	Fayetteville, NC	★★★
W	**Luke Harper**		

2463	July 20	Tampa, FL	★★1/2
W	**Bray Wyatt (Battleground)**		

2464	July 26	Edmonton, Alberta	★★★
W	**Bray Wyatt**		

2465	July 27	Calgary, Alberta	★★★
W	**Bray Wyatt**		

2466	July 28	Houston	★★★
NC	**Seth Rollins,** NO CONTEST		

2467	July 29	Corpus Christi, TX	★★
W	**Erick Rowan**		

AUGUST 2014

2468	Aug. 03	San Antonio	★★1/2
W	**Bray Wyatt**		

2469	Aug. 04	Austin, TX	★★★
W	**Luke Harper,** DQ		

2470	Aug. 07	Melbourne, Australia	★★★1/2
W	**Bray Wyatt**		

2471	Aug. 08	Sydney	★★★1/2
W	**Bray Wyatt**		

2472	Aug. 09	Perth, Australia	★★★
W	**6-man with The Usos (Jey & Jimmy) vs. Bray Wyatt, Luke Harper & Erick Rowan**		

2473	Aug. 16	San Jose, CA	★★3/4
W	**Bray Wyatt (Ric Flair referee)**		

| 2474 | Aug. 17 | Los Angeles | ★★★ |

L   **Bray Wyatt (Summer Slam)**

| 2475 | Aug. 18 | Las Vegas | ★★1/2 |

W   **Bray Wyatt**

SEPTEMBER 2014

| 2476 | Sept. 01 | Des Moines, IA | ★★★ |

W   **6-man with John Cena & Roman Reigns vs. Kane, Randy Orton & Seth Rollins**

| 2477 | Sept. 02 | Lincoln, NE | ★★★ |

W   **10-man tag with John Cena, Mark Henry, Roman Reigns & Big Show vs. Kane, Seth Rollins, Bray Wyatt, Erick Rowan & Luke Harper**

| 2478 | Sept. 08 | Baltimore | ★★★★ |

L   **Bray Wyatt (cage match)**

MATCH NOTES #2478

This was kind of a rubber match for Bray and me after two mediocre outings on the pay-per-views prior (#2463 & #2474), but we knocked it out of the park with this one. The match was highlighted by my first top-of-the-cage dive since 1993 … and probably my last! Earlier in the day, I climbed up to the top of the cage and standing in an empty arena 15 feet off the ground made me question my sanity. But only a few hours later (with Harper and Rowan preventing my escape by beating on the cage with chairs beneath me), I stood in that exact same spot looking at an action-figure-sized Bray below and the fear was gone. I shrugged my shoulders in a homage to HBK and launched myself into the great wide open. The landing was picture perfect and the stunt was a success. More importantly, we finally had the great match I knew we could have.

| 2479 | Sept. 09 | Wilkes-Barre, PA | ★★★ |

W   **Tag with Roman Reigns vs. Randy Orton & Seth Rollins**

| 2480 | Sept. 14 | Boston | ★★★ |

L   **Seth Rollins**

| 2481 | Sept. 15 | Lafayette, LA | ★★1/2 |

W   **Kane**

| 2482 | Sept. 21 | Nashville, TN | ★★★ |

L   **Randy Orton (Night of Champions)**

| 2483 | Nov. 10 | Bournemouth, England | ★★★1/2 |

W   **Bray Wyatt (street fight)**

| 2484 | Nov. 11 | Liverpool, England | ★★★ |

W   **Tag with Dean Ambrose vs. Bray Wyatt & Kane**

| 2485 | Nov. 12 | Newcastle, England | ★★★1/2 |

W   **Bray Wyatt (street fight)**

| 2486 | Nov. 13 | Glasgow, Scotland | ★★★★ |

W   **Bray Wyatt (street fight)**

| 2487 | Nov. 14 | Braunschweig, Germany | ★★★1/2 |

W   **Bray Wyatt (street fight)**

| 2488 | Nov. 15 | Frankfurt, Germany | ★★★1/2 |

W   **Bray Wyatt (street fight)**

| 2489 | Jan. 10 | Montgomery, AL | ★★★ |

W   **Luke Harper**

| 2490 | Jan. 11 | Mobile, AL | ★★★ |

W   **Luke Harper**

| 2491 | Jan. 16 | St. Louis | ★★★ |

W   **Luke Harper**

| 2492 | Jan. 17 | Las Vegas | ★★★ |

W   **Cesaro**

| 2493 | Jan. 18 | Houston | ★★★ |

W   **Cesaro**

| 2494 | Jan. 23 | Trenton, NJ | ★★★1/2 |

W   **Cesaro**

| 2495 | Jan. 24 | East Rutherford, NJ | ★★★ |

W   **Cesaro**

| 2496 | Jan. 31 | Edmonton, Alberta | ★★★ |

W   **Cesaro**

FEBRUARY 2015

| 2497 | Feb. 01 | Calgary, Alberta | ★★★1/2 |
| **W** | **Cesaro** | | |

| 2498 | Feb. 07 | Jacksonville, FL | ★★★ |
| **W** | **Luke Harper** | | |

| 2499 | Feb. 08 | Canton, OH | ★★★ |
| **W** | **Luke Harper** | | |

| 2500 | Feb. 14 | Tampa, FL | ★★★ |
| **W** | **Cesaro** | | |

| 2501 | Feb. 15 | Ft. Myers, FL | ★★★ |
| **W** | **Cesaro** | | |

| 2502 | Feb. 27 | New York City | ★★★1/2 |
| **W** | **Luke Harper** | | |

| 2503 | Feb. 28 | Toronto | ★★★ |
| **W** | **Luke Harper** | | |

MARCH 2015

| 2504 | Mar. 01 | Buffalo, NY | ★★1/2 |
| **W** | **Luke Harper** | | |

JUNE 2015

| 2505 | June 12 | Springfield, IL | ★★★ |
| **W** | **Luke Harper** | | |

| 2506 | June 13 | Terre Haute, IN | ★★★ |
| **W** | **Luke Harper** | | |

| 2507 | June 20 | Las Vegas | ★★★ |
| **W** | **Luke Harper** | | |

| 2508 | June 27 | Boston | ★★★ |
| **W** | **Team with Dolph Ziggler vs. Wade Barrett & Sheamus** | | |

| 2509 | June 28 | Reading, PA | ★★1/2 |
| **W** | **Wade Barrett (street fight)** | | |

| 2510 | July 03 | Tokyo | ★★★3/4 |
| **L** | **Finn Balor** | | |

| 2511 | July 04 | Tokyo | ★★★★ |
| **W** | **Neville (The Beast in the East)** | | |

| 2512 | July 10 | Philadelphia | ★★★ |
| **W** | **Luke Harper** | | |

| 2513 | July 11 | Pittsburgh | ★★★ |
| **W** | **Luke Harper** | | |

| 2514 | July 31 | San Diego | ★★★ |
| **W** | **Kevin Owens** | | |

| 2515 | Aug. 01 | Ontario, CA | ★★★1/2 |
| **W** | **Kevin Owens (cage match)** | | |

| 2516 | Aug. 02 | Fresno, CA | ★★★ |
| **W** | **Kevin Owens (cage match)** | | |

| 2517 | Aug. 15 | Detroit | ★★★ |
| **W** | **Kevin Owens** | | |

| 2518 | Aug. 21 | Bridgeport, CT | ★★1/2 |
| **W** | **Wade Barrett** | | |

| 2519 | Aug. 29 | San Juan, Puerto Rico | ★★★ |
| **W** | **Luke Harper** | | |

| 2520 | Aug. 30 | Tallahassee, FL | ★★3/4 |
| **W** | **Luke Harper** | | |

| 2521 | Sept. 11 | Edmonton, Alberta | ★★★ |
| **W** | **Kevin Owens** | | |

| 2522 | Sept. 12 | Calgary, Alberta | ★★★ |
| **W** | **Kevin Owens** | | |

In 2015, I worked house show matches almost exclusively with Brodie Lee, and we never had a bad one. Just an excellent performer.

2523	Sept. 20	Houston	★★★1/2
L	**6-man with Dean Ambrose & Roman Reigns vs. Bray Wyatt, Braun Strowman & Luke Harper (Night of Champions)**		

2524	Sept. 25	Toronto	★★★
W	**Luke Harper**		

2525	Sept. 26	Rochester, NY	★★3/4
W	**Luke Harper**		

2526	Sept. 27	Syracuse, NY	★★★1/2
W	**Luke Harper**		

IN THEIR WORDS: MR. BRODIE LEE (AKA LUKE HARPER)

At one point, Chris was working against either Cesaro or me for almost six months straight. We were in Syracuse, New York, and Jericho started his comeback. He ascends to the top rope and yells to the crowd as loud as he could, "Come on, Rochester!" to deafening silence and dropped an axe-handle on me. I told him, "Hey, we're in Syracuse." Without missing a beat, Chris gets up and goes, "Come on, Syracuse!" and the crowd gets right back behind him. That was my favorite memory of him among many, many good ones.

| 2527 | Oct. 02 | Trenton, NJ | ★★★ |
| **L** | **Kevin Owens** | | |

| 2528 | Oct. 03 | New York City | ★★★ |
| **L** | **Kevin Owens (Live From Madison Square Garden)** | | |

MATCH NOTES #2528, 25TH ANNIVERSARY MATCH

I claimed this was the exact 25th anniversary of my first match, even though it was a day late, because it seemed just too poetic to have my Silver in the world's most famous arena AND the place where I had some of my earliest memories watching my dad play hockey for the New York Rangers. The night was made even more special due to the fact that I flew in my three oldest friends in the business (Lance Storm, Don Callis, and Lenny Olson) to mark the occasion and sat them in the front row at Vince's insistence. The match was rushed as Vince decided to make the show a WWE Network special, so we had a set amount of time for our segment, but the best part was cutting a promo reminiscing about my career and my time in the business beforehand that tore the house down. Afterward the four of us celebrated at the best steak house in NYC and finished the night tracking one of my favorite and funniest episodes of *Talk Is Jericho* ever.

New York City on Oct 2, 2015, the night of my 25th anniversary of my first match, with my three oldest friends in the wrestling business. It's such a blast to be working with Don Callis and Luther in AEW in 2021.

MY TOP 5 MADISON SQUARE GARDEN MATCHES

#1174, TAG MATCH WITH RIKISHI VS. EDDY GUERRERO AND X-PAC, SEPT. 23, 2000

I was soooo hungover during this match after a night of drinking with Sebastian Bach, Paul Gargano, and Adrian Smith.

#1530, SHAWN MICHAELS, TRIPLE H, BOOKER T, ROB VAN DAM, AND KANE, ELIMINATION CHAMBER, NOV. 17, 2002

It was disastrous in so many ways between injuries and technical fuckups (they even opened the ring chamber door and let Kane out instead of HBK). But it was still the first EVER and a piece of history.

#1691, CHRISTIAN, WRESTLEMANIA 20, MAR. 14, 2004

An underrated match in Mania history, both in story line buildup and execution.

#2045, JOHN CENA, CAGE MATCH, DEC. 28, 2008

For all the reasons I stated in my favorite match list, plus the innovative, first-of-its-kind finish — an AA from the top rope.

#2199, TRIPLE THREAT TAG TITLE MATCH WITH BIG SHOW VS. KANE AND UNDERTAKER VS. TRIPLE H AND SHAWN MICHAELS, NOV. 16, 2009

Huge in star power in the ring AND out, as the cast of *MacGruber* was sitting in the front row.

2529 **W**	Oct. 08 **Big Show**	Jeddah, Saudi Arabia	★★★1/2
2530 **W**	Oct. 09 **Luke Harper**	Jeddah, Saudi Arabia	★★★1/2
2531 **W**	Oct. 10 **6-man with Cesaro & John Cena vs. Luke Harper, Big Show & Miz**	Jeddah, Saudi Arabia	★★★
2532 **W**	Oct. 16 **Wade Barrett**	Merida, Mexico	★★★1/2

| 2533 | Oct. 17 | Mexico City | ★★★1/2 |
| W | Wade Barrett | | |

| 2534 | Oct. 18 | Monterrey, Mexico | ★★★ |
| W | Wade Barrett | | |

JANUARY 2016

| 2535 | Jan. 08 | Houston | ★★★ |
| W | Alberto Del Rio | | |

| 2536 | Jan. 09 | Bossier City, LA | ★★★ |
| W | Alberto Del Rio | | |

| 2537 | Jan. 10 | Monroe, LA | ★★★ |
| W | Alberto Del Rio | | |

| 2538 | Jan. 23 | Ft. Myers, FL | ★★★ |
| W | Alberto Del Rio | | |

| 2539 | Jan. 24 | Orlando, FL | ★★★ |
| L | Royal Rumble, Eliminated by Dean Ambrose after 50:47 | | |

| 2540 | Jan. 25 | Miami | ★★★1/2 |
| L | A.J. Styles | | |

| 2541 | Jan. 26 | Tampa, FL | ★★★ |
| W | 6-man with Dean Ambrose & Roman Reigns vs. Bray Wyatt, Erick Rowan & Luke Harper, DQ | | |

FEBRUARY 2016

| 2542 | Feb. 05 | Calgary, Alberta | ★★★ |
| W | 6-man with Kane & Big Show vs. Bray Wyatt, Erick Rowan & Luke Harper | | |

| 2543 | Feb. 09 | Portland, OR | ★★★3/4 |
| W | A.J. Styles | | |

| 2544 | Feb. 09 | Portland, OR | ★★★ |
| W | Tag with A.J. Styles vs. Adam Rose & Curtis Axel | | |

| 2545 | Feb. 13 | Fresno, CA | ★★★ |
| W | Bray Wyatt | | |

| 2546 | Feb. 14 | Bakersfield, CA | ★★★ |
| W | Bray Wyatt | | |

| 2547 | Feb. 16 | Ontario, CA | ★★3/4 |
| **W** | **Miz** | | |

| 2548 | Feb. 21 | Cleveland | ★★★ |
| **L** | **A.J. Styles (Fastlane)** | | |

| 2549 | Feb. 22 | Detroit | ★★★ |
| **W** | **Tag with A.J. Styles vs. Adam Rose & Curtis Axel** | | |

| 2550 | Feb. 23 | Indianapolis | ★★★1/4 |
| **W** | **6-man with A.J. Styles & Mark Henry vs. Big E. Langston, Kofi Kingston & Xavier Woods** | | |

| 2551 | Feb. 29 | Nashville, TN | ★★ |
| **W** | **Tag with A.J. Styles vs. Kofi Kingston & Big E. Langston** | | |

MARCH 2016

| 2552 | Mar. 07 | Chicago | ★★★★ |
| **L** | **Tag with A.J. Styles vs. Kofi Kingston & Big E. Langston** | | |

| 2553 | Mar. 12 | Toronto | ★★★1/2 |
| **W** | **Jack Swagger (Roadblock)** | | |

| 2554 | Mar. 13 | Erie, PA | ★★★ |
| **W** | **Jack Swagger** | | |

| 2555 | Mar. 14 | Pittsburgh | N/A |
| **L** | **Neville, DQ** | | |

| 2556 | Mar. 19 | Buffalo, NY | ★★★ |
| **W** | **Jack Swagger** | | |

| 2557 | Mar. 20 | Binghamton, NY | ★★★1/2 |
| **W** | **Jack Swagger** | | |

| 2558 | Mar. 21 | Philadelphia | ★★★ |
| **W** | **Fandango** | | |

| 2559 | Mar. 28 | New York City | ★★3/4 |
| **L** | **Zach Ryder** | | |

APRIL 2016

| 2560 | Apr. 03 | Arlington, TX | ★★★1/2 |
| **W** | **A.J. Styles (WrestleMania 32)** | | |

| 2561 | Apr. 04 | Dallas | ★★★1/2 |
| **L** | **4-way vs. A.J. Styles vs. Cesaro vs. Kevin Owens** | | |

| 2562 | Apr. 05 | Houston | ★★★ |
| **L** | **Tag with Kevin Owens vs. A.J. Styles & Cesaro** | | |

| 2563 | Apr. 12 | San Diego | ★★★ |
| **L** | **Sami Zayn, DQ** | | |

| 2564 | Apr. 18 | London | ★★★ |
| **L** | **Tag with Kevin Owens vs. Dean Ambrose & A.J. Styles** | | |

| 2565 | Apr. 18 | London | ★★1/2 |
| **W** | **Sami Zayn** | | |

| 2566 | Apr. 19 | London | ★★★ |
| **W** | **Tag with Kevin Owens vs. Sami Zayn & Dean Ambrose** | | |

| 2567 | Apr. 20 | Newcastle, England | ★★★ |
| **L** | **A.J. Styles** | | |

| 2568 | Apr. 21 | Brussels | ★★★ |
| **L** | **A.J. Styles** | | |

| 2569 | Apr. 22 | Paris | ★★★1/2 |
| **L** | **A.J. Styles** | | |

| 2570 | Apr. 23 | Malaga, Spain | ★★★1/2 |
| **L** | **A.J. Styles** | | |

MAY 2016

| 2571 | May 01 | Chicago | ★★★ |
| **L** | **Dean Ambrose (WWE Payback)** | | |

| 2572 | May 14 | Raleigh, NC | ★★★ |
| **L** | **6-man with Karl Anderson & Luke Gallows vs. Roman Reigns & The Usos** | | |

| 2573 | May 15 | Columbia, SC | ★★★ |
| **L** | **6-man with Karl Anderson & Luke Gallows vs. Roman Reigns & The Usos** | | |

| 2574 | May 22 | Newark, NJ | ★★★1/4 |
| **L** | **Dean Ambrose (asylum match/Extreme Rules)** | | |

| 2575 | May 23 | Baltimore | ★★1/2 |
| **W** | **Apollo Crews** | | |

| 2576 | May 28 | Winnipeg, Manitoba | ★★★★ |

W   Dean Ambrose (street fight)

IN THEIR WORDS: JON MOXLEY (AKA DEAN AMBROSE)

We had the main event in Winnipeg. At the time, I was a good guy, and Jericho was a bad guy. But we knew going in he was the hometown guy. He's a returning hero, legend. He came from Winnipeg. It was literally Chris Jericho Day in Winnipeg on this day, so we knew the crowd would be solidly behind him. I'd been a good guy my entire (WWE) singles career to that point. We both knew we should switch roles for the night and not play around. He went out as a total babyface. I came out to massive boos as a total heel, and it was so much fun because I hadn't gotten to work as a heel for so long. It was a street fight, and it was intense. I was so happy to get the chance to work heel again, especially against a literal hero in his hometown. It was a Winnipeg classic.

| 2577 | May 30 | Green Bay, WI | ★★★ |

L   6-man with Alberto Del Rio & Kevin Owens vs. Cesaro, Dean Ambrose & Sami Zayn

---

JUNE 2016

| 2578 | June 06 | Oklahoma City | ★★★ |

L   Cesaro

| 2579 | June 07 | Wichita, KS | ★★★ |

W   Dean Ambrose

| 2580 | June 13 | New Orleans | ★★★ |

L   Dean Ambrose

| 2581 | June 14 | Biloxi, MS | ★★★ |

L   6-man with Alberto Del Rio & Kevin Owens vs. Cesaro, Dean Ambrose & Sami Zayn

---

| 2582 | June 17 | Salt Lake City | ★★★ |

L   Dean Ambrose (street fight)

| 2583 | June 18 | Los Angeles | ★★★1/2 |

L   Dean Ambrose (street fight)

| 2584 | June 19 | Las Vegas | ★★★★ |

L   6-way vs. Dean Ambrose vs. Alberto Del Rio vs. Cesaro vs. Kevin Owens vs. Sami Zayn (ladder match/Money in the Bank)

| 2585 | June 29 | Honolulu | ★★★1/2 |

L   4-way vs. A.J. Styles vs. Seth Rollins vs. Dean Ambrose

2586	July 01	Tokyo	★★★3/4
L	**Shinsuke Nakamura**		

MATCH NOTES #2586

This was a fun match that really opened my eyes to the brilliance and charisma of Nakamura. I only met him for the first time a few days earlier, but we had an excellent match that wowed the crowd in the Sumo Arena and really impressed me, to the point that the first thing I did when I got back to the States was suggest that Vince to bring him up from NXT to the main roster, ASAP! I told him the same thing after matches I had in Tokyo against Finn Balor and Neville the prior two years. He listened all three times.

2587	July 02	Tokyo	★★★★
L	**3-way vs. Dean Ambrose vs. Seth Rollins**		

2588	July 04	Columbus, OH	★★★1/2
L	**16-man tag with Alberto Del Rio, Cesaro, Kalisto, Kevin Owens, Sami Zayn, Sheamus & Sin Cara vs. Apollo Crews, Bubba Ray Dudley, D-Von Dudley, Jack Swagger, Kane, Mark Henry, Big Show & Zack Ryder**		

2589	July 05	Toledo, OH	★★★
L	**Sami Zayn**		

2590	July 16	New York City	★★★1/2
W	**Neville**		

2591	July 17	Glens Falls, NY	★★★3/4
L	**Neville**		

2592	July 18	Providence, RI	★★★
L	**Tag with Kevin Owens vs. Cesaro & Sami Zayn**		

2593	July 19	Worcester, MA	★★★
W	**Cesaro**		

2594	July 25	Pittsburgh	★★★
L	**4-way vs. Roman Reigns vs. Sami Zayn vs. Sheamus,** Reigns		

2595	July 30	Knoxville, TN	★★★
L	**Dean Ambrose (street fight)**		

2596	July 31	Asheville, NC	★★★1/2
L	**Dean Ambrose (street fight)**		

2597	Aug. 01	Atlanta	★★★1/2
W	**Mixed tag with Charlotte Flair vs. Enzo Amore & Sasha Banks**		

2598	Aug. 08	Anaheim, CA	★★1/2
W	**Enzo Amore, DQ**		

2599	Aug. 10	Auckland, New Zealand	★★★
L	**Finn Balor**		

2600	Aug. 11	Melbourne, Australia	★★★
L	**Tag with Seth Rollins vs. Finn Balor & Roman Reigns**		

2601	Aug. 12	Adelaide, Australia	★★★
L	**Tag with Seth Rollins vs. Finn Balor & Roman Reigns**		

2602	Aug. 13	Sydney	★★★1/2
L	**Finn Balor**		

"You Just Made The List!" became one of my biggest hit catchphrases in 2016. People still ask me to put them on the list to this day, but I always tell them that you can't request to be on the list ... it has to be bestowed upon you.

| 2603 | Aug. 15 | Corpus Christi, TX | ★★★ |
| **L** | **Tag with Seth Rollins vs. Dean Ambrose & John Cena** | | |

| 2604 | Aug. 21 | New York City | ★★1/2 |
| **W** | **Tag with Kevin Owens vs. Big Cass & Enzo Amore (Summer Slam)** | | |

| 2605 | Aug. 22 | New York City | ★★★1/2 |
| **L** | **Roman Reigns** | | |

| 2606 | Aug. 26 | Abilene, TX | ★★★ |
| **W** | **Neville** | | |

| 2607 | Aug. 27 | San Angelo, TX | ★★★ |
| **W** | **Neville** | | |

| 2608 | Aug. 28 | San Antonio | ★★★ |
| **W** | **Neville** | | |

| 2609 | Aug. 29 | Houston | ★★★ |
| **W** | **Neville** | | |

SEPTEMBER 2016

| 2610 | Sept. 05 | Kansas City, MO | ★★★ |
| **L** | **Seth Rollins** | | |

| 2611 | Sept. 07 | London | ★★★1/2 |
| **L** | **Roman Reigns** | | |

| 2612 | Sept. 08 | Manila, Philippines | ★★★1/2 |
| **L** | **Roman Reigns** | | |

| 2613 | Sept. 10 | Shanghai | ★★★3/4 |
| **L** | **Roman Reigns** | | |

| 2614 | Sept. 19 | Memphis, TN | ★★1/2 |
| **L** | **10-man tag with Karl Anderson, Luke Gallows, Epico & Primo vs. Big Cass, Enzo Amore, Sami Zayn, Big E & Kofi Kingston** | | |

| 2615 | Sept. 24 | Chicago | ★★★ |
| **W** | **Neville** | | |

| 2616 | Sept. 25 | Indianapolis | ★★★1/2 |
| **W** | **Sami Zayn (Clash of Champions)** | | |

| 2617 | Sept. 26 | Cincinnati | ★★★ |

W Tag with Kevin Owens vs. Big Cass & Enzo Amore

OCTOBER 2016

| 2618 | Oct. 03 | Los Angeles | ★★★ |

L 6-man with Kevin Owens & Rusev vs. Big Cass, Enzo Amore & Roman Reigns

| 2619 | Oct. 03 | Los Angeles | ★★★ |

L Tag with Kevin Owens vs. Big E & Xavier Woods

| 2620 | Oct. 10 | Oakland, CA | ★★★ |

L Seth Rollins

| 2621 | Oct. 14 | Edmonton, Alberta | ★★★ |

L Cesaro

| 2622 | Oct. 15 | Calgary, Alberta | ★★★1/2 |

L Sami Zayn

| 2623 | Oct. 17 | Denver | ★★★ |

L Seth Rollins

| 2624 | Oct. 22 | Milwaukee | ★★★ |

L Cesaro

| 2625 | Oct. 23 | Rochester, MN | ★★★ |

L Cesaro

| 2626 | Oct. 24 | Minneapolis | ★★★1/2 |

L 3-way vs. Seth Rollins vs. Kevin Owens

| 2627 | Oct. 31 | Hartford, CT | ★★★ |

L Roman Reigns, DQ

NOVEMBER 2016

| 2628 | Nov. 04 | London | ★★★ |

L Sami Zayn

| 2629 | Nov. 05 | Somerset, England | ★★★ |

L Sami Zayn

| 2630 | Nov. 06 | West Yorkshire, England | ★★★ |

L Sami Zayn

ALL OF MY WWE SPECIAL GUEST REFEREES/ENFORCERS/ CORNERMEN

(NUMBER OF MATCHES IN PARENTHESIS)

- Steve Austin (1)
- Batista (1)
- Ric Flair (2)
- Bret Hart (3)
- Jerry Lawler (1)
- Dean Malenko (1)
- Shaquille O'Neal (1)
- Roddy Piper (3)
- Dr. Tom Prichard (1)
- CM Punk (1)
- William Regal (1)
- Ricky Steamboat (2)

2631	Nov. 07	Glasgow, Scotland	★★★★
L	**5-way vs. Kevin Owens vs. Braun Strowman vs. Roman Reigns vs. Seth Rollins,** Owens		
2632	Nov. 08	Oberhausen, Germany	★★1/2
L	**Sami Zayn**		
2633	Nov. 09	Berlin	★★★
L	**Sami Zayn**		
2634	Nov. 10	Wien, Austria	★★★
L	**Sami Zayn**		
2635	Nov. 11	Lyon, France	★★★
L	**Sami Zayn**		
2636	Nov. 12	Strasbourg, France	★★★
L	**Sami Zayn**		
2637	Nov. 14	Buffalo, NY	★★★
W	**6-man with Braun Strowman & Seth Rollins vs. New Day**		

| 2638 | Nov. 20 | Toronto | ★★★★ |

L 10-man with Braun Strowman, Kevin Owens, Roman Reigns & Seth Rollins vs. A.J. Styles, Bray Wyatt, Dean Ambrose, Randy Orton & Shane McMahon (elimination tag/Survivor Series)

| 2639 | Nov. 27 | North Charleston, SC | ★★★ |

L Seth Rollins

DECEMBER 2016

| 2640 | Dec. 02 | Albuquerque, NM | ★★★ |

L Seth Rollins

| 2641 | Dec. 03 | Mexico City | ★★★ |

L Seth Rollins

| 2642 | Dec. 04 | Monterrey, Mexico | ★★★ |

L Seth Rollins

| 2643 | Dec. 05 | Austin, TX | ★★★ |

L Roman Reigns

| 2644 | Dec. 12 | Philadelphia | ★★★ |

L 3-way tag with Kevin Owens vs. Roman Reigns & Seth Rollins vs. Big E & Xavier Woods

| 2645 | Dec. 18 | Pittsburgh | ★★★1/2 |

L Seth Rollins (Roadblock)

| 2646 | Dec. 19 | Columbus, OH | ★★★ |

L Tag with Kevin Owens vs. Roman Reigns & Seth Rollins, DQ

| 2647 | Dec. 27 | St. Louis | ★★★ |

L Seth Rollins

| 2648 | Dec. 28 | New York City | ★★★ |

L Seth Rollins

| 2649 | Dec. 29 | Boston | ★★★ |

L Seth Rollins

TOP 10 INANIMATE OBJECTS
I GOT OVER

• PRINCE NAKAMAKI'S MAHI MAHI

I was doing a "collector" gimmick, where I would take something from a beaten opponent. Nakamaki was actually Prince Iaukea and the "mahi mahi" was actually his lava lava, which I wore for a few weeks.

Wearing Prince Iaukea's "mahi mahi" vs. Dean Malenko in Peoria, Illinois in 1998. Not sure what I'm reading, but could it be a precursor to The List? (Photo by an 18-year-old Justin Roberts)

• JUVI'S MASK

During the same time frame, I beat Juventud Guerrera for his mask (#813) and proceeded to wear it around my neck on a string.

• DX GLOW STICKS

We had a live event at the O2 Arena in London, and I was in the main event (brother) against Cena (#2193). I was cutting a promo on the English fans before the match with the typical "you have bad teeth" cheap heat, when suddenly they exploded and pelted me with dozens of DX rave-style glow sticks they bought for 10 pounds a pair at the merch stand. It looked like a neon-colored hailstorm — check it out on YouTube for yourself! This led to Stephanie McMahon, Triple H, and Shawn Michaels calling for my head and demanding that I be fined and suspended. Afterward, I left Vince a message threatening to quit for getting in trouble for creating genuine heel heat. He texted me back with a smiley face emoji, and I never heard another word about it.

• THE LIST OF JERICHO

A throwaway idea from WWE writer Jimmy Jacobs led to one of the biggest successes of my career. For the next year, I carried a silver aluminum clipboard into the ring for every match I had and sold dozens of them at the merch stand nightly. I still get daily requests from people asking me to put them on the list, so much so that I created a set of rules:

You can't ask me to put you on The List. It's solely my decision and I don't take requests.

You can't yell, "You just made The List" at me, since it's my creation and my list and therefore I am eternally exempt.

• PEN CLICK

Once The List got over, I started having some fun with different aspects of it; one of which was the overexaggerated pen click I would hit after saying, "You know what happens?" I would then hold the utensil in the air for the most pregnant of pauses, all the while never taking my eyes of my hapless opponent ... until finally, I would bring down the hammer. As a result, the ensuing pen click got a bigger pop than half the roster. And I'm not exaggerating!

• LITTLE BIT OF THE BUBBLY

When I won the AEW title from Hangman Page (#2693), I was supposed to walk through the backstage area, cut a promo on the assembled onlookers, and douse a backstage employee with champagne. After four takes that got busted for various reasons, I was in a goofy mood when I finally got back to the dressing room. There was a sole deli tray in my quarters, and to me the funniest part of the bit was when I grabbed an olive and recited the Nigel Tufnel line from *This Is Spinal Tap*: "There's a little guy in there." While nobody cared about that homage, the furor started after I stole a throwaway Lloyd Christmas line. "Little bit of the bubbly" gave me one of my most famous catchphrases and helped sell tens of thousands of bottles of said bubbly.

• THE OBSCENELY EXPENSIVE JERITRON 5000

The big-screen TV that served as my sidekick on every edition of "The Highlight Reel" became as popular and integral to these segments as Hank Kingsley was to Larry Sanders. Despite the fact that it didn't do much more than hang around — until we teamed up to take out Shawn Michaels.

• POTTED PLANT

The idea I had to assault Dean Ambrose with a heavy blunt object (that he had gifted me months earlier) in order to start an injury angle backfired on me the next day when some jackass at WWE.com christened the attempted murder weapon "Mitch the Potted Plant." That's all it took to influence fans to make pro-Mitch signs and have a good laugh, which in turn ruined the angle entirely. But at least they made a Mitch action figure, so I suppose not all was lost.

• SHAD KHAN'S FORD GT & CAR KEYS

We got permission to borrow Shad Khan's $750,000 Ford GT for an angle where I offered it to Moxley if he joined the Inner Circle. Of course, he didn't, but he ended up with the car anyway. We continued the story by taking out his eye with a spike from my jacket, which led to him doing the same to Santana with ... the keys to the GT. We used the car (and the keys) a few more times, and it even made another appearance on *Dynamite* months later during Moxley's next program. Talk about long-term planning!

• FLOYD THE BAT

I started carrying a baseball bat to the ring with me a few weeks prior to the Inner Circle destroying Matt Hardy's Vanguard 1, because I didn't wanna just show up with a random bat. I felt it was an "angle alert," a warning to the fans that something was gonna get smashed. I tried to come up with a nondescript name like Negan's "Lucille" on *The Walking Dead* and decided on Floyd, based on my dad Ted Irvine's old St. Louis Blues teammate Floyd Thomson, who apparently swallowed his own tongue after being knocked out by a vicious body check.

		JANUARY 2017	
2650 **L**	Jan. 02	Tampa, FL	★★★1/2
	Roman Reigns		
2651 **L**	Jan. 08	Mobile, AL	★★★
	Seth Rollins		
2652 **W**	Jan. 09	New Orleans	★★★1/2
	2-on-1 handicap with Kevin Owens vs. Roman Reigns (won WWE U.S. heavyweight title), Jericho pin		
2653 **L**	Jan. 14	Wichita, KS	★★1/2
	Seth Rollins, DQ		
2654 **L**	Jan. 14	Wichita, KS	★★★
	Tag with Kevin Owens vs. Roman Reigns & Seth Rollins		

2655	Jan. 15	Tulsa, OK	★★★
L	**Seth Rollins,** DQ		

2656	Jan. 15	Tulsa, OK	★★★
L	**Tag with Kevin Owens vs. Roman Reigns & Seth Rollins**		

2657	Jan. 16	North Little Rock, AR	★★★
W	**6-man with Braun Strowman & Kevin Owens vs. Seth Rollins, Roman Reigns & Sami Zayn**		

2658	Jan. 21	Indiana, PA	★★★
L	**Roman Reigns,** DQ		

2659	Jan. 21	Indiana, PA	★★
L	**Tag with Kevin Owens vs. Roman Reigns & Seth Rollins**		

2660	Jan. 23	Cleveland	★★★
L	**Roman Reigns,** DQ		

2661	Jan. 29	San Antonio	★★★1/2
L	**Royal Rumble,** Eliminated by Roman Reigns after 1:00:13		

2662	Jan. 30	Laredo, TX	★★★
L	**Sami Zayn**		

FEBRUARY 2017

2663	Feb. 06	Portland, OR	★★1/2
W	**Sami Zayn**		

2664	Feb. 11	Anchorage, AK	★★★
L	**Sami Zayn,** DQ		

2665	Feb. 11	Anchorage, AK	★★1/2
L	**Tag with Kevin Owens vs. Sami Zayn & Roman Reigns**		

MARCH 2017

2666	Mar. 06	Chicago	★★
L	**Samoa Joe,** countout		

2667	Mar. 10	Buffalo, NY	★★★
W	**6-man with Sami Zayn & Finn Balor vs. Kevin Owens, Samoa Joe & Triple H**		

2668	Mar. 11	Toronto	★★★
W	**6-man with Sami Zayn & Finn Balor vs. Kevin Owens, Samoa Joe & Triple H**		

ALL 46 WRESTLING OBSERVER HALL OF FAME SELECTIONS THROUGH 2020 WHO HAVE EITHER WRESTLED OR TEAMED WITH 2010 INDUCTEE CHRIS JERICHO

Kurt Angle

Atlantis

Steve Austin

Bob Backlund

Chris Benoit

Daniel Bryan

El Canek

Dos Caras

Negro Casas

John Cena

Masa Chono

Bobby Eaton

Ric Flair

Gedo

Eddy Guerrero

Hulk Hogan

Gene Kiniski

Konnan

Jerry Lawler

Brock Lesnar

Jushin Liger

Los Misioneros de la Muerte
   (El Signo, El Texano &
   Negro Navarro)

Mil Mascaras

Vince McMahon

Shawn Michaels

Rey Mysterio Jr.

Yuji Nagata

Shinsuke Nakamura

Kenny Omega

Atsushi Onita

La Parka

Roddy Piper

The Rock

The Rock 'N Roll Express
   (Ricky Morton &
   Robert Gibson)

El Satanico

Ricky Steamboat

A.J. Styles

Hiroshi Tanahashi

Genichiro Tenryu

Triple H

Ultimo Dragon

The Undertaker

Dr. Wagner Jr.

2669	Mar. 12	London, Ontario	★★★1/4
W	**3-way vs. Sami Zayn vs. Samoa Joe**		

2670	Mar. 13	Detroit	★★★
W	**Tag with Sami Zayn vs. Kevin Owens & Samoa Joe, DQ**		

2671	Mar. 18	Allentown, PA	★★★
W	**Tag with Finn Balor vs. Kevin Owens & Samoa Joe**		

2672	Mar. 19	Hershey, PA	★★★
W	**Tag with Sami Zayn vs. Kevin Owens & Samoa Joe**		

2673	Mar. 26	White Plains, NY	★★1/2
W	**6-man with Finn Balor & Sami Zayn vs. Kevin Owens, Samoa Joe & Triple H**		

2674	Apr. 02	Orlando, FL	★★★3/4
L	Kevin Owens (lost WWE U.S. heavyweight title/WrestleMania 33)		

2675	Apr. 17	Columbus, OH	★★★
L	Samoa Joe		

2676	Apr. 22	Bismark, ND	★★★
W	Tag with Seth Rollins vs. Kevin Owens & Samoa Joe		

2677	Apr. 23	Fargo, ND	★★★
W	Tag with Seth Rollins vs. Kevin Owens & Samoa Joe		

2678	Apr. 24	Kansas City, MO	★★
NC	2-on-1 handicap with Dean Ambrose vs. Miz, NO CONTEST		

2679	Apr. 30	San Jose, CA	★★★
W	Kevin Owens (won WWE U.S. heavyweight title/2nd time – Payback)		

2680	May 02	Fresno, CA	★★★
L	Kevin Owens (lost WWE U.S. heavyweight title)		

2681	June 28	Kallang, Singapore	★★1/2
L	Hideo Itami		

2682	June 30	Tokyo	★★★1/4
W	Hideo Itami		

2683	July 01	Tokyo	★★★★
W	Finn Balor		

2684	July 25	Richmond, VA	★★★1/4

L   **3-way vs. Kevin Owens vs. A.J. Styles (Styles wins WWE U.S. heavyweight title),** Styles beats Owens

MATCH NOTES #2684

I didn't realize it at the time it was happening, but this was my last official match in WWE (I was in the Greatest Royal Rumble a few months later for about three minutes, but this was the last actual bell-to-bell match) and it was a good one. If I never step through that company's ropes again, I'm glad my last match there was with two great opponents in a bout I can be proud of! I'm not sure why they brought me in for this, but I remember I did two podcasts that day before the show with Naomi and Breezango and a few episodes of *Southpaw Regional Wrestling* as Clint Bobski. Busy day!

NEW JAPAN– ALL ELITE WRESTLING

JAN. 04, 2018 - OCT. 07, 2020

MATCHES 2685 - 2722

2685   Jan. 04   Tokyo   ★★★★★

L   Kenny Omega (no DQ/Wrestle Kingdom 12)

IN THEIR WORDS: **KENNY OMEGA**

So, going into a Tokyo Dome show, whether it be dark match, 10-man tag, or main event, there's always been an ominous feeling for me. I wake up devoid of emotion, and the scale of what's to come never hits until I see the empty arena and only then can I imagine the production going into it, the attention of 40,000 in the house and however many else around the world. Then with the story that Jericho and I had built to this thing — my goodness — everything online, the eventual attack from behind, my first taste of non-accidental color, the very physical press conference ... long story short, I was geared up for the Dome months and months in advance before actually getting to January 4.

And then the anxiety hit. Like a wave, I'd remembered all of my experiences with legends on the indies or horrific stories from friends. I was sitting there in the taxi on my way to the Dojo to plan this thing, and I kept thinking to myself, "How do I not disappoint people if this is another legend collecting an easy paycheck?"

Then I arrived at the dojo, we exchanged pleasantries, did the standard, "So, you got any ideas?" and Jericho blew my mind.

I'd gotten to a point in Japan where I would always show up to an arena and my opponent would put their hands out to me and say, "Please. Idea."

I'd accepted it, I was used to it, but as soon as I'd opened my mouth, we were bouncing back and forth and pretty much finishing each other's sentences. We were arguing over who should take floor and table bumps. It felt like the times when wrestling was fun, and I think because of that, our ideas, mixed with just us having fun in the moment, made for a magical match that I'll never forget. Many others enjoying it was a huge bonus, too!

With Nick and Matt Jackson in Tokyo in 2019. I've liked these guys since I first met them in a studio for an episode of Talk Is Jericho and I have the utmost respect for them for becoming huge stars in the business by doing things their own way.

| 2686 | Apr. 27 | Jeddah, Saudi Arabia | ★★ |

L   **Greatest Royal Rumble,** Eliminated by Braun Strowman after 3:18

| 2687 | June 09 | Osaka, Japan | ★★★★ |

W   **Tetsuya Naito (won IWGP Intercontinental title/Dominion)**

When the idea was pitched for me to dress up as Pentagon for All In 2018, I thought it was tremendous. Only problem was Penta brought a costume that was a different color from the one he was wearing. So with literally only minutes to spare, my PA Jack Slade and I spray painted the white suit yellow and got it done and dried just in time for my appearance. If you look closely, you can totally see the paint.

Backstage in Osaka the night I won the New Japan Intercontinental Championship from Naito, with Kenny and his IWGP Championship and Cody with the IWGP US Championship in 2018. It's the only time in New Japan history that all the major championships were held by foreigners.

2688   Oct. 29   At sea   ★★★★

L   **6-man with The Young Bucks vs. Cody, Marty Scurll & Kenny Omega (Jericho cruise)**

MATCH NOTES #2688

This was a huge match for me, as it was the main event on the first Jericho Cruise and my secret weapon in case I needed a sales boost. Well, I did, and it worked. It was also an excellent match that once again proved to me that I could hang with the new generation and still perform at the highest of levels. It wasn't easy wrestling on the boat, and not because we were in the middle of the ocean. The match before us had taken a bump into the deck pool, and the ring was soaked and slippery as a result!

2689   Nov. 03   Osaka, Japan   ★★★3/4

W   **Evil (Power Struggle)**

2690   Jan. 04   Tokyo   ★★★★1/2

L   **Tetsuya Naito (lost IWGP Intercontinental title/Wrestle Kingdom 13)**

With Jado and Gedo, two of my oldest friends in the business in 2019.

TOP 10 BOSSES

- Genichiro Tenryu
- Paco Alonso
- Bob Puppets (He gave me my first match when nobody else would — I made 30 bucks — and I'll always respect him for that)
- Eric Bischoff
- Paul Heyman
- Jim Cornette
- Gedo
- Tony Condello
- Vince McMahon
- Tony Khan

	MAY 2019		

2691	May 25	Las Vegas	★★★★
W	**Kenny Omega (Double or Nothing)**		

	JUNE 2019		

2692	June 09	Osaka, Japan	★★★3/4
L	**Kazuchika Okada (Dominion)**		

I came up with the Painmaker character in preparation for my feud with Naito in 2018. My WWE Jericho look just wasn't clicking with the stronger style I was working in New Japan and I wanted to come up with something that would resemble what a serial killer might look like if he was a pro wrestler. This was it.

2693	Aug. 31	Chicago	★★★★

W **Hangman Adam Page (won AEW world title/All Out)**

MATCH NOTES #2693

I loved this match for obvious reasons, as it was essentially the one that kicked off AEW in a sold-out Chicago arena. Hangman was good then, he's better now, and will be even better next year. I still believe putting the title on me was the right move for the growth and legitimacy of the company, and I was proven right when only three months into our existence AEW was given a $175 million contract extension on the TNT network.

OCTOBER 2019

2694	Oct. 02	Washington, D.C.	★★★1/2

W **6-man with Santana & Ortiz vs. The Young Bucks & Kenny Omega (AEW Dynamite debut show)**

2695	Oct. 09	Boston	★★★1/2

W **Tag with Sammy Guevara vs. Dustin Rhodes & Hangman Page**

At Flair's 70th birthday party with Triple H in 2019. I can't say it wasn't a tad awkward to see him as I had already signed with AEW, but Paul and I had been to war together and the true respect we had for each other trumped any "rival company" animosity.

ALEX MARVEZ'S TOP 10 CHRIS JERICHO AEW MATCHES AND MOMENTS (SO FAR)

Alex Marvez is a long-time wrestling journalist who is now part of AEW's announcing and production teams.

10. ANNOUNCING DYNAMITE WITH TONY SCHIAVONE (APRIL 2020)

Upon learning that AEW would have to tape 20-plus matches in one day because of a COVID-19 shutdown being enacted by the Georgia governor, Jericho quickly sprung into action by booking an impromptu private flight from Tampa to join the crew and help on commentary because regular announcers Jim Ross and Excalibur were grounded. Chris' enthusiasm bubbled over to enhance the matches. He also displayed strong chemistry with Schiavone, a longtime foil he nicknamed "Skee-vone." Plus, Jericho's time behind the mic accidentally but fortuitously laid the groundwork for a mini-feud and future match. There was a Hawaiian-shirt wearing "enhancement talent" stationed as a fan at ringside whom he regularly insulted. That wrestler — Suge D — was bestowed a nickname by Jericho — Pineapple Pete (which was inspired by a bar where Chris drank with fellow WCW wrestlers following television tapings in Orlando during the mid-1990s). Pete got his 15 minutes of fame that would never have come his way otherwise in AEW.

9. MANITOBA MELEE (DYNAMITE, APR. 30, 2020)

With the COVID-19 pandemic temporarily keeping us from running shows, AEW was seeking content that would provide levity during a dark time and keep viewers glued to the telecast. Jericho and the Inner Circle delivered in a big way with their own rendition of a campy-but-not-cheesy, socially-distanced brawl featuring other wrestlers and some of Chris' celebrity friends, including Lou Ferrigno, Duff McKagan, and Jay and Silent Bob.

8. #2718, ORANGE CASSIDY, MIMOSA MAYHEM, SEPT. 5, 2020, JACKSONVILLE, FL

We'll never know the exact number of viewers this match attracted in particular, but the intrigue behind seeing who would win the rubber match between Jericho and Orange Cassidy combined with curiosity over what the "Mayhem" setup would look like surely helped All Out draw more than 100,000 pay-per-view orders. Chris lost on a sweltering summer evening, but getting dunked could have been worse. AEW's production crew wisely decided against adding milk to the juice and champagne in the ringside mimosa vats, as had been originally advised by one outside stunt director to make the liquid look more orange.

7. BACKYARD CONFRONTATION WITH VANGUARD 1 (DYNAMITE, APR. 1, 2020)

Who wears leather pants in a Jacuzzi? *Le Champion*, of course. Jericho's interaction with Vanguard 1 and subsequent releasing of his "hounds" to howl at Matt Hardy's drone was a show-stealer.

6. AEW SUPER WEDNESDAY DEBATE 2020 (DYNAMITE, AUG. 5, 2020)

The concept was fantastic for helping to further raise the bar in the feud between Jericho and Orange Cassidy. Chris thought he could humiliate a non-verbal opponent in a debate setting with Eric Bischoff as moderator in his return to TNT after almost two decades. Instead, Bischoff gave the suddenly verbose Orange the nod following a discourse on global warming.

5. #2705, JON MOXLEY, REVOLUTION, FEB. 29, 2020, CHICAGO

This was more than a fantastic match with an unforgettable entrance (a gospel choir singing "Judas"). It was a rewarding culmination of a well-planned story line that saw Moxley gradually go through Inner Circle members one by one to avenge being blinded in one eye by Jericho — only for Mox to then reveal he had been playing possum in this match to end Chris's 182-day reign as AEW world champion.

Face to face with Moxley, the man I recruited into AEW, who becomes a bigger and bigger star every time he steps into the ring.

4. #2691, KENNY OMEGA, DOUBLE OR NOTHING, MAY 25, 2019, LAS VEGAS

Besides being an outstanding bout with the post-match debut of Jon Moxley in the first AEW main event, Chris successfully introduced a new finishing move — the Judas Effect — that left the sold-out crowd at the MGM Grand Garden Arena in Las Vegas stunned when used to defeat another major superstar in Kenny.

3. "CHRIS JERICHO'S THANKSGIVING THANK YOU CELEBRATION FOR LE CHAMPION" (DYNAMITE, NOV. 27, 2019)

A huge smile crosses my face every time I think about the absurdity of Soul Train Jones serving as emcee, giant inflatable cartoon characters bopping around at ring-side, a marching band, Jake Hager trying to work with an uncooperative goat named Chris Jeri-GOAT, the Puerto Rican-themed gift basket from Santana and Ortiz, ring announcer Justin Roberts going down like he was shot after getting smacked, and Chris' dad Ted Irvine emerging from a box and bestowing New York Rangers jerseys to the Inner Circle in the middle of Chicago Blackhawks country.

2. INTRODUCTION OF THE INNER CIRCLE (OCT. 9, 2019)

In one fell swoop on the second episode of *Dynamite*, Chris allowed Jake Hager to re-invent himself post-WWE by shooting down a crowd chant with his prior wrestling gimmick and lifted the career of Sammy Guevara by bestowing upon him the nick-name "Spanish God." It was a sign of things to come as Chris would later elevate other AEW talent like Scorpio Sky, "Jungle Boy" Jack Perry, and Orange Cassidy by working with them.

Nick Jackson and I get blown away during Stadium Stampede.

1. #2710, STADIUM STAMPEDE, MAY 23, 2020, JACKSONVILLE, FL

Not only does Chris deserve credit for his multiple roles in crafting one of the most original and unforgettable matches in modern pro wrestling history. CJ also saved the day with a think-on-your-feet suggestion. Something in the original filming of the match finish went awry and it would have taken significant time to re-shoot the entire sequence of Kenny Omega giving Sammy Guevara a one-winged angel from the stands through a crash pad at least 20-feet below. It was already 5 a.m. and the fire marshal said he was leaving if we didn't shoot off the celebratory pyro by 5:15. Thanks to Chris offering a way to repackage the footage, we managed to salvage Kenny's pin on Sammy and then capture the closing scene of The Elite rejoicing with fireworks in the background as a fitting end to an all-time classic.

| 2696 | Oct. 16 | Philadelphia | ★★★3/4 |

W   Darby Allin (street fight)

IN THEIR WORDS: **DARBY ALLIN**

There was a lot I had to prove from a national TV wrestling standpoint because I had pretty much come up from the indies. Growing up watching a guy like Chris Jericho, it was put up or shut up for me. I got the ball handed to me in Week 3 of television on *Dynamite*, and I knew my whole trajectory in the company and how I would be used in the future was riding on that night and if I could hang in those main-event spots. But we did it. We fucking killed it. It was lots of fun. Whenever you can go in there and tell an awesome story, it's special.

Cody grew into a legit main-eventer in his first three months in AEW, and we had a tremendous feud for the title. He's bleeding here after landing on his head on a dive to the ramp, during our classic at Full Gear 2019.

2697	Nov. 06	Charlotte, NC	★★★1/2
W	**Tag with Sammy Guevara vs. Kenny Omega & Hangman Page**		

2698	Nov. 09	Baltimore	★★★★1/2
W	**Cody (Full Gear)**		

2699	Nov. 13	Nashville, TN	★★★1/2
L	**Tag with Sammy Guevara vs. SCU (Frankie Kazarian & Scorpio Sky)**, pinned by Sky		

IN THEIR WORDS: **SCORPIO SKY**
(AEW/NOV. 20, 2019)

Believe it or not, it wasn't the two matches we had between this show (#2699 & #2700) that is my favorite memory. I really enjoyed those, but it was the face-to-face promo that we had where I basically embarrassed him and tricked him into giving me an AEW title match. Jericho is one of the greatest talkers in the history of wrestling. Going into this, I was really nervous because I believe I'm pretty good at it, but people don't know me as a talker. They know me as a wrestler. But I couldn't have been happier with the way it turned out. It was funny, interesting, and entertaining. We sucked people in. It's really a testament to how great he is. He's so good that it's easy to play off what he's doing. That's why he's the GOAT.

2700	Nov. 27	Chicago	★★★3/4
W	**Scorpio Sky**		

2701	Dec. 18	Corpus Christi, TX	★★★1/2
DR	**Jungle Boy**, 10 minutes		

IN THEIR WORDS: **"JUNGLE BOY" JACK PERRY**

I was extremely nervous. It was the biggest night of my life up to that point. I kind of felt like that was a make-or-break moment because that was really my first big AEW opportunity. But once I finally got there that day and it was time to do it, some of the nerves went away. Obviously, I had never worked before with anyone at that level. He was another caliber. I'd never experienced anything like that. I started learning a lot just seeing how he put the match together immediately. The match was great. I loved it and I felt like it really set me up on a good path. And it really changed the way I thought about wrestling in general after that. It showed me what is actually important and what is not. I realized — as people had been telling me all along — it wasn't about how many cool moves you could do. It's the other stuff that's more important. This was the first time I felt it put into practice. People used to tell me that all the time but I was like, "OK, OK." But in the indie promotions, it really is about that stuff sometimes. Being with Chris, he showed me ... the one thing people remember about that match is me being in the Walls of Jericho and not tapping out. Nobody remembers any of the moves I did. Going in, I was thinking, "What cool moves might I use that people are going to remember?" None of it mattered. It was all about the end and getting there and telling that story. That was cool.

	JANUARY 2020		
2702	Jan. 05	Tokyo	★★★★★
W	**Hiroshi Tanahashi (Wrestle Kingdom 14)**		
2703	Jan. 21	Nassau, Bahamas	★★★★
W	**6-man with Santana & Ortiz vs. Jurassic Express (Jungle Boy, Marko Stunt & Luchasaurus/Jericho Cruise)**		
2704	Jan. 29	Cleveland	★★★1/2
W	**6-man with Santana & Ortiz vs. Darby Allin & Private Party (Isiah Kassidy & Marq Quen)**		

Using the Jericho/Moxley weigh-in for Revolution in February of 2020 to my advantage. The creative freedom afforded to us in AEW makes original ideas like this one possible. Hard to believe less than a month later, the entire world would lock down for the rest of the year.

I love this pic of me giving Darby the Judas Effect, mid tope. Darby is another talent (like Orange Cassidy) that I had never heard of prior to AEW who is a born superstar.

2705	Feb. 29	Chicago	★★★★★
L	Jon Moxley (lost AEW world title/Revolution)		

MY TOP 10 AEW OPPONENTS

(SO FAR)

• JON MOXLEY

As much as I enjoyed my feud with Dean Ambrose in WWE, Moxley is on a totally different level of intensity, promo, and performance in 2020. It was an honor to drop the AEW title to him at Revolution 2020 (#2705).

• JUNGLE BOY

I think Jack Perry is going to be one of the biggest stars in AEW in a year or two. I saw it from the start, especially when my twin 14-year-old daughters — who don't pay attention to wrestling — started paying attention to him.

Moxley is one of the most intense guys I've ever been in the ring with, and that's a good thing. We always had solid matches in WWE, but our AEW match for the world title was excellent. Funny thing is you can see the stitches on my face from his headbutt a week earlier, but about a minute after this picture was taken, Mox hit the post and got a stitch-worthy cut of his own ... in the exact same place.

• CODY RHODES

Cody broke away from being comfortable and focused on becoming legendary. As a result, he has become everything his father, Dusty, was and more. It was a pleasure to create and craft an amazing multiple-month story line with him that turned into one of my favorite AEW bouts (#2698) to date at Full Gear 2019.

• KENNY OMEGA

It's no surprise we have excellent chemistry, considering we come from the same small prairie town of Winnipeg. What's also no surprise is the anticipation for our imminent third classic "rubber" match.

• DARBY ALLIN

I worked with Darby in Week 3 of *Dynamite* (#2696), and that's when I realized how much charisma he has and recognized his potential to be a top guy for AEW. Plus, whenever you see fans of all ages — girls, guys, kids — dressing up as one of your performers, you know you have something special.

• ORANGE CASSIDY

When Orange was signed to AEW, I didn't get it. I thought his character was a mockery to the business. Then I got my head out of my ass and realized he had gotten over to a massive degree (fans of all ages dress up as him at the shows as well) by doing something different. That's when I became an OC fan and decided I wanted to do something with him. We put together an exciting 14-week story line that began with an attack on him with a bag of blood oranges and ended with the awesome Mimosa Mayhem match (#2718). I enjoyed every minute of it!

• THE YOUNG BUCKS

As great as the Bucks are and as classic as many of their matches have been, I think we've only scratched the surface with what these amazing athletes can do. I can't wait to work with them more often both in tags (the reunion of The Bucks of Jericho MUST happen) and in singles matches for years to come. Just a pleasure to be around and work with.

• ISIAH KASSIDY

With every match I have with this kid, he just keeps getting better and better. Our singles bout on *Dynamite* (#2721) was only his second ever, and the promo we did the week before was only his first. He was excellent in both, and I'm saying right now he's gonna be a main-event draw for AEW very soon.

• HANGMAN ADAM PAGE

Hangman was really good in our match to decide the first-ever AEW champion (#2693) at All Out 2019, and he's only gotten better since. The match between him and Dustin Rhodes vs. Sammy and me on March 11, 2020 (#2707), was not only the last match we had in front of people before the coronavirus lockdown, but it was also another forgotten favorite of mine.

• MJF

At just 24 years old, MJF is far more advanced as a well-rounded, exceptional performer than his age might suggest. A true student of the game, he is a blast to work and trade insults with. Our first promo in Nashville in November 2019 featuring our "Do you wanna be in the Inner Circle, Max?"/"Do you want me to be in the Inner Circle, Chris?" banter was an instant classic and for a virtual rookie to hold his own with Le Champion himself was something that the fans, critics, and — most importantly — I did not take lightly.

| 2706 | Mar. 04 | Denver | ★★★1/2 |

W   **Tag with Sammy Guevara vs. Jon Moxley & Darby Allin**

| 2707 | Mar. 11 | Salt Lake City | ★★★3/4 |

L   **Tag with Sammy Guevara vs. Dustin Rhodes & Hangman Page,** Guevara pinned

| 2708 | May 06 | Jacksonville, FL | ★★★★1/2 |

W   **Tag with Sammy Guevara vs. Kenny Omega & Matt Hardy (falls count anywhere street fight)**

| 2709 | May 13 | Jacksonville, FL | ★★★ |

W   **Pineapple Pete**

What people don't realize is our shows at the outdoor Daily's Place sometimes take place in 100 degree-plus temperatures.

Giving Jaxson de Ville the Judas Effect at the incredible spectacle known as The Stadium Stampede ... Jackass had it coming! Also gotta give credit to the amazing AEW crew for arranging the awesome Inner Circle football uniforms.

2710   May 23   Jacksonville, FL   ★★★★★

L   **10-man Stadium Stampede with the Inner Circle (Jake Hager, Sammy Guevara,**
Santana & Ortiz) vs. The Elite (Young Bucks, Kenny Omega, Matt Hardy & Hangman Page)
– Double or Nothing, Omega pinned Sammy

IN THEIR WORDS: **THE YOUNG BUCKS (MATT AND NICK JACKSON)**

MATT JACKSON: It was one of those things that would have been impossible if not for this entire terrible pandemic that has happened. It was a silver lining. We would have never thought of the concept. I don't remember exactly how long it took. The more the story grows, so does the time it took for us to shoot it. It was like making a movie in a day. We were rained out for an hour-and-a-half at one point. I broke my rib two nights before on *Dynamite,* so it was one of the most painful nights of my life. Sometimes when I think of Stadium Stampede, I think of misery.

NICK JACKSON: But you know what? At the same time, this was probably the most proud we ever felt. It was 10 guys plus a ton of production people. Tony Khan had a lot of ideas as well. It was everyone collaborating and having the time of our lives. Seeing it come to life was amazing. After one scene was filmed, they would cut and replay it on the big screen inside TIAA Bank Field. We would watch it back, and it would motivate us even more for the next scene to make it even better.

MATT JACKSON: We were trying to top each other. It would be like, "Hangman Page really killed it in the bar scene with Jake Hager. We'd better bring it in the next one." I remember the next night was Double or Nothing. We all had the night off, so we all got to sit in the bleachers and they put it on the big screen like we were at a movie theater. Everyone who was in the match sat together and watched it. It was fun to hear the boys and girls in our company pop and genuinely laugh and have a good time. By the end of it, I remember the fireworks shot off. Chris stood up and had tears in his eyes. I had tears in my eyes and we hugged. It was one of the greatest things I had ever done.

I realized the magnitude when Chris Jericho said it was one of his favorite things. He has done it all.

IN THEIR WORDS: **SAMMY GUEVARA**

There's a scene when the golf cart pops up behind me, and that face I made where I'm like, "Oh, no. Not again," and do that turn to run. Behind the scenes, we had to do that take more than once for some reason. Chris came up to me and said, "You need to do it slower. Just take your time and really sell it like, 'Ooooh, nooooo.' I listened, and what a genius he is because that moment became such a meme and GIF and made the match that much better, just the facials I was doing. He is so smart with certain little things that you wouldn't think about.

	JUNE 2020		
2711	June 03	Jacksonville, FL	★★★
W	**Colt Cabana**		
2712	June 17	Jacksonville, FL	★★★1/2
L	**Tag with Sammy Guevara vs. Best Friends (Trent? & Chuck Taylor),** Trent? pinned Guevara		

	JULY 2020		
2713	July 02	Jacksonville, FL	★★★★★
W	**Orange Cassidy (Fyter Fest)**		
2714	July 16	Jacksonville, FL	★★★3/4
W	**Tag with Jake Hager vs. Luchasaurus & Jungle Boy**		
2715	July 29	Jacksonville, FL	★★★
L	**10-man tag with Inner Circle vs. Jurassic Express (Jungle Boy & Luchasaurus), Best Friends & Orange Cassidy**		

	AUGUST 2020		
2716	Aug. 12	Jacksonville, FL	★★★1/2
L	**Orange Cassidy ($7,000 obligation match)**		

Ready for the debate with Orange Cassidy and Eric Bischoff. I absolutely loved working with Freshly Squeezed for 14 weeks in 2020.

Cassidy still owes me $7,000 for ruining my jacket by unleashing a flood of orange juice on me. Floyd the Bat agrees.

SEPTEMBER 2020

2717	Sept. 02	Jacksonville, FL	★★★
W	**Joey Janela**		

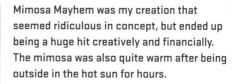

Mimosa Mayhem was my creation that seemed ridiculous in concept, but ended up being a huge hit creatively and financially. The mimosa was also quite warm after being outside in the hot sun for hours.

| 2719 | Sept. 08 | Jacksonville, FL | ★★★★ |

W Tag with Jake Hager vs. Sonny Kiss & Joey Janela

| 2720 | Sept. 09 | Jacksonville, FL | ★★★1/2 |

W Tag with Jake Hager vs. Private Party

| 2721 | Sept. 25 | Jacksonville, FL | ★★★★ |

W Isiah Kassidy

With Dr. Britt and Reba during the post match Saturday Night Live-esque celebration at the end of the Jericho 30 anniversary special. The rolling "Chris Jericho Does Everything" credits at the end are a personal favorite.

OCTOBER 2020

| 2722 | Oct. 07 | Jacksonville, FL | ★★★1/2 |

W Tag with Jake Hager vs. Chaos Project (Luther & Serpentico)

IN THEIR WORDS: **LUTHER (AKA LENNY OLSEN)**

The 30th anniversary match is obviously very special to me. For my jaw — not so much. I can tell you the Judas Effect is the real deal. Getting to do that match with the GOAT was great, and the fact he's my best friend really added to the excitement of the whole thing. Just being in there with him was like a dream, really. And just knowing when we started

357

wrestling in those little tiny towns in front of nobody, who would have thought he would get to where he is now. It's amazing how far he has come. I was proud of him when he went to WCW and WWF. I'm proud now. It's just a good feeling watching everything. He changes when he has to change, but at the core, he's still the same thing. He's just an ass-kicker all the way around.

What a great full-circle moment to have my 30th anniversary match vs. Luther on Oct 7, 2020 ... over 29 years after we had our first one on April 10, 1991.

DAVE MELTZER'S TOP 10 CHRIS JERICHO MATCHES

Dave Meltzer is the publisher and editor of the Wrestling Observer Newsletter.

When it comes to Chris Jericho's best matches, there are so many to choose from over 30 years. When making my list, the key points weren't necessarily the best matches because that has to do with time and place, but simply great matches that also stood out for historical reasons. The list would be matches that changed Jericho's career, had lasting impact, and in one case, changed the entire foundation of the industry as we know it.

But you'll see on the list some of the great performers of this and the last generation: Shawn Michaels, Kenny Omega, Triple H, Steve Austin, and Chris Benoit. The latter is a name kind of buried in history. Jericho had many of his best and most important career matches with Benoit. The name will always be uncomfortable to speak of — for obvious reasons — but Benoit was a major part of Jericho's career.

But to me, the real statement of Jericho as a worker is not having a great match with Michaels or Omega or Benoit, but matches that would never make this list but in other ways are just as impressive.

For example, in 2020, at the age of 49, Jericho wrestled Isiah Kassidy on *Dynamite* (#2721). Kassidy is a great athlete, is becoming a star, and very well could be talked about as a great worker someday down the line. But on that day, Kassidy had exactly one singles match in his entire career. But you would never have a clue of that watching the match. It wasn't perfect, but it was damn good.

Even more impressive to me was the night in San Jose where Jericho had just a normal match on a long show against Viscera (#1094), a 6-foot-7-inch or so, almost-500-pound wrestler who also was known as Mabel and Big Daddy V. This wouldn't be one of the best 100 matches of Jericho's career, but it was the best match I ever saw of Viscera's — and by a wide margin. Viscera worked with many of the biggest names in WWE and Japan at one time or another through different character incarnations.

[JERICHO NOTE: I remember this match! It was the second time I ever wrestled Vis. I also was ready to quit that day when I saw the card and the finish for this match (I got pinned after a belt shot from Eddy Guerrero behind the referee's back). I was about to storm into Vince's office to tell him I was walking out, but fortunately I ran into writer Tommy Blacha, who told me I was winning the title from Triple H the next week in State College, Pennsylvania.]

Even Hulk Hogan, when he was at the end of his career, wrestled Jericho on *Smackdown* (#1439). Jericho was literally the fountain of youth for Hogan, as the match was better than probably 95 percent of Hogan's matches during his heyday.

[JERICHO NOTE: I'm glad Dave pointed this out, because I totally agree with this statement.]

And there was a match that I never saw, other than photos, but I talked to many who were there who raved about it: a Jericho and Lance Storm tag match against the Heavenly Bodies on one of Smoky Mountain Wrestling's biggest shows in its history #362. Jericho wrestled a full match with a broken arm and full cast from an injury suffered that afternoon while he was practicing doing a shooting star press.

So here is my top 10:

10. #2690, TETSUYA NAITO, JAN. 4, 2019, TOKYO

This is not like any other match on this list. This was Jericho studying tapes of Bruiser Brody, a Japanese legend of the '80s. He gained weight for the purpose of doing an aggressive brawl with a wrestler who was willing to take an incredible amount of real punishment to get a huge match over on the biggest stage in Japan. This match, where Naito regained the Intercontinental title, along with Omega vs. Hiroshi Tanahashi, led to the first legitimate sellout of the Tokyo Dome for pro wrestling in nearly two decades.

[JERICHO NOTE: This is absolutely true. I was going through a big Bruiser Brody phase at this time.]

9. #1152, TRIPLE H, JULY 23, 2000, DALLAS

This last man standing match from Fully Loaded is notable because there is a big difference between being on the card and having a great match, and having a pay-per-view main-event championship match. Wrestling is weird in the sense that until you're put in the position to draw, the knock will be that you can't draw. Until you have a successful major show main event, you may be viewed as a great wrestler, but you are unproven as a headliner. Even though this match didn't lead to the next 20 years of being nothing but a headliner, or even completely remove any stigma that Jericho couldn't carry a company, they both proved here that he could not just headline successfully, but be part of an epic WWF-style main event.

8. #517, WILD PEGASUS (CHRIS BENOIT), SECOND SUPER J-CUP, DEC. 13, 1995, TOKYO

This was a great match; I wouldn't say the best match the two ever had, but it was their first singles match. It turned out to be one of the most important matches of Jericho's career due to a backstory. Shortly after this show, I pitched the idea to Zane Bresloff, a WCW promoter, of them doing a Super J-Cup idea. The idea would be a special episode of *Nitro* with nothing but junior heavyweights, a tournament that would naturally build to the main event and showcase talent that was not really being shown to its best advantage. I sent him a tape of this show, and the tape then, according to Eric Bischoff, wound up in his hands. He saw Benoit vs. Jericho, was intrigued by Jericho, and asked Benoit if Jericho was worth signing. Benoit gave his highest recommendation, and that led to Jericho getting his WCW deal. Unfortunately, we never did get that Super J-Cup, which, with the talent WCW had, would have been a show people would have talked about for years.

[JERICHO NOTE: This was our first singles match! As a matter of fact, it was the first time the two of us had ever been in the ring together. Similar to the classic matches I had with Shawn Michaels and Kenny Omega, Benoit and I just had amazing chemistry from the get-go.]

7. #1099 TRIPLE H, APR. 17, 2000, STATE COLLEGE, PA

This was a WWF title match where Jericho, who at this point would have been a huge underdog, beat Triple H to apparently win the title on *Raw*. You would expect a big reaction to a wrestler on the way up who was very popular winning the title in a match nobody expected him to win. But the reaction was two or three levels above that, largely because the match was one of the best TV matches of the era. It may have been remembered as one of the greatest matches in *Raw* history, but they ended up reversing the decision and taking the title from Jericho. I've always thought that if they listened to the reaction, they could have called an audible about taking the title away. But in those days, wrestling was booked on top long-term, and that wasn't the plan. Still, I don't know that Jericho as a young babyface was ever stronger in WWF than at that moment, and when it was over, there were simply other plans and it wasn't taken advantage of.

[JERICHO NOTE: What people forget is I wrestled twice that night. I was also in a six-man in the main event (#1100) where I was pinned by guess who? Triple H.]

6. #1227, CHRIS BENOIT, LADDER MATCH, JAN. 21, 2001, NEW ORLEANS

Everyone has an idea of a ladder match, which is mostly to take crazy bumps and do creative stunts using the ladder. This match was not that. This was one of the best wrestling matches of the year, and the idea was to use the ladder to make a wrestling match better, as opposed to doing the formula ladder match. For that reason, it is one of my favorite ladder matches ever.

5. #468, ULTIMO DRAGON, JULY 7, 1995, TOKYO

I'd probably seen Jericho wrestle consistently in different parts of the world from around 1992 on. A lot of that was in Mexico and some in Japan. Jericho and Dragon battled many times in Mexico and had great chemistry. At this point in time, Dragon was considered one of the most complete wrestlers in the world, in the sense he was a rare luchador whose style would fit in the U.S. and Japan. Really, he was the father of an entire generation in Japan, and promotions like Universal, Michinoku Pro, Osaka Pro, Toryumon, and Dragon Gate all came from the style Dragon was using. To me, this was easily Jericho's greatest match at this point in time. It was, for its time, a match of dueling great moves, lots of near falls, similar to what Jushin Liger pioneered in Japan a few years earlier. It is very different from Jericho's other career best matches, but to this day, it's one of the best matches I've ever seen him in. It also has an interesting story, similar to Match 8 on my list. Shortly after this match, Paul Heyman, who at the time was the head of ECW, called me up and asked me to send him a tape of Ultimo Dragon. He'd heard tons about Dragon for years and wanted to make a play for him, since Dragon had never wrestled in the U.S. up to this point. This was my single favorite Dragon match, the best I'd seen him in. So I sent him the tape. He knew of Chris Jericho, but he'd never seen a Chris Jericho match at quite this level. Ultimo Dragon never wrestled in ECW; it just didn't work out. Jericho got his job in ECW from that tape.

4. #2003, SHAWN MICHAELS, LADDER MATCH, OCT. 5, 2008, PORTLAND, OR

This was voted Match of the Year in the *Wrestling Observer*. As far as Jericho's WWF career goes, to me, the high point is 2008 and 2009, largely due to the entire Michaels program. There were multiple great matches, but this was the most memorable. With the Benoit ladder match, it was a super wrestling match where there happened to be a ladder. This was more of a modern ladder match: a brutal fight with a ladder intimately involved.

3. #2710, STADIUM STAMPEDE, MAY 23, 2020, JACKSONVILLE, FL

Wrestling is all about time and place. Pro wrestling is, in its purest form, a one-take play — at its highest level it has drama and convinces you that maybe the match isn't real, but the stakes or consequences are. The best matches combine athletics, timing, reading the audience, and storytelling. This, while having some of those elements, was nothing like a classic wrestling match. It was taped over hours, didn't air live, had a few stunts set up that you literally could never do without a crash pad without killing someone. And it was one of the most entertaining matches at a time when people needed simply to be entertained. Almost everyone understood that, but it had its detractors, who missed the point that the world wasn't normal, and people on that day simply needed for 45 minutes to have a smile on their face. Nothing more. If you show this match to people who are not wrestling fans, they will be far more entertained than by matches people would call the greatest ever. And on that day, that was all you could ask for.

2. #1284, TAG MATCH WITH CHRIS BENOIT VS. TRIPLE H AND STEVE AUSTIN, MAY 21, 2001, SAN JOSE, CA

When people talk about the greatest match ever on *Raw*, this one comes up more than any other. *Raw* has been on the air for 28 years, 52 weeks a year — more shows than all but a few pro wrestling television shows in history, and for that matter more than most entertainment shows other than soap operas in the history of U.S. television. There is an interesting backstory to this. WWF was on fire from early 1998, when Mike Tyson and Steve Austin had their angle, until WrestleMania in 2001, when the company made arguably its worst business decision ever, turning Austin heel. Things were going down fast: attendance, ratings, pay-per-view orders, and especially merchandise. WrestleMania 17 in Houston was a giant success, the biggest revenue show in the history of the company by a wide margin. Austin and Triple H did a pay-per-view main event with The Undertaker and Kane that was supposed to start a long program. Then Vince McMahon got the word that the show only did 300,000 buys. While at another time, that would have been a number to celebrate, after 1999 and 2000, it was considered a terrible number. McMahon decided they needed to do something new. Heyman was working for WWF by this time, with ECW having just shut down. His suggestion was to make Benoit and Jericho the top babyfaces, and to do so, they'd need to beat the company's two biggest active stars decisively to kick things off. McMahon signed off on it. The match was phenomenal. You had four of the best guys around, and it was a great crowd and everything was clicking. Nobody truly believed Benoit and Jericho could win, but the match was worked in a way where they looked on the verge of a giant upset. Then Triple H tore his quad. Under normal circumstances, in a match designed to elevate two people, an injury that severe at that moment would have been a disaster. To his credit, Triple H continued the match doing every planned spot, including being Boston-crabbed on a table. Benoit and Jericho shocked the world by winning. And, really, the story of Triple H working the last few minutes on a torn quad is probably the biggest part of the match's legacy. But there's an ironic part of the story that few know about. In those days, the reporting of pay-per-view numbers was haphazard at best. The company would get an estimate from its cable partners a few days after the show. The number could be off the real number by 20 percent, which is pretty significant. Vince McMahon had told me that his entire business at the time was about drawing big pay-per-view numbers and reacting to those numbers. He was having to make decisions on what was and wasn't working based on numbers that weren't completely accurate. He thought with tens of millions of dollars at stake, how could the cable industry not be able to give him an actual number the day after the event, or at least a few days after. Remember, he came from a business where decisions were based on the live gate, a number the promoter knew midway through the show, and you take that number and tweak your direction based on this. About a month or two later, McMahon found out that Austin and Triple H vs. Undertaker and Kane actually did closer to 450,000 buys, which wasn't a bad number. Had he known that before, Benoit and Jericho would have never been put over in what was essentially a panic move. Unfortunately, even as great as the match and the ending was, McMahon pivoted again, and Benoit and Jericho stopped being booked as the top faces just weeks after the decision made to anoint them.

[JERICHO NOTE: This is mind-blowing stuff! There is lots of info in here that even I had never heard before!]

1. #2685, KENNY OMEGA, JAN. 4, 2018, TOKYO

You could argue this as the best match of Jericho's career. And you could argue it wasn't. But you can't argue that it wasn't the most important match in the big picture. Three months earlier, this was not even a match you would think about or would even be viewed as possible. Jericho, wrestling part-time, was a WWE star. WWE stars only wrestled in WWE. Jericho had said he would never wrestle outside WWE. Don Callis, who, like Jericho and Omega, is from Winnipeg, was working as an announcer for New Japan, and suggested the idea to Jericho about a match with Omega. Omega had garnered a large cult following in the U.S. from insiders from being New Japan's top foreigner and for a series of matches with Kazuchika Okada. Callis convinced Jericho of the viability of the match. Boxing and MMA had just done monster business with a Floyd Mayweather vs. Conor McGregor battle of two worlds that nobody ever thought would merge. Jericho attacked Omega out of nowhere in Japan. The match was made. Immediately there was more interest outside of Japan in Jericho's Alpha vs. Omega match than any pro wrestling match ever held in that country. Subscriptions to New Japan World went from 60,000 to 100,000 the week of the show. The problem then became having to have a match to live up to the hype. Remember, the people most interested in Jericho vs. Omega were mostly New Japan fans, or fans of Jericho willing to sample New Japan, but above all, the nature of the match and build-up were that if the match was anything but great, it would have been excoriated. Jericho was 47, so he had to prove he could hang with one of the best of the modern athletic wrestlers. Just as many were hyped for success, many were waiting for failure. But even so, the most important legacy of this match is that Tony Khan, a fan of New Japan wrestling, saw the business and interest this match generated and, a few months later, when he really decided to try and start a wrestling company, it was the success of this match and TNT showing interest that were major keys in the formation of AEW. Even Callis, when he pitched the idea, couldn't have envisioned this match as a key point in starting a promotion that would change the entire foundation of the American wrestling business and at the top level: the salary structure of its top talent.

APPENDIX

CAREER RECORD

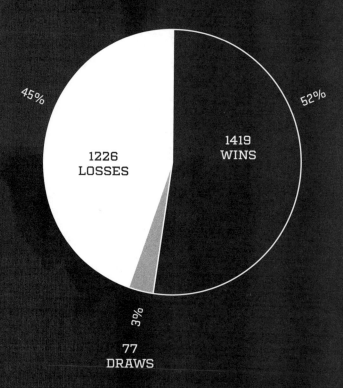

45%

52%

1226
LOSSES

1419
WINS

3%

77
DRAWS

WINS AND LOSSES BY YEAR

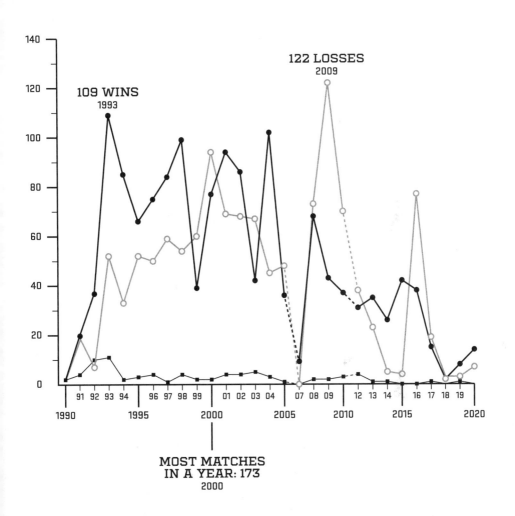

109 WINS
1993

122 LOSSES
2009

MOST MATCHES
IN A YEAR: 173
2000

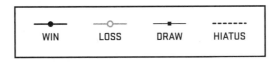

WIN   LOSS   DRAW   HIATUS

STARS

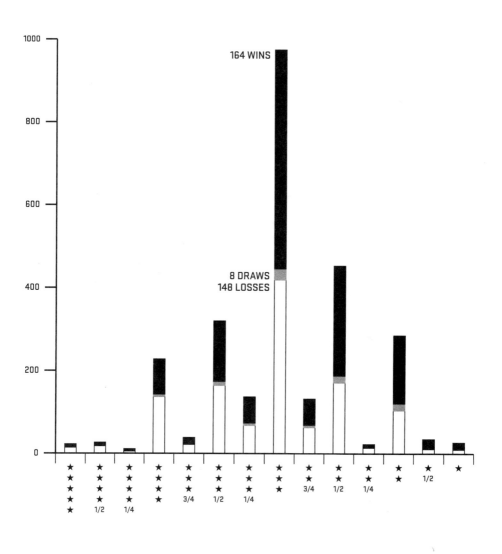

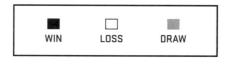

CHRIS JERICHO 5-STAR MATCHES

MATCH #	OPPONENT	DATE	CITY	RESULT
372	Ultimo Dragon	November 8, 1994	Tokyo	Loss
418	Ultimo Dragon	March 17, 1995	Mexico City	Loss
424	Gedo	March 26, 1995	Tokyo	Loss
468	Ultimo Dragon	July 7, 1995	Tokyo	Win
469	Ultimo Dragon	July 28, 1995	Tokyo	Loss
535	Tag With Gedo vs. Jushin Liger & Tatsuhito Takaiwa	February 26, 1996	Tokyo	Win
1099	Triple H	April 17, 2000	State College (PA)	Win
1132	Triple H	June 12, 2000	St. Louis	Loss
1152	Triple H	July 23, 2000	Dallas	Loss Countout
1284	Tag with Chris Benoit vs. Triple H & Steve Austin	May 21, 2001	San Jose	Win
1285	Tag with Chris Benoit vs. Dudleys vs. Hardy Boyz vs. Edge & Christian	May 22, 2001	Anaheim	Win
1363	Rock	October 21, 2001	St. Louis	Win
1464	Rock	June 15, 2002	Honolulu	Loss
1510	TLC with Christian vs. Bubba Ray & Spike vs. Jeff Hardy & Rvd vs. Kane	October 7, 2002	Las Vegas	Loss
1582	Shawn Michaels	March 30, 2003	Seattle	Loss
2003	Shawn Michaels	October 5, 2008	Portland	Win
2045	John Cena	December 28, 2008	New York City	Loss
2050	John Cena	January 9, 2009	Winnipeg	Loss
2685	Kenny Omega	January 4, 2018	Tokyo	Loss
2702	Hiroshi Tanahashi	January 5, 2020	Tokyo	Win
2705	Jon Moxley	February 29, 2020	Chicago	Loss
2710	Stadium Stampede	May 23, 2020	Jacksonville	Loss
2713	Orange Cassidy	July 2, 2020	Jacksonville	Win

CHRIS JERICHO ROYAL RUMBLE BREAKDOWN

MATCH NO.	YEAR	CITY	ENTRY	ELIMINATED	ELIMINATIONS	ELIMINATED BY	TIME
2661	2017	San Antonio	2	27	2	Roman Reigns	1:00:13
2539	2016	Orlando	6	26	1	Dean Ambrose	50:47
2398	2013	Phoenix	2	25	2	Dolph Ziggler	47:53
1554	2003	Boston	2	14	6	Test	39:00
2054	2009	Detroit	11	23	1	Undertaker	37:17
1826	2005	Fresno	11	21	2	Batista	28:22
1673	2004	Philadelphia	25	27	1	Big Show	14:58
2326	2012	St. Louis	29	29	2	Sheamus	11:34
1059	2000	New York City	15	10	1	Chyna	3:47
2686*	2018	Jeddah	50	46	1	Braun Strowman	3:18
2228	2010	Atlanta	28	26	0	Edge	2:24
*Greatest Royal Rumble in Saudi Arabia							
Total: WWE record for most time in a Royal Rumble: 4 hours, 59 minutes and 33 seconds							

CHRIS JERICHO WRESTLEMANIA HISTORY

MATCH NUMBER	WRESTLEMANIA NUMBER	DATE	CITY	OPPONENT	RESULT	JERICHO STARS
1091 / 1092	WM 2000	April 2, 2000	Anaheim	3-way vs. Kurt Angle & Chris Benoit	LOSS / WIN	★★★
1262	WM 17	April 1, 2001	Houston	William Regal	WIN	★1/2
1420	WM 18	March 17, 2002	Toronto	Triple H	LOSS	★★★1/2
1582	WM 19	March 30, 2003	Seattle	Shawn Michaels	LOSS	★★★★★
1691	WM 20	March 14, 2004	New York City	Christian	LOSS	★★★★
1850	WM 21	April 3, 2005	Los Angeles	6-way ladder match	LOSS	★★★★
1932	WM 24	March 30, 2008	Orlando	7-way ladder match	LOSS	★★★★1/2
2084	WM 25	April 5, 2009	Houston	3-on-1 vs. Ricky Steamboat, Roddy Piper & Jimmy Snuka	WIN	★★1/2
2248	WM 26	March 28, 2010	Phoenix	Edge	WIN	★★★1/2
2352	WM 28	April 1, 2012	Miami Gardens, FL.	CM Punk	LOSS	★★★3/4
2423	WM 29	April 7, 2013	East Rutherford, NJ	Fandango	LOSS	★★★1/4
2560	WM 32	April 3, 2016	Arlington, Texas	A.J. Styles	WIN	★★★1/2
2674	WM 33	April 2, 2017	Orlando	Kevin Owens	LOSS	★★★3/4
Record: 5-9						

COUNTRIES

COUNTRY	TOTAL NUMBER OF MATCHES	WIN	LOSS	DRAW	WINNING PERCENTAGE
1. United States	1851	954	855	42	52%
2. Canada	227	133	74	20	59%
3. Japan	227	110	115	2	48%
4. Mexico	223	145	75	3	65%
5. England	52	25	26	1	48%
6. Germany	45	20	16	9	44%
7. Australia	13	5	8	0	38%
8. France	12	0	12	0	0%
9. Scotland	8	3	5	0	38%
10. Ireland	7	3	4	0	43%
11. Spain	7	2	5	0	29%
12. Italy	4	0	4	0	0%
13. Saudi Arabia	4	3	1	0	75%
14. South Korea	4	3	1	0	75%
15. India	3	2	1	0	67%
16. Iraq	3	1	2	0	33%
17. United Arab Emirates	3	1	2	0	33%
18. Wales	3	2	1	0	67%
19. Austria	2	1	1	0	50%
20. Belgium	2	0	2	0	0%
21. China	2	0	2	0	0%
22. Ecuador	2	0	2	0	0%
23. Philippines	2	0	2	0	0%
24. Singapore	2	1	1	0	50%
25. At Sea	1	0	1	0	0%
26. Bahamas	1	1	0	0	100%
27. Brazil	1	0	1	0	0%
28. Chile	1	0	1	0	0%
29. Costa Rica	1	0	1	0	0%
30. El Salvador	1	0	1	0	0%
31. Finland	1	1	0	0	100%
32. Malaysia	1	1	0	0	100%
33. New Zealand	1	0	1	0	0%
34. Panama	1	0	1	0	0%
35. Peru	1	0	1	U	0%
36. Portugal	1	1	0	0	100%
37. Switzerland	1	0	1	0	0%
38. Taiwan	1	1	0	0	100%

COMPANIES

COMPANY	TOTAL NUMBER OF MATCHES	WIN	LOSS	DRAW	WINNING PERCENTAGE
World Wrestling Entertainment	1685	799	851	35	48%
World Championship Wrestling	373	222	144	7	60%
Consejo Mundial de Lucha Libre	203	137	63	3	67%
Wrestle Association R	147	69	76	2	47%
Smoky Mountain Wrestling	53	53	0	0	100%
West Four Wrestling Alliance/ International Wrestling Alliance (IWA; name change in 1994)	49	30	7	12	61%
New Japan Pro-Wrestling	43	23	20	0	53%
Catch Wrestling Association	34	16	9	9	47%
Canadian Rocky Mountain Wrestling	31	17	11	3	55%
All Elite Wrestling	30	21	8	1	70%
Extreme Championship Wrestling	23	10	12	1	43%
Canadian National Wrestling Alliance	19	9	7	3	47%
Frontier Martial Arts Wrestling	10	4	6	0	40%
No company name known or special one-off show	6	4	2	0	67%
Canadian Wrestling Connection	4	1	2	1	25%
Asistencia Asesoria y Administracion	3	1	2	0	33%
Bay Area Wrestling	3	2	1	0	67%
Ohio Valley Wrestling	2	1	1	0	50%
Heartland Wrestling Association	1	0	1	0	0%
Ring of Honor	1	0	1	0	0%
Stampede Wrestling	1	0	1	0	0%
West Coast Wrestling Alliance	1	0	1	0	0%

CHRIS JERICHO
BY THE NUMBERS

1-1	Record in the WAR 1995 Super J-Cup (#516 and #517)
2	Number of matches wrestling with or against referees — Nick Patrick (#638) and Mike Chioda (#1354)
2	(and counting) Rock 'N' Wrestling Rager at Sea cruises hosted — the only ones of their kind ever done
4	Slammy Awards won (including one for the time Michael Cole vomited on my shoes)
4-2	Record in New Japan's 1997 Best of the Super Juniors tournament (#s 705, 706, 710, 711, 714, and 716)
4:59:33	Hours, minutes and seconds logged in the Royal Rumble — the highest total in WWE history
9	WWE intercontinental title reigns — the most in company history
13	WrestleMania appearances
14	Women wrestled or teamed with — Desiree Peterson, Rhonda Sing, Chyna, Stephanie McMahon, Victoria, Trish Stratus, Stacy Keibler, Lita, Jackie Gayda, Jazz, Molly Holly, Beth Phoenix, Charlotte Flair & Sasha Banks
15	Cents in a 2000 check received from World Championship Wrestling — which was less than half of the postage it took to mail it
19	Different championships held
21	Wrestling companies worked for, not counting one-offs for stand-alone shows or small promotions whose names I can't remember
36	Matches wrestled at Madison Square Garden
38	Countries wrestled In
45	WWE Hall of Famers wrestled or teamed with
46	Wrestling Observer Hall of Famers wrestled or teamed with
49	States wrestled in. The only one missing — Montana
52	Career winning percentage (1422-1223-77)
90	Different opponents wrestled in 203 CMLL matches
182	Days as All Elite Wrestling's first world champion (Aug. 31, 2019, to Feb. 29, 2020)
400	Dollars paid to teach at the Hart Brothers Wrestling Camp in the summer of 1991
2010	Year voted into the *Wrestling Observer* Hall of Fame
80,709	Largest crowd wrestled in front of (WrestleMania 32 in Arlington, Texas)

CHRIS JERICHO
CHAMPIONSHIP LIST

CANADIAN ROCKY MOUNTAIN WRESTLING

CRMW HEAVYWEIGHT TITLE
WON: January 29, 1993 from Biff Wellington in Calgary (barbed wire match/#106)
LOST February 12, 1993 to Jason the Terrible in Calgary (#109)
TITLE REIGN: 14 days

CMLL (CONSEJO MUNDIAL DE LUCHA LIBRE)

WORLD WRESTLING ASSOCIATION TAG TEAM TITLES
WON: July 21, 1993 with El Dandy from El Texano & Silver King in Ciudad Lopez Mateos, Mexico (#182)
LOST September 1, 1993 to El Texano & Silver King in Mexico City (#205)
TITLE REIGN: 42 days

NWA MIDDLEWEIGHT TITLE
WON: December 4, 1993 from Mano Negra in Mexico City (#265)
LOST November 8, 1994 to Ultimo Dragon in Tokyo (#372)
TITLE REIGN: 11 months, 4 days

CRMW MID-HEAVYWEIGHT TITLE
WON: January 7, 1994 from Steve Rivers in Calgary (#277)
LOST February 4 1994 to Lance Storm in Calgary (ladder match/#281)
TITLE REIGN: 28 days

CRMW MID-HEAVYWEIGHT TITLE (II)
WON: May 12, 1995 from Lance Storm in Calgary (2 of 3 falls/#448)
LOST May 26, 1995 to Lance Storm in Calgary (ladder match#450)
TITLE REIGN: 14 days

WAR

WAR INTERNATIONAL JUNIOR-HEAVYWEIGHT TITLE
WON: June 4, 1995 from Gedo in Tokyo (#455)
LOST July 28, 1995 to Ultimo Dragon in Tokyo (#469)
TITLE REIGN: 54 days

WAR INTERNATIONAL JUNIOR-HEAVYWEIGHT TAG TEAM TITLES

WON: February 23, 1996 with Gedo from Lance Storm & Yuji Yasuraoka in Sendai, Japan (#532)

Loss: March 27, 1996 with Gedo to Lance Storm & Yuji Yasuraoka in Nagoya, Japan (#548)

TITLE REIGN: 33 days

EXTREME CHAMPIONSHIP WRESTLING

ECW WORLD TELEVISION TITLE

WON: June 22, 1996 from Pitbull #2 (Anthony Durante) in Philadelphia (#575)

LOST July 13, 1996 to 2 Cold Scorpio in a 4-way match also involving Shane Douglas & Pitbull #2 in Philadelphia (#579)

TITLE REIGN: 21 days

WORLD CHAMPIONSHIP WRESTLING

WCW CRUISERWEIGHT TITLE

WON: June 28, 1997 from Syxx (Sean Waltman) in Los Angeles (#725)

LOST July 28, 1997 to Alex Wright in Charleston, W.V. (#736)

TITLE REIGN: 30 days

WCW CRUISERWEIGHT TITLE (II)

WON: August 12, 1997 from Alex Wright in Colorado Springs (#742)

LOST September 14, 1997 to Eddy Guerrero in Winston-Salem, N.C. (#754)

TITLE REIGN: 33 days

WCW CRUISERWEIGHT TITLE (III)

WON: January 24, 1998 from Rey Mysterio Jr. in Dayton, Ohio (#801)

LOST May 17, 1998 to Dean Malenko in Worcester, Mass. (#860)

TITLE REIGN: 3 months, 23 days

WCW CRUISERWEIGHT TITLE (IV)

WON: June 14, 1998 from Dean Malenko in Baltimore (#872)

LOST August 8, 1998 to Juventud Guerrera in Sturgis, S.D. (Dean Malenko special referee/#892)

TITLE REIGN: 55 days

WCW WORLD TELEVISION TITLE

WON: August 10, 1998 from Stevie Ray in Rapid City, S.D. (#893)

LOST November 30, 1998 to Konnan in Chattanooga, Tenn. (#937)

TITLE REIGN: 3 months, 20 days

WORLD WRESTLING FEDERATION/
WORLD WRESTLING ENTERTAINMENT

WWF INTERCONTINENTAL TITLE
WON: December 12, 1999 from Chyna in Fort Lauderdale, FL (#1039)
Vacated: December 28, 1999 after a match vs. Chyna in Richmond, Va. (#1046)
TITLE REIGN: 26 days

WWF INTERCONTINENTAL TITLE (II)
WON: January 23, 2000 in a three-way match vs. Chyna & Hardcore Holly in New York City (#1058)
LOST February 27, 2000 to Kurt Angle in Hartford, Conn. (#1074)
TITLE REIGN: 35 days

WWF EUROPEAN TITLE
WON: April 3, 2000 from Eddy Guerrero in Los Angeles (#1092)
LOST April 4, 2000 to Viscera in San Jose, Calif. (#1093)
TITLE REIGN: 1 day

WWF INTERCONTINENTAL TITLE (III)
WON: May 2, 2000 from Chris Benoit in Richmond, Va. (#1109)
LOST May 8, 2000 to Chris Benoit in Uniondale, N.Y. (#1113)
TITLE REIGN: 6 days

WWF INTERCONTINENTAL TITLE (IV)
WON: January 21, 2001 from Chris Benoit in New Orleans (#1227)
LOST April 3, 2001 to Triple H in Oklahoma City (#1264)
TITLE REIGN: 72 days

WWF TAG TEAM TITLES
WON: May 21, 2001 with Chris Benoit vs. Triple H & Steve Austin in San Jose, Calif. (#1284)
LOST June 19, 2001 with Chris Benoit vs. The Dudley Boyz in Orlando (#1303)
TITLE REIGN: 29 days

WWF HARDCORE TITLE
WON: May 28, 2001 from Big Show in Calgary (#1288)
LOST May 28, 2001 to Rhyno in Calgary (#1289)
TITLE REIGN: 1 day

WCW WORLD TITLE
WON: October 21, 2001 from The Rock in St. Louis (#1363)
LOST November 5, 2001 to The Rock in Uniondale, N.Y. (#1369)
TITLE REIGN: 15 days

WWF TAG TEAM TITLES (II)
WON: October 22, 2001 with The Rock vs. The Dudley Boyz in Kansas City (#1364)
LOST October 30, 2001 with The Rock to Booker T & Test (#1367)
TITLE REIGN: 8 days

WCW WORLD TITLE (II)
WON: December 9, 2001 from The Rock in San Diego (#1382)
LOST N/A
TITLE REIGN: N/A (WCW world title and WWF world championship were unified into the Undisputed WWF Championship following Jericho's subsequent win over Steve Austin later that evening)

UNDISPUTED WWF WORLD CHAMPIONSHIP
WON: December 9, 2001 from Steve Austin in San Diego (#1383)
LOST March 17, 2002 to Triple H in Toronto (#1420)
TITLE REIGN: 3 months, 8 days
Note: Victories over Austin (WWF world title) and Rock (WCW world title) unified those two belts into the Undisputed WWF Championship

WWE INTERCONTINENTAL TITLE (V)
WON: September 16, 2002 from Rob Van Dam in Denver (#1502)
LOST September 30, 2002 to Kane in Houston (#1507)
TITLE REIGN: 14 days

WWE TAG TEAM TITLES (III)
WON: October 14, 2002 with Christian vs. Kane & Hurricane Helms in Montreal (#1513)
LOST December 15, 2002 with Christian to Booker T & Goldust in a four-way match also involving The Dudley Boyz & William Regal-Lance Storm (#1544)
TITLE REIGN: 62 days

WWE INTERCONTINENTAL TITLE (VI)
WON: October 27, 2003 from Rob Van Dam in Fayetteville, N.C. (#1634)
LOST October 27, 2003 to Rob Van Dam in Fayetteville, N.C. (cage match/#1635)
TITLE REIGN: 1 day

WWE INTERCONTINENTAL TITLE (VII)

WON: September 12, 2004 from Christian in Portland (#1761)
LOST October 19, 2004 to Shelton Benjamin in Milwaukee (#1781)
TITLE REIGN: 37 days

WWE INTERCONTINENTAL TITLE (VIII)

WON: March 10, 2008 from Jeff Hardy in Milwaukee (#1928)
LOST June 29, 2008 to Kofi Kingston in Dallas (#1966)
TITLE REIGN: 3 months, 19 days

WORLD HEAVYWEIGHT CHAMPIONSHIP

WON: September 7, 2008 in a 5-way scramble match involving Batista, Kane, JBL & Rey Mysterio Jr. (pinned Kane/#1990)
LOST October 26, 2008 to Batista in Phoenix (Steve Austin special referee/#2015)
TITLE REIGN: 49 days

WORLD HEAVYWEIGHT CHAMPIONSHIP (II)

WON: November 3, 2008 from Batista in Tampa (steel cage/#2018)
LOST November 23, 2008 to John Cena in Boston (#2031)
TITLE REIGN: 20 days

WWE INTERCONTINENTAL TITLE (IX)

WON: June 7, 2009 from Rey Mysterio Jr. in New Orleans (no holds barred/#2118)
LOST June 28, 2009 to Rey Mysterio Jr. in Sacramento (mask vs. title/#2130)
TITLE REIGN: 21 days

WWE TAG TEAM TITLES (IV)

WON: June 28, 2009 with Edge vs. Carlito & Primo Colon and Ted DiBiase Jr. & Cody Rhodes in Sacramento (three-way match/#2131)
LOST December 13, 2009 with Big Show (substituting for an injured Edge/Achilles) to Triple H & Shawn Michaels in San Antonio (tables, ladders and chairs/#2209)
TITLE REIGN: 5 months, 15 days

WORLD HEAVYWEIGHT CHAMPIONSHIP (III)

WON: February 21, 2010 in a six-way Elimination Chamber match also involving Undertaker, John Morrison, Rey Mysterio Jr., CM Punk vs. R-Truth in St. Louis (pinned Undertaker/#2235)
LOST March 30, 2010 to Jack Swagger in Las Vegas (#2250)
TITLE REIGN: 37 days

U.S. HEAVYWEIGHT CHAMPIONSHIP

WON: January 9, 2017 in a 2-on-1 handicap match with Kevin Owens vs. Roman Reigns in New Orleans
LOST April 2, 2017 to Kevin Owens in Orlando
TITLE REIGN: 83 days

U.S. HEAVYWEIGHT CHAMPIONSHIP (II)

WON: April 30, 2017 from Kevin Owens in San Jose, Calif. (#2652)
LOST May 2, 2017 to Kevin Owens in Fresno, Calif. (#2674)
TITLE REIGN: 2 days

NEW JAPAN PRO-WRESTLING

IWGP INTERCONTINENTAL TITLE

WON: June 9, 2018 from Tetsuya Naito in Osaka (#2687)
LOST January 4, 2019 to Tetsuya Naito in Tokyo (#2690)
TITLE REIGN: 6 months, 26 days

ALL ELITE WRESTLING

AEW WORLD CHAMPION

WON: August 31, 2019 from Hangman Adam Page in Chicago (#2693)
LOST February 29, 2020 to Jon Moxley in Chicago (#2705)
TITLE REIGN: 5 months, 29 days